Happy Dreams of Liberty

Happy Dreams of Liberty

An American Family in Slavery and Freedom

R. ISABELA MORALES

OXFORD
UNIVERSITY PRESS

OXFORD
UNIVERSITY PRESS

Oxford University Press is a department of the University of Oxford. It furthers
the University's objective of excellence in research, scholarship, and education
by publishing worldwide. Oxford is a registered trade mark of Oxford University
Press in the UK and certain other countries.

Published in the United States of America by Oxford University Press
198 Madison Avenue, New York, NY 10016, United States of America.

CIP data is on file at the Library of Congress

ISBN 978-0-19-753179-2

DOI: 10.1093/oso/9780197531792.001.0001

1 3 5 7 9 8 6 4 2
Printed by Sheridan Books, Inc., United States of America

Contents

Note on Quotations

Excerpts from the Townsends' letters and other documents from the Septimus D. Cabaniss Papers are rendered with original spelling, punctuation, and emphasis throughout this book. Brackets mark the few places where spelling has been edited for clarity.

Happy Dreams of Liberty

The Townsend Family in 1860

Underlined – Descendants of Edmund Townsend
Bold – Descendants of Samuel Townsend
= Indicates an unmarried union
+ Indicates a marriage under slavery
=/+ Indicates an unspecified union under slavery

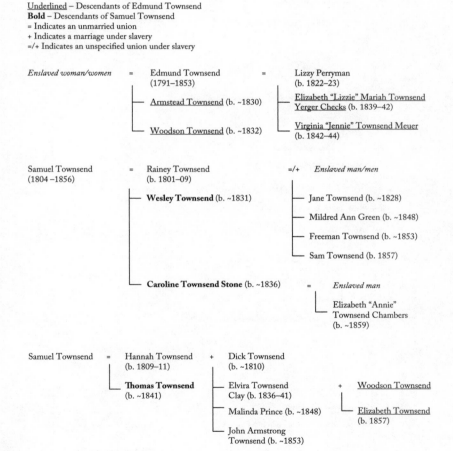

Enslaved woman/women   =   Edmund Townsend   =   Lizzy Perryman
(1791–1853)   (b. 1822–23)

   — Armstead Townsend (b. ~1830)   — Elizabeth "Lizzie" Mariah Townsend
Yerger Checks (b. 1839–42)

   — Woodson Townsend (b. ~1832)   — Virginia "Jennie" Townsend Meuer
(b. 1842–44)

Samuel Townsend   =   Rainey Townsend   =/+   *Enslaved man/men*
(1804 –1856)   (b. 1801–09)

   — **Wesley Townsend** (b. ~1831)   — Jane Townsend (b. ~1828)

                                      — Mildred Ann Green (b. ~1848)

                                      — Freeman Townsend (b. ~1853)

                                      — Sam Townsend (b. 1857)

   — **Caroline Townsend Stone** (b. ~1836)   =   *Enslaved man*

                                      — Elizabeth "Annie"
Townsend Chambers
(b. ~1859)

Samuel Townsend   =   Hannah Townsend   +   Dick Townsend
(b. 1809–11)   (b. ~1810)

   — **Thomas Townsend**   — Elvira Townsend   +   Woodson Townsend
(b. ~1841)   Clay (b. 1836–41)

                     — Malinda Prince (b. ~1848)   — Elizabeth Townsend
(b. 1857)

                     — John Armstrong
Townsend (b. ~1853)

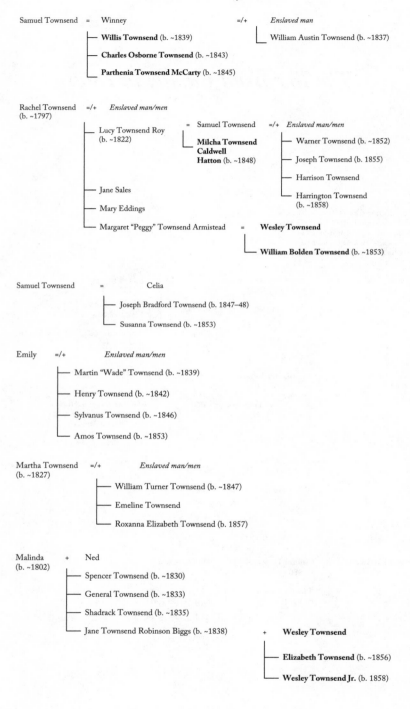

Samuel Townsend = Winney   =/+   *Enslaved man*

   — **Willis Townsend** (b. ~1839)   William Austin Townsend (b. ~1837)

   — **Charles Osborne Townsend** (b. ~1843)

   — **Parthenia Townsend McCarty** (b. ~1845)

Rachel Townsend   =/+   *Enslaved man/men*
(b. ~1797)

   — Lucy Townsend Roy   = Samuel Townsend   =/+   *Enslaved man/men*
     (b. ~1822)
                  Milcha Townsend   — Warner Townsend (b. ~1852)
                  Caldwell
                  Hatton (b. ~1848)   — Joseph Townsend (b. 1855)

                                      — Harrison Townsend

   — Jane Sales   — Harrington Townsend
                                      (b. ~1858)
   — Mary Eddings

   — Margaret "Peggy" Townsend Armistead   =   **Wesley Townsend**

                                  — **William Bolden Townsend** (b. ~1853)

Samuel Townsend   =   Celia

   — Joseph Bradford Townsend (b. 1847–48)

   — Susanna Townsend (b. ~1853)

Emily   =/+   *Enslaved man/men*

   — Martin "Wade" Townsend (b. ~1839)

   — Henry Townsend (b. ~1842)

   — Sylvanus Townsend (b. ~1846)

   — Amos Townsend (b. ~1853)

Martha Townsend   =/+   *Enslaved man/men*
(b. ~1827)

   — William Turner Townsend (b. ~1847)

   — Emeline Townsend

   — Roxanna Elizabeth Townsend (b. 1857)

Malinda   +   Ned
(b. ~1802)

   — Spencer Townsend (b. ~1830)

   — General Townsend (b. ~1833)

   — Shadrack Townsend (b. ~1835)

   — Jane Townsend Robinson Biggs (b. ~1838)   +   **Wesley Townsend**

                                          — **Elizabeth Townsend** (b. ~1856)

                                          — **Wesley Townsend Jr.** (b. 1858)

Introduction

WHEN SAMUEL TOWNSEND died at his home in Madison County, Alabama, in November 1856, he left behind hundreds of slaves, thousands of acres of rich cotton land, and a net worth of approximately $200,000. The fifty-two-year-old white planter was the antebellum equivalent of a multi-millionaire, though he did little in life to distinguish himself from other members of the elite slaveholding class that dominated the American South. He held no political office and rarely participated in the social life of the city of Huntsville, despite living just miles away. Samuel was "not fond of so-ciety," as his lawyer delicately phrased it, preferring instead the seclusion of his plantations and the pursuit of ever more wealth in land and slaves.[1] Samuel was not exceptional in that trait either. Most of the planter's money and property came to him by bequest, the posthumous generosity of shrewder elder brothers. But Samuel did make a name for himself in death when he de-cided to leave almost his entire fortune to five sons, four daughters, and two nieces: all of them his slaves.

Like countless men across the antebellum South, the unmarried cotton planter Samuel Townsend and his brother Edmund fathered children with enslaved women they owned on their vast estates. These women—at least two in Edmund's case and five or more in Samuel's—can be described as the brothers' concubines.[2] In the Townsends' era the term "concubine" had a specific legal meaning: any woman who cohabited with a man without being married.[3] In practice, concubinage in the United States was deeply intertwined with the institution of slavery, and the laws of that institution conspired to make enslaved women concubines.[4] By definition, a concubine had neither the rights nor status of a wife, and her children could not in-herit from their father. But because enslaved people were prohibited from marrying, an enslaved woman could never be someone's wife. And because slavery in the United States followed the condition of the mother, any children she had would necessarily be illegitimate and unable to inherit. This was a system accepted by custom and enshrined in law. As the famous escaped slave and abolitionist Frederick Douglass wrote in 1845, slaveholders established these practices "obviously to administer to their own lusts, and make a gratification of their wicked desires profitable as well as pleasurable."[5] Both Black and white Americans of the eighteenth and nineteenth centuries referred to enslaved women trapped in this system as "concubines." Madison Hemings, for example, one of six children of Thomas Jefferson and the enslaved woman Sally Hemings, used the term to describe his own mother.[6] Like Sally Hemings, a number of enslaved women on the Townsend plantations had extended sexual contact with their masters—though the length of these relationships should not imply consent or affection on the women's part.[7] As human property themselves, with no right or recourse to legal protection, enslaved women in the South were highly vulnerable to coercion, abuse, and rape from men with nearly unlimited power over their lives. One former slave from Alabama recollected that "back in the days when I came along us women couldn't help it if a white man wanted to take up time with us."[8] Another stated: "I didn't want him, but I couldn't do nothin.'"[9] For the mothers of Samuel and Edmund's children, this was no free choice.

As for the children, they were chattel too, subject to the same uncertainties and abuses as their mothers or any other enslaved person. They could be sold at a whim; they could be separated from the people they loved; they could be beaten and brutalized. The fact that their father was a wealthy white man granted them no special legal status in antebellum Alabama. In Samuel Townsend's mind, however, his children were a caste apart, superior to other slaves by merit of the Townsend blood he had bequeathed to them. Samuel expected his enslaved family to tend to him during his lifetime, but after his death he wanted his children freed, along with their mothers, their mothers' children by enslaved men, and his brother Edmund's enslaved children: forty-five individuals in total. Even more outrageous to his white relatives and neighbors, he wanted to leave his land and money to them.

Samuel wasn't the first Townsend to attempt this feat. Three years earlier, Edmund had tried to do the same for his own enslaved children. But Edmund's will was broken in court, leaving his two sons and two daughters neither the freedom nor fortune he'd promised them. Undeterred, Samuel, with the aid of his attorney S. D. Cabaniss, intended to make the wide white world beyond his plantation—or at least the Madison County Probate Court—recognize his sons and daughters as his legitimate heirs. In his own words: just as if they were "white children."[10] He named S. D. Cabaniss the executor of his estate, tasked with ensuring that his children enjoyed the elevated status to which Samuel believed his twin legacies of wealth and whiteness entitled them. In 1860, four years and several lawsuits after the cotton planter's death, Cabaniss succeeded in seeing the forty-five Townsends manumitted. They left Alabama, where state law prohibited free African Americans from settling, and migrated across the country in the following decades, seeking new homes in communities where they could exercise their freedom to the fullest.

From Samuel and Edmund's generation forward, the Townsends wanted what virtually all nineteenth-century Americans wanted: social and economic mobility. They pursued these goals in the American West, the region of the United States most closely associated with promises of opportunity and advancement.[11] When the white Townsend brothers left their home state of Virginia for Alabama in 1819, they were among the first wave of Anglo-American settlers on what was then the country's western frontier—advancing themselves at the expense of the hundreds of enslaved people who labored to build their plantations, as well as the Native Americans who had been removed from their ancestral lands to make room for a cotton empire. The freed Townsends, too, migrated westward after their master's death. When Samuel's eldest son Wesley was manumitted in 1858, two years before the rest of the family, S. D. Cabaniss arranged for him to settle near Cincinnati, Ohio, one of the country's major western commercial centers. In 1860, Samuel's other children, along with their mothers, cousins, and half-siblings, migrated to Kansas, where boosters promised cheap, fertile land and possibilities as boundless as the sky over the Great Plains. After the Civil War, Samuel's son Charles Osborne and other relatives ventured to the Rocky Mountains, lured by Colorado's silver mines. In all of their travels, the Townsends hoped to find the wealth and social status that Samuel and Edmund had found in Alabama, or at the very least a home where they might be treated with dignity and respect. They had "happy dreams of liberty," one of Cabaniss's colleagues would write contemptuously—dreams the man considered an illusion.[12] But as Edmund's son Woodson and his wife Elvira would later assert, they expected just as much respect and consideration "as any body."[13] They refused to settle for anything less.

The Townsends enjoyed certain advantages in their pursuit of social and economic advancement. Emancipation and inheritance gave family members access to freedom and property, a "hallmark of whiteness" in a country where blackness was associated with inferiority and enslavement.[14] Though white communities across the free states all too often met African American migrants with animosity and violence, some made exceptions for the Townsends, who brought desirable capital to those communities. As one neighbor in Ohio observed: "I have yet to see the first man that refuses to . . . sell a colored man anything they have for sale if the colored man can pay for it."[15] Money opened doors to schools like Wilberforce University, where the younger Townsend children joined other mixed-race sons and daughters of wealthy southern planters. It opened doors to furnished homes and well-stocked barns that the Townsends could own rather than working as hired labor. When trouble broke out, as it invariably did, Samuel Townsend's money opened the doors to lawyers' offices, indispensable for an African American family navigating a legal system dominated by bigoted whites. Unlike the fugitive slaves who fled to Ohio in the years before the Civil War, or the "Exodusters" who would leave the South for Kansas *en masse* in the decades after, the Townsends began their new lives in freedom with a measure of financial security and stability.

Samuel had also given his children another powerful, if less quantifiable, bequest: their mixed-race ancestry. Many Americans at the time believed that race was a biological fact, the foundation of innate differences between groups of people, as opposed to the present-day understanding that "race" is in fact socially constructed.[16] Then as now, racial prejudice damaged people's lives, while "whiteness" endowed privileges and advantages. Members of the Townsend family experienced both of these effects. White associates, acquaintances, and others they encountered over the course of their lives interacted with members of the Townsend family differently depending on their parentage—whether they were the children of Samuel Townsend, his brother Edmund, or two enslaved parents—and perceptions of their physical appearance. These perceptions were central to the Townsends' lived experiences both in freedom and under slavery, having a concrete impact on whether or not individuals within the family were emancipated, inherited money, or received a formal education. At the same time, some members of the family used their ancestry and appearance to consciously distance themselves from other relatives or their local Black communities. The Townsend's mixed-race background was an intangible quality that shaped their lives in very real ways.[17]

In the language of their day, the Townsends were considered "mulattos," individuals whose physical appearance indicated Anglo-American or European as well as African ancestry. Yet even those who believed in inherent racial differences often found themselves unable to agree on a single category in which to place men and women like the Townsends. Nineteenth-century Americans applied labels like "black," "white," "mulatto," and "colored" to neighbors and strangers based on their subjective, individual perceptions—and, accordingly, the Townsends' "race" could change depending on whom you asked. The lawyer S. D. Cabaniss commented that some of Samuel's children looked more Mexican than African American, and one government agent, after meeting Samuel's daughter Milcha, wrote a colleague that he wouldn't have guessed she was "an African" at all if he hadn't known she was married to a man with darker skin.[18] Even census takers were told to ask neighbors and other community members to confirm a given person's race if they couldn't tell from their own observation.[19] That was no foolproof strategy either. In 1870, federal census enumerators placed a "W" beside Samuel's grandson William Bolden Townsend's name, declaring him white; four years later, a city directory marked him "C," for colored.[20] It's impossible to assess what the Townsends' contemporaries saw, since few images of any of the forty-five enslaved people freed by Samuel's will appear to have survived. A sketch and a grainy newspaper photograph of William Bolden Townsend may be the only visual representations of one of them that remain.[21] The Townsends remain as unclassifiable today as they were in life.

Men and women like the Townsends, whose mixed ancestry belied the idea that racial lines were permanent and impermeable, occupied a shifting space between Black and white. Being in-between had its advantages. Samuel and Edmund's children, as well as other family members with mixed-race ancestry, benefited from widespread color prejudice among white Americans. In line with practices common throughout the antebellum South, mixed-race individuals held privileged positions on the Townsend plantations. Samuel and Edmund's daughters, along with certain concubines, were exempt from field labor, and their sons learned skilled trades and owned personal property that neighbors acknowledged as theirs—even if the laws of Alabama did not. Most significantly, they were the ones who received their freedom.[22] Of the forty-five freed Townsends, at least thirty-seven of them were related by blood to the planter brothers or the mothers of their children.[23] Even after their emancipation, Samuel and Edmund's heirs continued to benefit from their mixed-race ancestry. White neighbors and associates—including S. D. Cabaniss, who exercised extensive control over their finances—assumed that Samuel and Edmund's children were more intelligent, capable, and trustworthy than their relatives without Anglo-American or European heritage.

To understand how race shaped the Townsends' experiences of freedom, the family must be situated in their own time. At the turn of the twentieth century, as Jim Crow segregation hardened social, political, and economic divisions between white Americans and people of color, the color line hardened too. White Americans settled on a "one-drop rule" whereby any African ancestry, however distant or visually imperceptible, made a person "black," a label subjecting all who bore it to indignity, violence, and exploitation. When the Townsends lived and settled around the country as free men and women, however, this system had yet to develop.[24] The second half of the nineteenth century was one of the most radically transformative periods in American history, throwing the country's racial regime into a state of flux. Between the Townsends' manumissions in 1860 and the rise of Jim Crow in the early 1900s, a bloody civil war ended slavery throughout the nation, collapsing the planter aristocracy of the South and challenging a system of white supremacy that had undergirded American politics, economics, and society since the founding of the United States. Millions of African American men and women won their freedom and recognition as citizens, and half of them won the right to vote. Across the country, Black men held public office, while their constituents demanded justice and equality from a political system that had never before represented their interests. This was a time of change and possibility, an in-between moment as fluid as the mixed-raced Townsends' identities.[25]

Nineteenth-century racial hierarchies across the Americas covered a wide span between "black" and "white." In the British West Indies, "free coloureds" or "browns" formed a third class, at times allying with whites against "blacks" both slave and free. In Jamaica, individual free coloreds could petition for civil rights—effectively becoming legally "white." In Barbados and Brazil, though skin color granted no special legal privileges, free people of color formed a distinct social group with their own institutions and hierarchies. Indigenous peoples further complicated the picture, especially in Latin America, where Europeans and their descendants at times considered Native Americans more "other" than the Black or mixed-race descendants of Africans. In the United States, lower South cities like Charleston, Mobile, and especially New Orleans (with its Spanish and French colonial history) also bore similarities to the Caribbean's three-tiered society. Though all such racial systems harbored a great deal of anti-Black prejudice, they provided mixed-race individuals with the maneuverability to shape their own identities and, perhaps, climb to a higher rung on the social ladder.[26]

The Townsends never saw the Caribbean, and they would have known New Orleans only as the terrifying slave-trading hub where Samuel and Edmund shipped their crops. Their homes were in Alabama's cotton country, Ohio's river towns, Kansas's rolling prairies, and Colorado's towering Rocky Mountains. Yet they, too, experienced—and sought to take full advantage of—the porousness of racial divisions in their time. The clothes they wore, the jobs they held, the eloquence of their speech, and the identities of their friends and neighbors could all play as important a role in how the Townsends were perceived as the exact color of their skin. As historian Martha Hodes has written, factors such as class and education, in addition to skin color, might serve to "shade" a person closer to the social status of whiteness.[27] Perhaps the Townsends could pay their way, work their way, or educate their way out of racial prejudice. Perhaps even into whiteness.

Geography, like money and mixed-race ancestry, played a key role. Take antebellum Ohio. Though a far cry from the Caribbean or cosmopolitan port cities of the lower South, this state was another place where mixed-race individuals might enjoy freedoms denied to them elsewhere. In the 1856 *Dred Scott v. Sandford* decision, the United States Supreme Court declared that African Americans had no rights of citizenship. Yet in Ohio, state courts held that men with more than 50 percent Anglo-American or European ancestry, whether they had "visible" African ancestry or not, were entitled to vote.[28] When Wesley Townsend moved to Ohio just two years after *Dred Scott v. Sandford*, he may have been considered legally white, entitled to the same civil rights that the Supreme Court would have prohibited him exercising. Despite the existence of this legal loophole for mixed-race men, not every Ohio community welcomed migrants like Wesley. So in Xenia, the southern Ohio town where Samuel Townsend's younger children attended school, propertied African Americans created their own insular enclave of "colored elites."[29] The community included multiple other families with mixed-race children, manumitted mothers, and inherited wealth. Within their small settlement, these "elites" defined their own social and racial hierarchies.

The Black community in eastern Kansas had a different set of rules. When members of the Townsend family settled in Leavenworth in the 1860s, they entered a city with one of the largest Black populations in the state—as well as one of the most politically organized. Black Kansans had the numbers to form social networks and independent community institutions, protect fugitive slaves from recapture, and mobilize large numbers of African American recruits to serve in the Union Army during the Civil War.[30] Community

leaders stressed unity above intra-racial divisions, and mixed-race people neither occupied a distinct legal category nor created an exclusive social stratum
within the wider Black community. Nevertheless, the Townsends occupied an
ambiguous racial category from the perspective of white Kansans, and mixed-
race members of the family were at times classified as "white" in censuses and
city directories.[31] Some also benefited from the color and class prejudices of
local whites. When Woodson Townsend, Edmund Townsend's youngest son,
was falsely accused of rape in 1864, his money and links to influential white
Leavenworth residents likely saved him from a death sentence even as Black
community leaders declared with disdain that he had "always considered himself a white man."[32]

Farthest west, in Colorado Territory, Charles Osborne Townsend experienced an exceptional level of social and political equality in his small
community. Georgetown was an isolated silver mining town in the Rocky
Mountains, and when Charles Osborne and his half-brother William Austin
settled there in the 1860s, they were two of fewer than five hundred African
Americans living in the vast Colorado Territory.[33] Here, white Americans
saw native peoples and Chinese migrant laborers as outsiders—not the Black
settlers who joined them in such small, unthreatening numbers and adopted
their distinctly western politics, marked by populist sentiment and distrust of
the federal government. In Georgetown, white residents and monied, often
mixed-race, African Americans attended social events together, formed business partnerships, and played on the same baseball team.[34] Charles Osborne
Townsend became a local "celebrity" feted for his military service in the
Union Army and his successful barbershop, patronized by white and Black
customers alike.[35] In this relatively liberal racial climate—at least for African
American migrants—region took precedence over race, and Charles Osborne
came to consider his interests and identity more closely aligned with white
farmers and miners in the West than striving African Americans like his
family members elsewhere in the country.

Even in post–Civil War Alabama, Samuel's son Thomas Townsend found
avenues for social and economic mobility as well as local political promi-
nence. A teacher, journalist, and businessman, Thomas returned to Madison
County in 1868 and purchased a part of his father's old plantation. This
was his birthplace and birthright. From the site of his former enslavement,
Thomas worked to reclaim the elite status the white Townsends had once
enjoyed. As an educated man and a landowner, Thomas was a natural leader
in northern Alabama's Black community during Reconstruction, funding an
African American newspaper in Huntsville and assisting Black Union Army

veterans to claim their government pensions. His political career began in 1880—three years after federal troops left the former Confederacy, and six years after white Democrats regained control of Alabama's state government. Thomas's mixed-race ancestry, middle-class respectability, and willingness to form strategic alliances with white southerners protected him at a time when African Americans across the country faced increasing violence and repression. Alone among Samuel Townsend's heirs, Thomas retained the trust of the lawyer S. D. Cabaniss. When he died in 1916—well into the Jim Crow era—a white newspaper eulogized him as a man, a "capitalist" no less, "respected and esteemed by white citizens as well as negroes."[36]

In some ways, the Townsends' story is a small one. The Townsends weren't major actors in the affairs of the nation. Like so many others, they were ordinary people seeking stability in an extraordinarily tumultuous time. To date, only one full-length narrative of their experiences has been written.[37] Yet small stories can provide valuable perspectives on the bigger picture. Detailed studies of individual lives often yield insights lost in broad, sweeping histories of a time or place.[38] In this case, details of the Townsends' lives and travels reveal a sometimes surprising landscape of opportunity and oppression where meanings of race and freedom—as well as concrete opportunities for social and economic mobility—were dictated by highly local norms and values. At different moments throughout their lives, the Townsends' race, place, and money gave them the space to define their own identities and experience freedom on their own terms: as "colored elites," as western everymen, as Black community leaders, or perhaps as white men and women. Samuel's teenaged daughter Susanna was engaged to a white man in 1868, stating that she would be a "Townsend" no more and possibly planning to "pass" as white, though the man left her before they could marry.[39] Edmund Townsend's daughter Lizzie did cross the color line; she married a white Union Army officer in 1868, moved with him to North Carolina, and was subsequently listed as "white" in federal census records.[40] Her husband may never have known that his wife was once held as a slave—or perhaps he was passing too.[41] Few of the Townsends, however, sought to permanently cross the color line. Instead, they attempted to move toward the social status of whiteness at a time when racial lines were more flexible and color and capital could transform a former slave's prospects. But flexibility was fragile. The opportunities the Townsends' ancestry and inheritance provided them were always dependent on the people and institutions with the greatest authority in their communities. When those people challenged the Townsends' self-chosen identities, the Townsends rarely won.

Huntsville attorney S. D. Cabaniss exercised more influence over the Townsends than any single person after their emancipation, as Samuel Townsend's will gave the lawyer virtually unilateral control over the use and disposal of his property. He chose where the Townsends would first settle after they left Alabama in 1858 and 1860, since he had the power to withhold money from the estate if they refused to comply. He and the white agents he appointed to oversee matters in Ohio and Kansas could, and did, veto decisions made by the Townsends. Land purchases, business dealings, and contracts were all subject to the executor's approval. He policed the Townsends' friends and associates, charging local whites with keeping an eye on them and reporting back if anyone in the family drank, gambled, or kept what Cabaniss considered bad company. Only when the Civil War intervened in 1861—and the Confederate government demanded that Cabaniss cut off all contact with citizens of the enemy United States—did the Townsends begin to experience freedom without the executor's oversight, if also without payments from Samuel's estate. Afterward, the lawyer never regained the same grip over their lives as he had held before the war, but his ability to withhold payments from the will undoubtedly influenced their choices. Cabaniss was a diligent executor, but his racial prejudices and assumptions about the Townsends' intelligence and abilities continued to limit the ways in which they could exercise their freedom. In the end, Samuel Townsend's estate was not fully settled until 1890, a year after Cabaniss's death.

By then, changing attitudes and ideas about race had begun to shrink the space between Black and white that the Townsends once occupied.[42] Perhaps only Lizzie—accepted as a white woman by wider society—escaped the contraction of privileges that her relatives who had "shaded" toward whiteness saw as the nineteenth century came to a close. In 1871, Charles Osborne Townsend was shocked at being forced to ride in a second-class train compartment on a trip to Kansas; in 1889, he swore to his brother Thomas that his self-respect would never allow him to set foot in the South again.[43] Sure enough, white legislators pushed Thomas out of Alabama politics in 1884. Meanwhile, Samuel's grandson William Bolden Townsend, once taken as a white man by federal census agents, regularly faced death threats and lynch mobs on account of his civil rights activism in Kansas. The qualities that William Bolden's father, aunts, and uncles had relied on to advance themselves—money and mixed-race ancestry foremost among them—could no longer protect the Townsends in the age of Jim Crow. Maybe, William Bolden said in 1901, "now and then one of us might be able to overcome the storm of combined oppression and fight his or her way to the stars; but he or she is an exception to the rule."[44] As their local communities' flexible color lines hardened into impassable barriers, the mixed-race Townsends were relegated to the same side as the relatives and community members who had never had a say in how they were defined.

———⚬———

In slavery, hoping that Alabama courts would uphold their father and master's will, the Townsends imagined their lives in freedom. In Ohio, Kansas, and Colorado, they imagined new identities for themselves—their visions competing with those of white Americans who saw them as something less. The process of reconstructing their experiences requires imagination as well. The same people and institutions that determined how and whether the Townsends could exercise their freedom also shaped how they're remembered today. Detailed information about their lives after emancipation comes largely from S. D. Cabaniss's personal and legal files. A careful lawyer, he left behind nearly 15,000 individual items: receipts, account books, inventories, depositions, petitions, and calculations scratched on the backs of envelopes. He also kept two boxes of correspondence from the freed Townsends themselves, letters that provide a rare opportunity to recover the voices of Samuel and Edmund's children, their mothers, and their half-siblings—all former slaves. Tantalizing and frustrating, the letters the Townsends wrote to the lawyer reveal only pieces of their minds. At times stiff, terse, and designed to flatter the attorney's ego, they were crafted for the eyes of a powerful white southerner with a slave-owner's mentality and did not record the Townsends' private thoughts and experiences. Even the few extant letters that the Townsends wrote to each other, in which family members discussed political opinions and personal life events more freely, were colored by their shared interest in Samuel's property. Some of the Townsends lived hundreds of miles apart and went years without seeing one another. The status of their promised inheritance, however, kept them in contact, and when the Townsend siblings corresponded, they rarely failed to ask for news about the estate. Without the decades-long litigation over the old cotton planter's property, there might be no record of the Townsends' voices at all.[45]

Cabaniss's papers found their way to the University of Alabama in 1952, a gift of his granddaughter Frances Cabaniss Roberts, who wrote her master's thesis on Samuel Townsend and his children in 1940. For decades, "An Experiment in the Emancipation of Slaves by an Alabama Planter" was the first and last word on the Townsend family, with Roberts framing their lives as a test of African Americans' ability to sink or swim without the guidance of a benevolent master.[46] In her view, the experiment failed. She told a story of men and women too ignorant to succeed in freedom. Mismanaging their inheritance, she said, many of the Townsends faced poverty and hardship, unable to make more than a "bare living."[47] Too stubborn to accept the well-meaning advice of their long-suffering executor, some fell into vicious, immoral habits. A few managed to "rise above the others" through education and hard work, true, but they were the exceptions; "a very short, unstable kind of life" proved closer to the rule.[48] Considering the evidence, Roberts concluded that the freed Townsends might have fared better as slaves, where at least they would have been "well cared for and protected from the time they were born until they died."[49] Her analysis bears the signature of early twentieth-century scholarship on slavery and emancipation, which denied the violence and inhumanity of slavery in the antebellum South, asserted the innate inferiority of African Americans, and ultimately served to justify the racial segregation and white supremacy of her own day.[50] In the end, Roberts's thesis depicted the Townsends as undeserving of their freedom and inheritance due to their race and status as former slaves—the same arguments that Samuel's white relatives had made when they challenged his will in 1856. Nearly a century after the antebellum planter's death, the story was largely unchanged.

Yet there are other stories to be told about the Townsend family. About an egotistical master whose affection for his children didn't forestall violence and cruelty toward other enslaved people he did not father. About a powerful executor who struggled to see his client's mixed-race children as fully capable of exercising their freedom or inheritance. About individuals seeking autonomy for themselves in ways both large and small: homesteaders settling on the country's ever-shifting western frontier; women leaving the partners pressed on them under slavery to marry men of their choice; a young man joining the Union Army to fight for emancipation; a politician buying the old plantation where he had once been enslaved; an activist, the son of a slave and grandson of a slave owner, fighting for justice and equality. About brothers and sisters linked to each other across vast distances by bonds of kinship and money, and how the one reinforced the other. It's a story about men and women whose money, mixed-race ancestry, and geographic dispersal opened doors to economic and social mobility in a hostile society—and the times and places where prejudice closed those doors and frustrated their choices. This is the story of one family living in a turbulent time, a testament to the unexpected opportunities and all-too-common obstacles they faced as they pursued that most American dream: moving up in the world.

I

This Happy, Free, and Flourishing Country

"HE WAS A wealthy man."[1] When Edmund Townsend died in 1853, the relatives he had left behind in Virginia more than thirty years earlier knew little more about him than his net worth, but apparently that was enough. "His reputation as a man of singular character," a niece and her husband eulogized, "who, commencing life without patrimony, had accumulated so large a fortune," was widely known in his old home county of Lunenburg, Virginia, even to those who had never met him.[2] That was a topic worthy of conversation, and there was plenty to talk about. At a time when the average farm size in the United States was two hundred acres, Edmund Townsend owned more than six thousand.[3] Modest farmers like his relatives in Virginia counted anyone a rich man who had land and personal property worth more than a $1,000; Edmund was worth $500,000—more than $16 million in present-day currency.[4] Perhaps most impressive of all to the Townsends in Virginia, who claimed they had "always been poor and humble," Edmund Townsend controlled the lives and labor of the three hundred men, women, and children he owned as slaves on seven sprawling cotton plantations in northern Alabama.[5]

While he was alive, he lived the nineteenth-century American dream.

Edmund Townsend was among the first generation of children born into a new nation after the end of the Revolutionary War. Awash with ideals of liberty and equality, northeastern states from Vermont to New Jersey passed gradual emancipation laws intended to abolish the institution of slavery over the next few decades. Others, however, were less convinced. The Declaration of Independence might have trumpeted the right to "life, liberty, and the pursuit of happiness," but some Americans preferred philosopher John Locke's version from a century before: life, liberty, and property.[6] In 1784 and 1785, just a few years after the war, more than 1,400 Virginians signed proslavery petitions bound for the state legislature. Antislavery acts were "rash," they said, the "chimerical Flights of a fanatic spirit." Slaves were "the most valuable and indispensable" property they owned. Had they "waded thro' Deluges of civil Blood" just to lose them? "No!" one petition answered, "we have sealed with our Blood, a Title to the full, free, and absolute Enjoyment of every species of Property." In Lunenburg County, where Edmund Townsend's parents made their home, 161 men signed the petition. Take away their slaves, Virginians warned their lawmakers, and bring total ruin to "this once happy, free, and flourishing Country."[7]

The petitions read as more desperate than defiant. Postwar Virginia was far from a "flourishing" country. Tobacco was no longer the cash crop it had been a century before. Generations of wasteful cultivation had left the soil exhausted of nutrients and even poor land was growing scarce. By the time Edmund Townsend was born in 1791, one out of every four white Virginians of his parents' generation had already left the Chesapeake, hoping they could make a better living in Maryland, Kentucky, or the Carolinas.[8] But the Townsends stayed. Family tradition holds that Edmund's father, William, married up, to a widow named Elizabeth who brought some money to the household by way of her first husband.[9] Perhaps they bought a little land, purchased a few slaves—not much of either but enough to make the prospect of uprooting themselves and their six children too risky to seriously consider. They were comfortable enough as they were, the sort of independent yeoman farmers fellow Virginian Thomas Jefferson called "the most virtuous citizens" in the Republic, "the chosen people of God."[10] When they died sometime before 1819, this kind of modest success was the best they could have hoped to leave their sons and daughters. At the end of the eighteenth century, Virginia wasn't a place for dreams of social mobility.

But the country was changing, bringing new opportunities for Edmund and his siblings. Developments in transportation, communication, industry, and commerce made it possible for small-scale farmers to participate in an ever more interconnected national economy. Instead of producing food and goods solely for their families and local communities, rural Americans increasingly turned their attention—and their labor—toward generating the commodities demanded by national and international markets. At the turn of the nineteenth century, no product was more central to these markets than cotton. Before the Revolution, cotton production in North America had been limited to small amounts planted on the Sea Islands off the South Carolina coast. Native to subtropical areas, this strain of long-staple cotton didn't grow well on the mainland. The bolls of the hardier short-staple strain could grow virtually anywhere south of Virginia, but the short-staple bolls were riddled with small seeds that had to be removed by hand. This arduous process made planting cotton a losing game for most farmers until 1793. That year, American inventor Eli Whitney created a machine that could quickly and easily remove the seeds from short-staple cotton fiber, mechanizing what had long been one of the most time-consuming aspects of cotton production. The cotton gin changed the landscape of agriculture in the United States. It made short-staple cotton profitable to grow, creating a new commodity in demand by textile mills in the Northeast. And by fueling the expansion of market-oriented cultivation, cotton generated demands for another sort of expansion as farmers sought that holy grail Anglo-Americans coveted above all else: cheap land.[11]

From the founding of the republic, the idea of a vast, "virgin" continent to the west had captured Americans' imaginations—and the United States government had been trying to acquire more of that land for as long as that government had been in existence.[12] With the Louisiana Purchase in 1803, President Thomas Jefferson presided over the acquisition of more than 800,000 square miles of French territory west of the Mississippi River. Jefferson's administration obtained another 15,000 square miles of land in the fertile Tennessee River Valley in 1805, when a small number of Cherokee chiefs sold the tribe's hunting grounds. In exchange, the chiefs received privately owned land parcels, lifetime annuities, cash gifts, and valuable farming equipment—including cotton gins.[13] The final impetus for mass westward migration, however, came with the War of 1812.

As Britain fought France in the Atlantic and the United States fought Britain on the eastern seaboard, General Andrew Jackson engaged in battle with a faction of Creek Indians called the Red Sticks. Like the Cherokees, the Creeks had been facing increasing pressure to cede land to the US government, adopt Anglo forms of property ownership, and in the process abandon much of their traditional culture and lifestyle.[14] The Red Sticks opposed white settlers' encroachment and the threat of cultural assimilation, and their rebellion began as a civil war within the Creek Confederacy. But the victory of Red Stick warriors over an American militia that attacked them in 1813—and the subsequent Red Stick takeover of a military garrison in lower Alabama—pushed jumpy US officials into more direct involvement in the conflict. At the Battle of Horseshoe Bend in 1814, forces commanded by Andrew Jackson defeated the Red Sticks, definitively eradicated native people's influence in the region, and, under the terms of the treaty of surrender, acquired nearly 36,000 square miles of Creek land across Alabama and Georgia. "The power of the creeks is I think forever broken," Jackson wrote after the battle.[15] For prospective migrants, that was nothing to mourn. After all, as the man who crushed the Red Sticks would ask as president: "What good man would prefer a country covered with forests and ranged by a few thousand savages to our extensive Republic?"[16]

The hundreds of thousands of white settlers who flocked to the region after the Red Sticks' defeat certainly did not. Between 1810 and 1820, Alabama's population increased by more than 1,000 percent, with most of the migrants arriving after the end of the war in 1815. "Alabama fever" swept across the eastern seaboard as the opening of seemingly endless, fertile lands to the west heralded what must have felt like an age of unlimited opportunity.[17] "I have no doubt but in a few years," Jackson prophesied, "the Banks of the allabama will present a beautiful view of elegant mansions, and extensive rich & productive farms."[18] This was a vision of empire, but not the one Thomas Jefferson had foreseen a decade earlier. A large landowner and slaveholder himself, Jefferson had imagined modest yeoman farmers along the lines of Edmund Townsend's parents spreading "an empire for liberty" across the continent.[19] But Edmund and his siblings, along with countless others like them, were starting to imagine riches more like Thomas Jefferson's. Suddenly, social mobility seemed not just possible but destined. With Native American power shattered, millions of square miles of "wilderness without an owner" open to settlement, and a new cash crop to make them rich, Alabama was ripe for the taking.[20] Virgin land was not meant to remain untouched. Jefferson had said: Be fruitful and multiply.

What followed was the first great land rush in American history. In 1818, the federal government's land office in Huntsville, a northern Alabama boom town only established in 1810, sold nearly 1 million acres of land to prospective settlers.[21] Migrants—predominantly from Virginia and South Carolina—flooded Huntsville for the sale. The rules were simple: pay one quarter of the purchase up front and the rest over the course of the next three years. One hundred sixty acres was the smallest tract of land the government offered for sale, but demand for cotton had risen so high that even men of "poor and humble" circumstances were confident they could buy land on credit and pay back the debt when their first crop came in.[22] "The town was literally crammed with people," one Alabama resident would write decades later; the local bank was so overwhelmed that "the hotel keepers were coining money."[23] To farmers disillusioned with their limited prospects on the eastern seaboard, the fertile Tennessee River Valley looked like heaven. One Baptist preacher back east, searching for a metaphor for God's kingdom that his congregation would understand, described heaven as "a fair Alabama of a place."[24] Another man, his mind on more secular matters, called the new state El Dorado.[25]

Edmund Townsend arrived in 1819. He had missed the government sale but found plenty of cheap land anyway. As it turned out, not all of the migrants caught up in the previous year's speculation could pay their debts. A nationwide economic depression in 1819 forced thousands of overly optimistic farmers to surrender their land to the federal government or else sell at a loss to men with a little more capital—men like Edmund Townsend.[26] Along with his younger brothers Parks, Stith, and Samuel, and his sister Henrietta and her husband—some of whom arrived later—Edmund established himself in Hazel Green, Madison County, just north of Huntsville.[27] Only Virginia Townsend, the eldest sister, chose to remain in the state she was named for. Others Edmund brought had no choice, because despite what his Virginia relatives would say in later years, Edmund Townsend had not been left entirely without patrimony. As, if not more, important than the land he bought were the slaves he brought to work it, men and women uprooted from their homes and families to build the opulent mansions and productive farms Andrew Jackson had foreseen. Over the course of the next four decades, these forced migrants would carve the Townsend siblings an empire out of the wilderness, but it was no empire for liberty.

———

Lizzy arrived in Alabama the year the stars fell. She was ten or eleven—she couldn't say for sure—but for the rest of her life she would remember that night in 1833 when the world seemed to be ending.[28] Around midnight on November 13, shooting stars began to fill the skies east of the Rocky Mountains, with Alabamians receiving the most spectacular view. Flashes of light and booming sounds woke people and drew them outside as meteors passed through the earth's atmosphere, dozens per second and hundreds per minute, according to some estimates.[29] It was "as if the planets and constellations were falling from their places," one newspaper reported the next day.[30] As the shower continued unabated for hours, witnesses started to wonder whether this was the long-awaited second coming of Christ. "And the stars of the heavens fell unto the earth," the book of Revelation reads, "for the great day of his wrath is come; and who shall be able to stand?"[31] Terrified onlookers cried, or prayed, or simply stared in wonder. Up north in Illinois, a young man named Lincoln heard his innkeeper shouting "Arise, Abraham, the day of judgment has come!"[32] For a century after, Alabama residents would mark time by "the years the stars fell," the dividing line for local and personal histories. It was the dividing line for Lizzy too, a night the sky seemed to reflect what must certainly have felt like the end of her world: the year she was forced to leave her home in Virginia, sent west on a seven-hundred-mile trek to Alabama, and sold to a man named Edmund Townsend.

In the first decades of the nineteenth century, the political and economic developments that gave men like the Townsend brothers new opportunities for wealth and status had a different—and devastating—effect on enslaved people in the United States. At the time of the Revolution, conventional wisdom held that American slavery was a dying institution. During and after the war, antislavery and gradual emancipation laws were passed across the northern states; the importation of slaves into the United States from Africa and the Caribbean was abolished in 1808; and in places where slavery did remain legal, falling tobacco prices and limited land led even slave owners themselves to believe that their economic system might not be viable for much longer. Cotton changed everything. With the discovery of a new cash crop that required year-round labor, white southerners' demand for slaves skyrocketed—and the massive territorial expansion that followed the War of 1812 spread that demand westward.[33] Migrants to new cotton states like Alabama, Mississippi, and Louisiana hungered for laborers to work land that was, in their eyes, still a wilderness. One white settler described northern Alabama as "the most broken mountainous country I ever saw." Another called it wild, untrodden, tomahawk-marked.[34] Clearing dense woods, burning underbrush, building cabins and fences and outbuildings—there were countless tasks to complete before cotton planting could even begin. As far as these migrants were concerned, slave labor was the solution. As early as 1820, enslaved people already comprised nearly half the population of Madison County, Alabama, a larger percentage than anywhere else in the Tennessee River Valley. By 1850, Madison County would have a Black majority.[35]

The Townsends were avid participants in the slave trade, with Parks Townsend and his nephew Thomas regularly traveling back east to purchase enslaved men and women on behalf of the other brothers.[36] While Samuel, the youngest, had been only fifteen when the family moved to Alabama, he soon joined his brothers among the ranks of Alabama's slave owners. Samuel was buying slaves before he owned an acre of land; his first recorded purchase was "a Negro boy named Jack" in 1827.[37] When his brother Stith died the following year, Samuel inherited two more enslaved men as well as Stith's home plantation of 260 acres, one third of the proceeds from his current cotton crop, and more than $400 in notes due him by the end of the year.[38] Samuel wasted no time investing that money in the commodity that was making his family rich. He bought dozens of enslaved people in subsequent years: a girl named Polly ("Healthy and a slave for life") in 1831, Hannah and her son Richard in 1832, Mariah and her infant child ("sound Both in body & mind") in 1833, and twenty-nine men, women, and children on a single day in February 1835, purchased for more than $10,000 on a trip to the slave-trading hub of Richmond, Virginia.[39] Samuel and his brothers favored young women, many nearly children, knowing that they could buy them more cheaply than adult workers and, in time, watch their net worth accumulate with every child the women bore.[40] In the United States, slavery followed the condition of the mother. Whether the father was slave or free, any child born to an enslaved woman would be, like Polly or Hannah or Mariah, or the young girl named Lizzy whom Edmund purchased in 1833, "a slave for life."

To men like the Townsends, the domestic slave trade was a business, soon the largest business in the South apart from cotton production. Between 1810 and 1861, slave owners and slave traders wrenched more than 1 million men, women, and children from their homes and families to sell them west.[41] Although slave traders may have considered themselves ordinary men trying to get a leg up in a competitive market, the people they bought and sold had a different name for them: soul drivers.[42] "The idea is like this," a former slave named John Boggs told an interviewer in 1863, "when a man goes out in the morning, he may have a wife and a parcel of children, and maybe when he comes back at night, he will find nobody who will tell him anything about them." He added: "That is what our people dread the most."[43] The possibility of sale hung like a pall over enslaved people's daily lives. The rice swamps of South Carolina, the sugarcane fields of Louisiana, the cotton plantations of Alabama and Mississippi—"we had them held before us as terrors, by our masters and mistresses, all our lives," an escaped slave from Kentucky said in 1853. "We knew about them all; and when a friend was carried off, why, it was the same as death, for we could not write or hear, and never expected to see them again."[44] Separating wives from husbands and parents from children was of little concern to men in pursuit of profit. Enslaved people were property under the law, and their ties to friends and family or the places they were born had no legal standing whatsoever.

Once sold, bondsmen and women destined for the cotton states could expect a grueling five to seven weeks of travel, most of it on foot, before they reached journey's end.[45] "The great Highway from Virginia to Alabama during the years 1818–1819 was more like an army of occupation than an ordinary public highway," a Madison County man would recall in the 1880s. Travelers could journey for days without ever losing sight of "emigrant wagons, accompanied by long files of Negro slaves tramping southward."[46] These "perfect caravans" (as one Alabama newspaper called the slave coffles) could be forced to cover as many as twenty-five miles a day.[47] The trek took its toll. Exhausted and malnourished, enslaved people relocated west were more susceptible to sickness, and the low-lying land of the Tennessee River Valley that planters preferred for its rich soil teemed with malaria and other mosquito-borne diseases.[48] James Tait, a cotton planter who migrated from Georgia to Alabama in 1818, recalled that for a long while "my plantations were very sickly and I lost a great many Negroes"—about three hundred in the first twenty years, he estimated. "Besides the fever about seven years ago," he noted in 1853, "the pneumonia got in among them and killed off in five years about thirty grown ones."[49] An opportunity for social advancement for Tait or the Townsends, migration to the cotton frontier was a matter of life and death for the enslaved people who accompanied them.

If they survived the physical rigors of the journey and the dangers of disease—alongside the grief and isolation that followed forced removal from their homes and communities—enslaved migrants faced the challenges of building a plantation from the ground up. While cotton cultivation was less technically complicated than tobacco (which required considerable skilled labor both to grow and harvest) or sugar (whose highly involved processing made it a nearly industrial enterprise), the labor patterns associated with cotton were unfamiliar to enslaved migrants from the Chesapeake or the Carolinas. In tobacco farming regions, enslaved people performed a wide range of different tasks: preparing seedbeds in February, harvesting in August or September, and curing and pressing tobacco leaves in late autumn. After relocating to cotton country, however, planters required enslaved workers to transition to a year-round agricultural calendar. The growing cycle for cotton was longer than for tobacco. The picking season alone could start in late summer, continue through Christmas and the new year, customarily a period when enslaved people were granted time off, and last until as late as February.[50]

Cotton stretched the workday as well as the work year. On tobacco farms, enslaved men and women organized their labor according to the "task system," performing a set amount of work for the day and using the rest of their time for themselves. Some grew crops of their own on small plots in order to supplement their diets or raise produce they might trade or sell in town on free Sundays or half-Saturdays.[51] They often worked in family groups directed by enslaved foremen, with little close supervision from planters. But cotton growers came to realize that the tedious, repetitive work of planting and picking could be done more efficiently—and thus more profitably—if they abandoned the task system, as James Tait did in 1848. "Done, forever done, working Negroes by task after this year," he wrote in his journal. "The evils attending to it are too numerous to mention here."[52] Planters avoided the "evils" of tasking (that is, free time and a modicum of autonomy for enslaved workers) by imposing dawn-to-dusk gang labor, subjecting enslaved people to longer days and tighter plantation discipline. Gang labor kept enslaved men and women in the cotton fields for as long as there was light in the sky, while the other jobs they were expected to perform—drying and ginning, carding and spinning—could continue even after nightfall.

Planters monopolized enslaved people's time as a method of control, but the job of enforcing that control from day to day fell to white overseers, who took the place of Black foremen on many cotton plantations across the South. Edmund Townsend still had enslaved foremen on his plantations in the 1840s and '50s—like Ned at Mullens Place and Edmund at King Place, a "foreman 1st class" even at fifty-seven years old.[53] But all of his enslaved field hands were subject to the authority of white overseers. Some planters placed their sons or younger relatives in overseer positions, training them for their own futures as plantation masters; for a short time, Edmund hired his namesake Edmund G. Townsend, the son of his nephew Thomas, in just this manner.[54] Most overseers, however, including most of Edmund's, came from the ranks of poorer, non-slaveholding whites whose prospects in El Dorado had proven disappointing. These were men who would have occupied the lowest rungs of society's ladder if not for the presence of a vast enslaved underclass. For them, a sense of racial superiority to enslaved African Americans was their only form of power, and they enacted that power in their interactions with the people under their control.[55] Responsible for working and punishing slaves, overseers were despised by enslaved people and, at times, even by their slave-owning employers, who could imagine themselves benevolent by comparison. Accounts of overseers' cruelty were a fixture of writings by former slaves and abolitionists both white and Black, as well as newspaper notices about runaways or slaves in jail. Rare though it was, if an enslaved person committed murder, the most common target was the overseer.[56]

Enslaved people used a variety of tactics to try to influence plantation owners' choice of overseer. Breaking tools, feigning illness, and truancy (running away for a few days) were small-scale forms of resistance that could, nevertheless, put pressure on planters to listen to their grievances.[57] As vulnerable as they were to sale and brutality, enslaved people still had some leverage, and denying slave owners their labor—especially during the cotton picking season, when any dip in productivity could cut into planters' profit margin—was one form of it. In 1850, slaves on Edmund Townsend's home plantation used this leverage to plot a protest against Edmund's overseer Joseph Atkins. "They had Determined on Burning up my Jin house for the purport of making me turn him of," Edmund wrote in April, "as they had said he was Very Bad to them and that would make me do it."[58] The picking season usually ended by February, meaning that Edmund's slaves were right in the middle of processing his cotton, and most (if not all) of the year's crop would be stored in the cotton gin house. Burning it down would have been a disaster for Edmund, who was producing so much cotton by 1850 that, when he considered changing the firm he relied on to sell his crop in Charleston later that year, the firm's representative sent a panicked letter pleading that he "would rather lose the business of any man, than yours."[59] Had the plan not been discovered in time to save Edmund's gin house, the plotters may have succeeded in getting rid of Atkins. Hiring a new overseer was unquestionably cheaper than losing tens of thousands of dollars in cotton sales.

The failed plot resulted in stricter control of enslaved people on Edmund's plantations. Atkins, seeing he had lost the respect (or rather, the fear) of the men and women he had been hired to oversee, called on Edmund to "assist him in Correcting some of the negrows under his Command"—whipping slaves himself, perhaps, or threatening them with sale.[60] Edmund Townsend was known to be a rich man, not one who showed restraint. In 1828, he and his brothers Parks and Stith had been sued for trespass and assault by a white farmer who claimed that they, "with force and arms," did "beat, bruise, wound, and ill-treat him."[61] The plaintiff's injuries must have been extreme: he asked for $10,000 in damages. A violent man with a violent temper, Edmund employed similarly rough men to do his bidding. Even Atkins may have been an improvement on his former overseer Daniel Curry, whose reputation in the white community was as bad as among the enslaved. In 1848, one of Edmund's neighbors, seventy-six-year-old Mary Dale, confronted him about hiring Daniel: "Now that you have Curry back," she told him, "we shall have no peace." Edmund flew into a rage, repeating several times that "Curry is a very clever fellow, and does nothing more than I wish him to do!"[62] Edmund Townsend's slaves were undoubtedly aware of their master's temperament—they would have borne the marks of it on their bodies—making their plot to burn his cotton crop all the more audacious. Perhaps it was fear of extreme consequences that led one of them to reveal the plan to Atkins before the fire could be lit.[63]

Slaveholders like Edmund believed that preserving the status quo demanded vigilance from all white men, because there were always enslaved people willing to risk everything to escape their bondage. In 1852, on Samuel Townsend's behalf, his nephew Thomas purchased a man named Miles Felton from a farmer in Richmond.[64] In the next year, Miles would run away from Samuel's plantation at least twice—perhaps attempting to return to the family he had been sold away from in Virginia. A man named Bill tried to escape twice in two years, as did two men named Harry. Between 1853 and 1856 alone, Samuel paid more than $175 in what he called "runnerway fees," the costs of jailing fugitives who had been caught plus rewards for the patrollers who captured them.[65] Slave patrols had been a fixture of Alabama's cotton country from the earliest days of statehood. In 1819, Alabama's first general assembly passed laws establishing procedures to restrict enslaved people's mobility: a "pass" system and a patrol law.[66] Under the pass system, no slaves could leave their masters' plantations without a written note granting them permission and explaining why they were permitted to leave—like the note Samuel wrote in 1856 for his blacksmith George, sent off the grounds to buy leather for aprons and shoe soles.[67] Any white person could demand to see a pass if he suspected permission hadn't been granted, and this practice was formalized with the 1819 patrol law, which required local militia captains to organize all white men in their districts into regular patrols to hunt down runaways, break up assemblies of more than five or six enslaved people, search for firearms, and administer up to twenty lashes to any slave apprehended without a pass after dark.[68]

The Townsends, like other white slaveholders, were strongly invested in preserving the social and economic system that kept them at the very top, sometimes going out of their way to recapture other men's runaways. In a letter to one of Parks's sons, Samuel addressed his nephew John E. Townsend as "Colonel," likely his militia title, as John had never fought in a war. In his letter, Samuel suggested that the "colonel" get a posse together to track down another planter's escaped slave, commenting that he believed men would go "if they thought the prospect was good to get the Reward."[69] Samuel was a rich man, even if he wasn't as successful as his eldest brother Edmund. When he wrote the letter in 1856, Samuel was worth $200,000 in land and slaves; he hardly needed the reward. But passes and patrols were about more than planters losing money when enslaved people ran, or patrollers making money if they could catch them. Enslaved people comprised 45 percent of Alabama's total population in 1860 and more than 50 percent of Madison County's, and white Alabamians feared slave conspiracies more than almost anything else.[70] Edmund Townsend chalked up the near success of his slaves' plan to burn the cotton gin house to the fact that "all of them negrows" frequently "Visit" in secret.[71] Controlling where enslaved people could go and when they could meet was a means of guarding against such plots.

By the 1840s and '50s, Madison County was no longer the western cotton frontier; it was the Cotton Kingdom. In Alabama, Mississippi, and Louisiana—states that made up what was coming to be called the Deep South—the institution of slavery formed the foundation of both the economic and social order.[72] Slave owners across the cotton South held wealth and power vastly disproportionate to their numbers. Large planters, men who owned fifty or more slaves, made up just one fifth of 1 percent of Alabama's population but owned 30 percent of its real estate. At the time, an average white man in the free states was worth about $700; an ordinary white Alabama man owned twice as much; and the average large planter in Alabama was eighteen times wealthier than that.[73] Edmund Townsend, worth $500,000 in 1853, was another eighteen times richer than even the large planters. Slave owners held disproportionate political power as well, dominating elected and appointed positions in Alabama from the local sheriff's office up to the governor's mansion. Meanwhile, mandatory patrol laws enlisted every white man, slave owner or not, into a paramilitary force with the sole purpose of preserving slavery. In antebellum Alabama, the master class was indisputably the ruling class.

For the Townsend brothers, managing their plantations and accumulating wealth in cotton and slaves seemed to have been their primary concern. None of the Townsend men showed much interest in politics. The official positions they did hold in Madison County—Edmund as a justice of the peace a handful of times, his nephew Samuel C. Townsend as the overseer of a twelve-mile stretch of road in Hazel Green—were unimpressive.[74] But that hardly meant the Townsends were not interested in power. Three decades after their arrival in northern Alabama, Edmund and his brothers had found the success they had dreamed of, and on their plantations they enacted their supremacy in their relationships with the enslaved men, women, and children who were the casualties of that success. Victims of the Townsends' American dream, enslaved people struggled to endure and resist the system that commodified their bodies and the white slave owners who held so much power over their lives.

———•———

The posse arrived on horseback—Edmund, Parks, Samuel C., and the Curry men—armed with hickory sticks and the largest bullwhip Adam Dale had ever seen.[75] They stopped at the gate outside the house, shouting for someone to come out and meet them. This was the estate of Willis Routt and his wife Elizabeth, along with William Jeffries, Elizabeth's teenage son from a previous marriage, and her elderly parents Adam and Mary Dale.[76] With sixty slaves and $12,000 in real estate, Routt was one of Madison's County's large planters— but even he didn't come close to Edmund Townsend's wealth. Though Edmund and the Routts lived only two miles apart, Adam Dale's family was far from friendly with the Townsends. When he heard men shouting outside on Monday May 15, 1848, and spotted Edmund at their head, Dale knew there was going to be trouble.

With the Routts away in Tennessee, eighty-year-old Adam Dale was the only white man on the plantation, so he had no choice but to go out and meet the posse alone. When Dale reached the gate, Edmund wasted no time telling him that four enslaved men from the Routt estate—Lewis, Jacob, Solomon, and Henry—had killed two of his hogs the previous Saturday night. They had conspired with two enslaved men from his own brother Samuel's plantation, he said, another case of the dangers of letting slaves "visit in secret." Dale didn't believe it. Edmund hadn't caught anyone in the act; he had only the word of Harrison Curry, his overseer's son, and neither Dale nor his wife had much faith in the Currys' integrity. Harrison said he had been walking to his father Daniel's house when he spotted six slaves with one of Samuel Townsend's horses and two dead hogs. When they realized they'd been seen, the men dropped the hogs and ran into Samuel's cornfield to hide. Harrison said he'd left the horses and hogs undisturbed and continued to his father's house; on the way he saw four or five of the men on the road to the slave cabins, but he didn't pursue them.

"Were the negroes riding or walking?" Dale asked. Harrison said he couldn't tell. "The moon near full, a bright moonlight night, and you couldn't tell whether they were riding or walking?" Dale was incredulous. "And they fifteen or twenty steps ahead of you!" With a bright moon out, enabling him to see their faces, Harrison should have been able to tell if the enslaved men were on horseback or not. The story didn't hold up—and the old man told Edmund so. Harrison's testimony proved nothing.

Dale, who had called eight or ten of the Routts' slaves over to listen to Harrison's account, asked one of them—a man named George—what he had to say. George hadn't been involved in the alleged theft, but he had an alibi for one of the accused, Lewis. According to George, Lewis had been sick in his mother's cabin on Saturday night, not off the plantation at Edmund or Samuel's place. But the fact that Dale, a white man, would take an enslaved person's word over his own infuriated Edmund, and before George could finish speaking he jumped up with his hickory stick raised.

"Shut your damned big mouth or I'll split your damned brains out!" Edmund shouted. "Clear yourself—damned son of a bitch!" Rightly frightened for his safety, George left the scene, but the posse wasn't about to let the accused men get away too. As Edmund swore he would have them whipped and the elderly Adam Dale protested, the two Curry men and Parks Townsend's son Samuel C. went out into the lane by the water well, where the enslaved people had congregated, to keep them from dispersing. Still arguing with Edmund, Dale was unnerved to see Daniel and Harrison Curry sitting on the fence, methodically braiding another thong into their massive bullwhip. Desperate, he pleaded with Edmund to wait until the Routts returned from Tennessee—he said he'd send for them immediately. But Edmund wouldn't be swayed. "I'll whip them *now*," he insisted. Parks Townsend, who had been trying to convince Edmund that the slaves should receive only a "light" whipping, gave up and joined the others in the lane. Dale tried one last time to persuade Edmund to drop the matter, but Edmund ignored him and left him by the well. "I remained alone, with my head down, not knowing what to do," Adam Dale would later say. Dale was a veteran of the Revolutionary War and the War of 1812, but this was "the first time, in a long life" that he had ever "felt intimidated."

The crack of the whip moved Dale to action. He found Parks guarding Jacob, tied up in the lane. Harrison and Samuel C. were chasing after Solomon and Henry, who had managed to ride off on the plow horses they had brought with them when Dale called them away from their work. But Lewis, hands tied above his head to a small tree, had blood streaming down his sides and back. He had eight or ten gashes from the whip, so deep Dale could have buried his finger in them, and on his hip Lewis was cut to the bone. Daniel Curry had the whip raised to strike again, and just behind him stood Edmund Townsend, watching with approval.

Dale was horrified, but no longer intimidated. Eighty years old, unarmed, and outnumbered, Adam Dale stepped forward and shouted at Curry to stop. "Don't strike him another lick!" he said, and very deliberately placed his hand in his pocket, as though reaching for a gun. It was a bluff, but it worked. "There will be no more whipping," Dale told Edmund, then directed another enslaved man to untie Lewis. Edmund was furious, but he left, still bellowing at Dale and his wife Mary (who joined her husband outside when she heard the shouting) that he would shoot any of Routt's slaves found on his property again. Lewis, meanwhile, was taken to his mother's cabin—where he was bed-ridden for the next three weeks. According to Dale, Lewis had been a "first rate plough-man," his labor easily worth fifty cents a day; in May, at the height of planting season, they couldn't have spared him for twice that much. But on Edmund Townsend's orders, Daniel Curry had almost killed him—and after that, Dale said, Lewis "never has had the same use of himself that he had before."

The Routts would later sue Edmund (along with Parks, Samuel C., and the Currys) on behalf of the teenage William Jeffries, to whom the enslaved man Lewis belonged. Legally speaking, Jeffries was the injured party, since he had "lost the benefit of his labor in performing and transacting the affairs & business" of the plantation. Whipping a slave nearly to death wasn't Edmund's crime—the issue was that Lewis wasn't *his* slave. On his own plantations, Edmund and other planters like him had the power to commit incredible acts of violence against enslaved people with near impunity. Even in this case, however, Edmund never had to face the consequences of his actions. Although the court ruled that he owed Jeffries financial compensation, Edmund had the means to appeal the judgment and continue appealing until after his own death.[77] Edmund's preeminence in Madison County shielded him from the censure of other white men—allowing him to flout community norms. The Townsend brothers were not men to let anyone, Black or white, stop them doing exactly what they wanted. But whipping was only one form of violence committed against enslaved people, and Lewis was not the sole casualty of Edmund's appetite for power and domination. The most vulnerable people in the planter's orbit were the enslaved women he owned—like Lizzy, Edmund's twenty-seven-year-old concubine, who remembered the sky falling around her when she first came to Alabama.

Lizzy's background, like that of so many enslaved people, remains something of a mystery. She was born in Virginia and spent her early years in the household of a white Richmond man named Anthony Perryman, who occasionally identified Lizzy as his daughter with an enslaved woman named

Mary.[78] But that wasn't the only story. Anthony Perryman told some of his friends that Lizzy was actually his sister Fanny's child. Fanny, being dead, could neither confirm nor deny, but several of the Richmond Perrymans affirmed that around 1820 Fanny had been "familiar" with "a negro man (Randolph) of the Perryman family."[79] It was a surprisingly candid admission, considering the scandal attached to a white woman's sexual liaisons with a Black man.[80] But they asserted that Fanny "was but little removed from an idiot" and couldn't be held responsible for acts committed when she wasn't in her right mind.[81] This excuse is questionable, but it gave the Perrymans a way to save face, just as Anthony's periodic claims that Lizzy was his daughter did. A white woman giving birth to a mixed-race child was unthinkable; an enslaved woman giving birth to a white man's child was, sadly, business as usual. Avoiding scandal wasn't the only reason the Perrymans would have wanted to conceal the true identity of Lizzy's mother. The daughter of a white woman like Fanny Perryman, whether the father was Black or white, slave or free, would be born free herself. But the daughter of an enslaved woman— say, Mary—was a slave for life, human property with a dollar value. Anthony could sell her, putting the evidence of his sister's disgrace out of sight and out of mind while making a profit, and that's exactly what he did.

In February or March of 1833, Anthony Perryman sold Lizzy to a slave trader named Fox, who sold her to another trader named White, who sold her to a third man named Collier, who finally sold her to Edmund Townsend.[82] If Lizzy really were Fanny's child—as Lizzy's daughters and others would later claim—then selling her into slavery was illegal. But if she protested, it was the word of a mixed-race child against a wealthy white man, and Anthony Perryman, Fox, and the others had a financial interest in Lizzy remaining enslaved. In the antebellum slave market, enslaved men usually sold for more than women, and adult women for more than children. Skin color, however, could change the equation. Lighter skin could add hundreds of dollars to an enslaved woman or girl's value at sale. In the language of the slave trade, these were "fancy girls"—female slaves sold for purposes other than cotton planting and picking, and at times for stratospheric prices.[83] In the New Orleans markets, a strong, healthy young man (a "prime" field hand) sold for around $500 at the turn of the century and more than $1,800 by the 1850s.[84] In the city's "fancy trade," however, prices could reach as high as $5,000 for one girl.[85] These sales had nothing to do with physical labor or plantation productivity; no one would spend such a sum on an enslaved person intended for use solely as a field hand, cook, or maid. Slave owners bought "fancy girls" for sex. Young and light-skinned, with the appearance of white women but none of their legal protections or social status, these girls were sold into an established system of concubinage.[86] Slave owners sexually exploited enslaved women of all skin colors, but only the wealthiest, most powerful men could satisfy their desires so openly and at such exorbitant expense. Edmund Townsend saw himself as one of those men. When he purchased Lizzy and brought her back to Alabama, keeping her in his house, preserving her from field labor, everyone knew his reasons.

Lizzy knew too. In Virginia, she had been acquainted with Anthony Perryman's enslaved woman Mary, after all. In Alabama, she would have gained insight into her new master's character as soon as she set foot in his home and saw his enslaved sons Armstead and Woodson. Lizzy may have met their mother, perhaps helped her care for the boys—Armstead was three years old in 1833, and Woodson still an infant—and in just a couple more years she would take their mother's place with Edmund.[87] When Lizzy "arrived at the age of puberty," her daughters recounted decades later, "she was treated by him as his wife," though the meaning of "wife" in this context and Lizzy's own description are matters of speculation.[88] She may have been terrified, like Harriet Jacobs, an escaped slave who described the unwanted attentions of her master when she turned fifteen. "Sometimes he had stormy, terrific ways, that made his victims tremble," Jacobs wrote in her autobiography, and "sometimes he assumed a gentleness that he thought must surely subdue."[89] But however Jacobs's master approached her, and however Edmund approached Lizzy, the power difference between master and slave was simply too great to make consent possible under any circumstances. "No matter whether the slave girl be as black as ebony or as fair as her mistress," she was still a slave who could be sold at any time, for any reason.[90] For Lizzy, like Jacobs, there was nowhere for her to turn. And no one in Madison County had ever accused Edmund Townsend of gentleness.

Lizzy's position in Edmund's household was precarious. By the age of nineteen she had given the fifty-one-year-old cotton planter two daughters, Elizabeth and Virginia (called Lizzie and Jennie), one named for herself, perhaps, and one for the home she had been sold away from.[91] Lizzy may have hoped that one day, Edmund might free all three of them in exchange for her sexual favors or out of affection for their children.[92] Edmund never hid his attachment to his daughters. The slave owner who would order a man whipped to the bone raised his own daughters as if they were free. The girls wore hoop skirts and crinolines like the white belles of the South; they learned to read and write in their father's house, a crime in antebellum Alabama.[93] Though their enslaved status made Lizzy's daughters vulnerable to sale and abuse, there were reasons to harbor hope. Edmund Townsend never married. There was no white plantation mistress to resent Lizzy's presence or demand that she and her daughters be sold. When Elizabeth and Virginia later stated that Edmund treated their mother as "his wife," they may have meant that, with no white woman on the plantation, Lizzy was closer to being "Mrs. Townsend" than anyone in Hazel Green.

Around 1850, two men from Virginia called on Edmund Townsend at his home and confronted him about Lizzy. Asserting that the woman he kept as a slave was freeborn, they accused him of abducting her and threatened to involve the courts. Perhaps Edmund defended himself by saying that he had not known about Lizzy's mother when he purchased her, but it seems that he did not challenge the Virginians' claim that she was a free woman. Then, in an uncharacteristic move for the planter, Edmund acted diplomatically. In the presence of his neighbor Elias Wellborn and his overseer Daniel Curry, Edmund Townsend made a solemn pledge: he would emancipate Lizzy and their daughters and, as restitution for holding them in slavery unlawfully, he would give them his fortune when he died. Edmund's promise must have satisfied the men from Virginia; neither they nor their threats of prosecution were heard of again.[94] But Edmund never had any intention of keeping his word—at least as it related to Lizzy. Shortly after the unexpected visit, he did what Anthony Perryman had done two decades earlier when Lizzy's parentage became a problem: he sold her.[95] Lizzy Perryman had been the closest person to Edmund Townsend for nearly thirty years, the unofficial mistress of his plantation and born free, but because she had been kidnapped and sold into slavery illegally and so few would take her word over a wealthy white man's, her life had no guarantees.

When Edmund Townsend and his brothers migrated west in 1819, they dreamed of conquest: of the wild Alabama frontier, of a cutthroat commercial market, and of the enslaved people they owned as property. Over the next three decades, Edmund would have all of these things in excess. He accumulated wealth in land and slaves, power in the aristocracy of the Cotton Kingdom. Out of this power, he developed a sense of supremacy over everyone below him, whether they be enslaved people on his plantations or white Alabamians less successful in their pursuit of the American dream. He could separate families by sale; he could beat a man half to death; he could rape the women he owned, and he would still earn the admiration of the relatives and neighbors he had left behind in Virginia. The social order of the South rested on an impassable dividing line between Black and white, slave and free, and none of these actions fundamentally challenged that division. As long as wealth and power remained firmly in the hands of white slave owners, the habits of men like Edmund Townsend could be overlooked.

Trouble arose in 1853 when someone tried to blur that line, and to the horror of the white relatives who had praised him so highly, the culprit was Edmund himself. When the cotton planter died at the age of sixty-two, family members and acquaintances from Alabama all the way back to Virginia were shocked to find that he had left his estate almost entirely to his two daughters, upholding at least one part of his 1850 promise to the visitors from Richmond. With the stroke of a pen, Edmund made Elizabeth and Virginia ("two mulatto wenches," as the white Townsends described them) heiresses to $500,000 in land, cotton, and slaves.[96] The wealthy planter had long lived by the doctrine that he could do anything he liked with his property. It was American economic dogma that citizens were entitled to full, absolute control of their property, lest their "happy, free, and flourishing Country" fall into ruin. This was what the Townsend family's neighbors in Lunenburg County, Virginia, had argued back in 1785, and it's what Edmund Townsend believed until his last breath in 1853. The way Edmund saw things, slave owners had a fundamental right to buy, sell, own, and treat their human property however they saw fit. No one dared stop him doing just that when he was alive, and he couldn't imagine they would start trying after he was dead. He was wrong. In Alabama's Cotton Kingdom, allowing non-white, unfree people to join the ranks of the elite was one line not even Edmund Townsend could be allowed to cross.

2

The Strangest Will He Ever
Knew a Sensible Man to Make

THE WILL BEGAN in an ordinary way: "Know all men by these present that I, Edmund Townsend of the County of Madison & State of Alabama Being in Tolerably good helth and of sound mind and noing the uncertainty of Life and the Surtainty of Death, do make this my Last will and Testamony." Aside from the spelling, there was nothing unusual in the will's opening lines. The rest of the document, however, would leave relatives and neighbors questioning Edmund Townsend's claim to a "sound mind."[1]

To Elizabeth, Virginia, Armstead, and Woodson—"Children I have a Rite to Believe are my own"—he left his seven plantations, more than six thousand acres of prime farming land. He granted them his farming tools and equipment, his household and kitchen furniture, his livestock and slaves, "all of my negrows consisting of Men wimmen Boys and Gurls & children amounting in number from Two to three hundred," everything necessary to run his plantations successfully when he was gone. He wished his "negro man Ned," enslaved foreman of the Mullens Place, to be freed and paid an annual salary of $100 to oversee his plantations and "attend to business as he had done for many years." He wished his executors (his brother Samuel, his nephews Thomas Townsend and Robert Johnson, his grand-nephew Edmund G. Townsend, and his neighbor Charles Patton) to maintain the plantations "as they are now kept up," selling his cotton and collecting income to support his four children. Finally, to the "Two Small Gurls" alone—Elizabeth and Virginia, daughters of his former concubine Lizzy—he gave "a Separate Legacie" of $100,000, "a special share over and above" the estate they would draw on with their brothers.[2]

Edmund's white relatives were appalled. They had had no idea what the old planter intended to do with his estate until the document was read aloud in the county Probate Court four days after his death. When they finally heard it, they were shocked.[3] At half a million dollars in land and personal property, Edmund's will accounted for the largest bequest made by a master to his slaves in Alabama history.[4] Adding insult to injury, he expected his white relatives— men who stood to considerably increase their own property and social status if they inherited even a piece of the estate—to be advocates for "two yellow boys" and "two mulatto wenches."[5]

The affront was too much for his grand-nephew Edmund G. Townsend to bear. At some point in late April or early May, he vented about the will to a friend named Thomas Redmond.[6] A slave trader by profession, Redmond lived a peripatetic life, leaving his wife at their home in Virginia for weeks or months at a time during his regular trips to the cotton states.[7] Redmond had tried farming once, like his planter brother in Mississippi, but his attempts hadn't been successful. Slave trading proved more lucrative. Like Edmund G.'s position as his great-uncle's overseer, slave trading was a job that gave Redmond power over enslaved men and women. Yet neither man could call himself the equal of a large planter like Edmund Townsend. This was what they dreamed of: joining the ranks of the most elite class in the South, standing at the center of white society instead of on the periphery. If they could acquire even a fraction of the land and slaves that a man like Edmund Townsend owned, their status in society would be utterly transformed. Bitter at the loss of his chance, Edmund G. may have sought out his friend for a sympathetic ear when Redmond arrived in Huntsville with a coffle of slaves to sell. Or perhaps Redmond approached Edmund G. first, expressing disbelief and asking for details. One way or another, the slave trader acquired a copy of the elder Edmund Townsend's will, and—ever ready to seize an opportunity for advancement—Redmond, leaving his slaves unsold, caught the first train back to Virginia.[8]

The way Redmond saw it, there was money to be made off the white Townsends' resentment. Edmund's relatives in Alabama were already hiring lawyers and submitting petitions to have the Probate Court void the planter's will, but there were other Townsends who lacked the resources to mount a challenge—the children of Edmund's sister Virginia, for example, who had remained in the state of Virginia when her five siblings went west. These were the Alabama Townsends' less fortunate relatives, poor farmers whose only asset in society was the fact that their skin was white. They were uneducated (only a few could write their own names) and untraveled (leaving the farm untended when they had no laborers to till it in their absence was impossible). According to Jones D. Crow and his wife Rushia, the daughter of Virginia Townsend, they had "set out in life without education & learning and dependent upon their own manual labor, for their maintenance upon a poor & comparative barren soil." They were humble and unambitious, Crow said, with "neither the means nor the opportunities of acquiring learning about matters of business not falling within the sphere of their little farming operations and household duties."[9] Their lives were exactly what Edmund had migrated west to escape. And as far as the slave trader Redmond was concerned, their ignorance was going to make him rich.

Redmond was betting that news of Edmund Townsend's death had not yet reached the old planter's nieces and nephews in Virginia. Redmond would get to them first and stir up their prejudices against Edmund's enslaved children, ask them why slaves—"two mulatto wenches" the old man claimed were his daughters—should inherit half a million dollars in land and personal property while hard-working white families like them lived hand to mouth.[10] He would remind the Townsends that Edmund had been like them once, a small Virginia farmer "born without patrimony," but that his success was proof social mobility was possible. It would be difficult, Redmond told them, but "he thought there was a <u>chance</u>" to break the will if the family acted immediately. Of course the slave trader understood that it would be impossible for them to leave their farms in the middle of planting season and go to Alabama for a series of long, drawn-out legal proceedings—but as another of Virginia Townsend's daughters and her husband explained, "Redmond said he had been a poor man himself and would be a friend to the poor."[11] He would go to Madison County as their agent and undertake the litigation at his own expense, he said, even though everyone back in Alabama considered it a losing proposition. All the Virginians had to do was sign a contract giving Redmond a share of whatever inheritance they might ultimately get from the estate. Redmond, a generous man, would give each of them $100 up front, maybe $200. He claimed that the Alabama Townsends "had in fact employed all the lawyers in the county . . . to prevent [the will] from being broke." Should he succeed against all odds, however, he would be content to take just half of the proceeds.[12] Sign now, Redmond said, or throw away your future.

They signed.

One week later, Edmund Townsend's nephew Thomas arrived with word that his uncle's will had been broken. None of Edmund's relatives in Alabama had ever intended to uphold the will; there was no complex legal maneuvering required. The Townsends in Virginia would inherit a total of $15,000 from their uncle's estate—if they could somehow get out of the contracts they had made with Thomas Redmond. Redmond had lied to the Virginians, "coaxed and frightened" them into the execution of the contract with "the most unmitigated bad faith."[13] But that was the price of doing business. Redmond felt no remorse over the matter. He had seen an opportunity to raise his status in society, and he had taken it.[14]

Edmund Townsend's will stirred up passions—outrage, resentment, greed—because of what it promised: transformation. With some of that money, Thomas Redmond could stop selling slaves to planters and become a planter himself. Edmund's relatives in Virginia could buy slaves to work their land, perhaps plant cash crops instead of farming for subsistence. Their wives could stop working in the fields and live like ladies instead. Money, and the opportunities it afforded, would make them "whiter" by elevating their social status.[15] It was the possibility that Edmund's mixed-race children might also experience that transformation that stirred up the most virulent passions. Inheriting Edmund's estate would turn his enslaved children into free men and women with greater wealth than most whites in Madison County. For the racial and social order to be preserved, emancipated slaves—especially those whose mixed-race heritage may have allowed them to "pass" across the color line into white society—had to remain subordinated even as free people. Edmund Townsend's will directly challenged that principle. It was, his younger brother Samuel Townsend remarked to a neighbor after the Probate Court declared the document invalid, "the strangest will he ever knew a sensible man to make."[16]

It also happened to be illegal. When Edmund died in April 1853, Alabama's laws regulating African American life were at their most restrictive. The southern defense of white supremacy had never been so strong. Since the state's founding, white residents had defended slavery as the foundation of the social and economic order. Many of the early migrants had brought enslaved people with them or at least dreams of someday joining that powerful slave-owning class. But enslaved people were not the only objects of white Alabamians' contempt, anxiety, and brutality. As Alabama transformed into the Cotton Kingdom, slave owners and non-slaveholding whites alike increasingly came to see free people of color—men and women who had either been born free or were manumitted by former masters—as threats to their chokehold on social and political power. These so-called slaves without masters threatened the social order of the South, a society divided, ostensibly, between Black slaves and free whites.[17] Neither property nor citizens, nominally "free" but legally and socially subordinated to whites, free people of color occupied an ambiguous and precarious position. Where did they fit into southern society? Where could they find some degree of peace and autonomy for themselves and their families? As far as white Alabamians were concerned, the answer was simple: not here.

Throughout the first half of the nineteenth century, state legislators and slaveholders (often one and the same) passed laws designed to make Alabama one of the least hospitable places in the country for a free person of color. The 1819 patrol law, instituted to guard against slave conspiracies, authorized white men to invade the homes of free African Americans under the pretense of breaking up meetings or searching for firearms, or for no reason at all.[18] Free people of color were, as Huntsville newspapers constantly repeated, potentially more dangerous than slaves—"a source of demoralization" liable to stir up resentment or even that perennial nightmare of the planter class, rebellion.[19] Although free people of color never made up more than one half of 1 percent of Alabama's total population, with most of them concentrated in the large port city of Mobile rather than rural, planter-dominated counties like Madison, white Alabamians continued to push for laws limiting the growth of a free Black population.[20] In 1832, one year after Nat Turner's rebellion in Virginia sent southern planters into a panic, the state legislature passed an anti-immigration act prohibiting free people of color from moving to Alabama, on penalty of whipping if they remained in the state for longer than thirty days. In 1839, a draconian "seizure act" empowered white citizens to enslave for life any African American who had entered the state after 1832 but had not left according to the terms of the anti-immigration law. As of 1834, any slaves freed by their masters were required to leave Alabama immediately or risk re-enslavement for life.[21]

Those masters who, for whatever reason, wished to manumit enslaved people faced their own set of obstacles. Freeing a slave in Alabama had never been easy; the 1819 constitution stated that emancipation could only be granted by individual petition to the state legislature. To avoid this lengthy process, some planters sought alternatives—most commonly, freeing slaves in their wills. White southerners clung to the doctrine of absolute property rights perhaps more strongly than any other Americans, defending their prerogative to use and dispose of possessions however they liked. If those possessions included slaves, then, intuitively, it followed that a master was entitled to free some or all of those men and women in his will. While Alabama law never challenged a master's right to transfer the ownership of enslaved people to another master, by the time of Edmund Townsend's death decades of Alabama Supreme Court rulings had made emancipation by will a legal minefield.

The 1838 case of *Trotter v. Blocker* set the most powerful precedent, with the Alabama Supreme Court nullifying the will of a farmer who had attempted to free eleven slaves and leave them enough money to move out of the state. The court ruled that if slaves were themselves property, they could not legally receive a gift of property. The gift in this case? Their own bodies.[22]

Allowing masters to emancipate slaves by "mere volition"—as the court stated in a similar 1828 case—could be "disastrous to the quiet of the country."[23] Even in Alabama, the supposed public interest could occasionally win out over private property rights. In the antebellum South, a society ruled by slave owners and dependent upon enslaved labor, state supreme court justices weren't the only ones to consider white supremacy to be in the public interest. Huntsville's *Southern Advocate* enthusiastically supported each new measure put in place to halt the "morbid growth of free niggerdom."[24] Gleefully speculating about what might happen if every southern state passed anti-immigration laws as strict as Alabama's, the *Advocate* predicted that "the North would in a few weeks, be so completely over run with free negroes that the Yankee abolitionist would die in agony, with disgust."[25] This was not a community likely to uphold a will that would, with the stroke of a pen, turn four slaves into four of the wealthiest landowners in Madison County. So, as scandalized as they were the day Edmund's will was read in court, the white Alabama Townsends also knew they had little to worry about. As one niece and nephew commented, it almost immediately became "a notorious fact, throughout the community" in Madison County that Edmund's bequests to his enslaved children were unlawful.[26] Chalk it up to one last case of Edmund Townsend's disregard for social conventions. The will was voided without incident (with *Trotter v. Blocker* cited as precedent), Edmund's children remained enslaved, and the old planter's immense wealth was divvied up by his surviving siblings and their families.[27] When Samuel Townsend told his friend Elias Wellborn that his brother's will was "the strangest will he ever knew a sensible man to make," he was saying what the white residents of Madison County were already thinking.

The difference was, Samuel was lying. He did know of a stranger will, and quite intimately. He was the one writing it.

————◆————

Samuel Townsend was fifteen years old and orphaned when he followed his family to Alabama. The youngest Townsend sibling, he grew up the ward of his older brothers, raised, essentially, by the family's ad hoc patriarch Edmund.

In Alabama he lived with Edmund for close to a decade before establishing his own household, and when he did, he modeled himself after his eldest brother. He bought land in Madison County, invested in slaves and cotton, and established himself as a successful planter—albeit less successful than Edmund. Samuel's most striking similarity to Edmund was in how he arranged his family life. Like his brother, Samuel never married, but between 1830 and 1853 he would have nine children, all of them his legal property. Their mothers, Samuel's "concubines," were enslaved women who lived and labored on his home plantation, uniformly young and usually light-skinned.[28] But none of Samuel's children would ever claim that their father had been looking for a surrogate wife.

Samuel's sexual contact with enslaved women rarely lasted longer than a few years at a time, and they often overlapped. His earliest known concubine was a woman named Rainey, who may have been among the original coffle of slaves the Townsend brothers brought to Alabama in 1819. In 1831, the year after Edmund's son Armstead was born, Rainey gave birth to Samuel's first child—also a boy, Wesley. While Rainey was pregnant with his daughter Caroline, Samuel began a sexual liaison with another enslaved woman named Winney, who would give him a second son, Willis. Hannah, an enslaved woman from Virginia, was probably already pregnant with Samuel's son Thomas when Willis was born in 1839—after which Samuel would have two more children by Winney, a boy named Osborne and a girl called Parthenia. Samuel's daughter Milcha and son Joseph Bradford were born just months apart in 1848. Samuel would have had sexual contact with their mothers— Lucy, who had been sold west from Virginia along with her sisters and mother Rachel, and a woman named Celia—around the same time, with Samuel continuing his liaisons with Celia long enough to have one last child, his daughter Susanna, in 1853.[29]

On his home plantation, Samuel made himself a patriarch in the Old Testament sense: the founder of a large family, with supreme mastery over the lives and fates of his children and chosen concubines.[30] His desires took precedence over the families that these women had already created. Hannah had an enslaved partner named Dick for years before Samuel decided to make her his concubine. Hannah and Dick likely considered themselves husband and wife; even Samuel described Dick as Hannah's "husband," a term he did not use for any of the other women's enslaved partners.[31] But slaves could not legally marry, and Samuel apparently had no compunctions about separating Hannah and Dick. There was little either of them could do to stop him. Years later, when Hannah's daughter—seventeen-year-old Elvira, half-sister to

Samuel's son Thomas—may have become the latest object of Samuel's desire, Hannah couldn't help her either.[32] Samuel may have also temporarily or permanently separated Rainey, Winney, and Lucy from other partners, as they each had children by enslaved men both before and after their relationships with their master. He certainly took Lucy from her children and family. Samuel didn't sell his former concubine, but by the time of his death Lucy was living on his Martin plantation while her mother, three sisters, daughter Milcha, and two eldest sons remained on the "Home Place."[33]

Edmund Townsend may have thought that Samuel, his last living brother, with a household that mirrored his own, was the natural choice to be an executor of his will. If any white relative was likely to understand Edmund's wish to provide for his enslaved children, it was Samuel. But Edmund underestimated his brother's rapacity, a mistake the enslaved women on Samuel's Home Place would never have made. Samuel had inherited the family lust for wealth and social status—as well as Edmund's stormy temper, what Samuel's lawyer would later call "a family characteristic"—but he didn't have his elder brothers' business acumen.[34] The first house, farm, and slaves Samuel could call his own had belonged to Stith Townsend before him, a brother's last bequest to the youngest of the family.[35] While Samuel could count himself among Madison County's large planters in 1850, with his eighty-six slaves and $20,000 in real estate, much of that property could be traced back to another inheritance: the money he received after his brother Parks Townsend's death.[36] Perhaps Samuel resented Edmund for his success. Or perhaps it was only a coincidence that Samuel insisted on being buried directly beside his brother, with an eight-foot marble pillar throwing Edmund's modest tombstone into eternal shadow.[37] Whatever the reason, when the Probate Court confirmed him as Edmund's executor, Samuel immediately hired a Huntsville law firm to petition to have the will declared void—and, in the process, inherited more than $150,000 from his late brother's estate.[38] At last, in the spring of 1853, Samuel was the wealthiest, most powerful Townsend in Madison County. All he had to do was outlive the others.

But Samuel was not long for this world. Whether he was already suffering from the same "consumption" that had taken his brother, or Edmund's death had simply been a sharp reminder of his own mortality, he quickly began preparing for the end.[39] Just months after Edmund's death in 1853, Samuel finished the first draft of his own will, whose contents revealed that he had one last quality in common with his late brother. A man who bought and sold human beings, broke up enslaved people's families, and separated wives from their husbands to satisfy his own desires, Samuel nevertheless wanted to provide for the children he had produced through violence. Slaves could be treated cruelly, but his sons and daughters were a class apart. They were to be treated as though they were "white children," he said, and after he died, they "never should serve any body else."[40]

Samuel Townsend's Home Place was a world unto itself. Fields of cotton, wheat, corn, and oats surrounded barns for horses, tools, and equipment, herds of hogs and goats and cattle, bee stands for honey, spinning wheels to

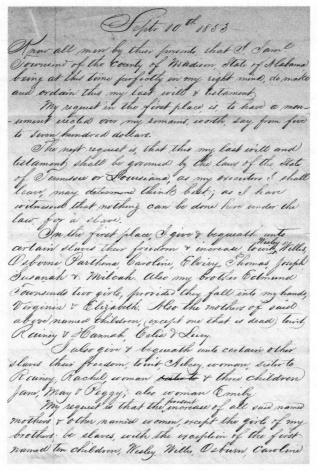

FIGURE 2.1 Page of Samuel Townsend's will dated 10 September 1853. University of Alabama Libraries Special Collections.

make cloth, a fully functioning blacksmith shop, and a cotton gin house large enough to accommodate not only Samuel's crop but also the cotton of his planter neighbors in Hazel Green.[41] Just one among Samuel's eight plantations, the 1,700-acre Home Place was more like a small village than a farm: the antebellum South in microcosm. In 1940, one local historian puzzlingly remarked that the planter had lived "a very simple life."[42] Yet Samuel slept on a feather bed in his big house, a stand of fruiting pecan trees shading it from the Alabama sun, while hundreds of bondsmen, women, and children worked for his benefit.[43] They lived in a cluster of small cabins west of the house—what the residents of Hazel Green called, simply, "Townsend's Quarters."[44] On the Townsend plantations, as in southern society more broadly, a small group of white elites lived in incredible luxury, an aristocratic lifestyle supported by the forced labor of enslaved people. Also like southern society at large, on the Home Place an intermediate class existed: not free people of color, not yet, but Samuel Townsend's children.

A slave owner having children by his slaves was not, in itself, anything unusual, and it was virtually impossible to keep secret. Though theoretically taboo in a society that preached the innate racial inferiority of African Americans, sex across the color line was a fact of life in the antebellum South and one tacitly accepted by white communities.[45] Even when a white man did attempt to hide his relationships with enslaved women, the presence of children bearing a resemblance to the plantation master could be hard to explain away—though of course they could always be sold away. "You couldn't tell the difference between the children he had by his slaves & those he had by his wife," an ex-slave named John Boggs recalled in 1863, when asked about his old master's family. "He used to have some Irishmen on the plantation, and he said these children were theirs, but everybody knew they were his. There were as much like him as himself."[46] Family who knew or saw or guessed, friends and neighbors who gossiped, enslaved people meeting in town on half-days or visiting kin on other plantations: it was only a matter of time before a white man's dalliances became common knowledge. The trick was not talking about it. Demonstrating extravagant favoritism for an enslaved child or concubine violated the rules of polite society and, if a slave owner went as far as manumission, the rules of white supremacy.[47] Some plantation mistresses insisted that slaves they suspected of any sort of relationship with their husband, sexual or familial, be whipped or sold. But in exchange for a modicum of discretion, at least in public, others simply looked away. As South Carolina diarist Mary Boykin Chesnut famously quipped: "Every lady tells you who is the father of all the Mulatto children in everybody's household, but those in her own, she seems to think drop from the clouds." Or at least, Chesnut added, "she pretends so."[48]

The Townsend brothers had never worried much about the rules of polite society, but as lifelong bachelors Samuel and Edmund had even fewer curbs on their behavior than married slave owners. With no wives to challenge how they arranged their private or public lives, the Townsend men spoke openly about their children with friends and neighbors—Samuel "kindly and tenderly," and Edmund in such a way that the sheriff of Madison County came to believe that Elizabeth and Virginia were in fact free girls "much beloved" by their father.[49] Samuel's children knew that their mothers were slaves—they saw them working in their father's fields, enduring chronic pain and injuries from decades of hard labor—so they knew, as their cousins had not, that they were not legally free people of color.[50] Under Alabama law they could be beaten, bought, and sold just like any other person owned as property. But they were also Samuel's children, as recognizably so as those of John Boggs's former master. Multiple descriptions of the enslaved Townsends noted their "light complexion"; later in life, a white government official describing Samuel's daughter Milcha would write that "The Woman is nearly white."[51] The resemblance went beyond skin color. One neighbor commented that Samuel's children "generally favored him very much," and Samuel's lawyer would later tell Willis Townsend that his child by a local woman, likewise, "favors the Townsend family very much."[52] Perhaps Osborne Townsend's gray eyes came from his father's side.[53]

Samuel's children occupied privileged positions on their father's plantation, with his sons learning skilled trades and his daughters exempted from fieldwork. Elvira, Hannah's daughter, also had a special status as, possibly, Samuel's latest, youngest concubine. Visitors to the Home Place in the 1850s called the seventeen-year-old girl his "housekeeper"—a common euphemism at the time.[54] Like her half-brother Thomas, she had mixed-race ancestry: in 1865, Elvira would be marked "mulatto" in a state census, and in 1866 a city directory would take her for a white woman.[55] Like her mother Hannah, she was a seamstress and dressmaker, a skill that kept her out of Samuel's cotton fields.[56] It was a pattern repeated across the antebellum South. In a society where whiteness was social capital and blackness was a mark of degradation, slaveholders' racial prejudices could occasionally benefit enslaved people with a mixed-race heritage. In the minds of southern whites, slaves with "light complexions" were more intelligent, more trustworthy, and better suited for skilled work, housework, or even freedom.[57] Deep South slave owners manumitted lighter-skinned men and women at a much higher rate than those without mixed-race ancestry. In Alabama alone, roughly 70 percent of free people of color had mixed-race ancestry.[58] But Edmund and Samuel Townsend's racial prejudices—evident in their preference for lighter-skinned concubines, for example—weren't the only factors involved. The enslaved Townsends didn't just have mixed-race ancestry; they had Samuel and Edmund's ancestry. In Samuel's estimation, his children were among but not of the other slaves on the Home Place. He called them "servants" instead, to mark the difference. The word "slave" was reserved for bondspeople without Townsend blood.[59] Although semantics alone couldn't free them, it did indicate how their father perceived them and what opportunities they had that weren't shared by non-relations.

Samuel's eldest son Wesley was a talented blacksmith and carpenter, trained by an enslaved man named George who had run the blacksmith shop on the Home Place for decades, forging tools and shoeing horses.[60] Wesley would have taken over from George sometime in the 1850s, when George grew so "Rheumatic" that an inventory of Samuel's property declared the man worth precisely "0.00" dollars. Wesley, on the other hand, performed work that netted his father a small fortune. One project alone—"a good work of a wagon" that twenty-four-year-old Wesley built and painted for a local farmer in 1855—cost the man $100.[61] The money, of course, went to Samuel. By age eighteen Samuel's second-eldest son Willis would also work as a blacksmith on the Home Place, first assisting Wesley and then "striking in the shop" on his own.[62] But decades later, when the younger Townsend brothers reminisced about their childhoods, they recalled incidents that suggested they had a special status in Hazel Green even before they were old enough to take up a trade.

Do you remember, Osborne wrote his brother Thomas in 1888, "the old fellow that caught us kids one Sunday morning going chestnut hunting"?[63] It was Abner Tate, a neighboring cotton planter, who had caught them on his property—alerted perhaps by the barking of the boys' hounds getting in among his livestock.[64] Furious, Tate threatened to "lick us for having the dogs on his hogs," but their friend Harrison (perhaps the property of one Townsend or another) "jumped up on the fence and hollered" for Mrs. Tate, who promptly appeared and scolded her husband to leave the boys alone.[65] Their relation to Samuel and Edmund shielded Osborne and his brothers from the worst brutality regularly meted out to other enslaved people in Madison County. Slave patrols hunted and terrorized runaways by setting dogs on them; Samuel's sons took their father's dogs out to run wild on another slave owner's farm. Edmund Townsend had a man whipped to the bone because he suspected him of killing two of his hogs; caught red-handed among a neighbor's hogs, Edmund's nephews escaped with no more than a reprimand. Perhaps if Harrison had been alone, that Sunday morning would have had a very different ending.

When the Townsend name alone couldn't protect their children, Edmund and Samuel's money and connections could. In 1850, Edmund wrote a letter to Huntsville lawyer James Robinson, who was defending his son Woodson in court for a crime Edmund cryptically referred to only as "this other matter." Woodson had been a part of the plot to burn Edmund's cotton gin house earlier that year, and the planter suspected that "this other matter might have been Brought abought [instead] of Burning the Jin for the Same purport"— that is, driving off the white overseer Joseph Atkins. Woodson's unnamed crime might have been an assault on Atkins. Because he had been "Very unwell for Several weeks" Edmund had been unable to attend the trial and was anxious to know that Robinson was doing everything he could to defend Woodson. "Do what you think Best as I cant be thair," he wrote, though he couldn't help including advice on who the lawyer should call as a witness.[66] Apparently Robinson did handle the case well because Woodson was out of jail, at the latest, by the time Edmund died in 1853. In 1851 or 1852, when some of Samuel's slaves (likely his children or their half-siblings) were arraigned on a criminal charge, he too hired attorneys to defend them—Brickell & Cabaniss, one of the most prominent law firms in Madison County.[67] In 1853, although Samuel had led the charge to have Edmund's will declared void in court, he did fulfill one of his brother's last requests: find legal counsel for his son Armstead, who was awaiting trial after being indicted for murder.[68] He hired Brickell & Cabaniss, and Armstead went free.

It was behavior that belied Samuel's assertion in his petition against Edmund's will that his brother had "left no widow, children, or descendants of children," or at least none that the court should recognize.[69] Samuel would say what he had to in order to inherit Edmund's estate, but that didn't mean he would let his brother's sons face prison time or death at the end of a rope. And it didn't mean he would allow his brother's children to be owned by someone outside the family, or even a white family member marked by an "absence of sympathy" for Edmund's sons and daughters.[70] When Edmund's property was put up for sale, Samuel purchased Woodson himself and jointly bought Armstead, Virginia, and Elizabeth with his nephew John E. Townsend—for $1,000 each.[71] His brother's children were Townsends too, and Samuel was willing to expend considerable resources to ensure they were treated as such.

But the fact that the two planters recognized and favored their children in some respects did not mean that the enslaved Townsends weren't subject to the control that masters held over people legally considered property. In fact, their lives on the Home Place may have been under greater scrutiny precisely because the brothers did consider them family. Samuel and Edmund's desire to maintain a separation between their "servants" and slaves may have led them to go so far as arranging marriages for their children, specifically choosing enslaved men and women they considered to be of comparable elite status. While enslaved on the Home Place, Wesley married a woman from his uncle's Mullens plantation: Jane, daughter of the "negro man Ned" Edmund had attempted to free and pay a $100 annual salary in his will. Ned had been the foreman on one of Edmund Townsend's plantations and the only enslaved person mentioned in Edmund's will who wasn't one of his children. Distinguished in this way, perhaps Ned, his wife Malinda, and their five children seemed like a suitable household for Samuel's eldest son to join.[72] Wesley and Jane had two children together, and in letters to his wife he expressed genuine affection and concern for her, so personal choice—or perhaps his own desire to maintain status, if Wesley shared Samuel's sense of his difference from other slaves—seems to have influenced his marriage to Jane.[73] But that's less likely for his sister Caroline. Samuel's eldest daughter married even closer to the family: her first husband was her first cousin, Edmund's son Woodson. Woodson and Caroline probably never considered their union a true marriage.[74] While alive, Samuel appeared to suspect that Woodson either wasn't or wouldn't be faithful to his daughter, and in the final draft of his will he included a $5,000 bequest to Woodson only if he remained married to Caroline.[75] But Woodson and Caroline had no children together and separated immediately after their emancipation, with even Samuel's lawyer assuring her that she would "not be under any obligation to continue as his wife."[76] Samuel had been right; Woodson preferred another woman all along, though he wisely gave no hint of who she was. The year after Samuel's death, he would father a child with the late planter's former "housekeeper" Elvira.[77]

Samuel Townsend's intimate management of his children's private lives was an exercise in power and control, the same mastery he wielded to separate enslaved spouses when he wanted a new sexual conquest. Yet even in their vulnerability, the enslaved Townsends may have seen their relationship to their master as something they could leverage into permanent liberty. Most enslaved people on the Home Place knew the only way they would ever go free was if they ran—like Dick and Owen, who took advantage of the upheaval over their master's death to successfully escape in 1856.[78] The enslaved Townsends, however, saw other possibilities. They knew what Edmund had tried to do for his daughters Elizabeth and Virginia and his sons Armstead and Woodson. They knew that they could rely on Samuel to expend time and money getting them out of even the direst legal trouble. Local whites recognized their special status too: their parentage, their skilled work, the way Samuel and Edmund treated them. At the same time, Samuel's children and concubines also knew just how fragile that status was. While their relation to their master gave them certain opportunities and immunities, the fact of their enslavement made their privileged positions inherently unstable. In a community as committed to slavery and white supremacy as Madison County, Alabama, all it took was one man's death to see those opportunities destroyed. Edmund Townsend's children had experienced that firsthand. Perhaps their cousins told themselves, *just look what happened to Lizzie and Jennie.* Even so, the enslaved Townsends knew that Samuel's acknowledgment of them as family was their best hope for emancipation. When Wesley's mother Rainey gave birth in 1853—the same year Edmund's will was broken and Samuel began writing the first draft of his own—she named her infant son "Freeman."[79]

Samuel Townsend was a month from death when he spoke with his overseer John J. Busby about his plans for his property when he was gone. For the last three years he'd been keeping the provisions of his will a strict secret, but on this particular day in 1856, Samuel wanted to talk.

"Well, Jeff, I wrote my will," he said. Samuel "reckon[ed] they'll try to break it after I'm gone," *they* being the white nieces and nephews who would doubtless be as eager to inherit his property as Samuel had been to acquire Edmund's. "But they're welcome to press their whips at it." Samuel had total confidence in the legal soundness of his will. After all, he added, he "got Sep Cabaniss to write it."[80]

Septimus Douglass Cabaniss, professionally known as S. D. Cabaniss, was one half of the successful Huntsville law firm Brickell & Cabaniss when Samuel hired him to defend some of his slaves against a criminal charge and to represent Edmund's son Armstead. But the lawyer had known about Samuel Townsend for decades. Cabaniss's mother and father had migrated to Alabama from the same county in Virginia as the Townsends, though they had made the move nine years earlier. Septimus Cabaniss, born in Madison County, was four years old when the Townsend brothers arrived.[81] "When a boy I lived several years in the same neighborhood" as the Townsends, Cabaniss later recalled, "but there was no intercourse between us and I have no recollection of his recognizing me as an acquaintance prior to the year 1848."[82] That was probably no accident. The Cabanisses were among the first families of Huntsville, proudly tracing their lineage back to the French Huguenot Henri Cabaniss of LaSalle, who had arrived in North America in the late seventeenth century.[83] They'd been slaveholders for generations: Septimus Cabaniss's father Charles had signed his name to the 1785 Lunenburg County petition in which white residents rabidly insisted on their right to life, liberty, and the pursuit of property, particularly "the most valuable and indispensable Article of our Property, our Slaves."[84] One of thirteen children, Septimus Cabaniss went into law, attending the University of Virginia before returning to Alabama and passing the state bar at the age of twenty-three.[85] He had a plantation of his own, but cotton wasn't his primary occupation. Born into wealth and status, Cabaniss was more Virginia gentleman than social-climbing Alabama migrant. In background and temperament, he was the Townsend brothers' opposite, as were his employees. While John Busby practiced his shaky signature all over the back of Samuel's farm book, Cabaniss's overseer wrote him erudite letters discussing the state of Alabama politics.[86] In spite of their differences, the two men worked well together. Cabaniss had watched Samuel from afar since he was a child; perhaps the well-bred lawyer found something appealing about the coarse, uncultured planter's utter disregard for public opinion. So when Samuel asked to meet with him privately—to discuss a matter he told Cabaniss to keep secret even from his business partner Robert Brickell—the lawyer agreed.[87]

Samuel invited Cabaniss to the Home Place in late April 1853, just days or weeks after his brother Edmund's death. He was thinking ahead. Like Edmund, Samuel counted his enslaved children as family, and as long as he was alive (and those children remained enslaved) Madison County's white community indulged his behavior. But if his children's privileged status were to last beyond his lifetime, Samuel needed to guarantee that his will didn't meet the same fate as Edmund's. Never mind that Samuel was, even as he met with Cabaniss that day, fighting his brother's will in court. To Samuel, it made perfect sense: with Edmund's fortune augmenting his own estate, Samuel's children would inherit a massively larger sum when he died. He was even happy to name his brother's children among his heirs, provided they received less than his own. Samuel had no doubt his white relatives would have contested Edmund's will without his help, and he knew they would try again with his. "He did manifest much anxiety about his will," Cabaniss noted, and "a great dread of his childrens becoming the slaves of some of his relations."[88] The overseer John Busby agreed, commenting that Samuel told him "he had rather strangers had his property than such men" as his white nephews.[89] Samuel Townsend was under no illusion that he could rely on his white relatives' family feeling. He needed to bring in reinforcements, and S. D. Cabaniss—analytical, detail-oriented, and above all discreet—would be at the vanguard.

"The dominating object of his will," Cabaniss said, was threefold. First, to emancipate his children, Elvira, and "my brother Edmund's two girls"; second, to leave them the bulk of his estate; and third, to see that they had the education and resources to manage it in freedom. Cabaniss made a point of noting that Samuel "never changed his purposes in those respects from the first to the last conversation he had with me."[90] The lawyer must have realized, in those first conversations, that he had his work cut out for him. Samuel didn't know much more about Alabama law than his brother had, only that it wasn't on his children's side. "I have witnessed," Samuel wrote in the earliest draft of his will, "that nothing can be done here, under the law, for a slave." Samuel's solution—to ask that his will be probated under Louisiana state law, where laws regulating slavery and manumission were more lenient than elsewhere in the South—wouldn't have passed muster, as he owned no land in Louisiana to justify choosing that jurisdiction. His proposed bequests added further complications. Edmund had wanted to emancipate his children and leave them the proceeds from the sale of his land and slaves; Samuel wanted his children to live on that land as slave owners themselves.[91]

To Elvira: the ownership of her mother Hannah, her mother's children, her mother's husband Dick, and all their increase—along with a special $5,000 bequest "to dispose of as she please."

To Wesley and Caroline: the blacksmith George, their mother Rainey, their mother's two children by an enslaved man, and all her increase.

To Willis, Osborne, and Parthenia: their half-brother Austin, the three sons of a woman now deceased, Wesley's aunt Dinah and her three boys, and all her future increase.

To Joseph Bradford and Susanna: three female slaves and two male slaves, their mother Celia, and all their mother's increase.

To Milcha: her mother Lucy, her half-brother Warren, and her mother's increase thereafter.

And there was more to bequeath: "Milly, old woman + daughter; Martha, + Martha's son William + increase; also Miner fellow + wife Jinny + son Marshall, also two boys sons of Miner by other women, Walter + Washington, also Thomas + wife Jane, also two young women Eliza + Frances, also Jim + wife Tempa + four children, Emma and Anny, Kinchen + Burl, also two little girls Martha Betsy sisters, also two boys Ned + Reuben, also girl Easter in Jackson County + two boys in Jackson Black William and cross-eyed William." Samuel's children were to inherit these slaves too once they came of age and to divide them equally among themselves. Promising them the "increase," or future children, of his female slaves, Samuel planned that his children would be slaveholders for a long time. He wrote: "my request is that all the above twelve children shall live together, until they become twenty one years of age, + then his portion given up to him, as in white children."[92]

Cabaniss nixed all of it. While free people of color did own slaves in Alabama, even in Madison County, these were almost exclusively former slaves who had managed to purchase their own freedom before buying their spouses' or children's.[93] The Townsend children wouldn't be purchasing themselves or their extended families: they were being manumitted by their master, and Alabama law prohibited slaves emancipated in this way from remaining in the state. The $5,000 bequest to Elvira was another problem. Visiting the Home Place to advise Samuel on his will, Cabaniss would have come into contact with Elvira regularly; perhaps she moved in and out of the room where their discussions happened, bringing the men food or drink. The lawyer likely worried that Samuel was making himself vulnerable to accusations of "undue influence." When his white relatives inevitably contested the will, they could argue that Elvira was using her proximity to Samuel to manipulate him.[94] Samuel had hired Cabaniss to make his will unassailable, and anything that might prove a liability in court had to go.

In his next draft, Samuel proposed an alternative: sell his plantations and other personal property and use the proceeds to remove the "favorite objects of my bounty" to a more hospitable state "where emancipated slaves are permitted to reside and hold property under the protection of the laws." His executors would purchase land for them—contiguous farms, ideally—along with a whole host of other things Samuel considered necessary "for the comfort of my servants." He wanted his executors to buy them horses, mules, and cattle, hogs and poultry, household and kitchen furniture, one year's provisions, "comfortable beds & bed clothing," and six months' supply of new clothes. After that, Samuel estimated he could leave his nine children, Elvira, and his nieces Lizzie and Jennie $12,000 each. Until all this could be arranged, Samuel expected the remainder of his slaves to continue cultivating the plantations for his children's benefit, with his "female servants" (that is, his daughters, nieces, and Elvira) exempted from "laboring in the crops." It was a division Samuel wished to maintain even off the Home Place. Though the second draft of his will freed his children's mothers and other half-siblings,

Samuel still intended them to "remain with said legatees as long as they shall live" and work as their servants for "a liberal wage." Cabaniss may have convinced Samuel that his children couldn't be slaveholders in Alabama, but the planter remained determined to make their lives as close to it as possible.[95]

Between 1853 and 1856, Samuel Townsend re-wrote his will at least three times. Each new draft bore more of Cabaniss's stamp, with talk of "defraying costs" and "residuary trust funds," and the replacement of "children" and "favorite servants" with "legatees of the first and second class." The lawyer was indefatigable—but instead of trying to guarantee that Samuel's children would live like planter elites in freedom, Cabaniss focused on guarding against legal attacks that would keep those children from being freed in the first place. He divided the slaves Samuel wished to emancipate into two groups: legatees of the first class (Samuel's children, Elvira, and his brother Edmund's daughters), and legatees of the second class (Samuel's other concubines and their children by enslaved men). Though the terms were common legal designations, they also captured Samuel's priorities. The twelve legatees of the first class were to be emancipated first and share equally in a trust fund of over $200,000, or more than $16,000 each. The fund would comprise the proceeds from the sale of Samuel's real estate and personal property—including enslaved people less fortunate than they. The second class would be freed only after the first class was removed from the state and would inherit a smaller amount: $200 each. *Trotter v. Blocker* had established that slaves couldn't receive a "gift" of their own freedom, let alone sums like this, but Cabaniss found a loophole. "In order that there may be no question as to the power and legal authority of my Executors to remove and emancipate said slaves," Samuel's final will read, "I do hereby bequeath to the Executors of this my will, such property and title in and to each and all of my above named slaves . . . in order to entitle them in law to have said slaves and their said increase so removed and emancipated . . . and for no other purpose." Emancipating slaves by will was illegal, so Samuel wouldn't emancipate them at all. Instead, he was leaving them to his executors and trusting that they would do it. He just needed executors he could trust.[96]

Again, Cabaniss's guidance proved invaluable. In his first will Samuel named S. D. Cabaniss and Robert Brickell as his executors, but Cabaniss had a better idea: co-opt one of Samuel's white relatives. Cabaniss's strategy throughout had been to make the will so ironclad as to "prevent the commencement of any litigation in relation to its probate."[97] Making an ally of one of the white Townsends—having a member of Samuel's supposedly legitimate family defending his will—was one way to discourage the others.

In the first draft of his will, Samuel didn't leave a penny to any white nieces or nephews except his sister Henrietta's son Robert, whom he wanted to employ as a financial advisor for his children. By 1854, however, he had added his "beloved nephews" John E. Townsend and Samuel C. Townsend to his list of beneficiaries.[98] John and Samuel C. were the two eldest sons of his late brother Parks, and two of the only white Townsends with whom Samuel was friendly. The temperamental planter was "at outs" with most of the others: he and Parks S. had quarreled about a fence, Muntford rarely visited, Michael was "almost a stranger to him," and the rest lived out of state. John had long been Samuel's favorite. After Edmund's death they decided to go into business together, putting $28,000 into a "partnership plantation" they called the Mountain Place.[99] Samuel named John an executor alongside Cabaniss in 1854 because "he supposed him to be so well off & so thrifty that he would risk nothing in doing so."[100] A wealthy man, Samuel thought (conveniently forgetting his own past actions), would have no reason to seek further enrichment by challenging his will.

As it turned out, John E. Townsend was neither well-off nor thrifty. He had "squandered" his inheritance from his uncle Edmund, and by the time of Samuel's death was completely insolvent.[101] To make matters worse, as Cabaniss recorded in his meticulous notes on the Townsend family drama, "in July 1856 in the night time he ran off with his overseers daughter."[102] After that, Samuel lost all confidence in his nephew. It may seem hypocritical for a man with a history of sexual violence against enslaved women to criticize John E. Townsend for an affair with a free and, presumably, willing woman. But perhaps John's behavior offended Samuel's sense of family duty. Even Samuel provided for his blood, and they were slaves. Meanwhile, John was abandoning his wife, Sarah, who had lost three children in the past three years—all under the age of seven.[103] While in the past Samuel had spoken of his nephew in glowing terms, he now denounced John to his friends as a "rascal," "dissipated and reckless," a man who had "forefeited all claim on him" or his estate.[104] Samuel cut John off entirely, putting John's brother Samuel C. in his place. Samuel C. was a "good man," the elder Samuel Townsend said, "and nearer like the old stick than any of them."[105]

S. D. Cabaniss seemed to suspect that Samuel was more right about his namesake than he knew. If Samuel C. Townsend really were "nearer like the old stick" than his other white relatives, he probably wouldn't defend his uncle's will for love—but he might for money. In the final will Cabaniss wrote for Samuel, penned two months before the planter's death, Samuel C. Townsend was appointed co-executor with Cabaniss, with a reward that far exceeded even the lawyer's generous annual salary of $3,000.[106] "With affection and for services to be rendered as executor," the will concluded, Samuel left his nephew the Home Place, slaves worth more than $10,000 total, and an additional $20,000 with the possibility of "further compensation."[107] Just in case Samuel C. were to change his mind about emancipating his enslaved cousins after Samuel's death, there was one last stipulation: the inheritance would be handed over to Samuel C. Townsend only after the successful probate of his uncle's will.[108]

On November 19, 1856, the last Townsend brother died. Just as he had feared, Samuel's white nieces and nephews, led by a furious John E. Townsend, contested the will that disinherited them in favor of his enslaved children. They said Samuel hadn't written the will, and if he had, then he hadn't been in his right mind. They said the beneficiaries he named had influenced Samuel to leave his property to "persons who were not his heirs at all."[109] It was similar to the argument made against Edmund's will in 1853: that they, the white Townsends, were Samuel's only living relatives and only proper heirs. Everyone in Madison County knew it wasn't true. But whether they were willing to admit it in the public record—to state once and for all that the enslaved Townsends were not only a wealthy white planter's kin, but more deserving of his property than white relatives—was another matter.

John E. Townsend and his cousins dragged out the litigation for a year, repeatedly delaying the jury trial ordered by the Probate Court. In the meantime, Samuel and Edmund's children remained in limbo on the Home Place while the depositions and hearings on Samuel's will dragged on. Samuel's executors Cabaniss and Samuel C. had been charged with making an "inventory and appraisement" of the late planter's estate in order to determine how to divide his property in the event John E. Townsend's challenge succeeded. So as the enslaved Townsends waited, the "legatees of the first class" learned, perhaps for the first time, precisely what they were worth to a slave society. Samuel's eldest son Wesley was far and away the most valuable human property the planter had owned, his executors determined, worth $2,000. Samuel's daughter Caroline and likely former concubine Elvira were worth $1,200 each, the highest-valued women on Samuel's eight plantations. Altogether, Samuel and Edmund's children were worth more than $15,000 dollars.[110] They would either inherit a fortune or be sold for one. But when a jury of twelve "good and Lawful men" was finally allowed to meet on January 20, 1858, they found in favor of Samuel Townsend's executors.[111] The will S. D. Cabaniss had written for his client was airtight. He had made it impossible for anyone in Madison County to claim that Samuel's bequests were illegal, however much they may have wanted to.

While enslaved, Samuel and Edmund Townsend's children navigated between two families on the Home Place—the wealthy, privileged world of their white planter fathers and the extreme vulnerability of their enslaved mothers. Like free people of color in the antebellum South more broadly, they upset categories of a social hierarchy that equated African ancestry with powerlessness and inferiority. Children of a master and slave weren't meant to be acknowledged; they weren't meant to be freed; they certainly weren't

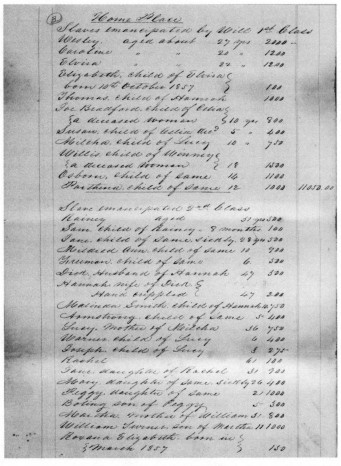

FIGURE 2.2 Page from an 1858 inventory listing the monetary value of Samuel Townsend's children and their family members. University of Alabama Libraries Special Collections.

meant to inherit. But Samuel Townsend's will guaranteed that they would. By declaring the will valid under Alabama law, the Madison County Probate Court made official what Samuel and Edmund had always insisted: that their children were something more than slaves. Even so, they couldn't remain in Alabama. In the following years, the process of finding a place where they could belong—as men and women whose dual inheritances of mixed-race ancestry and promised wealth made them perhaps more difficult to categorize in freedom than in slavery—would prove just as complicated as the litigation that preceded it.

3

Where Shall the Free Negro Go?

HUNTSVILLE LAWYER S. D. CABANISS had met all of Samuel Townsend's expectations. He made the cotton planter's will unassailable; he fended off jealous relatives in court; he ensured that Samuel's enslaved children received the freedom and wealth to which he believed their Townsend blood entitled them. Just months before he died, Samuel encouraged his sister Henrietta to let his lawyer write her will too. The white Townsends were a litigious family, and Samuel believed that Cabaniss—"Sep," as the old planter companionably called him—would keep Henrietta's sons and daughters from squabbling over her own estate.[1] Samuel's confidence in Cabaniss extended even beyond the grave. As his attorney, Cabaniss was responsible for defending the planter's will before the Madison County Probate Court, which he accomplished in 1858. As his executor, however, Cabaniss's duties were not so neatly bounded. Samuel had said in his will that he wished his "favorite servants" to live in "some land where they can enjoy liberty & own property under the protection of the law."[2] But where and how, he left to Cabaniss—and even outside the South, the rights and freedom of African Americans were in no way guaranteed.

In the preceding decade, conflict and compromise at the highest levels of government had created new, dangerous threats to free people of color. The key, as when the Townsend brothers left Virginia decades before, was territorial expansion. At the close of the Mexican-American War in 1848, Mexico ceded more than 500,000 square miles of land to the United States—territory that would come to comprise large parts of present-day Arizona, California, Colorado, Kansas, Nevada, New Mexico, Oklahoma, Utah, and Wyoming.[3] Add to that the Texas annexation of 1846 and the Oregon Treaty with Great Britain that same year, and the United States was looking at its largest geographical expansion since the Louisiana Purchase. American settlers wasted no time pushing westward with their visions for the future. Would-be gold miners struck out for California to dig for their fortunes. Fleeing persecution in the Midwest, a growing Mormon population sought to establish their own government in Utah Territory. And just as they had since men like Samuel and Edmund Townsend flooded into Alabama, southern planters envisioned extending their empire for slavery all the way to the Pacific. This time, however, they had a more difficult fight on their hands.

Since 1820, the spread of slavery throughout the country's western territories had been restricted by the Missouri Compromise—a federal law that kept the balance of slave and free states in the Union even and (excluding Missouri itself) prohibited slavery above Missouri's southern border. Northerners' and southerners' opposing visions for the lands opened by the Mexican-American War tested the strength of that compromise. Northern whites had never been immune to racial prejudice, and African Americans had long faced hostility in the form of discrimination, mob violence, and anti-immigration laws across the "free" states.[4] But broad antislavery sentiment had been building throughout the North, and by mid-century opposition to slavery's expansion was reaching a head. Thomas Jefferson's vision of free, independent farmers spreading agriculture across the continent still held a great deal of cultural power, and that future seemed under attack by southern planters who wished to use their wealth and political influence to spread their vast plantations ever westward. The Compromise of 1850 seemed to ease some of this tension, at least at first. California entered the Union as a free state; the domestic slave trade was banned in Washington, DC; and residents of the Utah and New Mexico territories would vote on whether to allow slavery within their borders under the principle of "popular sovereignty." But the most controversial aspect of that compromise—and the one that directly threatened the safety and freedom of African Americans in the North—was the 1850 Fugitive Slave Act.

From the beginning, the United States Constitution had included a clause that required free states to extradite escaped slaves back to their masters. In the sixty years since the Constitution was ratified, however, state governments and private citizens in the North had devised methods to weaken and skirt the law. Some jurisdictions passed "personal liberty laws" requiring jury trials for alleged fugitives or simply prohibiting state officials from capturing and returning them.[5] Throughout the country, freeborn African Americans, escaped slaves, white abolitionists, and members of antislavery religious denominations cooperated to create a secret network of safe houses and escape routes that would come to be called the Underground Railroad.[6] To counter these tactics, the 1850 Fugitive Slave Act empowered federal marshals to force private citizens to assist them in capturing runaways—with failure to do so resulting in a $1,000 fine or six months' imprisonment. In the words of one ex-slave who fled to Canada out of fear that even the North was no longer safe for him, the law made "every man a slave catcher."[7] Jury trials for suspected fugitives were outlawed. As an added inducement to rule in favor of slave owners, federal commissioners were paid $10 when they sent runaways back to slavery; those who ruled in favor of the accused received $5.[8] The dangers to free Black people in the United States continued to multiply. In the infamous 1857 *Dred Scott v. Sanford* case, the Supreme Court ruled that the federal government had no power to regulate slavery in the territories, effectively repealing the Missouri Compromise.[9] Chief Justice Roger Taney further declared that no African Americans—slave or free—could be considered American citizens. They were "beings of an inferior order," he wrote, and "they had no rights which the white man was bound to respect." Not even free states were safe for African Americans, who might at any time be accused of escaping slavery and sold back South with little legal recourse.

In the final draft of his will, Samuel Townsend, almost certainly acting on Cabaniss's advice, made a provision for just this possibility, setting aside money for his executors to purchase his children's freedom if they "being emancipated, should again become slaves."[10] Perhaps this fear was what led Samuel (or his attorney) to recommend the colony of Liberia as a place of settlement for the enslaved Townsends. Founded in 1822, Liberia began as a scheme of the American Colonization Society, an organization whose members believed that people of different racial backgrounds could never co-exist on a basis of equality in the United States and therefore supported emancipating slaves with the purpose of sending them to West Africa.[11] By the time Samuel Townsend wrote his will, however, the colonization movement had lost much of its popularity among all but the most conservative opponents of slavery. Free Black people were particularly vehement in their rejection of colonization as a solution for southern slavery and northern racism. For the vast majority of them, the United States was their native home—as it was for the enslaved Townsends, whose protestations may have been what led Samuel to backtrack on his original recommendation. "I do not wish my Executors to be influenced by the preference expressed in my will aforesaid for the settlement of the legatees of the first and second class in Liberia," he wrote in October 1856, weeks before his death. "I now prefer that they should be settled at some place on the North American Continent."[12] Someone had persuaded Samuel to change his mind. Although Cabaniss had been the guiding hand behind

much of Samuel's will, this added piece didn't sound like the lawyer. Cabaniss
had no desire to see a larger free Black population in the United States. "If
they cant stand a few thousand," he wrote of northerners advocating anti-
immigration laws, "how can they expect us to stand half a million"?[13] But
Samuel's codicil said he "preferred" North America, and it's most likely that
the preference was his children's. They would leave slavery happily, but they
wouldn't leave their country.[14]

So where to send them? In January 1858, as soon as Samuel's will was declared
valid, Cabaniss began gathering information. He wrote to Stephen Douglas,
the Illinois senator whose debates later that year would propel his challenger,
Abraham Lincoln, to national fame. Cabaniss explained to Douglas that he
had the task of emancipating and finding a new home for more than forty
slaves and hoped the senator would send him information "relative to any
laws touching the privileges and disabilities of free negroes" in the Midwest
or new western territories.[15] He wrote to New York senator William Seward,
asking his opinion of the free Black population in the Northeast. He wrote
to C. C. Clay, yet another senator and friend from Huntsville, regarding the
political situation in Mexico and Central America as well as the Liberian "experiment," which, Cabaniss said, he had been discouraged but not entirely
"precluded" from pursuing.[16]

Cabaniss hoped that the Townsends' inheritance—both their wealth
and mixed-race ancestry—would help to shield them in a hostile country. In
his letter to Douglas he made sure to note that, with Samuel's estate worth
$200,000, "it is not probable that they will ever become a charge upon the
charitable institutions of the state."[17] To the contrary, they would be property owners themselves. Cabaniss fixated particularly on skin color. More
than the threats the Fugitive Slave Act or the *Dred Scott* decision posed to the
Townsends' freedoms, color was the reason Cabaniss wanted to send them
out of the country. In Mexico, Central America, Liberia, Haiti, or Indian
Territory—he believed—the African ancestry that marked the Townsends
as inferior among white Americans wouldn't matter so much.[18] "Townsends
children are some of them nearly as bright as Mexicans and are sprightly," he
wrote Clay, and "the relatives & family connexions of his children . . . are
also said to be smart."[19] Again, with reference to Edmund's daughters Lizzie
and Jennie: they were "two Mulatto girls (very bright)."[20] When he used the
words "bright" and "smart," Cabaniss wasn't referring to intelligence—he was
describing the Townsends' physical appearance in terms slave owners and
slave traders across the South used to distinguish lighter from darker-skinned
chattel.

Cabaniss shared the racism of his class. He owned slaves himself and justified it with the paternalism of so many southern planters: that African Americans were naturally suited to slavery and ultimately happier and better cared for as slaves than they could be as free people.[21] He had a low opinion of the character of "free negroes," convinced as he was that they were ever "apt to seek the society of the lowest class in the community in which they live and consequently fall under their influence."[22] When William Seward warned Cabaniss against New York and New Jersey—citing the higher labor competition the Townsends would face from both whites and free Black people in densely populated Northeastern cities—the lawyer chose to take Seward's advice as confirmation of his own prejudices. "I think Mr Seward is right in his conclusion that free negroes fare better in the newest portions of the Western States than in the old States," he told C. C. Clay, but for Cabaniss the fundamental reason was "remoteness from large cities." Free Black people were "prone to flock" to large metropolitan centers, he wrote, where they "soon become victims of the most degrading vices."[23] It was an imagined fate he wished the Townsends to avoid. Never mind that freeborn and manumitted African Americans might wish to live in cities for the community, support, and strength in numbers that a concentrated Black population provided. Cabaniss was confident that white men from slaveholding states were the "best friends" free Black people could find. "Understanding the Negro character and his proper sphere," he asserted, southerners were "above that prejudice to which Mr Seward alludes."[24]

In February 1858, Cabaniss settled on a location: the state of Ohio. Just a river's breadth from Kentucky and Virginia, its geographical proximity to the slave South made travel to Ohio a less expensive proposition than, say, Liberia. That proximity also meant that many of the state's river counties were home to a large number of white migrants from slaveholding states—just the kind of people Cabaniss trusted. Outside of Cincinnati to the south and Columbus to the north, Ohio had no major cities to worry about, and though the state had the fifth largest absolute population of free Black people in the country (third in terms of percentage), most Black immigrants to Ohio settled in rural townships.[25] Perhaps most critical for Cabaniss was the anomalous legal status of African Americans with mixed-race heritage. Ohio law restricted voting rights to white men but, according to legal precedent in the state, African Americans with more than 50 percent white ancestry could not properly be considered "negroes."[26] According to the Ohio Supreme Court, then, the Townsends may have been legally "white." Most Ohio communities didn't agree, and the state legislature would attempt to deny suffrage to men with any "visible admixture of African blood" in 1859. But this formal legal distinction indicated that mixed-race immigrants to the state might have benefited from lighter skin informally, in employment opportunities and general social interactions, for example.[27] As Cabaniss told Samuel's eldest son Wesley, Ohio seemed the "most convenient" place for the Townsends to settle—at least in the short term.[28] There, perhaps, they could exercise the rights the Supreme Court said white Americans weren't bound to respect.

***

Wesley Townsend arrived in Cincinnati on February 14, 1858.[29] It was the largest city he had ever seen—the seventh most populous in the country— a buzzing, bustling hub of commerce, manufacturing, and all shades of humanity. Stepping off a steamboat at Public Landing, Wesley and William D. Chadick, a white Presbyterian minister Cabaniss had appointed to accompany him out of Alabama, were greeted by the cacophony of one of the nation's great port cities. On the Ohio River, bells rang from arriving steamers; deckhands and dockworkers shouted and swore in English, Gaelic, and German as they loaded and unloaded heavy cargo; and Black roustabouts sang as they worked on the wharves, slave songs from the South and new ballads about their lives in "old Ragtown."[30] Merchants and tradesmen advertised the wares piled high along the waterfront, while public horse-cars shared the streets with herds of hogs and cattle making their way to the slaughter. Linked to the Mississippi River by the Ohio, to Lake Erie by canals, to St. Louis and the Chesapeake Bay by railroad, Cincinnati at mid-century was the "Queen City of the West"—the crossroads of northern, southern, and western markets.[31] It was home to more than 160,000 people, 3,500 of whom (more than Huntsville's entire population, Black and white) were African American.[32] All of them were free.

Four days after entering the city, Reverend Chadick spent $22.65 from Samuel Townsend's estate to hire a Cincinnati legal firm to obtain a court order for Wesley's emancipation.[33] In 1841, the Ohio Supreme Court had ruled that any slaves who entered the state—with or without their master's consent—were automatically freed.[34] But Chadick worried about the implications of the new Fugitive Slave Act and the *Dred Scott* decision, noting the "difference of opinion here, among the Judges and Lawyers," as to how a slave became free in Ohio.[35] Better for Wesley to have formal emancipation papers should anyone question his legal status. So, at twenty-seven years of age, Wesley became the first Townsend legatee to go free, and he did it in style. While in town he and Chadick stayed at the best hotels Cincinnati had to offer: the Burnet House, which the *Illustrated London News* called "the finest hotel in the world," and the Spencer House, whose accommodations were only slightly less lavish.[36] The evening Wesley received his manumission papers, he and Chadick stayed up in the hotel together. When Chadick had to break off their conversation to pen an update for Cabaniss, Wesley was still sitting by his side, "a broad grin" stretched across his face.[37] Wesley was a free man. He was the son of a wealthy white cotton planter and heir to a fortune, and for the first time he was living like it. When Cabaniss wrote to him from Alabama, he began his letters with two words Wesley had never heard as a slave: "Dear Sir."[38]

Wesley Townsend's first experience of freedom was to share the luxury of merchants, planters, politicians, and other members of the white elite, but he couldn't stay at the Burnet House forever. He had been sent to Ohio ahead of his family to assist Reverend Chadick in selecting a temporary home for the forty remaining legatees. They were looking for farmland to buy, schools for the younger children, and, crucially, communities where the Townsends might enjoy the elevated social status their late father had envisioned for them. Cincinnati itself, with its large, concentrated population of African Americans whom Cabaniss and Chadick considered "worthless free negroes," was out of the question.[39] So on the lawyer's instructions, Wesley and Chadick toured Ohio from February to March of 1858—a trip the minister likened to a religious duty and a grueling one at that. In a ten-page letter he titled "Mission to Ohio," Chadick reported back to Cabaniss in minute detail. He wrote about the climate of the state, its soil, its farmlands; he described its schools, which ones accepted Black students, which ones had students with "the lightest possible tinge of Negro blood"; he warned against towns where the prospects for employment seemed slightest.[40] But he was most concerned with how Ohio's white population would receive a large number of Black immigrants—and his conclusions weren't promising.

While traveling, Chadick met with "quite a number of the most intelligent clergymen, lawyers and other prominent citizens of the place," soliciting their advice and asking for letters of introduction to members of the state legislature and other local leaders. "I found them cordial in giving me the advantage of their knowledge of the physical + moral circumstances of the country generally," he wrote Cabaniss. He corrected himself, adding two telling words: "I found some of them cordial." Chadick and Wesley received a cold welcome virtually everywhere they went in their month-long tour of Athens, Albany, Chillicothe, Columbus, Dayton, Hamilton, Springfield, Xenia, "&c.

&c." Chadick was perplexed. "The majority of those with whom I conversed said, frankly, 'we prefer never to see a free negro land on our shores.'" But when he asked them "'But why?'" Chadick said, "many of them seemed not to know why." Ohio had been antislavery from its founding in 1802, but that didn't mean its white population wanted to see more free Black migrants settle among them. There was "an indefinable aversion to the man of color" in Ohio, Chadick wrote, even "confessedly felt by free-soilers."[41]

Part of the reason lay in the state's history: Ohio had deeper cultural and economic ties to the South than arguably any other free state. Many of its early pioneers were small farmers from Virginia, Maryland, and Kentucky—migrants from regions where slavery didn't play a meaningful role in the economy, or who had never managed to break into the planter aristocracy themselves. Shut out of political and economic power in their old homes, white settlers brought their resentment of slave owners with them to Ohio.[42] Fearing that wealthy planters would buy up land and dominate agricultural production, or that enslaved people would practice the skilled trades of white artisans, they determined to keep slavery out of their state. Yet, at the same time, many white Ohioans saw an upside to supporting slavery where it was. Southern commerce had helped transform Cincinnati from a boomtown into a booming city, and it continued to drive the economies of river towns across the state. Writing in 1838, one historian imagined the economic benefits Ohio could reap if slavery continued for another hundred years: "As a state, it is our interest, in Ohio, to have slavery continued in the slave holding states, for a century yet, otherwise our growth would be checked. The broad and deep streams of wealth, numbers, enterprise, youth, vigor, and the very life-blood of the slave holding states, now rolling into Ohio like mighty floods, would be stayed, and even rolled back." If excessive cotton or tobacco cultivation turned the South into a desert, he wrote, well, "that is none of our business."[43] On the Ohio River, free-soil politics and proslavery pragmatism flowed together.

Unsurprisingly, white settlers also brought the anti-Black attitudes of a class of people whose chief asset was their sense of racial superiority. Ohio's 1802 constitution prohibited slavery within its borders, but the state legislatures of 1804 and 1807 instituted some of the most restrictive "Black Laws" in the country—denying free Black people rights of citizenship more than fifty years before *Dred Scott*.[44] African Americans within the state could not serve on juries, join the state militia, enter contracts, testify in court, vote (excluding some mixed-race men), or attend public schools.[45] The restrictions on Black settlement were stringent too: among other requirements, migrants were obligated to post a prohibitive $500 bond pledging good behavior and proving they could support themselves financially.[46] (An explanation of the Townsends' inheritance would have undoubtedly been at the top of Chadick's talking points when he met with prominent Ohioans, as it had been for Cabaniss writing to Stephen Douglas.) Decades of activism on the part of Black Ohioans led to the repeal of most of these laws by 1849, but the racism they had emerged from didn't disappear. "It is a fact beyond dispute," Reverend Chadick wrote, "that a free negro in the streets of Cincinnati is not shown half the kindness and courtesy awarded to an honest slave in the streets of Huntsville."[47] Especially in Ohio's southern counties—home to the state's largest numbers of Black residents as well as the most white southerners— white hostility led to discrimination, segregation, and outbreaks of mob violence against African Americans.[48] In 1829, for example, white Cincinnatians launched a series of violent mob attacks against Black neighborhoods with the express goal of expelling the city's African American population. As a result of the attacks, between 1,100 and 1,500 Black residents left the city, forming their own new settlement far to the north—in Ontario, Canada. There's a reason Cincinnati's other nickname was "Queen City of Mobs."[49]

But Ohio's geographical proximity to slave states made it an attractive destination for more than poor to middling white southerners. The thousands of fugitive slaves who fled to Ohio throughout the antebellum period would have had plenty to dispute about Chadick's assertion that they would find more "kindness" and "courtesy" in a slave state. For enslaved people in Kentucky and Virginia, the Ohio River—in some places just half a mile wide—was all that separated them from freedom. Abolitionist Henry Bibb, born into slavery in Kentucky, remembered standing on a bluff overlooking the Ohio River, where he "eagerly gazed upon the blue sky of the free North." To Bibb, the river seemed "an impassable gulf."[50] Nevertheless, he and thousands of others risked their lives to escape to freedom. And after Harriet Beecher Stowe's 1852 novel *Uncle Tom's Cabin* sold more than a million copies in the United States and England, the image of a desperate runaway leaping onto ice floes to cross the Ohio River was indelibly etched on the public imagination.[51] Twenty-odd towns dotted the northern side of the river, and virtually all of them had Underground Railroad "stations": safe houses where free Black people and sympathetic whites fed, clothed, and hid runaways from slave-catchers and their former masters.[52] Though the southern character of cities and towns along the river made public antislavery activism a dangerous endeavor, Ohio abolitionists engaged in perhaps more Underground Railroad activity than those in any other free state.[53] Residents with strong southern ties and deep anti-Black sentiment lived next door to men and women willing to risk their livelihoods and very lives to help those seeking freedom.[54]

For Reverend Chadick, however, abolitionists were no more appealing than white Ohioans who balked at the thought of Black immigration into the state, and he had plenty to say about these men who "aid the negroes in flight from the custody of a good master."[55] Sharing Cabaniss's paternalistic belief that free Black people would be happier as slaves and incapable of imagining that an enslaved person would ever leave slavery without being seduced away by "fanatics," Chadick had only contempt for abolitionists. The Townsends would be welcomed in "some 'under-ground-railroad' neighborhoods," the minister wrote Cabaniss, "but this would be the worst thing that could be done for them." The communities were "colonies of worthless free negroes," and no less distinguished a man than the governor of Ohio had told Chadick that Black immigrants were received there simply so "they may get their labor for little and fleece them of what little money they may chance to bring with them."[56] Chadick insisted that white abolitionists and the free Black people they associated with were "vagabonds" and "thieves" who would only befriend the Townsends for their money. Chadick trusted neither "the rushing, restless yankee" nor the "Western Freesoiler."[57] He wanted to find "conservative, sensible" men for the Townsends to live among, ideally well-to-do southerners "to whom the free negro might entrust his interests with the greatest safety."[58]

For his part, Wesley agreed. "Some of the colored people want to make me prejudice against Mr. Chadick," he wrote Cabaniss, "but I see them out of such is that."[59] African Americans in southern Ohio would have been understandably wary when Reverend Chadick rode into town asking pointed questions about the area's Black population. Experience with slave-catchers and masters seeking fugitives had taught them to question the motives of strangers from the Deep South. But Wesley didn't see it that way. Chadick had brought him safely out of Alabama, arranged for his formal emancipation, and had instructions to buy him a farm of his own and all the tools and supplies necessary to manage it. Perhaps more importantly, Chadick listened to him and treated him nearly like an equal. "Wesley is a Noble Negro," the minister wrote Cabaniss the day Samuel Townsend's eldest son was formally emancipated. "A little of the right sort of training in his earlier years would have made him far superior to most of his race."[60] So when local residents tried to tell Wesley to be careful, he took it as confirmation of all the warnings the minister had given him about "notoriously dishonest" free Black people.[61] It solidified his own prejudices, inculcated by his father Samuel, that Wesley was of a different, superior class. He trusted Cabaniss and Chadick because—as a free man, with mixed-race ancestry and a fortune to inherit—he believed he had more in common with wealthy white southerners than runaway slaves and common laborers.

In March 1858, Chadick and Wesley believed they had found a suitable place of settlement for the Townsends: Albany, a village in southeastern Ohio's Athens County. By Chadick's account, Albany had a good school, a mild climate, productive soil, and a population of industrious farmers. "Here," he informed Cabaniss, "the negro, as a general thing, is contented with his appropriate sphere in society, attentive to his business," and "moral in his habits."[62] Best of all, it was one of the "communities of Virginians and Marylanders who are said to be well disposed toward good negroes and will do them justice in every way" that Chadick had been searching for— and he had encountered only two outspoken abolitionists during his visit.[63] Though Chadick had worried that it would be difficult to acquire farms for the Townsends so late in the growing season, he was able to find two small farms for rent about a mile outside the village. The first, which the minister designated for Wesley, along with his wife Jane and their children, when they arrived, had between fifteen and eighteen acres of "very rich and fresh" corn land; the remaining eighty acres were pasture for livestock. "There is on this place, fine water, a valuable orchard, (an important attachment to a farm in this country) and a good dwelling house and barn," Chadick reported, along with a garden, "potatoe grounds," and a few smaller cabins that Wesley might use to lodge whatever laborers he chose to hire.[64]

It was a typical farm for the area, where virtually everyone was involved in agriculture in some capacity—though not the sort of agriculture Wesley was accustomed to. Planters in Madison County, Alabama, raised cotton on sprawling plantations staffed by scores of slaves. In and around Albany, a village of under five hundred people, the average farm size was just 120 acres, with most food grown for subsistence or local trade and wheat the only cash crop.[65] Yet, if the farm seemed modest to Wesley, it nevertheless placed him in the upper ranks of Albany's community. Many if not most of Albany's Black residents were southern migrants working as farmhands or servants in private homes. They were "'hired help,'—so these Western Yankees call it," Chadick said. But Wesley's inheritance allowed Chadick to rent him a comfortable house and a productive farm, as well as buy horses ("they cannot do with less than 4"), furniture, and "a years provision, utensils to work with &c."[66] Wesley wouldn't have to start his new life from the ground up.

Or so he thought. The same day Chadick wrote his glowing description of Albany, back in Huntsville, Cabaniss had just learned that he would be

fighting another legal challenge to Samuel Townsend's will. He telegraphed
Chadick with a terse message: "Negroes wont be sent this spring — Rescind
your contracts or sell out — Leave Wesley."[67]

Cabaniss had finalized his plans to send Samuel Townsend's remaining "first
class" legatees to Ohio in early March 1858, making arrangements for them to
take a train to Memphis and from there a steamer to Cincinnati. Although
he inquired of one steamboat captain how best to "ship" and "store" them
on board, adopting the language of the slave trade, he was a diligent executor nonetheless.[68] Cabaniss had everything in place to send Samuel's eight
remaining children, Elvira, and Wesley's wife and daughter out of Huntsville
on Tuesday, March 9, when disaster struck. The four daughters of Samuel
Townsend's sister Henrietta had brought another suit to court. Almost entirely disinherited by their mother in favor of two brothers, they had challenged Henrietta's will and failed. So they turned their attention to their uncle
Samuel's estate. On Monday, March 8, just one day before the Townsends were
scheduled to leave the Home Place, they filed a petition to overturn the original ruling of the Madison County Probate Court.[69] Cabaniss sent Wesley a
letter with the full story:

> Dear Wesley — Mr Chadick will inform you that in consequence
> of a suit in Chancery commenced by some of the heirs of Henrietta
> Johnson for the purpose of trying to set aside the will of Mr Samuel
> Townsend & prevent the removal of the negroes . . . we cannot now
> send to you your wife & children & the other emancipated negroes —
> This will probably prevent their removal before the beginning of next
> year — If the will should be broken, they will be sold as slaves — I have
> no fear of that result however, if I should live until the suit is decided.
> You may rely upon my using all proper exertions to sustain it & secure
> to you & the others their rights under the will.[70]

"I am truly glad that you were emancipated before they commenced their litigation," Cabaniss added, and considering what would have happened had
the lawyer waited to send him north, Wesley must have been glad too.[71] But
his relief would have been mixed with fear, guilt, and disappointment, as he
learned that his family and friends might never follow him to Ohio.

With money from the estate tied up in yet more litigation, Wesley's comfortable life vanished. Instead of settling on a fully provisioned farm of his own, he moved into the home of the white Drake family in Athens County as "hired help." He assured Cabaniss that the Drakes were "very clever people" and he was "treated as one of the family," but perhaps he was simply telling the lawyer what he wanted to hear.[72] In early June, Wesley sent word that "I wood not stay there no longer." He had moved to Albany, hoping he could practice his trade as a blacksmith for the local farmers and earn more money than he had with the Drakes. "As for a black smith I can make $5 dollar where I can not make one dollar there," he calculated.[73] But that didn't pan out either. By July, Wesley was "working a bout in town in the gardens" for seventy-five cents a day, taking the occasional odd job building fences or clearing roads. Wesley told Cabaniss he understood that "I can not expect money from you until you get things fix up" with the lawsuits, so he took what work he could find, however beneath his station he considered it.[74] He wanted to be able to pay back the money Cabaniss had already expended on him in the event that his father's will was broken.[75] If he could save extra, perhaps he also hoped to buy his wife and daughter out of slavery should the worst happen.

When he wasn't working, Wesley told Cabaniss, "Ima putting all my time in school," practicing his reading on a spelling book and the lawyer's missives from Alabama.[76] At first he could decipher only a few words per letter, but he was determined to improve. Wesley was tired of relying on others to read him the news from Alabama, and he was tired of dictating his own news through them. He wanted to send his love to "my little girl Lisebeth" (his two-year-old daughter) and "my poor Wife" Jane (six months pregnant with a second child) without strangers knowing what he said.[77] So he practiced tirelessly: two months after Chadick left him in Athens County, Wesley wrote to Cabaniss entirely on his own. It was a single short paragraph, and he worried that the lawyer wouldn't be able to make out his shaky handwriting ("if you can read it let me know"), but the next was longer, and his hand was steadier.[78] He told Cabaniss that this second letter took him three hours to finish; he had stayed up late on Sunday, painstakingly writing by candlelight.[79] The effort was worth it. He needed to know what was happening in Alabama, and he hadn't heard from Cabaniss in twenty-four days.

For Cabaniss, the litigation over Samuel's estate was time-consuming enough for him to quit his law firm to manage the Townsend case full-time, but fundamentally it was a business matter. For Wesley, and for the friends and relatives left behind in Alabama, the case was profoundly personal. It would

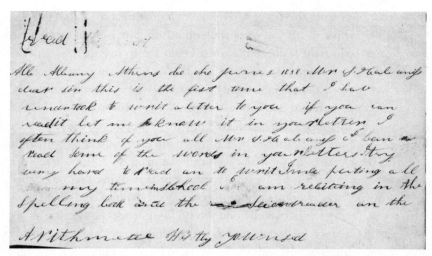

FIGURE 3.1 Letter from Wesley Townsend to S. D. Cabaniss dated 2 June 1858. This letter was the first Wesley wrote in his own hand. University of Alabama Libraries Special Collections.

determine whether Samuel's children, their mothers, and their half-siblings went free or remained slaves for life. It would determine whether Wesley ever saw his wife and daughter again. So when Cabaniss was too preoccupied with other aspects of the case or simply forgot to write to Wesley, the waiting was agony. In every letter he sent the lawyer, Wesley asked after his family and tried to send them encouragement. "Please talk to my wife an keep her in good heart about me," he wrote in July 1858.[80] And again in August: "tell her I hope to see her free if life last."[81]

Cabaniss did pass on Wesley's messages when he visited Samuel's plantations to appraise the estate (including its slaves) in the event that Samuel's nieces succeeded where his nephews had failed, and he told Wesley to "rest satisfied of Janes constancy & affection for you."[82] Jane had previously been given the choice to move to the Home Place but decided to stay with her mother and brothers instead, on the Mullens plantation where her father was foreman. On one occasion when he visited the property, Cabaniss found Jane working alone near the house; due to her pregnancy, the plantation's new administrator had given her a reprieve from field labor. The lawyer told Jane that he had been receiving letters from Wesley, and she was momentarily shocked. Jane knew Wesley was a free man now, but she had never imagined him reading and writing. She was proud of him, "surprised and gratified" to hear about his progress. Although Jane was the one enslaved in Alabama, possibly for life, with an unborn child who might never meet its father, she still worried about Wesley—and whether he had anyone to take care of him. When given the chance to speak with Cabaniss in person, her first question was: do you know who does Wesley's laundry?[83]

In August 1858, Jane gave birth to a healthy son and named him Wesley Jr., but when Cabaniss wrote to Wesley about the birth a month later he couldn't remember the child's name.[84] Tell "my wife to take good [care] of her little boy and her Selfe," Wesley replied by letter, helpless to do anything for them from Ohio.[85] Though he continued to ask for news about the estate of "my poor old father," as the lawsuit dragged on and 1858 turned to 1859, Wesley knew he had to learn how to manage on his own.[86] His predicament wasn't unique. In 1849, former slave Henry Bibb wrote about his own separation from his wife Malinda when he saw an opportunity to escape for Canada alone. Knowing he could never "consent to live and die a slave," Bibb chose to leave Malinda and their daughter behind—but the separation, he said, "was almost like tearing the limbs from my body."[87] After multiple failed attempts to rescue his wife from slavery, Bibb was forced to contemplate what once seemed impossible: he would never see Malinda again. Wesley, too, came to the painful realization that his separation from Jane and all the enslaved Townsends might be permanent. He visited a photographer's studio and had his portrait taken; he sent it to Cabaniss to give to Jane, to remember him by.[88] Then, like Bibb, he set about building a new life for himself.

When he was able, Wesley attended the Albany Manual Labor Academy.[89] Founded in 1848 by a white New Englander, William S. Lewis, the academy admitted students regardless of race or sex and taught them together in the same classrooms—an experience Lewis had first had as a student at Oberlin College.[90] Oberlin, in northern Ohio, had been the first college in the country to admit Black and white men and women on a basis of equality. Reverend Chadick had rejected Oberlin and other similar schools for the Townsends, saying "the men who, and who alone, have any thing to say in favor of their merits, are the strongest Abolitionists in the Country, while the sound conservatives all speak disparagingly of them."[91] Lewis wanted to bring Oberlin's egalitarianism south. There was "a spirit of aristocracy, that is spreading itself throughout the land," the Albany Academy's constitution stated—a not-so-veiled reference to slavery in the South and racial prejudice in free states like Ohio—and Lewis created his academy to break down these "oppressive distinctions on account of caste and color." Slave owners were prohibited from becoming shareholders in the joint stock company that managed the school, the board was required to have at least one woman and one

African American member, and students of limited means could offset their tuition by cultivating the school's farm, milling lumber, or making bricks.[92]

Wesley's time at the Albany Manual Labor Academy would have put him in contact with Black and white students and teachers who shared Lewis's opposition to "oppressive distinctions on account of caste and color." As it turned out, there were more of these than Reverend Chadick had been able to identify. The minister had told Cabaniss that there were only two "ultra" radicals in town, but that was probably because they'd known better than to speak openly about abolitionism with an Alabama man.[93] Albany merchants, bankers, and one county sheriff were "station keepers" on the Underground Railroad, hiding fugitives in their homes and places of business until they could send them to the Northeast or Canada. The small farming village was fertile ground for moral reform movements, and its Black residents played a significant role. One of the Albany Academy's board members was himself a fugitive slave from Virginia who had been sheltered by a local white merchant and felt safe enough in Albany to settle there permanently as a shoemaker. African Americans were active in the town's religious life as members of Albany's Methodist and Methodist Episcopal churches, as well as the Albany Free Will Baptist Church, formed after a religious revival in the winter of 1853 drew large numbers of converts from the Black population.[94] Wesley—studying at the academy during the week and attending Sabbath school on weekends—met more abolitionists, runaway slaves, and free Black men and women than during his twenty-seven years in Alabama.

He wanted nothing to do with them.

Wesley took full advantage of the educational opportunities available to him in Albany, but he had no desire to involve himself with the town's anti-slavery element. In February 1859, almost exactly one year after his arrival in Ohio, he was writing long letters to Cabaniss, studying "practical arithmetic" with multiplication and division tables, and reading "a great many of the interesting books and newspapers" he could find in town—but if any of those were abolitionist publications, he kept his opinions about them to himself.[95] "Attend to your books & your work and let politics alone," Cabaniss wrote. "You cant make any thing by going to public political meetings."[96] Wesley followed the lawyer's advice, but he limited his allies in the process. Albany's white population harbored the anti-Black characteristics of southern Ohio generally, and Wesley, especially now that his economic status had been diminished, was not exempt. Chadick had commented that the average African American resident in Albany was "contented with his appropriate sphere in society," but where the minister saw contentment, Wesley saw subjugation.[97]

As Wesley put it: "the people in Albany got so down on the Neggrows so that they wood say most anything about them toward running them down."[98]

Unlike most of Albany's Black residents, however, Wesley was able to rely on prominent white men in town to act on his behalf when he needed assistance—benefiting, perhaps, from the color prejudice that worked in favor of mixed-race individuals in Ohio. When he got tangled up in a lawsuit for trespassing on a local white man's property and ended up in court in November 1858, Wesley was confident that the connections he had made through Reverend Chadick would keep him out of serious trouble.[99] As he told Cabaniss, he had "friends that say they will tend to mind for me."[100] In February 1859, when a blacksmith shop went up for sale in town, Wesley asked Cabaniss to send him $500 to make the purchase—adding that his "great friend" C. D. Lindley, a town trustee, would ensure that he wasn't cheated.[101] Cabaniss was pleased to hear that Wesley was associating with "intelligent & well-informed persons," and continued to remind him that he and Chadick only wanted to see him succeed in life.[102] But Cabaniss's concern was laced with condescension. The lawyer corresponded privately with Wesley's supposed friends, asking them to monitor Wesley's behavior and habits and report back to Cabaniss.[103] Lindley's response—that "Wesley was a thrifty negro who conducted himself very differently from most of his race in that area"—revealed the town trustee's racial prejudice as well.[104] Harassed by white residents and unwilling to associate with abolitionists or free Black people he considered to be of a lower social status, Wesley remained isolated in Albany. "Mr. S. D. Cabaniss," he wrote, "you are all the friend I have."[105] Yet Cabaniss, Chadick, and Lindley did not consider the former slave their true equal.

Wesley and Cabaniss's letters to each other grew fewer and further between in 1859, as Cabaniss continued to fight Henrietta's daughters in court and Wesley gradually stopped asking for updates. Stranded in Albany, Wesley's prospects continue to decline. Despite good progress in school, the twenty-eight-year-old blacksmith met with disappointment in business. Despite his association with men like C. D. Lindley, he continued to occupy a lower social and economic stratum than he felt he deserved, working as a common laborer and unable to purchase a shop of his own. He had been known among his neighbors in Alabama as "industrious" and "economical" but also fond of liquor, and at some point living in Albany, lonely and frustrated with his prospects, Wesley began to drink more heavily. He gambled, racking up considerable debts.[106] He resented being unable to practice his trade in Albany, just as local whites resented him having the gall to try. Add to that Wesley's rejection of Albany's Black community, and his isolation was deeper than ever. Then, after a year of diminishing contact, Cabaniss wrote him again.

In the first week of December 1859, the case against Samuel Townsend's will was tried in court for a second time and Cabaniss won for a second time. The lawyer wrote to tell Wesley that he would be sending the legatees of the first class out of Alabama at once. "I wish you to write me immediately and tell me what you think of that country," Cabaniss said, meaning southern Ohio. "How do you like . . . where you are? — Tell me something of the schools there, and the manner in which people of your class are treated there — Write frankly I want your views & not merely those of your friends who may wish you to stay or go away."[107] Cabaniss suggested Mexico again and remarked that he had heard "a great many people have gone from Louisiana to Hayti" in recent months, though he did acknowledge that "the continuous revolutions" and "instability of these governments, is a serious objection."[108] Kansas was another option, though he was still waiting to hear back from an acquaintance there he had consulted about its suitability. Cabaniss even considered bringing Wesley back to the South and settling the Townsends in a slave state, if he could find one without anti-immigration laws.[109]

As they had when he first arrived, free Black people in Albany (neighbors, fellow students, or perhaps Adelaide, the devout young Methodist from Mississippi with whom he had struck up an acquaintance) warned Wesley to be careful, suspicious that Cabaniss was merely a subtler kind of soul driver. Wesley didn't listen this time either. "I was gratified to learn from your letter that you could not be persuaded that I wished to allow you back into slavery," Cabaniss replied when Wesley told the lawyer about their misgivings. "I have no doubt but that your friends here, altho they are proslavery men, would sacrifice more to protect your rights than those who gave you that advice."[110] The lawyer made clear that he wanted to help the Townsends acquire the elevated "social position" to which their wealth and paternity entitled them.

It was exactly what Wesley wanted to hear.

———◆———

Reverend Chadick returned to Cincinnati on January 9, 1860, bringing with him fourteen more of Samuel Townsend's former slaves—Cabaniss's "legatees of the first class."[111] These were Samuel's children: Wesley's only full sister Caroline (age twenty-two) and her infant daughter Annie; Willis (twenty years old), his full brother Osborne (sixteen), and their sister Parthenia (fourteen); Thomas (nineteen); Milcha and Joseph Bradford, called Bradford by his family (both twelve, the children of different mothers); and Samuel's youngest child Susanna, only seven years old. Twenty-four-year-old Elvira also joined them with her young daughter Elizabeth. Finally, there was Wesley's wife Jane, their daughter Elizabeth, and Wesley Jr., soon to meet his father for the first time. After four years of waiting, they were free—though many of their friends and family were still suspended in legal limbo on the Home Place. Thirty legatees remained on Samuel Townsend's plantations in Alabama, including Edmund's daughters Lizzie and Jennie, his son Woodson, and Samuel's other former concubines and all their children by enslaved men. Apparently, Henrietta's daughters were threatening to appeal to the state supreme court. Cabaniss thought this empty bluster, but he had to be careful. If they did appeal and managed to break the will, the estate's executors would be liable to reimburse them for the value of any slaves who had already been emancipated. While Cabaniss felt secure enough in his own abilities to say he "would not be afraid to risk eight or ten thousand dollars on the validity of the will" (the monetary value of Wesley and his fourteen newly freed family members), he wouldn't chance "so much as might reduce me to poverty."[112] The rest of the Townsends would continue to wait.

Wesley was already in Cincinnati when his family arrived, having left Albany the previous week to find them accommodations in the city. Reverend Chadick "cannot be absent from home long without neglect of his congregation," Cabaniss wrote him, "and you must therefore be prompt" and "gather sufficient information to be of service to him." The lawyer had always intended Wesley to act as his agent in Ohio—managing the Townsends' disbursements from the estate and keeping him apprised of their progress—and it was Wesley's job to see his family safely out of Cincinnati and settled in the new home Cabaniss had chosen for them. Though the lawyer confessed that Wesley's description of Albany had convinced him "Ohio is not the most desirable place for the permanent settlement of yourself & your friends," it would have to do until the seemingly endless litigation over Samuel's estate was put to rest.[113] The Townsends would be moving sixty miles northeast of Cincinnati to Xenia in Greene County.

Xenia was a larger, more energetic community than Albany. With a population of over six thousand in 1860, the local newspaper—the *Torchlight*—was quick to point out that Xenia qualified as a "city of the second class" rather than a mere town.[114] In 1860, the *Torchlight* proudly ran an article informing residents that their city's facilities had impressed even a distinguished "New England Doctor of Divinity" returning home from a western tour.[115] Most of Greene County's population was engaged in agriculture, but Xenia was also a manufacturing center for the area—producing cordage and twine for wheat farmers, as well as wagons and carriages, farm tools and furniture, glassware and gunpowder.[116] The small city had Presbyterian, Reformed Presbyterian, Methodist Episcopal, and African Methodist Episcopal churches, as well as a Colored Baptist Association and multiple Bible societies; white men could join the Sons of Temperance or the local Odd Fellows lodge; white women could attend one of Xenia's two female seminaries; and large crowds turned out for temperance meetings, whatever the weather.[117] Lecturers passed through the city on occasion, discussing the issues of the day. Abolitionist and suffragist Lucy Stone spoke on women's rights in 1856, followed two weeks later by the famous escaped slave, orator, and abolitionist Frederick Douglass.[118] Xenia's residents were adamantly antislavery and staunchly Republican voters. When President Abraham Lincoln's train from Cincinnati to Columbus stopped at the Xenia platform for precisely five minutes in February 1861, the city organized a cannon salute.[119]

Xenia had a vibrant, politically active Black population of nearly four hundred residents, numbers that allowed them to form independent churches and schools and organize more publicly than African Americans in rural communities like Albany. The same week in January 1860 that the Townsends arrived in Cincinnati, Xenia's "Ohio Antislavery Society"—an association formed by the city's Black men—held their first anniversary, unanimously passing a resolution endorsing John Brown's raid on Harper's Ferry and recommending that the people of Virginia "secure a place in a lunatic asylum" for their governor. Black Xenians participated in the Underground Railroad, with multiple "stations" located in or just outside the city. In 1860, when a Virginia man entered town seeking to recapture an escaped slave, locals acted quickly. "The alarm was given, the runaway set his nose toward the North Star, and is probably now in Canada," the *Torchlight* reported, and the Virginian returned home empty-handed, "a wiser if not a better man."[120] White Xenians as well as Black opposed slavery. They loudly decried the South's "relic of barbarism," expressed horror at news of a slave burned alive across the river in Kentucky, and gloated over the story of five enslaved men whose winter "sleigh ride" took them across the Ohio River into freedom.[121] But in Xenia, as throughout southern Ohio, Black immigrants were hardly welcomed with open arms.

In an 1858 article titled "Negrophobia," the editor of the *Torchlight* described what he considered the city's most pressing problem: "How is the influx of negroes to be stopped?" "The truth is, we are getting more than a desirable number of this negroe population," he said, and proposed that white Xenians cease all economic interaction with Black residents. Farmers and merchants who sold them land or goods, doctors who treated them when they fell ill, lawyers who acted as their agents, and neighbors who patronized their saloons and drank their whiskey only encouraged them to stay and attract more migrants. But, the author concluded, "if we can stop all this—and not till you can stop it all—you will put an end to their settling among us."[122] One white resident scoffed at the proposed boycott as implausible: "I have yet to see the first man that refuses to . . . sell a colored man anything they have for sale if the colored man can pay for it," he wrote.[123] Most, however, agreed with the general sentiment that Black immigrants were an unwanted element. Though Xenians roundly opposed a bill proposed in the state legislature to ban Black immigration into Ohio entirely—"to say that they shall not come into this State, while they have no choice but to come here, or elsewhere north, or to be sold into slavery, looks too harsh"—they conceded that southern states might yet drive them to that extremity by "hurling upon us a very undesirable number of a very undesirable class of population."[124] Precisely how to stop this in-migration, however, remained an open question.

Some white citizens reconciled their conflicting desires to see enslaved people freed from slavery without settling in Xenia by promoting foreign colonization efforts. When Arkansas passed a law in February 1860 to remove free Black people from the state, the *Torchlight* printed an editorial titled "Where Shall the Free Negro Go?" The article quoted a Black Arkansas woman's "Appeal to the Christian World" and sympathized with her statement that "we are exiles . . . a race oppressed by power, and proscribed by prejudice." Rather than condemn that prejudice, the *Torchlight* took it for granted that African Americans would always be outsiders in the United States: "It must be admitted that it would be the better part of wisdom for these 'outcasts,' and for all who would really assist them, to look for some home for them where the foot of the white man will not grind them into the dust, and then 'appeal' to all free Black people to avail themselves of the rights and advantages which such a home would give them."[125] The *Torchlight* regularly advertised lectures and meetings organized by local colonization societies. In August 1860, the Reformed Presbyterian Church planned to host Mr. Chester, a newspaper editor who had lived in Liberia for six years. "The public are invited to be present," the *Torchlight* noted, and then, pointedly: "our colored population especially are requested to come and hear for themselves from the mouth of one of their own class."[126] (Mr. Chester never actually showed, no doubt to the great disappointment of the colonization society and the *Torchlight* editors.)[127] Sounding much like S. D. Cabaniss in Alabama, white Xenians floated Central America, South America, and Haiti

as alternatives. "Every black man, who desires to be a man, will look with interest to the progress of the Republic of Hayti," one editorial read—the im-
plication being that no Black man who remained in the United States would
ever be treated as a man.[128] "With us they are negroes," the *Torchlight*'s editor
wrote, and "never will be anything but that."[129]

Fifty-nine percent of Xenia's Black residents originally came from the
South, and these new arrivals—rather than native-born Black Ohioans—
were the primary targets of local whites' animosity.[130] This in itself wasn't unusual. From the state's earliest years, white citizens had blamed immigrants
from slave states for turning Ohio into a supposed "dumping ground."[131]
What distinguished Xenia from most southern Ohio communities, however, was how the city's Black population had come to settle there. When
white Xenians complained about Black immigrants settling among them,
attempting to "claim equal privileges with our own colored people," they were
not referring to fugitives arriving by the Underground Railroad but to a very
specific subset of migrants: the "half breed children" of southern planters and
their concubines, emancipated legally and sent to Xenia with the money and
resources to buy land, build houses, and receive an education.[132] They were
talking about families like the Townsends.

Four miles outside Xenia, a fashionable summer resort called Tawawa
Springs had operated in the early 1850s. Well-heeled free people of color from
Cincinnati, Cleveland, Louisville, and New Orleans visited on their summer
vacations—filling the resort's eighty-odd rooms, relaxing in the shade of the
beech trees or beside the fountain on the front lawn, socializing on the wide
verandah of the main building, and taking the famous mineral spring water
from which the resort took its name.[133] The vacation spot declined over the
years, but the Black population around Tawawa Springs continued to grow
as southern slave owners made the area a place of permanent settlement for
their emancipated concubines and mixed-race children. Maria Holland, from
Louisiana, lived in a "commodious brick house . . . among fine evergreen
trees" with her three sons. Priscilla Harding was rumored to have arrived
from Nashville with a pillowcase half-full of gold coins, which she used to
build a two-story frame house, a barn, a saw mill and grist mill, and buy
"two spirited black horses, bedecked with silver mounted harnesses" to draw
her fine carriage. White planter Philip Piper lived openly with his "colored
family" near Tawawa Springs, and Captain Smith, from Mississippi, settled
his mixed-race sons there, the eldest of whom was described as "blue eyed,
golden haired and handsome as a Greek god."[134] By 1855 the resort had closed,
but Tawawa Springs thrived as a community of the propertied "colored elite."

Their numbers swelled after 1856, when the Cincinnati Conference of the Methodist Episcopal Church established Wilberforce University on the grounds of the defunct summer resort.[135]

Unlike Oberlin, Wilberforce served African American students exclusively; unlike the Albany Manual Labor Academy, it didn't reject fellowship with slave owners. To the contrary, Wilberforce was dependent upon them. Some of the school's male and female students came from free states—Ohio, Pennsylvania, Illinois, and as far afield as California. But a large proportion, by multiple accounts the majority, were the "natural children of Southern and South-western planters."[136] When Reverend Chadick visited Xenia with Wesley in 1858, he noted that Wilberforce had a student body "representing nearly all the Southern states." Believing as Cabaniss did that skin color was an indicator of intelligence and ability, he made sure to tabulate the students' phenotypes. According to Chadick, Wilberforce's pupils presented "every conceivable modification of the features and Color of the African . . . from the depressed forehead, broad flat nose, thick, protruding lip and unmitigated blackness of the skin, to the lightest possible tinge of the negro blood and the nearest approach to the bodily conformation and features of the Caucasian race."[137] The presence of mixed-race families, especially mixed-race families

FIGURE 3.2 Lithograph of Wilberforce University in Xenia, Ohio, by Middleton Wallace & Co., ca. 1860. Library of Congress Prints and Photographs Division.

of means, appealed to Chadick and Cabaniss. Wilberforce was not one of the "colonies of worthless free negroes" that the minister disdained.[138] It was instead, as one graduate would describe the school, "a community of Negroes of high character and considerable material possession"—or "the best element of colored people."[139] Cabaniss was sold.

Wesley brought the newly freed Townsends to Xenia from Cincinnati in early January 1860. He, Jane, Caroline, Elvira, and their young children lived together in a rented house in town, while "the children" (Willis, Thomas, Osborne, Bradford, Parthenia, Milcha, and Susanna, ranging in age from seven to twenty years) boarded at Wilberforce with the school's two hundred other pupils.[140] Like Wesley had in Albany, they dedicated their time to study. By March, Willis wrote Cabaniss that "We three Large ones" (Thomas, Osborne, and himself) could read the Bible well, and he had been through the second reader two or three times.[141] By the end of their first term, they were finishing the third reader, studying geography, and participating in the school's spring exhibition. Willis proudly reported that he and the two older boys could "stand upon the stage and speak small [pieces] as declamations."[142] He noted that Susanna, Parthenia, and Milcha were "not geting on verry fast in there study," but the girls had been sick with bad colds since they arrived in Ohio; Bradford too, subject to chronic illness from a young age, was "very poorly."[143] Still entangled in lawsuits over their own father's estate as well as Samuel's, Edmund Townsend's daughters Lizzie and Jennie did not arrive at Wilberforce until July. They made good use of their delay, though, assisting an enslaved man, Lizzie's future husband, to escape from a neighboring plantation before leaving Alabama.[144] Nineteen and seventeen years old, respectively, Edmund's daughters could already read, and soon their spelling and penmanship far exceeded their cousins'.[145] But the Townsend children's education at Wilberforce extended beyond reading, writing, and geography. The school's most influential course of study was in the subject of self-improvement.

African Americans throughout the country had long fought to combat the racist idea—widespread among white citizens—that they were mentally inferior to Anglo Americans. Thomas Jefferson wrote perhaps the most notorious exposition of this viewpoint in his *Notes on the State of Virginia*, where he asserted that slaves and free Black people lacked intellect ("I think one could scarcely be found capable of tracing and comprehending the investigations of Euclid"), imagination ("never yet could I find that a black had uttered a thought above the level of plain narration"), or even the ability to experience profound emotions ("their griefs are transient . . . their love is ardent, but it kindles the senses only").[146] Black abolitionists, orators, ministers, teachers, and tradesmen were determined to prove him wrong. Confident that they could change white Americans' opinions by demonstrating their abilities and accomplishments, Black moral reformers encouraged their communities to cultivate their minds and display a spotless moral character through education, hard work, temperance, Christian devotion, and mutual aid. If they collectively committed to "elevate" the race through education and moral improvement, one reformer said, "then, and not till then, will we be able to enjoy true equality, which can exist only among peers."[147] These "racial uplift" reformers believed that if free Black people improved their social and economic status through self-help and self-improvement, they might demonstrate to white society that African Americans were as capable and deserving of respect as anyone else.[148]

Wilberforce University's founders and educators worked to instill this ethos in their students. In 1860, one of the school's agents described their mission in a catalogue printed and distributed to parents and potential donors: to "*demonstrate* the capability of the African to receive the light of science, the stamp of Christianity, and the polish of general cultivation." A Wilberforce education emphasized "self-respect, self-control, and self-development," but its goal wasn't only individual progress—the school's "great object" was "*the elevation of the entire colored race*, by means of literary, social and religious culture." School rules prohibited alcohol, tobacco, profanity, and "games of chance"; they mandated attendance at church and Sabbath school on Sundays; and on weekdays all students were expected to report to the chapel at 8:30 for morning prayers, and to their classrooms at nine. After all, the school catalogue proclaimed, "the success of an enterprise is strictly proportional to its moral and religious tone."[149] The Townsends expressed their commitment to their academic and religious education in letters to Cabaniss, who told Wilberforce University's president in turn that the students' letters evinced "remarkable progress."[150] So remarkable was their progress that Cabaniss was "half inclined to suspect they got some school fellows to write for them."[151] The lawyer's suspicions, however, were ill founded. In May 1861, Edmund Townsend's daughter Lizzie wrote to her brother Armstead, still enslaved in Alabama, that her sister Jennie, cousins Thomas, Milcha, Bradford, and many of their friends had professed religion at a revival held at the school. She regretted that she couldn't write more, but she was herself "very busy now fixing for the exhibition."[152] Meanwhile, Willis was making an effort to attend more concerts and educational lectures in town.[153] Perhaps he had been inspired by influential newspaper publisher Horace Greeley's recent visit to Xenia: his speech had been titled "Self made men."[154]

But not even Wilberforce could completely shield its students from the outside world. There, the Townsends experienced threats and harassment similar to what Wesley had endured in Albany. White Xenians blamed the school for the influx of Black southern immigrants they called "Greene County's dark streak of luck."[155] Wilberforce's more advanced students would have remembered—and told the new arrivals—how rhetoric had turned to mob action when white men from Xenia set one of the school buildings on fire in 1858. No one was seriously injured or killed in the fire, but the event caused one teacher to suffer a nervous breakdown and resign her post.[156] Fannie Parker Currier, twelve years old when her father was named Wilberforce's first president, remembered the fear students felt in those early years. "I was much of the time in dread of the rough white element in Xenia who threatened to burn us out," she wrote decades later. "At that time I could go to sleep much more comfortably when I could hear the rain pouring down upon the roof, for I thought the ruffians would not come out from Xenia, in the rain to harm us."[157]

Though the Townsends at Wilberforce would certainly have shared that anxiety, they were not discouraged. Nor did it impact them the same way it had Wesley, whose isolation in Albany had led him to see white allies as his only means of advancement. At school, they were surrounded by students with histories strikingly similar to theirs and teachers who supported them. Wilberforce's mission—its promise of "prosperity and happiness" for individuals, and integration into American society for the race—introduced the younger Townsends to a politics of both social mobility and community. The students responded. When Cabaniss wrote Willis inquiring whether he and his siblings might be happier elsewhere, perhaps assuming they shared Wesley's displeasure with Ohio's prospects, Willis quickly set the lawyer straight. "In your last letter you wanted to know whether I wanted to come back or not," Willis wrote. "Well," he continued flatly, "I dont want to come back."[158]

In southern Ohio, the Townsends straddled North and South, Black and white, acceptance and rejection. Though their experiences were mixed, these first years in freedom shaped how they would continue to see themselves and their place in American society. Either pursuing a formal education or striving to make a living for themselves, the Townsends were developing strategies for how best to move forward in a hostile country. Their range of choices was still limited: as the late Samuel Townsend's executor, S. D. Cabaniss retained full control of the Townsends' inheritance. He chose their place of residence, selected their schools, and dispersed funds from the estate when, how, and to whom he saw fit. But the Townsends were no longer slaves, and they were gaining confidence in their new lives as free people. As the lawyer would shortly discover—when the twenty-eight remaining legatees were finally freed and the coming Civil War hampered his ability to monitor their finances or behavior—the Townsends' plans for their freedom bore little resemblance to his.

4

I Ain't Satisfied Here at All

DAVID L. LAKIN wrote Cabaniss from the steamer *J. H. Dickey*, rain pounding against his cabin as the Mississippi River churned around the vessel. It had been "raining hard and incessantly" since the *Dickey* left Memphis, Tennessee. The "dense foggy rain" had slowed their progress and Lakin was getting impatient. He was a young businessman traveling upriver to St. Louis, Missouri, where he would transfer to a second boat heading west to Kansas Territory. Cabaniss was paying him good money to transport $30,000 worth of cargo the thousand-odd miles from Huntsville to Kansas. Nonetheless, Lakin had hardly expected his cargo to have so many opinions.[1]

After three lawsuits and four years of waiting, twenty-eight enslaved men, women, and children Cabaniss had designated "legatees of the second class" were on their way to freedom. They were Rainey, Hannah, and Lucy (the last living mothers of Samuel Townsend's children); Hannah's husband Dick and Lucy's elderly mother Rachel; Rainey's children Jane, Mildred Ann, Freeman, and the infant Sam; Hannah's daughter Malinda and son John Armstrong; Rachel's daughters Jane, Mary, and Peggy; Peggy's seven-year-old son William Bolden; Lucy's sons Warner, Joseph, Harrington, and Albert Milton; William Austin, half-brother to three of Samuel's children; the four brothers Wade, Henry, Sylvanus, and Amos; a woman named Martha and her children William and Roxanna Elizabeth; and Woodson, Edmund Townsend's twenty-seven-year-old son.[2] The daily lives and routines of the "second class" hadn't changed much after Samuel's death in 1856, and Cabaniss's legal designation captured their subordinate status all too well. While their late master's children and other "favorites" were sent to Ohio to be manumitted, these twenty-eight remained on Samuel's plantations in northern Alabama. They planted and harvested cotton as they always had, and they served another Samuel Townsend, his nephew and heir Samuel C., in the same big house on the Home Place. As the years passed, they may have begun to wonder whether the promise in Samuel's will—that they wouldn't live the rest of their lives as slaves—was an empty one. At last, Cabaniss introduced them to D. L. Lakin ("a gentleman of great moral worth and excellent sense," the lawyer said), hired to accompany them on the train from Huntsville to Memphis, and then by steamboat to Kansas, where they would finally be free.[3]

On board the *Dickey*, the Townsends were ebullient, hopeful about their new lives as free people. Lakin found their optimism contemptuous. Reverend Chadick had at least made an effort to befriend Wesley and earn the young man's trust when they toured Ohio in 1858. Lakin didn't bother to hide his sense of racial superiority. The women's outspokenness especially irked the businessman, who wrote that he had "been forced Several times to Speak to them in tones of unmistakeable command." Though he admitted he had not conversed with the Townsends much on the trip, Lakin claimed to have "studied" the legatees. He concluded that "their freedom papers will only be a <u>pass</u> to want & misery"—and if Cabaniss thought otherwise, then the lawyer entertained "more hope for them than their capacities warrant." The Townsends had "happy dreams of <u>liberty</u>," Lakin wrote disdainfully, but "if they could realise, as clearly as I do, how much more happy they would be back on an Alabama plantation, than in any <u>free</u> condition they can be placed in, they would certainly be sad enough." As with Reverend Chadick, Cabaniss had hired Lakin to act as his agent abroad. He was to purchase homes for the Townsends and land for them to farm, ideally in communities friendlier to Black settlers than Wesley had encountered in southern Ohio. But unlike the minister—who had spent nearly a month crisscrossing the state, interviewing white Ohioans, and gathering information—Lakin doubted it mattered where he "disposed of" the Townsends. As far as the new agent was concerned, emancipation was a mistake regardless of where the legatees settled. "Send them where you will," he wrote Cabaniss. "You may Chide yourself for the location."[4]

The location was Leavenworth County in the easternmost part of Kansas Territory. Four years earlier, it had been a war zone.

In the late 1850s, Kansas Territory's prairies and steppes stretched west from the Missouri River to the Rocky Mountains: 100,000 square miles of the 800,000 the United States had acquired through the Louisiana Purchase in 1803. The Kansa, Osage, Pawnee, and Wichita tribes had occupied the land for centuries—trading with the Spanish and French and hunting vast herds of bison across the Great Plains—and as far as Anglo-Americans were concerned, they could keep it.[5] The vast semi-arid grasslands bewildered early travelers and explorers, who couldn't envision farmers prospering in a land-scape so bare of trees and water. On an early expedition to the Louisiana Purchase territory, US brigadier general Zebulon Pike compared the region to the "sandy deserts of Africa," speculating that its presence to the west would finally stop the territorial expansion of the United States. American citizens, "so prone to rambling and extending themselves on the frontiers," he wrote, would be forced to leave the plains to "the wandering and uncivilized aborigines of the country" instead.[6] Henry M. Brackenridge, who traveled up the Missouri River with a group of fur traders, wrote in 1817 that "there is scarcely any probability of settlers venturing far into these regions." US top-ographical engineer Stephen Harriman Long agreed, stating in 1823 that the area was "of course uninhabitable by a people depending upon agriculture for their subsistence."[7] For much of the first half of the nineteenth century, Americans had a different name for the Great Plains: the Great American Desert.

Over the following decades, opinions changed. In 1843, explorer John C. Fremont, leading another government expedition, reported an abundance of grazing land for livestock, along with fertile soil he considered "admirably adapted to agricultural purposes."[8] By mid-century, Anglo farmers had begun to move onto the eastern plains, ignoring restrictions on settlement in Indian Territory. Zebulon Pike had been wrong: white Americans wanted this land too. Under pressure from would-be settlers and squatters gambling that their illegal seizure of Indian lands wouldn't be illegal for long, the federal govern-ment incorporated Kansas Territory into the United States in May 1854.[9]

Settlers and speculators made their way to Kansas as soon as the territory was opened. Its first boomtown—the optimistically named Leavenworth "City"—sold fifty-four lots in its first two days of existence.[10] If Leavenworth could be called a city at all, it was a "squatter city," one man wrote in 1855, "lately composed of tents only."[11] So were the other early settlements: Atchison twenty-odd miles up the Missouri River and Kansas City twenty-odd miles down; Lawrence, Lecompton, and Topeka west on the Kansas River; and small villages like Grasshopper Falls, Wyandotte, and Quindaro springing up all around.[12] Never mind the tents and cheap frame houses, the lack of "the slightest improvement of any kind"—these were destinations for "settlers of enterprise."[13] As river towns, they were well positioned to facilitate trade between commercial centers like St. Louis and new farm settlements on the eastern plains. In 1858, when prospectors discovered gold in the Pike's Peak region of the Rocky Mountains, towns like Leavenworth, Atchison, and Kansas City became launching points for travel to the gold fields in the west.

Tens of thousands of fortune-seekers made their way to eastern Kansas, spurring growth one 1859 guidebook called "so extraordinary, it might almost be said magical."[14] Cities competed for the custom of these passers-through, but also for a more permanent population—because as guidebooks, directories, editorials, and testimonials increasingly emphasized, Kansas was more than just a way station. For the ambitious farmer, it could be paradise. As the Leavenworth *Daily Conservative* declared: "The great American desert is a myth."[15]

Kansas boosters swore that the fecundity of the new territory's "rich luxuriant prairies" bore no comparison to "the rugged hills of New England" or "the sterile valleys of the Middle States."[16] Kansas soil could support "corn, potatoes, wheat, rye, oats, barley" and "almost every variety of field crops," vegetables and berries of all kinds found on the eastern seaboard, orchards for pears, apples, cherries, and "peaches as large and fine flavored as ever tickled the palate of a Jerseyman."[17] As for livestock, grazing land for cattle, horses, and mules on the plains was "unsurpassed"; hogs fattened cheaply and easily; and, some said, sheep grew thicker wool on the high prairies than anywhere else in the country.[18] If the reports could be believed, Kansas land was "a sure mine of wealth" for every industrious farmer, "without the risk and privations of a life in the gold regions." This was no arid wasteland. "The Creator has done his best work here," one commercial directory asserted, "and invited his children to come and partake of the blessings prepared with so liberal hand."[19] With rolling plains as "fresh as when they came from the plastic hand of the Creator" and a boundless blue sky travelers called "the clearest and loveliest that over-arches the earth," the territory was like a "vast garden."[20] By 1860, S. D. Cabaniss had settled on Kansas as a permanent place of settlement for the Townsend legatees, perhaps influenced by the deluge of writings on Kansas in the late 1850s.[21] When the lawyer informed Wesley of his decision in February 1860, he echoed some of the boosters' talking points, if not their overblown language. "We are thinking of the Southern part of Kansas territory," he wrote, "where you can get rich lands cheap."[22]

In many ways, Kansas boosterism of the 1850s recalled the excitement that drew men like Samuel and Edmund Townsend to northern Alabama after the War of 1812. "The West! the West! where is the West?" Leavenworth's *Daily Conservative* asked its readers: "Where is that undescribable and undefinable land, to which the American youth turns a wistful eye ere his chin is ready for the sickle?"[23] Once, the answer had been the cotton frontier of Alabama and Mississippi. Now it was Kansas. Land bought or seized from Native American tribes for Anglo farmers' use, the promise of wealth and social mobility, the rhetoric of divine Providence blessing the endeavor—these were patterns that had typified American territorial expansion since the nation's founding. Yet the country had also changed in the intervening decades. When the Townsend brothers emigrated from Virginia to Alabama in 1819, no one questioned their right to bring a coffle of slaves to work the land for them. When Kansas Territory opened for settlement in 1854, however, slave-owning and proslavery migrants faced unprecedented opposition from a growing number of Americans unwilling to allow another slave state into the Union. Kansas, with its "soil of unsurpassed richness, and a fascinating, undu-lating beauty of surface," was virgin land just as Alabama had been before. Only this time, slaveholders were unwanted suitors. As Massachusetts sen-ator Charles Sumner trumpeted in 1856, slave owners' "lust for power" and "depraved longing for a new Slave State" had resulted in a violent assault: "the rape of a virgin Territory."[24] Territorial expansion was one thing. At mid-cen-tury, slavery's expansion was another entirely.[25]

The Missouri Compromise, a federal law prohibiting slavery in Louisiana Purchase lands north of Missouri's southern border, had governed the na-tion since 1820. Because the area comprising what would become Kansas Territory lay above that latitude, by the terms of the Missouri Compromise, Kansas should have been free soil. But the 1854 Kansas-Nebraska Act in-corporated the territory under a different rule: "popular sovereignty," which permitted territorial residents to vote for themselves on whether or not to allow slavery within their borders.[26] Threatening the compromise that had kept the peace between North and South for more than three decades, the Kansas-Nebraska Act stoked fears of a vast "Slave Power" conspiracy, a supposed plot by southern planter aristocrats to take control of the fed-eral government and spread slavery throughout the entire nation.[27] The re-sult was an electoral battle turned bloody. As emigration societies funded passage to Kansas for antislavery families who wished to settle in the terri-tory, proslavery Missourians crossed the border to cast fraudulent votes and intimidate free-soilers.[28] "Language is too feeble to give you an idea of the scene that took place at Leavenworth city," Kansas settler J. A. Davies wrote his friend in 1856, describing a municipal election that had devolved into anarchy. "For 3 or 4 days previous the Southerners & 'border ruffians' came into the city in order to vote," threatening antislavery residents "till every free state man was driven out of the city excepting 3 or 4 who took up arms with the mob." One man, he reported, was killed and scalped; Davies saw the body himself.[29] The violence continued to escalate. Proslavery militants sacked and looted Lawrence, an antislavery town founded by northeastern settlers, and targeted other free soil strongholds.[30] In retaliation, free-soilers formed bands of armed men to battle the "border ruffians." James Lane commanded militant free soil "Jayhawkers," and abolitionist John Brown led raids across the Missouri border to free slaves and kill their masters—violent tactics he would take to Virginia in 1859 with his failed raid on Harpers Ferry.[31] Five years before the Civil War tore the nation apart, "Bleeding Kansas" was engulfed in a guerilla war over slavery.

Enslaved people in nearby Missouri took full advantage of political turmoil to escape to freedom. They would "listen carefully to what they heard their owners say while talking to each other on political matters"— H. C. Bruce, a former slave who escaped to Kansas in 1864, wrote in his memoirs—"and as soon as opportunity would admit, go to the quarters" and share what they had learned. Bruce and his fiancée crossed the Missouri River into Kansas during the Civil War, when social and political chaos once again provided new opportunities to flee. But secret conversations like these, times when "the Colored people could meet and talk over what they had heard said about . . . the chances for their freedom," had always taken place.[32] After the fighting died down in Kansas and free-soilers gained control of the territorial legislature in 1858, enslaved men and women saw their chances rise. In Missouri, where the majority of enslaved people lived in river counties along the state's northwestern border, Kansas and freedom lay just across the Missouri River. Underground Railroad activity increased in the region, with Lawrence in particular earning a reputation as "the best-advertised antislavery town in the world."[33] One abolitionist claimed that roughly three hundred fugitives had passed through the city between 1855 and 1859; another estimated the monetary value of the escaped slaves at $100,000.[34] But flight remained perilous. The growing number of runaways prompted slave-owning Missourians to post patrols along the Kansas border, and with or without help from sympathetic abolitionists, fugitive slaves knew they were taking their lives into their own hands. "I had carefully weighed the cost before starting," H. C. Bruce wrote of his and his bride's escape, "had nerved myself for action and would have sold my life very dearly had they overtaken us in our flight." Decades later, he still felt that "I was braver that night than I have ever been since."[35]

When the Townsends arrived in Kansas in 1860, they did not risk their lives, and their economic situation was far stronger than Bruce's. The Townsend legatees had free papers to prove their legal status, and Cabaniss's agent Lakin had orders to purchase them houses and farmland with money from Samuel Townsend's estate. Still, the Townsends followed the politics of the day, and the territory's anarchic recent past worried them. Eager to move and increasingly anxious about their family and friends still in Alabama, Samuel's children wanted to leave Ohio. Even "the Boys and girls that you want to go to School says that they dont want to stay here be hind," Wesley reported. Yet they hesitated to commit to Cabaniss's plan. "I think a good deal about Canses," Wesley wrote apprehensively. "Is the questtion Settle . . . a bout that being a free State yet or not"?[36] After all, as late as 1860, Xenia newspapers were reprinting reports from Leavenworth, Kansas, of "companies of armed pro-slavery ruffians" prowling the countryside, "endeavoring to kidnap several of our citizens, and to assassinate others."[37] Perhaps Cabaniss could choose a less dangerous region. Unlike Bruce or other fugitives from slavery, the Townsends' inheritance gave them options. Or at least they thought it did.

In his response to Wesley's inquiries about Kansas, Cabaniss wrote that "the people of the territory have adopted a constitution which will, when the territory shall be admitted as a state, exclude slavery." While this seemed reassuring, Cabaniss included a pointed addendum hinting that he, like Lakin, resented having his judgment questioned: "It may be well for you to read and consider the 11th item of the will."[38] Wesley and the other legatees of the first class had brought copies of Samuel Townsend's will to Ohio along with their free papers. When they examined the documents, they would have found that the "11th item" Cabaniss mentioned was a clause giving Samuel's executors full authority to select his former slaves' new home—and leaving the Townsends themselves no power to contest the location.[39] "Send them where you will," Lakin had written Cabaniss. It was no one's decision but his.

———·———

Lakin telegraphed Cabaniss from Leavenworth City on March 13, 1860: "All here."[40] Samuel Townsend's legatees of the first class (minus the nine young people at Wilberforce University) had left Xenia for Kansas about a week before in order to greet the second class upon their arrival in Leavenworth.[41] They may have met at the docks, Wesley, Jane, Caroline, Elvira, and their children watching for friends and family among the passengers disembarking from the steamers. Or perhaps they met on the boat itself. Uncertain whether Lakin would be able to find a boarding house or hotel willing to accommodate twenty-eight freed slaves when the *Dickey* docked at St. Louis, Cabaniss had sent instructions to leave the Townsends on the steamboat "until he can learn where he can stow them"; they may have had a similar arrangement in Leavenworth.[42] Wherever the reunion took place, news of it spread quickly through the city. Leavenworth may have been the largest settlement in Kansas at the time, but in 1860 its total population still numbered fewer than eight thousand residents, and only 627 African Americans lived in the entire territory when the Townsends reached Kansas.[43] Thirty-six free Black settlers accompanied by a white businessman drew attention, and just two days after their arrival Wesley wrote Cabaniss that "the Whit people is right down on us for coming here and they are Doging Mr. David Lakin all about Town for bringing them Neggrows here."[44] This wasn't Lawrence. A large proportion of Leavenworth's early settlers had been proslavery migrants from Missouri, and the city had served as a headquarters for proslavery forces during the violent "Bleeding Kansas" period. By 1858 the city had a free-soil majority, but, as in Ohio, free-soilers could also harbor strong anti-Black sentiments.[45] "I have got to Kansas at last," Wesley wrote, perhaps with a sense of déjà vu, "and I don't think that I will like here very much."[46]

While Wesley's first letter from Kansas described the hostility of Leavenworth's white residents, Woodson's hinted at tension and divisions within the Townsend family as soon as he arrived. "When we met with those folks, they appeared to be glad to see us," he told Cabaniss, "but they did not give me much satisfaction."[47] Edmund's son saw rivalry and resentment simmering under the surface of what should have been a happy reunion. There was no love lost between the cousins. Woodson resented Wesley and his siblings' promised wealth, which derived largely from Edmund Townsend's estate—an estate Woodson and his sisters would have inherited in its entirety if Samuel and his other white relatives hadn't broken their father's will. Meanwhile, Wesley distrusted Woodson for how he had treated his sister Caroline. Woodson and Caroline's unhappy "marriage" had never been a secret. As early as 1858, Cabaniss had assured her that because the law did not recognize marriages between enslaved people, "upon being emancipated she will not be under any obligation to continue as his wife."[48] Caroline was pregnant at the time, though not by Woodson, and she may have been relieved to know that she wouldn't be bound to him as a free woman. According to the terms of Samuel Townsend's will, Woodson's emancipation depended on his remaining married to Caroline as long as the two remained in Alabama, but once they were both emancipated she would make her own decisions about who to marry.[49] "Caroline seem to care but little [about] him," Wesley wrote Cabaniss in January 1860.[50] In February, once plans for the legatees of the second class's journey were in progress, he conveyed his sister's wishes "not to put her property in Woodson hands for if you do it wood not do her any good."[51]

Wesley had no doubt that Woodson would cause trouble when he arrived. While traveling with W. D. Chadick, Wesley had managed to convince the minister that his cousin was nothing less than "a demon in human shape." Wesley claimed that Woodson "horribly abuses his wife" Caroline, and "keeps a mistress under her eye," not even bothering to hide his relationship with another woman. According to Wesley, Woodson was guilty of murder—a reference, perhaps, to the unspecified crime that had landed him in jail in 1850. Furthermore, Wesley said, Woodson spent all the money he could get his hands on buying guns. Woodson's ability to acquire firearms while still enslaved was an impressive demonstration of the Townsends' privileged positions on their fathers' plantations; not even free Black people in Alabama could safely own guns if they wanted to avoid the risk of white slave patrols assaulting them. To Wesley, it was also a sign of how dangerous his cousin was. "From what he has already been guilty of, under the lash," Chadick wrote Cabaniss, "I think he would be intolerable if set free."[52] Chadick recognized that the terms of the will required Woodson's manumission but wondered if Cabaniss could find a way to free him but send him away from the rest of the family. Two years later, Wesley suggested the same. "If you want us to get long well," he warned Cabaniss, "don't send him here."[53] Cabaniss assured Wesley that Woodson entertained no "unkind feelings" toward him and that he had promised to "meet you friendly & be friendly with you" in Kansas.[54] Wesley suspected his cousin was simply telling the lawyer what he wanted to hear. Woodson had a history. He had been trouble for his father Edmund, ending up in court after conspiring to burn the planter's cotton gin house to drive off a cruel overseer in 1850.[55] He had certainly been trouble for Caroline; he was an unfaithful husband at the least, and perhaps physically violent, if that was what Wesley meant when he told Chadick that Woodson "horribly abuses" her. No one in the family wanted him around, Wesley insisted, "save his Concubine."[56]

Even before he reached Kansas, Woodson was making life difficult for Wesley through Elvira, perhaps the only person among the freed Townsends eager to be reunited with Edmund's son. Like Woodson, Elvira felt at odds with "Uncle Sams children."[57] She was the only legatee of the first class unrelated to Samuel Townsend by blood, and among Samuel's former concubines she alone was to receive an inheritance equal to his children's. Though Samuel's infatuation with Elvira in his last years may have led him to single her out in his will, his unwanted attention seems also to have kept her separated from the man she preferred: Woodson Townsend. Eleven months after Samuel's death, Elvira gave birth to Woodson's daughter, but the couple was separated again when Elvira was sent to Ohio ahead of him with the rest of the first class.[58] "Miss Alvira she is fretting," Wesley wrote Cabaniss in January 1860; "Say that she is going back to Ala. Say she don't wont me to have any thing to do with her. Say that she want her money that was left to her."[59] Twenty-four years old, with a three-year-old daughter, Elvira wanted to begin her new life as a free woman with Woodson, not under Wesley's roof.

Cabaniss had originally intended Wesley to help the minister W. D. Chadick superintend the other Townsends in Ohio, managing the disbursements of money from the estate, purchasing food, household goods, and supplies, and effectively serving as the new patriarch of the family. He was Samuel Townsend's eldest son; to the lawyer, the arrangement seemed perfectly natural. But Elvira didn't trust Wesley, and neither did Wesley's wife Jane. "We write to inform you that we are not getting along as well as expected," Jane began a joint letter from the two women, and laid out their grievances succinctly:

> We have not got any money from Wesley which was placed in his hands for us — he has been acting very dishonorably — has sent money twice in a letter to a woman living in Albany — he does nothing for me, has quit me, and write to this woman in Albany ever week — and we have found out that he has been telling secretly — that he is going off with this woman, as soon as he can get all the money in his hands — We are very much dissatisfied — and want you to get some way to take us back home — we do not want you to send us any more money — unless you place it in the hands of some one, in whome we can place more confidence than we can in Wesley.[60]

Elvira added the postscript: "Wesley has not been doing anything for us" and "treats Jane very badly." Caroline was "pretty well satisfied," Elvira said, since Wesley "buys a great many things for her"—but Elvira and Jane would have preferred to return to Alabama and their families while the second class waited to be emancipated, rather than remain with Wesley. It was a plan quickly abandoned once they realized they could not return south without being re-enslaved. Cabaniss's proposal that they return and choose him as their master instead wasn't as appealing as the lawyer thought.[61] "Write soon," they finished, "& let us know what we are to do."[62]

Wesley denied everything, but he was lying. Elvira and Jane's suspicions about his affair with a woman from Albany were correct, and he was in fact using some of the money Cabaniss sent to pay his gambling debts.[63] At the same time, Wesley didn't want to lose the lawyer's good opinion. When Cabaniss confronted him with the women's accusations, Wesley blamed Elvira. "All of them will be governed by what I say to them" but her, he insisted.[64] She was a "torment," a troublemaker like Woodson. Also like Woodson, he said, "Elvira hates me and all the family of us."[65]

They were a perfect match.

Woodson and Elvira Townsend legally married on Saturday March 24, 1860, rejecting the control Samuel Townsend had exerted over their private lives and choices while enslaved.[66] They rented a house, bought a horse and buggy, and were—as Willis believed, when the news reached him and his siblings some weeks later at Wilberforce—"enjoying that life sumptiously."[67] They "is gone to they Selfs, is man and Wife," Wesley reported even before the wedding took place.[68] Elvira had left Wesley's house to live with Woodson just a day or two after the second class arrived in Leavenworth and, after that, Wesley never mentioned them in his letters to Cabaniss again. Woodson didn't want to cause trouble for his cousins; he was simply tired of feeling second-class in his own family. "I considered myself as free as they are," he wrote Cabaniss in the same letter he announced his nuptials, "and I was tired of their foolishness."[69]

Elvira's mother Hannah moved in with the newlyweds sometime that spring, along with her sixteen-year-old sister Malinda and seven-year-old brother John Armstrong.[70] John had been ill on the journey from Alabama, probably with the "complicated type" of whooping cough that Lakin reported had attacked a number of the children.[71] Rainey's three-year-old son Sam— born the year after Samuel Townsend's death and perhaps named for him— died from the disease in April, though Lakin informed Cabaniss that the rest of the children were "generally convalescent." The Townsends' inheritance probably saved John Armstrong and his relatives. Lakin informed Cabaniss that he had ensured "they have all had the attention of good physicians," receiving medicine and treatment not available to less fortunate families in Leavenworth, Black or white, or to most enslaved people.[72] The money, as distributed by Lakin, also gave the Townsends economic security during a devastating year for Kansas settlers, since they had arrived at the midpoint of a two-year drought.[73] "Literally and truly no grain nor vegetables have been raised this year," a Xenia paper claimed, and farmers were reduced to feeding their livestock with "a limited supply of cornstalks."[74] One town in Shawnee County, about seventy miles west of Leavenworth, had raised only ninety-two bushels of corn that year, as opposed to more than 30,000 the year before, and a mere ten bushels of wheat.[75] Bleeding Kansas had become "Starving Kansas."[76]

Leavenworth County, in the northeastern corner of the state, was spared the worst effects of the drought—but even if it had not been, the Townsends were in little danger of starvation. Back in Alabama, Cabaniss was confident that he would have Samuel Townsend's estate wrapped up soon. He had put Samuel's property up for auction: seven plantations and more than one hundred slaves whose sale, tragically and ironically, was intended to make Samuel's children a fortune.[77] One of the casualties of this sale was Armstead Townsend, the only one of Edmund's children not freed in Samuel's will. Before his death, Samuel had told Cabaniss that he'd already done "his share" for his brother's children by providing for Woodson, Lizzie, and Jennie. Cabaniss seemed to have mixed feelings about the arrangement: in one letter to a fellow planter, he wrote both that he thought Armstead "ought to be emancipated too," but, at the same time, that "he would doubtless be happier with a good master than in freedom."[78] The lawyer tried to convince a local planter to purchase Armstead so that he wouldn't be sold away to a distant plantation; he expected that Edmund's eldest son would be freed eventually when his sisters received their full inheritance and could buy his freedom from his new master.[79] Armstead's siblings pushed for a quicker reunion. Lizzie and Armstead wrote each other letters while she was at Wilberforce and he was left behind in Alabama; she sent her love and signed off as "your absent sister Elizabeth."[80] The young woman wrote Cabaniss too, imploring him to send Armstead to Kansas or Ohio with the rest of the second class. The lawyer asked Wilberforce president R. S. Rust to convey his regrets: "I have always desired that he should be emancipated and sent off," he said, but "I could not emancipate him without buying him, and there are many persons both white & black who have higher claims upon me for assistance than he has."[81] Years later, Woodson would still harbor resentment against Cabaniss for his inaction, accusing him of neglecting Armstead when he and his sisters "begged" the lawyer to find a way to free him.[82] But Cabaniss did have some scruples about separating relatives. Corresponding with planters seeking more information about the enslaved people for sale on the Townsend estate, he wrote one Louisiana man that he "will not consent to separate any children under ten years from their parents." He added, however, that "there are many field hands who have no parents with them" and could therefore be sold individually.[83]

Though most of the buyers made their purchases of land and slaves on credit, Cabaniss still declared the estate "abundantly solvent."[84] In July 1860, he sent Lakin a bank check for exactly $2,563.48, enough to pay each of the thirteen adult legatees of the second class their $197.19 legacies down to the penny—$200 each, minus the court costs for their emancipations in Kansas.[85]

Most of them attended local free schools or found work as farmhands or domestic servants in Leavenworth City and nearby Grasshopper Falls, their inheritances giving them the ability to rent houses for themselves rather than rely on employers for accommodation.[86] Demonstrating the assertiveness that so irritated Lakin aboard the *Dickey*, the Townsend legatees of the second class even petitioned the Madison County Probate Court for wages from their last two years of labor in Alabama, arguing that they were owed back pay from 1858 to 1860, the period after the court declared Samuel's will valid but before they were freed.[87] As for the first class, Lakin received another two checks that month for a total of more than $2,000, money to be used to purchase farms and homes for Wesley, Caroline, and Elvira. In the meantime, Lakin wrote, "I see them all every few days & furnish with the provisions & clothing they need, but not all they sometimes <u>desire</u>."[88]

The old cotton planter Samuel Townsend had believed that his enslaved children, who had received no formal education at the time of his death, would be incapable of protecting their newfound wealth responsibly on their own. His goal, according to Cabaniss, was simply "to guard as well as he could against them being fooled out of" the money "before they could be taught how to manage and take care of it."[89] For his part, the lawyer agreed. In a letter to Wilberforce University president R. S. Rust, Cabaniss commented that the Townsend were "liable to be injured by free use of money at this time," believing that "it is much better for them to be stinted, than freely indulged for the present."[90] By doling out money sparingly, Cabaniss may have believed he was simply fulfilling his role as a responsible trustee. Yet race certainly played into Samuel's and the lawyer's doubt about the Townsends' good judgment. After all, Cabaniss said in another note to Rust, Samuel Townsend had been "fully sensible of the danger of much money even to intelligent white persons"—and the Townsend legatees were former slaves.[91]

Whether Cabaniss acted solely out of a sense of professional duty or was influenced by his own racial prejudices, his piecemeal distribution of money from the estate frustrated the Townsends. They were adults—Wesley twenty-nine years old, Woodson twenty-seven, Caroline and Elvira both twenty-four, and Willis (the eldest Townsend at Wilberforce) twenty-one—but the lawyer insisted on treating them as if they were still children or still enslaved. "If you will conduct yourself with propriety you shall be supplied with whatever may be necessary to promote your comfort as well as your improvement," he wrote Willis on one occasion, but "if you were left to manage for yourselves and do as you please, some designing person would probably fool you out of your money."[92] In another letter, he told Wesley: "By reading the will of Mr

Townsend you will see that the Executors will not be authorized to pay the legatees of the 1st class their legacies, until they prove themselves qualified to take care of it."[93] And again: "If you have read the will, and have not been able to learn from it, that I could not with propriety pay your share <u>now</u>, you certainly have not sufficient capacity to manage affairs of such importance." Cabaniss assured the Townsends that he didn't enjoy constantly superintending their affairs, for if they only had the skill and knowledge to fend for themselves then "that will relieve me from the <u>labor</u> and <u>responsibility</u>" he endured as their father's executor.[94] Everything he did, he vowed, was "for the benefit of the negroes."[95] This was what the lawyer had been telling Wesley for the last two years, and Samuel's son was at first inclined to believe him; he had once written that Cabaniss was "all the friend I have."[96] But Wesley was losing faith in him, and the other Townsends had never had much to begin with. Seeking the autonomy denied them while enslaved and the wealth and status to which they believed their ancestry and inheritance entitled them, the Townsends chafed under the lawyer's control. Perhaps Cabaniss came to regret advising Elvira to "get a husband" to manage her inheritance, because the husband she did choose had no illusions that the lawyer or his agent would ever be their friends.[97] Samuel Townsend had said that his children, his brother's children, and his other manumitted slaves "never should serve anybody else." For Elvira and Woodson, "anybody else" included S. D. Cabaniss.

In March 1861, Woodson and Elvira found the farm they wanted. It belonged to a man named Powers, and he was asking $2,600 for the 240 acres—eighty acres of prairie and the remainder upland timber, about seven or eight miles outside of Leavenworth City. Lakin thought the price a little steep (Cabaniss had authorized him to pay no more than $1,200 or 1,500 for a farm for any of the first class legatees), but the married couple insisted. "They have been to see me 3 or 4 times a day about it since my arrival," Lakin wrote Cabaniss, saying Powers's land was "the only piece they want."[98] That very morning they had found him at the Planters' House, the hotel where Lakin was staying while in Leavenworth. The four-story brick building was the finest hotel in town and one of the most imposing structures in this "metropolis of Kansas," which was still composed primarily of cheaply constructed frame houses.[99] The Planters' wouldn't have been a welcoming environment for Woodson and Elvira; it had a reputation as a proslavery stronghold during the territorial conflict, and Lakin, less democratic than his predecessor Reverend Chadick, was embarrassed to be seen with the two in such an establishment.[100] He ducked into the general store on Main Street to avoid them, but Woodson and Elvira followed him into the store "& there took me through quite a drilling" in the presence of a white colleague. Perhaps simply to convince them to leave, Lakin promised to visit the Powers farm the next day, but Woodson and Elvira knew that was no guarantee of anything. Even if the agent decided the farm was worth the money, he would still have to write Cabaniss for the lawyer's permission to make an offer, and then again to confirm the price. This sort of back and forth had been going on for a full year since the family had arrived in Kansas, and no purchases of land had yet been made for any of the Townsends. "They burst into a stubborn passion" there in the store, Lakin wrote, "& said unless I got that place & that too right away, they did not want any & that they would not go on any that you might buy for them."[101] Woodson and Elvira were tired of waiting, and if they had to cause a public scene in order to extract a promise from Lakin, that's exactly what they would do.

When Lakin finally did visit Mr. Powers at his property more than a week later, he was shocked. The farm for which Woodson and Elvira seemed so "terribly anxious" was nothing like Powers had advertised.[102] Lakin supposed sixty acres of the prairie land might be tillable, but little more than that, and Powers had made no improvements to the place except to construct "a miserable cabin." The timber ground was even worse: "The whole of it consists of rocky cliffs or bluffs, deep ravines, narrow hollows," with "old snaggy roots," stones, and "a craggy sort of Black Oak & Scrub Oak—of but little value."[103] David Lakin knew Kansas real estate. He had moved to Grasshopper Falls from the South in 1858 and made a small fortune speculating in land; by 1860 he owned more than four thousand acres worth $16,000 in nearby Jefferson County.[104] And this Powers farm, he said, was "the roughest tract of land I have ever seen in this State, save one." Worst of all, Powers might not even have been the legitimate owner. With a little digging, Lakin discovered that he had purchased the property in 1857 from one "Mr. A" ("I have forgotten his name," Lakin confessed). Powers had a deed from Mr. A but the document had not been signed by any witnesses, and all in all it was "an extremely fragile title." Powers was effectively a squatter, and Mr. A having died, his heirs were claiming the land. Even if the title was legitimate, Lakin wrote Cabaniss, "you, I am certain, would not want to buy a law suit."[105]

The two white men could only imagine Woodson and Elvira wanted the farm because they lacked the intelligence to recognize a bad deal when they saw one. Elvira especially was in Cabaniss's opinion "very ignorant" and therefore susceptible to manipulation; the lawyer even suspected Woodson had pressured her into marriage after Caroline left him, since Samuel's will left no provision for him without the consent of a "wedded wife" from among the first class.[106] "Woodson leads her after his whims," Lakin agreed.[107] When it came to her demand that Lakin buy the Powers farm for them, he believed "Woodson put the inclination in her mind & the words in her mouth."[108] Never mind that Elvira's challenges to Wesley's authority and her intention to rejoin Woodson in Alabama if he wasn't freed in early 1860 demonstrated anything but a weak will. Woodson's under-the-table dealings with Powers only solidified Lakin's impression that he was untrustworthy. Though he affected an aversion to sending Cabaniss "Free negro gossip," Lakin didn't hesitate to write that he'd "found out a little secret." Apparently, "Powers was to give to Woodson, individually—a pair of ponies & a buggy provided he, W. succeeded in getting me to buy this place."[109] Lakin believed the motivation to be simple greed. But it's likely that Woodson's secret deal with Powers was an attempt to acquire some personal property for himself and his wife that Cabaniss didn't control.

Samuel Townsend's executor had little interest in the Townsends' opinions, and he certainly didn't trust their judgment. When Elvira and Jane had informed the lawyer about Wesley's gambling and affair, he hadn't believed them, though they were later proven right. When Woodson told Cabaniss he thought Lakin was using money from the estate to benefit himself—purchasing property for the Townsends that either Lakin or his friends owned—Cabaniss upbraided Woodson for his "vile suspicions" and lack of "proper deference" and then immediately wrote the land speculator to be careful not to do exactly what Woodson suspected he was doing.[110] "It is not for you to say what place shall be bought or how much shall be invested," Cabaniss told Woodson.[111] Cabaniss had no doubt that, if left to themselves to choose how to spend their inheritance, the Townsends would soon fall into "abominable idleness" and ruin themselves.[112] To him, their insistence that they had the right to make their own decisions smacked of ingratitude. He was only trying to protect them, he said: "You ought, all, to be well satisfied."[113] Lakin shared the lawyer's condescension. "The poor things are to be pitied," he wrote Cabaniss after Woodson and Elvira confronted him at the general store. "They have passion without sense, 'notions' without reason, & presume that they ought to be like other people that are as 'rich' as they, & ought to demand as much consideration 'as any body.'"[114]

But the Townsends demanded respect and continued to push back against Cabaniss's control. Most confusingly to Lakin, they refused to leave Leavenworth. Cabaniss had wanted to do in Kansas what he had done with

Wesley in Ohio—settle the Townsends "in the country & as near as practicable to some honest & understanding men, who would take some interest in trying to elevate them." White men, he meant. Cabaniss had a low opinion of "free negroes," especially those in cities, whom he considered ever "apt to seek the society of the lowest class . . . and consequently fall under their influence." Lakin would be able to buy them larger tracts of land farther from established settlements like Leavenworth City, but the Townsends didn't feel safe in the countryside, isolated among white Kansans who had no interest in elevating anyone. Even in Jefferson County, where Lakin's wealth and influence might have swayed his neighbors, local whites aggressively protested any influx of Black settlers. Cabaniss asked whether Lakin could "shame your fellow citizens out of the idea of driving off the unfortunate creatures," to no avail.[115] He and Lakin joked that Woodson, buying what seemed to them an unusually large number of weapons, "must be contemplating a buffalo hunt."[116] But Kansas had a violent history, and white residents were already threatening Lakin and the Townsends. Woodson was being prudent. So were the rest of the family, who were "so averse to going back into the interior" that Lakin had no choice but to search for smaller, less desirable farms in Leavenworth County.[117]

It proved but a short-lived victory. As it turned out, the Townsends wouldn't actually own the land Lakin purchased for them; Cabaniss would. As executor, Cabaniss held almost unlimited authority over Samuel's estate for ten years after the probate of the will, meaning he wasn't legally obligated to give the legatees anything until 1868. Though the lawyer permitted them "absolute" rights to movable personal property such as horses, wagons, and furniture ("I am not willing to be troubled with the title to that"), he considered title to the land too great a responsibility. "Let the title be made to me," he told Lakin. "It is best I think to retain control" at least for a year or two, "to see how they will do."[118] For Woodson and Elvira, this was business as usual. Elvira may have been sexually exploited by her master, just as her mother had been, and Woodson's hopes of emancipation and inheritance under his own father's will had been dashed by his uncle. They had reason to expect the worst from white men with power over their lives. So they did what they could to circumvent Cabaniss's plans—making a deal with Powers, for instance, to buy out his questionable land claim in exchange for items they knew they could own outright. But Wesley felt betrayed. Samuel's eldest son had been raised to believe he was different, superior to other slaves and free Black people by merit of his mixed-race ancestry, just as Chadick had told him in Ohio. Cabaniss's refusal to sign over the deed to his own land was stark proof that the lawyer didn't feel the same. Infuriated, Wesley broke ties with Cabaniss and the rest of his family too. He pulled together all the cash he could—selling his horse to a drayman in Leavenworth, "borrowing" the $197 legacies of his wife Jane, his mother Rainey, and another legatee of the second class named Martha—and took the Atchison stagecoach "for parts unknown."[119] He left word for Cabaniss before he departed: that "he would not suffer me any longer to make a negro of him."[120]

Undermining or completely rejecting Cabaniss's attempts to control their financial decisions, offering demands rather than supplication, Woodson, Elvira, and Wesley were making claims to the social status and privileges of whiteness. But their urgency to receive full shares of the estate, the "anxiety to get immediate possession of their inheritance" that so annoyed Cabaniss, was more than a matter of pride.[121] The country was once again in a state of upheaval over slavery. On November 6, 1860, Abraham Lincoln was elected president of the United States under the banner of the antislavery Republican Party. The very fact that he could win without electoral college votes from a single southern state threw slave owners into a state of panic. Planter aristocrats had lost the national political influence they had enjoyed since the founding of the republic, and beginning in December 1860, eleven slave states seceded from the Union. With war looming, the estate Cabaniss once considered "abundantly solvent" was at risk. Three days after Lincoln's election, the lawyer wrote a Mississippi planter that he was "almost in despair" over the state of the country.[122] With an antislavery president in office and Alabama likely to secede, Cabaniss "entertained some doubts as to the propriety of proceeding with the sale" of the rest of Samuel Townsend's land and slaves.[123] If there was a possibility that slavery could be abolished throughout the United States, cotton plantations in Alabama might not be the wisest investment—and if buyers went bankrupt on account of war or the emancipation of their human property, how could they pay Cabaniss? He had already sold land and slaves on credit; if he made the wrong decision now, the Townsends might never receive their full inheritance. Little wonder Elvira told Lakin, one month before the outbreak of civil war, that she needed a farm and full title to it "<u>now</u> or <u>never</u>."[124]

Cabaniss and Lakin, certain of their superior judgment, refused. As a result, when the rebel Confederate States of America prohibited its citizens from sending funds to "alien enemies" in the United States, and Cabaniss was forced to cut off all contact with the Townsends, they were left without the land or money they could have used to support themselves for the duration of the war.[125] Too bad he had not sent them to Canada or Mexico or Liberia like he once wanted, Cabaniss mused in a letter to R. S. Rust—the Confederacy wasn't at war with them.[126] Or perhaps Lakin had been right all along, and the Townsends really would have been better off as slaves. Still, Cabaniss thought, "if we have wronged them by emancipation, it does not seem right to deprive them of the pecuniary compensation made by their old master for the wrong which he caused to be done to them."[127] But it was too late for regrets.

The Townsends were on their own.

——◆——

Samuel Townsend's younger children and their cousins Lizzie and Jennie left Wilberforce University in the summer of 1862. Bound by the same Confederate laws that prevented Cabaniss from sending the Townsends money, the southern men who had sent their mixed-race children to Ohio to be educated could no longer pay the tuition that kept the school afloat. Facing bankruptcy, the board of trustees was forced to temporarily shut down operations.[128] Cabaniss tried to reassure R. S. Rust that the conflict would be over within the year. "The authorities at Washington" would yield to pragmatism and "conclude that peace even with a dissolution of the Union is better than a war of Extermination"; business would resume as usual; and if Rust would only support the Townsends until then he would certainly be repaid. "The two countries being at war, I cannot as a citizen of this country make any contract with you which would be valid in law," the lawyer hedged, but if he could do so, "I would as Executor propose to you to keep them at your school until the close of the war or until they could support themselves, and then present your claim against the estate." Cabaniss, of course, would not accept individual liability for the Townsends' debts to Rust, but he insisted that the estate was still worth between $175,000 and $200,000, and that "no debts shall be lost" during the course of the war. Anyway, he asked, "are there not some persons at the North who have sufficient sympathy for their race" to "take the chances of getting paid out of the Estate at the expiration of the war"?[129] If there were, Rust wasn't one of them. As Samuel's son Thomas wrote Cabaniss years later, "R. S. Rust indeed ceased to be a friend to us shortly after funds ceased arriving from South."[130] Like their family in Kansas, the Townsends at Wilberforce were at once freed from Cabaniss's control and cut off from his financial support—their newfound independence fraught with insecurity.

Edmund's daughters Lizzie and Jennie and Samuel's children Thomas and Milcha headed west after Wilberforce closed, reuniting with their family in Kansas at last. Samuel's second-eldest son Willis found a job on the Ohio

River, waiting tables on a steamer for $30 a month.[131] Osborne and Bradford remained in Xenia, wanting to be close to Wilberforce when it reopened—though Bradford, Samuel's youngest son, was fatally weakened by "scrofula," a form of tuberculosis infecting the lymph nodes.[132] Half-sisters Parthenia and Susanna, meanwhile, ended up with Wesley in New Richmond, the small river town where he lived in self-imposed exile with his new wife Adelaide.[133] The girls were both orphans, with no extended family members to join in Kansas. Bradford, Susanna's only full sibling, was too frail to help support her. Parthenia's eldest brother Willis had his job on the river, which didn't lend itself to him settling down, and her other brother Osborne was occupied caring for Bradford. Perhaps they ended up with Wesley because the other Townsends thought they would only be a burden. Perhaps no one else would take them.

Wesley was nearly a stranger to nine-year-old Susanna when she and Parthenia arrived in New Richmond in the summer of 1862. She had been five years old when Wesley left Alabama for Ohio in 1858 and had only been in Ohio for three months before he departed to meet the legatees of the second class in Kansas. Sixteen-year-old Parthenia might have remembered Wesley better, though she wouldn't have had much opportunity to spend time with him while studying at Wilberforce. What the girls knew about the much-older half-brother Susanna called "Uncle" would have come from stories of the other Townsends at school or correspondence with their extended family in Leavenworth—three of whom had $600 worth of reasons to think ill of Samuel Townsend's eldest son. Susanna and Parthenia probably didn't expect too warm a welcome from Wesley, who complained to Cabaniss that Willis and Osborne had foisted the girls onto him as if "they had not been any kin to them."[134] But at least his wife Adelaide ("Ada" for short) might have felt grateful to add the two of them to her household. When they joined her and Wesley in New Richmond, Ada had an infant daughter and a second on the way.[135] Seven or eight months pregnant, she probably hoped that her young sisters-in-law could help with housework and childcare. A year later—when Wesley was conscripted by the Union Army in Nashville, Tennessee—their help would prove more necessary still.[136]

Ada may have taken in laundry, like some of the Townsend women in Kansas did to make ends meet. It was a laborious, time-consuming job, but one that at least she could do from home, while caring for her two daughters.[137] Parthenia likely worked as a domestic servant for families in New Richmond or nearby Cincinnati, her long days tiring and tedious. So when the teenage girl had a little time for amusement, she took advantage of it.

Living and working in the suburbs of Cincinnati, the largest city she had ever seen, Parthenia experienced her freedom in a new way. With no moralizing schoolteachers or family patriarch to stop her, she befriended some other young women, perhaps joining them at the city's raucous public dance halls on Saturday nights. When her family eventually found out, they didn't approve. In the nineteenth century, Black working-class women's leisure activities—drinking, dancing, and mixing freely with men in places like dance halls—scandalized moral reformers and those who adhered to middle-class values of sobriety, propriety, and, for women, chastity.[138] The Townsends' Wilberforce education had emphasized respectability as a means of elevating the entire Black community, and the way her brothers saw it, Parthenia's leisure activities and choice of company, what Wesley would later describe as "cutting up and running with bad girls," were damaging the family's reputation.[139] By 1865, Willis had removed Parthenia from New Richmond and sent her to live with extended family in Kansas. Willis no doubt hoped that Leavenworth would be a more wholesome atmosphere for his sister, who had so far failed to adhere to the gospel of racial uplift introduced to the Townsends at Wilberforce. Susanna, meanwhile, remained in Wesley's home. Only twelve years old at the end of the Civil War, she would have been too young to accompany Parthenia on her leisure activities, though like her sister, the youngest Townsend daughter wanted to experience freedom on her own terms.

Susanna never shirked from hard work. She may have been a child when the war started, but she grew up quickly. Willis, whose work on the Ohio River sometimes took him by New Richmond, remembered Susanna caring for Wesley's children and working around the house "from the time she first went there" at age nine.[140] By war's end, she was earning her own wages, spending about a third of her time "working out for other people" as a domestic servant.[141] Years later, when Wesley petitioned Cabaniss to reimburse him for the money he had spent supporting Susanna when she lived with him in the 1860s, he would claim that she had been too small and sickly to contribute anything to the household. No one else agreed. As Willis remarked, his indignation almost palpable in the transcript of his conversation with one of Cabaniss's agents, "if she was so diseased I did not know any thing about it—I saw her about and at work" with "never a word of complaint."[142] A neighbor, Thomas Wood, described Susanna as "an industrious girl," the sight of her carrying armfuls of coal from his coal yard to Wesley's house etched deep into his memory. "If exact justice was done," Wood added, "Wesley would be indebted to her—instead of her being indebted to him."[143] Susanna more than earned her keep. With Wesley in Nashville and Parthenia banished to Kansas, only she and Ada remained to bear the full responsibilities of the household during the Civil War. Don't worry, Susanna told Cabaniss on New Year's Day, 1866, when wartime restrictions lifted and he was able to send the girl a $50 check: "I will not spend one [cent] of it foolishly and I am capable of taking cair of that much money my self for I am large enough to not let any body cheat me out of it."[144] She was thirteen years old.

Accustomed to shouldering adult burdens, Susanna expected to be treated as an adult in return. Wesley's homecoming near the end of 1865, however, complicated matters. When he mustered out of the Union Army and rejoined his wife, children, and half-sister back in New Richmond, Wesley Townsend wasted no time acting as head of the household again. Ada and Susanna had lived frugally during the war, but within weeks of his return Wesley put all of their savings into the purchase of a new house. In October, he proudly wrote Cabaniss that he had acquired "a large two story house with 4 room in it and in a good part of the Town" for $500 cash and a $200 mortgage.[145] Wesley had high hopes for his family's future. He wanted them to enjoy the social station he had always believed he deserved, and the price of the house was a mere fraction of the windfall he expected from his father's estate. What Wesley didn't wait to learn before putting money down was that his inheritance wasn't arriving any time soon. Back in Alabama, Samuel Townsend's estate remained mired in lawsuits, with the situation only exacerbated by the postwar bankruptcy of so many of the late planter's debtors. Meanwhile, an influx of fugitive slaves into southern Ohio—"contrabands neggroes" Wesley wrote contemptuously, some working for food alone—was driving down wages and lowering the prices he could charge as a blacksmith. Three months after he bought the house, Wesley was forced to sell it at a loss, leaving the family hundreds of dollars in debt. He wrote Cabaniss regretfully: "I wish that I had the money that I have spent foollish."[146]

Susanna didn't suffer fools gladly. "I aint satisfied here at all," she wrote the lawyer that spring. Wesley "quarrels with me like I was a dog and I want to leave as soon as possible."[147] More than anything, Susanna hoped Cabaniss would send her back to school. She was then attending the "free school" for African American pupils in town, but the rudimentary curriculum was no challenge after Wilberforce.[148] She had her eye on Clermont Academy, an elite preparatory school just outside of New Richmond, run by James K. Parker, a former president of Wilberforce University. At Clermont, Susanna could continue her education cut short by the Civil War, studying grammar, algebra, trigonometry, geometry, geography, book-keeping, history, logic, and rhetoric instead of the basic reading, writing, and arithmetic offered at the free school. But Clermont Academy was expensive—$1 a week for tuition, and $4 a week for room and board.[149] Wesley wasn't inclined to pay. He only made $1.50 a day, and, Susanna noted, "it takes all to feed us."[150] Only money from her father's estate would get Susanna into Clermont, and, as she fully understood, Cabaniss held the key. "Mr cabaniss I don't want to grow up ignorant without an education or a trade," she explained. She didn't want to be a servant or laundress for the rest of her life, and she remembered what her teachers had taught her back at Wilberforce: that education was the way to move up in the world. With the right schooling, she might be a teacher herself someday, one of the few skilled professions available to African American women at the time, and one her own half-brother Thomas was already pursuing in Kansas. "I would like to go to school before it is to late," she pleaded with the lawyer, "as I am now getting to be a large girl and if I dont get my learning now while I am young when I get old it will be to late."[151]

Cabaniss sympathized. "I am anxious that Susanna shall go to school," he wrote Osborne Townsend, who had expressed concern about his half-sister's welfare, "and so soon as I can I will send money to enable her to do so."[152] He asked Rust for suggestions for "some suitable boarding school" for Susanna, nothing that "her situation at Wesley Townsends" was "quite unpleasant."[153] He assured her that "in view of your being the youngest of the legatees & without a mother, or full brother or sister," he considered it his duty to send her disbursements from the estate even "when not able to supply the wants of all."[154] True to his word, Cabaniss had been sending small sums Susanna's way—$4.75 for shoes, $20 for clothing.[155] It wasn't enough, however, to pay for room and board at Clermont Academy. Thirteen-year-old Susanna didn't give up. "There is to or three exhibitions going" at "mr parkers school," she wrote Cabaniss, "and they wont do without me." Assertive and persistent, she continued to negotiate with James K. Parker until he finally agreed to a compromise: she could attend classes during the day if she roomed at home with Wesley and Ada at night. Parker "wants me to walk up every mournening and come back at night if i cant board there by week like the rest of the students," she explained—a daunting prospect for a young girl who was already doing housework and childcare for Wesley and working for wages as a servant. Susanna hoped her plight would move Cabaniss to find the funds for room and board at Clermont. If not, she said, "i would rather go to some other place or go to Kansas."[156]

Even if she couldn't attend school full-time, getting out of Wesley's house was paramount. But to do so, Susanna needed control over her own money.

Years earlier, while living with Wesley in Xenia, Elvira had demanded the same, leading Wesley to call her a "torment" who wouldn't be "governed by what I say."[157] Now it was Susanna he complained about, the "saucy" girl who "wont mind me."[158] Once again, Wesley Townsend faced the force of will of a female relative who wouldn't accept his authority. Both Elvira and Susanna understood that financial independence meant autonomy from Wesley's—and anyone else's—control. Perhaps that's why Susanna worked so hard. In addition to the small disbursements she periodically received from Cabaniss, she earned her own wages, around $1.50 a week when she "worked out" as a domestic servant.[159] As head of the family, however, Wesley considered Susanna's money his to manage. "Uncle takes all my money and spend it for his self," she wrote Cabaniss in May 1866. "He gose and drause it and do as he please with it and treater me so mean." So she devised a plan. Instead of sending checks made out to Susanna Townsend, she suggested, Cabaniss could send them to her employer, a man named Joseph Lamb. With Lamb's name on the checks, Wesley couldn't cash them and take her money. Susanna wasn't worried about Lamb cheating her, either. He was a decent employer and, just as important, a wealthy one. "Mr Joseph Lamb is Rich," she said, speculating that a man of means would have no reason to steal the dribs and drabs of money that she expected from Cabaniss. Send the next check to the post office as usual, she instructed the lawyer, but "send it to him this time."[160]

Whether or not Cabaniss followed Susanna's instructions, the Townsends' finances and relationships continued to deteriorate in New Richmond, and saving any money at all would prove impossible. In May 1866, Wesley was bedridden for three weeks and unable to work, likely due to the "very bad" rheumatism that had broken his health.[161] In August, someone broke into his blacksmith shop and cleared it out.[162] In September, Wesley was once again in poor health, so weak, Susanna wrote with some sympathy, that "it is just as much as he can do" to care for the family.[163] Susanna, too, was sick, showing signs of the same disease that had killed her brother Bradford.[164] Even so, by October, she had been forced to quit school and work full-time to help support the household.[165] In December, Wesley was arrested for robbery— wrongly, he claimed—and had to mortgage their furniture to make bail.[166] Plus, Ada was pregnant again, and the family would soon have another mouth to feed. Life with Wesley had become untenable for Susanna, and, in the new year, she finally left. Cabaniss would later write that he had been willing to assist Susanna financially because she was "more helpless and dependent than her brothers & sisters," but she was done being dependent on Wesley.[167] When Willis Townsend visited New Richmond in 1867, he was surprised to find Susanna out of school, "nursing child for a lady" and living with the same. She wasn't at Clermont Academy, as she would have preferred, but at least she was out from under Wesley's roof. Soon, she hoped, she would have a home of her own.

"Mr Cabaniss I write to you in haste," Susanna began her letter of June 4, 1868. There was a man in New Richmond, "the nicest young man I ever did see," who wished to have her for a wife. If Cabaniss could simply send her some money for a dress and shoes ("common enough" apparel, for she was "very plain in dressing"), and if he would pay for their train fare to Kansas, Susanna could marry the man within the month. She didn't want a church service, just to take her vows in the mayor's office and be off to her new life as fast as the train could take her. Susanna's wishes were modest: a simple gown for a simple ceremony, a husband who "says he will [do] his best for me as long as he lives," and a small sum of money out of her inheritance to join her extended family in Leavenworth and buy "a little house in Kansas if there is no more than three rooms and an acre" of land. "He has lent me money when I was sick and had no more nor no friends and I paid him the money he would not take it he said but I made him take it," she wrote of her suitor, breathlessly. After years spent sacrificing her health and her hopes to support others, Susanna had finally found someone willing to support her, telling the lawyer that "he says I have been going around long enough without anyone to take care of me." She didn't need him to—she had reimbursed him the money he lent her, after all—but the mere fact that this man cared enough to think of her needs amazed her. "He is a gentleman," fifteen-year-old Susanna Townsend assured Cabaniss, and also, she added almost as an afterthought, "he is a white man."[168]

Consciously or not, Susanna had become adept at presenting herself in a manner guaranteed to appeal to the lawyer's sensibilities. In some letters she had emphasized her youth ("i believe that you will do the best you can for me because i am the youngest as you say"); in others, her maturity ("i am old enough not to let any body cheat me").[169] Cabaniss valued industriousness, and Susanna worked hard to support herself. He valued respectability and education, and she and shown herself single-mindedly determined to finish her schooling. At fifteen, Susanna took on a role she had long rejected: the vulnerable, innocent girl in need of a man's protection.[170] With a little money from her father's estate, the lawyer could rescue Susanna from a life of hardship and dependence on unscrupulous relatives. Cabaniss, born into the planter aristocracy of the antebellum South, considered himself a gentleman as well as a businessman, and Susanna was offering him a chance to prove it. Calling him "a friend when all others have forsaken me," she wrote: "mr cabaniss you have favored me like a gentleman, and i think you will this time." This was, Susanna believed, her last chance—"i am lost here" in Ohio, she said—and she was desperate. She told Cabaniss that she would never "bother you no more" if he would only send her the money by the 10th of the month. "Please write as soon as you read this and let me know I want to go I want to g—" Here Susanna ended mid-sentence, as though someone's shadow had fallen across the page momentarily, compelling her to stop, turn the paper over, and hide what she'd written. On the next page, she continued: "Uncle wesley treats me like I was a dog or some kind of an animal Mr Cabiness let me go let me go for my sake let me go."[171] It was now or never.

For years, Susanna had struggled to assert her independence—seeking to finish her education, demanding control over her finances, ultimately leaving Wesley's home to make her own way. By June 1868, she must have felt that she had exhausted her options. Marriage, at least, would provide Susanna with her own home, a family of her choosing, and a level of security and stability that she had never known. All she needed now was one last check from Cabaniss, just enough to cover their train fare. With that, she could make her own fate. Perhaps Susanna planned to "pass" across the color line; that same year, her cousin Lizzie married a white Union Army officer and relocated to North Carolina, where she was later listed as "white" in federal census records.[172] If Susanna and her young man moved to Kansas, where she would be known as a member of the mixed-race Townsend family, passing for white would prove more difficult. But maybe they didn't care. Kansas, unlike Ohio, had no laws against marriage across the color line—"miscegenation," in the language of the time.[173] Theoretically, they could have lived openly as man and wife. However they chose to present themselves in Kansas, it would be a new start. "Susanna forever," the would-be bride signed her letter, "but not the Townsend."[174]

Cabaniss didn't send train fare on the 10th. "I did not have time to write so that my answer could reach her," he told Wesley a few weeks later, inquiring whether she had married after all and, if so, the name and residence of her husband.[175] If the lawyer harbored any suspicions about the young white man's motives—why Susanna hadn't given his name, why they had been in such a hurry to move, whether he had simply been after her inheritance—he didn't say. Wesley's reply provided some answers. "She is not married and she aint going to be married," he told Cabaniss. Susanna was living with his family again, four months pregnant. According to Wesley and Ada, Susanna was "in a delicate situation by some man" and, for whatever reason, "she will not tell *uncle wesley treats me like i was a dog or some kind of and animal Mr cabaniss let me go let me go for my sake let me go to kansas on the fourteenth i want to go with him to kansas he is a gentleman he has lent me money when i was sick and had no money nor no friends and i paid him the money he would not take it he said but i made him take it he says i have been going around long enough with out any one to take care of me i want and answer on the tenth of this month any how i am not going to have any wedding atall i am going to get maried in the mayrs office and then get on the cars and go to kansas Mr cabaniss dont refuse dont refuse me on the 10 of this month*

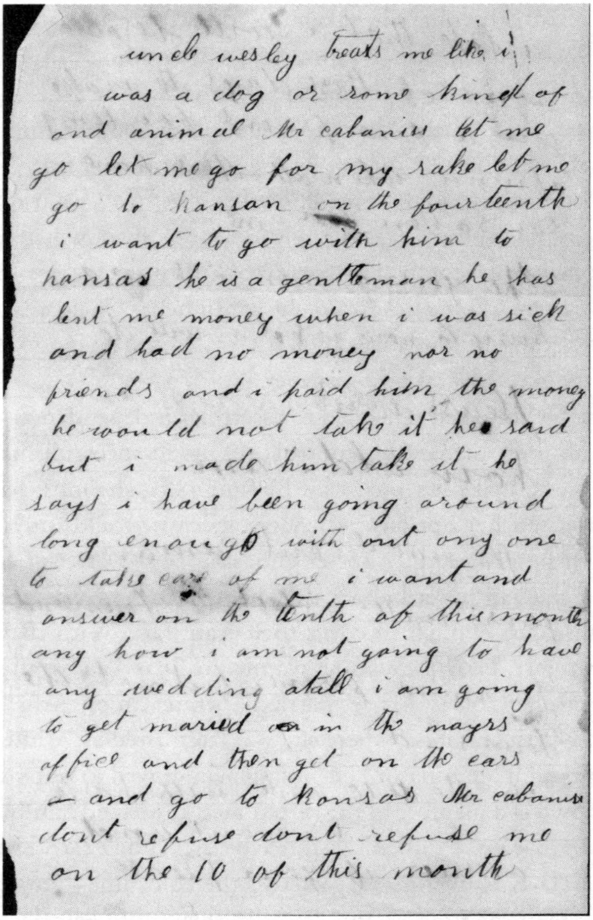

FIGURE 4.1 Page of a letter from Susanna Townsend to S. D. Cabaniss dated 4 June 1869. University of Alabama Libraries Special Collections.

the Father of the Child."[176] (Whether they meant she wouldn't inform the father of the child that she was pregnant, or whether she wouldn't tell Wesley and Ada his name is unclear.) When Susanna wrote to Cabaniss in June, she had been less than three months along; she might not have known she was pregnant. Or perhaps she had hoped to hide her condition until she was a respectable wife. Whatever the case, Susanna's secret was out, and the wedding was off. Remarkably, Cabaniss seemed willing to give her the benefit of the doubt. He asked Wesley for the name of the man who had "seduced" Susanna, implying that she had been taken advantage of.[177] Though Cabaniss had not sent the money she asked for, Susanna's letter had at least convinced him of her innocence. After all, no one ever said Parthenia had been seduced. Wesley, "sorry and ashamed," wrote that he and Ada were doing their best to protect her reputation and "keep her from being expose" to the world. "Susan has grown up to be a woman," Wesley wrote, "and she has acted wrong."[178] It was, ironically, the first time he had acknowledged his sister's capacity to make her own choices.

Susanna gave birth sometime around December 1868. By January 1, she was back at school, still determined to finish her education and build a better life—for herself and her infant child.[179] In the following months she would again leave Wesley's home to live and work for wages in Cincinnati.[180] Things were looking up. Wesley assured Cabaniss that, this time, he wouldn't interfere with Susanna's money: "I dont want a cent of her money every cent of it she will have the pleasure of spending it her self." He seemed genuinely apologetic about the way he had behaved in the past, telling Cabaniss that he knew he had acted poorly and wanted to repay the $600 he had taken from Rainey, Jane, and Martha. "I am sorry nuf for it," he admitted, "an I am man a nuf to own to it."[181] This rare peace didn't last long. Wesley and Ada lost one of their children to "lung fever"—pneumonia—that spring.[182] Susanna's child died too. Then, on May 10, Ada wrote Cabaniss to report that Susanna had passed away just days before. Already weakened by the tuberculosis that had troubled her for years, she had likely succumbed to the same fever and infection that killed the children. Dead at sixteen years of age, Susanna would never start over in Kansas as she had hoped. She would never have the independent life she had dreamed of, as a schoolteacher, or wife, or mother. Buried in Ada's graveyard plot in New Richmond, she would never even leave her brother Wesley's household.[183]

But no one could say she hadn't tried.

——◆——

If Susanna had managed to make it west to Leavenworth, Kansas, she would have found a world far different from southern Ohio—and different, too, from the "squatter city" Leavenworth had been when the legatees of the second class arrived in 1860. Leavenworth's population exploded during the Civil War, soldiers, ex-slaves, and refugees joining the rough-and-ready settlement in large numbers as wartime violence once again made the Missouri-Kansas border bleed. Though Missouri never seceded from the Union during the Civil War, it was still a slave state, and southern sympathizers comprised a considerable part of the white population. Skirmishes between Union and Confederate forces took place throughout the state, along with fighting between proslavery and antislavery guerillas. Leavenworth became a refuge. The city was situated just two miles down the Missouri River from Fort Leavenworth, a federal garrison established in 1827 to protect traders and travelers heading to the Southwest.[184] For decades, most Kansans had considered the word "fort" an honorific. It "can lay but little claim to the title," one man wrote in 1859, "as it is without defensive works of any kind, except two block houses."[185] The Civil War brought thousands of Union Army soldiers through Fort Leavenworth, and the increased military presence attracted civilians seeking asylum in a violent region.[186] As a result, the population boom stimulated trade and economic activity to an even greater extent than the rush to Pike's Peak had in the 1850s. War was turning Leavenworth City into the metropolis its boosters had long promised.

Fugitive slaves from Missouri played a pivotal role in Leavenworth's rapid expansion. Tens of thousands of enslaved people escaped to Kansas during the Civil War, radically changing the landscape of race along slavery's western frontier. Between 1860 and 1866, Kansas's Black population rose from 627 individuals to more than 12,500, the majority of them runaways fleeing bondage in Missouri.[187] Lawrence's antislavery history and Underground Railroad activity made it an attractive destination for fugitives, but the largest numbers of Black migrants settled in the Leavenworth area. State census takers counted 3,375 African Americans in Leavenworth County in 1865, with 2,455 (nearly 20 percent of the state's total Black population) living and working in the city proper.[188] Some white residents resented the growing Black population, many of whom they lamented were "wholly destitute of the means of living."[189] Like Cabaniss and Lakin, white Kansans failed to understand why these new arrivals would risk poverty in a crowded city when they could go to the country and farm good land for free. After all, the federal government had just passed a new Homestead Act promising 160 acres to any settler, Black or white, man or woman, who would live on and work the land for five years.[190] But with numbers came security, and thousands of Leavenworth's African Americans chose to stay where they were. They established social networks and community institutions—churches like the city's African Methodist Episcopal congregation in 1861 and the First Baptist Church in 1862, and the "Emancipation League's Labor Exchange and Intelligence Office," an informal employment agency—and formed their own companies of armed men to aid and protect runaway slaves.[191] For the most part, Leavenworth's white residents resigned themselves to the city's changing racial composition. After the war, perhaps, something would have to be done, but as one Kansas newspaper declared in

1863, the growing number of free Black people was a "side issue." They would "kill off the rebels first" and worry about the rest later.[192]

The legatees of the first class who relocated to Leavenworth from Xenia after Wilberforce closed in 1862 had never lived in a city with such a large free Black population. Except for Wesley and Susanna, who had each spent time in Cincinnati, none of the Townsends had. But the differences between Leavenworth and Xenia weren't simply a matter of numbers. Xenia's Black residents had been families much like the Townsends: the concubines and children of white southerners, manumitted legally and sent north with the capital to afford homes and an education. They were the "colored elite," wealthy mixed-race landowners even Cabaniss considered suitable associates for the Townsends.[193] Leavenworth's latest free Black residents, on the other hand, were fugitives carrying little more than the clothes on their backs. In the language of wartime, they were "contrabands"—fugitives from slavery whose "confiscation" from bondage, by their own efforts, deprived slave owners of the human property whose labor supported the Confederate cause.[194] In New Richmond, Wesley resented the "contrabands neggroes" he considered no better than slaves. But few of the Kansas Townsends expressed a similar contempt for the changing demographics of the free Black people they worked with, lived alongside, and in time made a part of the family.

When the Civil War threw the country and their inheritance into turmoil, many of the Townsends coped by relying on kinship ties, finding emotional and economic support living in tight-knit family groups in Leavenworth. The family continued to grow as Townsend women married local men. Samuel's eldest daughter Caroline wed Daniel Stone, a Kentucky-born man who worked as a day laborer in Leavenworth City.[195] Her half-sister Mildred Ann married Henry Green, a farmer around ten years her senior, with land worth a tidy $900; Mildred and Caroline's mother Rainey stayed with the Greens in Kickapoo, near Leavenworth City.[196] Three of elderly Rachel Townsend's daughters, sisters of Samuel's concubine Lucy, also married Leavenworth men during the war. Jane chose a carpenter named Lloyd Sales; Peggy another carpenter, George Armistead; and Mary a farmer living ten miles out from the city, Jessie Eddings. Samuel's daughter Milcha Townsend, following a familiar pattern, married a carpenter named John Caldwell, after which the couple moved into her mother Lucy's house with Lucy's four young sons.[197] Members of the Townsend family would remain in the Leavenworth area for decades, raising large families and establishing themselves in the local community. By the 1890s, Rainey's son Freeman, seven years old when he arrived in Kansas, would be working as a prison guard in the city with eight children of his own, all of them born free.[198]

Other Townsends supported themselves by working at the limited number of occupations available to African Americans at the time. Lucy supplemented her son-in-law's income by taking in laundry, one of the most common and laborious jobs for Black women.[199] Brothers Wade and Henry worked as a waiter and cook at the Mansion House, one of the city's oldest hotels.[200] Unlike the Planters' House, the Mansion House had been the favorite choice of free-soil men during the 1850s, leading proslavery whites to derisively call the establishment "Abolition Hill"—a nickname that may have made it an appealing workplace for Leavenworth's Black residents.[201] Their younger brother Sylvanus found a job as a clerk for a local drug store, becoming known as "Sylvanus the druggist" among extended family members.[202] Woodson Townsend made his living as a teamster. The freighting industry was booming, with wagoners like Woodson in high demand to transport

FIGURE 4.2 Photograph of Leila Townsend in Leavenworth, Kansas, at around sixteen years of age. Leila was the daughter of Freeman and Laura Townsend and the granddaughter of Rainey Townsend. Unknown, *Leila Townsend*, ca. 1901, gelatin dry plate negative, Amon Carter Museum of American Art, Fort Worth, Texas, P1978.127.171.

supplies to gold mines in the Rocky Mountains and military outposts across the western territories.[203] Woodson's wife Elvira took up work as a seamstress.[204] Meanwhile, Elvira's younger half-brother Thomas taught school. By 1866 he held positions in both Leavenworth and Atchison, his Wilberforce University credentials in high demand from the large numbers of African American children and adult freedpeople eager for a formal education.[205] Another of Samuel's sons, Osborne, joined the Union Army.[206]

From the very start of the war, free Black men and fugitive slaves alike had offered their services to the United States military as soldiers—recognizing, considerably earlier than white Americans did, that the Civil War would be a war for emancipation. Initially, white political and military leaders rejected them out of hand. "*It wasn't a black man's war,*" General Benjamin Butler told Virginian ex-slave Henry Jarvis in 1861, when Jarvis asked to enlist. But the would-be soldiers persisted. "I told him it *would* be a black man's war before they got through," Jarvis replied.[207] Two years into the war, when President Lincoln's Emancipation Proclamation went into effect on January 1, 1863, the federal government officially authorized the Union Army to enlist and train Black soldiers. In Kansas, however, the process had already begun. In October 1861, James Lane—a United States senator and Union brigadier general, formerly the leader of the free-soil Jayhawkers during the Bleeding Kansas period—returned to Kansas from Washington, DC, with, he claimed, instructions from Lincoln to raise a volunteer regiment of Black soldiers.[208] By the summer of 1862, he had established a recruitment center in Leavenworth City and commissioned "colored battery" recruiting officers to sign up men from the local Black community.[209]

W. D. Matthews led the recruitment effort in Leavenworth. Matthews was the son of a free Black farmer from Maryland and an enslaved woman manumitted when her master died. From Maryland he had moved to Leavenworth in 1856, opened a boarding house that also served as a station on the Underground Railroad, and organized a group of armed men who protected fugitive slaves entering the city from Missouri.[210] In later years, the man with bushy gray muttonchops and straight-backed military bearing would become one of Leavenworth's most prominent Black citizens.[211] He served as a city police officer; he was a successful business owner; he became grand master of the Royal Arch Masons in Kansas and grand master of all York Rite Masons in the United States.[212] By the time of his death in 1906 he would be known across the city as "Captain" Matthews—a title he earned in 1862, when James Lane appointed him captain of Company D in the U.S. Colored Light Artillery, the first Black unit raised during the Civil War and the only one to serve entirely under the command of Black officers.[213] Thanks in large part to Matthews's skill as a recruiter, 208 Black men joined the "colored battery" between 1864 and 1865, nearly 80 percent of whom came from Leavenworth.[214] Advertisements ran in the Leavenworth papers throughout the war, urging the city's African American men to enlist and fight for the freedom of their enslaved brothers and sisters in the South and the rights of free Black people in the North. At a ceremony celebrating the Emancipation Proclamation and his unit's official mustering into the Union Army in 1863, Matthews described military service as a way for Black men to prove themselves to the country's prejudiced white population. "Now is our time to strike," he said. "Our own exertions and our own muscle make us men. If we fight we shall be respected." He added: "I see that a well-licked man respects the one who thrashes him."[215]

Black community leaders like W. D. Matthews advocated racial unity during the Civil War. Though he, like the Townsends, came from a more privileged background than the majority of Leavenworth's free Black residents, Matthews rejected the idea that this entitled him to greater respect or consideration than a fugitive from Missouri or a slave in the South—a viewpoint that would have put him at odds with Wesley Townsend, who decried the influx of escaped slaves into Ohio as strongly as his white neighbors. Matthews never met Wesley, but the captain did know Woodson, and he didn't think very highly of him. For all their mutual animosity, Wesley and Woodson did share this: their demands for equality had always been based on their perceived differences from, not camaraderie with, other free Black people. With that kind of thinking, Matthews said, Woodson was still "a citizen of Alabama," or he might as well be.[216] The country was embroiled in a war that would determine the fate of millions of Black men and women across the country, and Matthews had no patience for color and class prejudices that would divide the Black community. Woodson's special status in Alabama—among but not of the larger slave community—had given him certain advantages, eventually leading to his emancipation in 1860. But Woodson's tendency to isolate himself proved a liability in January 1864, when Elizabeth McFarland, a white woman of Leavenworth City, accused him of rape.

———

This was what she said at the trial:

She was a married woman, four or five weeks pregnant, when she paid Woodson Townsend to take her to the Hannibal & St. Joseph Railway depot near Atchison, Kansas. She had shopping to do in Missouri and Woodson agreed to take her in his wagon for a fee. They left sometime on Sunday, January 17, and arrived at Atchison that night; she caught a train the next morning, bought the goods she had come for, and headed back to Leavenworth with Woodson. But when they neared town and started down Government Lane—the major freighting route from the city to Fort Leavenworth and Missouri destinations—Woodson pulled out two revolvers and threatened to shoot her if she refused to comply with "his hellish demands." She screamed and tried to fight him, but he choked her, tore her clothes, and after a fight lasting two or two-and-a-half hours finally overpowered her and had his way. She showed the jury her neck, bruised and sore from what he had done.[217]

This was what the defendant's lawyer said:

Elizabeth McFarland paid Woodson to take her to the railroad depot on Sunday the 17th—that much was true. They reached Atchison that evening and spent the night with a local Black family, where accommodations were tight: Woodson, Elizabeth, and five or six others all lodged in the same single-room house. Then, on Monday, Woodson retrieved Elizabeth and her parcels from the depot and started back for Leavenworth. Taylor Turner, "a colored man," saw them on the road; he worked as a farm laborer in Leavenworth County and recognized Woodson's wagon and team.[218] Taylor was on foot, and the thought of a long walk back to the city after dark couldn't have been appealing, so he hopped up onto the back of the wagon and hitched a ride. Woodson and Elizabeth didn't know he was there, but Taylor didn't see the harm. They were going to the same place, after all, and it's not as though Woodson was a stranger.

They reached Government Lane about sunset.

Taylor didn't hear the desperate fight Elizabeth reported—"no scuffle, no contest, no hallooing in the wagon"—but he did hear raised voices. They were arguing about the war and Woodson must have taken issue with something Elizabeth said. The Townsend temper, famous in Madison County, got the better of him, and in his anger Woodson called her a "rebel," a Confederate sympathizer. Furious and insulted, Elizabeth got out of the wagon and continued down Government Lane alone, but not before threatening Woodson that, one way or another, she would see him arrested. She made good on that threat. Elizabeth reported Woodson's "assault" to the police, who arrested him and held him on a $5,000 bail, an amount he couldn't pay. By Tuesday, Woodson was in the custody of the county sheriff, awaiting trial.[219]

Woodson's attorney said Elizabeth McFarland wasn't a reliable plaintiff. Yes, Woodson and Turner were Black men and perhaps the gentlemen of the jury wouldn't ordinarily be inclined to take their word over a white woman's, but what kind of white woman was she? She lived among the city's Black residents, was Woodson and Elvira Townsend's close neighbor, in fact, and had stayed overnight with that Black family in Atchison. If these were her associates, why should her word count for more than theirs? If this weren't convincing enough, the defense had white witnesses as well. Three physicians testified that Elizabeth wasn't actually pregnant; one woman said she had met Elizabeth at the milk-man's house the day after the alleged attack, where Elizabeth told her Woodson had been too drunk to assault her; another neighbor went to look in on her a day later and "found her with a low-necked dress on, neck bare, limber and white as usual," with no bruises or discoloration; and Elizabeth herself had told a pregnant Elvira Townsend to her face that Woodson tried to assault her "but thank God, he was not quite strong enough." "This McFarland woman's reputation for truth and veracity is bad," a final (white, male) witness stated—so bad that he wouldn't believe her even under oath.[220]

In the end, the jury came back with what the newspapers called a "compromise verdict."[221] They agreed that Elizabeth's story had too many inconsistencies to be entirely credible, but even if Woodson wasn't guilty of rape he was probably guilty of something, so six years' imprisonment and hard labor seemed reasonable to them. The "compromise" outraged some of Leavenworth's white residents. On February 17, 1864, the *Daily Times* decried the verdict, which they considered an insufficient punishment, but speculated that if a new trial were granted Woodson might, in time, receive "all the justice he so richly deserves."[222] One week later, Woodson's attorney protested the bias in the press, publishing a letter to the editor detailing all the evidence for his client's innocence. "There are good and honest men who heard the trial, who cannot think the defendant guilty of the offense," he concluded, and it was their job and his to fight the "others, born along by their vilest prejudices," who "seem ready to convict a colored man of this or any other crime." "Yours for justice," he signed the letter, "C. H. Chase."[223]

Woodson's status as one of the Townsend legatees likely helped him engage an attorney with a different definition of "justice" than the city's other white residents. As the Civil War neared its close, Leavenworth whites increasingly and with increasing violence lashed out against local African Americans. The uneasy truce put into place when they determined to "kill the rebels first" and then deal with the growing Black community had reached its end.[224] Attacks on African Americans took place across the state throughout 1864 and 1865, concentrated in areas with the largest Black populations—and Leavenworth had the largest of all. In this hostile environment, Elizabeth McFarland's accusation of rape could have easily been a death sentence. For almost any other Black man in the city, it probably would have been. But Woodson was known to Leavenworth's white community, and especially its legal professionals, due to Cabaniss and Lakin's work on the Townsends' behalf before the war.[225] He couldn't afford to post bail, but he must have convinced C. H. Chase that he would be able to pay his legal fees in full once the war ended and the Townsends received their inheritance. Chase, unlike Wilberforce president R. S. Rust, seemed willing to take the risk. Woodson continued to leverage that promised inheritance as he served out his jail sentence in Leavenworth. In 1866, Cabaniss discovered that the people of Leavenworth, including prison administrators, were under the impression that Woodson possessed a considerably larger share in the Townsend estate than he actually did.[226] Woodson, of course, knew that anything he inherited would only come to him through Elvira's portion; Cabaniss had made that very clear before the war. But he also knew that if the white Kansans clamoring for his execution believed he had access to wealth and influence, they might hesitate before turning to extralegal justice. Still, there was only so much Woodson could do, and his reliance on connections to local white men alienated others who could have been his allies: Leavenworth's Black community leaders.

On January 19, 1864—the day Woodson was arrested—Captain W. D. Matthews, of the U.S. Colored Light Artillery, held a meeting at the city's First Baptist Church. The gathering had a single object: "to denounce the outrage committed by one Woodson Townsend." Concerned that Leavenworth's white citizens would use the rape charge as an excuse to retaliate against the entire Black community, the captain of Company D launched a counteroffensive, formally and publicly disavowing Woodson. Joined by a committee of other local Black leaders, Matthews proposed the following resolution:

WHEREAS, A man by the name of Woodson Townsend has committed a brutal crime, justly outraging the feelings of every decent and law abiding citizen;

And, whereas, it is alleged that the said Woodson Townsend is a person of color, and as some are, in consequence of said allegation, disposed to blame all the colored citizens of the city; therefore be it

Resolved by the colored citizens of Leavenworth, in public meeting, that the said criminal has never identified himself with the colored citizens of this place, never having attended our churches, public or social meetings, and that whether he be a colored man or not, he alone is guilty, and he only should suffer for his crime.

The resolution passed unanimously: Woodson would receive no help from Leavenworth's Black community. "Townsend had always considered himself a white man," Matthews said. Perhaps his fellow white men would help him.[227]

Unsurprisingly, Woodson received little assistance from that quarter either. By February 1866, after two years' hard labor in a Kansas prison, he was desperate. Elvira, who had three young daughters with Woodson, may have felt she had no choice but to leave him and find another husband who could support her and her children. Their divorce in 1866 cut off Woodson's only legal claim to the Townsend estate.[228] When Cabaniss was once again able to send the Townsends disbursements from the estate after the Civil War, Edmund's son wouldn't be one of the recipients. Woodson wanted out of prison, badly, but there were four years left on his sentence and neither he nor his family held out much hope that he would be freed even then. "The people are pleading against him every day," his cousin Milcha wrote. The white folks in town wanted a new trial and a harsher sentence, and if they didn't get it she feared they might take "justice" into their own hands.[229] "I hope I hope that I will get out of here some day and I wish to get out of here honerable," Woodson said, for "god knows I am not gilty of the charge."[230] But Black men across the country were killed for less than what Elizabeth McFarland claimed he had done, and Woodson knew it. Within the year, he would make his escape from prison, not the "honerable" release he had hoped would clear his name, and if any of the Townsends knew where he went from there, they weren't telling.[231] Perhaps Woodson thought it was the only way out, save at the end of a rope. But before he disappeared from that Kansas prison cell, Woodson was going to speak his mind. He was Edmund Townsend's son, with Edmund Townsend's temper, and he had nothing left to lose. "Uncle Sams Children" had taken everything already.[232]

"Mr Cabaniss Sir it is with the greatest of pleasure that I have the opportunity of wrighting to you," Woodson began his last extant letter, scathingly polite. The only pleasure he took from writing was in telling Cabaniss exactly what he thought of him, very little indeed. Woodson knew that Cabaniss had recently visited the other Townsends in Kansas, but "when you was here you did not talk to the jailer for me and you did not try to do anything for me or in my behalf." The lawyer hadn't spent a cent or lifted a finger to help get him out of jail, and while Woodson acknowledged that Cabaniss had the power to "just do as you pleas about it," the hypocrisy galled him. "If it had been one of Uncle Sams Children," he was certain, "you would have had him out long ago." Samuel Townsend's children had been emancipated first; they had received a formal education; their father had left them $200,000 when he died. S. D. Cabaniss had been part of the problem from the beginning, starting in 1853 when Samuel hired his law firm to break Edmund's will in court—defying his own brother's last wishes to leave Woodson and his siblings his fortune. Things might have been different "if my Father had have let you be guardien over his property," Woodson wrote. He would have another life entirely if Edmund had hired the lawyer first. But as things were, Woodson's cousins were benefiting from his loss: of time, seven years he could have been a free man, and money, an inheritance that he believed Cabaniss was "trying to swindle me and my sisters and my brother out of." The way Woodson saw things, he had always gotten the short end of the stick.[233]

Woodson blamed Cabaniss for abandoning him in prison; he accused the lawyer of persuading his wife to leave him; he condemned his cousins for stealing his inheritance. Woodson's accusations appalled the lawyer. They were "offensive" and "insulting" and didn't merit a reply, he fumed.[234] But there was a hint of despair—and perhaps confusion—to Woodson's angry, accusatory letter to Cabaniss. This wasn't the first time he had seen the inside of a jail cell, but the last time, when he was still enslaved in Alabama, Woodson's relationship to Edmund Townsend had gotten him out of trouble. Now he was locked up and alone in the place where he had been promised freedom and wealth, without a friend "in Kansas or in the wourld."[235] W. D. Matthews's committee of Leavenworth's Black residents had confirmed that Woodson would no longer benefit from holding himself apart from the rest of the country's free Black population. And the only white man who would have helped him, his father Edmund, was dead.

Woodson's sense of superiority—his belief that his access to whiteness through Edmund's ancestry and money entitled him to status and respect—won him no allies in Leavenworth. Nor had Wesley, isolating himself in Ohio while he waited for his long-promised inheritance, escaped debt and difficulty. Wartime exigencies, white residents' prejudice, and her husband's own pride conspired to separate Elvira from the man she had loved and waited for.

Even Susanna, for all her determination, saw her dreams of independence and autonomy frustrated by her youth, gender, and poor health. But in the following years, mixed-race ancestry and a modicum of wealth would bring one of "Uncle Sams children" closer to the acceptance and social status Woodson and some of the other Townsends had failed to find. He just had to go six hundred miles west to the silver mines of Colorado Territory.

5

Some One of Us Will Have It Good

THE MILITARY RECRUITER looked Osborne up and down. *Five feet and eleven inches,* he jotted on an enlistment form—tall for his time, when the typical native-born white man measured 5′ 7″ and African Americans, so many enslaved, malnourished, and overworked, averaged an inch shorter.[1] The favored son of a wealthy white cotton planter, Osborne Townsend had never gone without food. He had never stooped under the hot sun in his father's cotton fields. At twenty-one years old, Osborne was an impressive-looking man. Along with his height, the recruiter noted his black hair, gray eyes, and—of course—his "fair" complexion. He had Osborne swear an oath of allegiance to the United States. He issued him a knapsack, clothes, and a canteen. It was February 23, 1865, four long years into the Civil War, and Samuel Townsend's son was a Union Army soldier.[2]

After war erupted in 1861 and Wilberforce University was forced to close, Osborne and his siblings were set adrift. With no money from the estate coming out of Alabama, they couldn't have continued their education at Wilberforce even if the school hadn't shut its doors. But when his cousins and siblings found work outside of Xenia or moved to Kansas to marry and build lives alongside their extended family, Osborne stayed behind. His teachers at Wilberforce had emphasized education as the best means of personal advancement as well as "elevation of the entire colored race," and the lesson stuck, leaving him sharing his half-sister Susanna's strong desire to complete her studies. As Osborne wrote Cabaniss, "I am very anxious to finish my education now before I get too old to study."[3] With his fifteen-year-old half-brother Joseph Bradford, whom he affectionately called "little Bradford," Osborne hunkered in place—hopeful that the war might end, that Cabaniss might find a way to send them money, that he might return to school.[4] A year later, his faith was rewarded. In June 1863, leaders of the African Methodist

Episcopal Church in Ohio raised the funds to purchase Wilberforce University from its original trustees.[5] In July, the school re-opened for its six remaining students. One of them was Bradford Townsend.[6]

Managed by African American trustees and administrators for the first time in its history, Wilberforce University had entered a new era, and its president—AME minister John G. Mitchell—was likely sympathetic to the Townsends' situation. He accepted Bradford on credit, something the last president, Richard S. Rust, had refused to do. But for some reason, Osborne didn't return to school with his half-brother. Perhaps he didn't want to strain the family's finances. For the first time in their lives (as Thomas Townsend wrote from Kansas), they were afflicted with "the pangs of poverty."[7] Meanwhile, the tuberculosis that had plagued Bradford since childhood had returned.[8] Osborne was a responsible brother, habitually looking after his younger siblings even in preference to himself. After the war, when the Townsends could communicate with Cabaniss again, he wrote the lawyer asking for money to return to Wilberforce.[9] When he learned that thirteen-year-old Susanna was working as a servant, however, his requests shifted. He still wrote to Cabaniss and Rust, but on his half-sister's behalf, imploring the men to get her into school—and continuing to pester them by post when they failed to reply.[10] Osborne made no distinction between his full brother Willis and Samuel Townsend's other children; he only ever called them sisters and brothers, not half-siblings.[11] While Osborne knew the value of an education, he valued his family too. In 1863, he sent Bradford back to school. Osborne was older, and there were other ways for a healthy young man to advance himself during wartime.

African American men had been trying to join the fight for years before President Lincoln's 1863 Emancipation Proclamation authorized the Union Army to enlist Black soldiers. But in southern Ohio, as in other parts of the Union, military leaders initially rejected the would-be recruits. In 1861, Cincinnati police told African American volunteers to leave the fighting to the white soldiers: "We want you d—d niggers to keep out of this."[12] In Xenia, Black men heard much the same thing. When Confederates fired on Fort Sumter in April 1861, one hundred Wilberforce University students, nearly half of the entire student body and virtually all of the young men, formed their own volunteer regiment. In later years, Richard H. Cain, a US congressman who had attended Wilberforce, recalled the reception the students received. "We were told," he said, "that this is a white man's war, and that the Negro has nothing to do with it." These young men—many of them former slaves who had been taught at Wilberforce that they needed to prove their worth to white America if they wanted to be respected—were eager to join up. Osborne may have been among them. The Townsends were still in school when the war began; they would have seen the fervor among their classmates, what Cain remembered as a "thrill that ran through my soul."[13] Whether he shared that zeal or not, by February 1865 Osborne saw few other options. If nothing else, the $100 enlistment bonus would have been enticing.[14]

Osborne was not the first Townsend to serve in the Union Army. About six months earlier, in September 1864, Wesley found himself shoeing mules for the war effort in Nashville, Tennessee—though the eldest Townsend brother found nothing thrilling about that.[15] Wesley claimed to have been drafted much against his will while living in New Richmond.[16] He was the last man to risk his neck, even for the cause of freedom. "I have no friends in town but whit peoples," he told Cabaniss, owing to the fact that the local Black community resented him "because I am not a black abolitions."[17] New Richmond was an Underground Railroad station, but Wesley felt only disdain for the fugitive slaves who worked for food alone, driving down what he could earn as a blacksmith.[18] They, in turn, scorned him as a "butter nut"— perhaps a disparaging reference to the light skin color he valued so highly, or worse, a comparison to the hated Confederate soldiers, called "butternuts" in the 1860s press for the color of their uniforms.[19]

Osborne's military service bore little in common with Wesley's. Within days of enlisting, he was in Vicksburg, Mississippi, with Company B of the 5th U.S. Colored Heavy Artillery.[20] This was the heart of occupied Confederate territory. Vicksburg was the key to the Mississippi river, and its capture by General Ulysses S. Grant in 1863 had divided the South, disrupting supply lines and isolating Confederate states to the west.[21] When Osborne arrived two years later, he entered a new world in the making. Thousands of black soldiers manned the garrison, huge numbers of them ex-slaves recruited from plantations outside the city. Freedpeople formed refugee camps along the river, tens of thousands of men and women working as cooks, laundresses, vendors, teamsters, and laborers.[22] At the center of it all was the army, tasked with everything from protecting against guerilla raids and punishing deserters to staunching disease in the camps. They built shelters, hospitals, orphanages, and schools; leased confiscated plantations to loyal men; enforced labor contracts; and answered petitions from former slaves seeking land to farm and from former masters demanding it back.[23] In occupied Vicksburg, the Union Army was beginning the slow process of reconstructing the slave South into a free society, and Osborne was an active participant.

Osborne began his military career in March 1865 as an orderly, performing menial work, heavy labor, and garrison duty—tasks that white officers considered best suited to Black soldiers.[24] He wasn't an orderly for long. Osborne, likely one of the best-educated enlisted men in the regiment, was transferred to the Provost Marshal of Freedmen's office as a clerk in May.[25] The precursor to the federal Bureau of Refugees, Freedmen and Abandoned Lands (most commonly known as the Freedmen's Bureau), the Provost Marshal's office provided legal assistance and arranged employment for former slaves, primarily seeking to settle freedpeople on confiscated southern plantations as farm laborers.[26] All of this generated paperwork. Clerks reviewed contracts from employers seeking to hire former slaves for wages; they issued marriage certificates for the thousands of newly free men and women who could be husband and wife in the eyes of the law for the first time; they drew up permits for refugees seeking to trade, work, or build in the city; they processed requests for aid and supplies from missionaries, teachers, doctors, and farmers.[27] Their work was so vital that Colonel Samuel Thomas, Provost Marshal for Vicksburg, arranged to have his clerks excused from mandatory militia duty, writing that "we have about half the number of Clerks in our Offices necessary to conduct our regular business, and often work them till midnight and always till nine o'clock."[28] In the hectic, harried Union Army, a recruit like Osborne Townsend—who could read, write, and figure—was a godsend. By July, he had been promoted from clerk to quartermaster sergeant.[29] In August, he was named acting sergeant major of the battalion.[30]

Osborne mustered out of the army in February 1866, with $490 in his pocket and an unspecified injury acquired during his year in Vicksburg.[31] He kept his government-issued Springfield rifle, perhaps suspecting a weapon might come in handy as the country reconstituted itself.[32] The Confederate Army may have surrendered, but Osborne knew that white southerners wouldn't change their minds about the rights of African Americans overnight. He may not have seen battle in occupied Vicksburg, but in the Provost Marshal's office he had been on the front lines as the federal government began to pull the former Confederacy back into the Union, the prelude to a tumultuous decade of Reconstruction. He had observed its failures too. Osborne saw the Union Army fail to protect civilians in the countryside just north of Vicksburg, where Confederate guerilla forces ambushed federal soldiers and abducted freedpeople.[33] He saw thousands of refugees, many of them the wives and children of soldiers, forcibly removed from the city to plantations in that same undefended countryside—more than ten thousand in the summer of 1865 alone. In Washington, DC, President Andrew

Johnson, who ascended to the office after Abraham Lincoln's assassination in 1865, was pardoning one hundred Confederates a day.[34] In Vicksburg, clerks like Osborne processed reams of paperwork recommending ex-slaves go to work under these ex-rebels, instead of supporting their requests to own the land they had toiled on for years with no pay and no power.[35]

"We were the only true and Loyal people that were found in possession of these Lands," a committee of freedpeople from South Carolina wrote in October 1865, petitioning the Freedmen's Bureau for "the Privilege of purchasing land."[36] In January of that year, Union General William T. Sherman had issued an order granting four hundred thousand acres of southern plantations to former slaves in South Carolina, Georgia, and Florida. In July, Freedmen's Bureau head Oliver O. Howard issued a similar order, directing bureau agents to favor freedpeople over pardoned Confederates when it came to selling confiscated farmland.[37] Redistributing land during wartime was no new idea in American history: during the Revolutionary War, "confiscation laws" passed in every state allowed for the seizure and sale of known loyalists' property.[38] For freedpeople after the Civil War, land ownership would have meant an unprecedented level of autonomy—freedom not just from slavery but from economic dependence on white southerners. Yet President Johnson quickly reversed Sherman and Howard's orders, and freedpeople's dreams of "forty acres and a mule" failed to materialize. Instead, the Freedmen's Bureau came to favor wage labor over land ownership, variously encouraging and coercing freedpeople to work under their former masters.[39] Emancipation hadn't meant full autonomy for the Townsends in 1860, and it certainly didn't mean that for the 4 million African Americans freed after the Civil War. After a year in Vicksburg, Osborne, perhaps more than any of his family members, knew firsthand the legal, social, and economic obstacles free Black men and women would continue to face in the South during Reconstruction.

It was an understanding that would shape how Osborne Townsend saw his opportunities for economic and social mobility over the course of the following decades—and, most significantly, where he saw them.

—◦—

After mustering out of the army, Osborne returned to Xenia only to find that "little Bradford" had died of his illness and Wilberforce University's main building had been burned down by local whites during the war.[40] But the school was still running, and with the money from his military service, Osborne paid for his brother's funeral and resumed study at Wilberforce for a couple months. He tried to save as much as he could, but by the end of term Osborne was nearing the end of his resources. He had started thinking about going into "some other business" if he couldn't remain at school and decided to spend the summer in Leavenworth visiting "the Kansasees."[41] Osborne hadn't seen his family in four years, and there was plenty to catch up on. Thomas—who had stayed in school in Kansas during the war—was a teacher, much in demand as freedpeople migrating from the South eagerly sought qualified instructors.[42] Willis waited tables on a steamboat, making $30 a month plying the Ohio River from Cincinnati to Louisville, Kentucky.[43] Thomas thought Osborne might do well to join Willis on the river, a suggestion that likely pricked Osborne's pride, coming from the brother who had exactly what he wanted most: a more advanced education and respected position in his community. Fortunately, and just in time, twenty-seven-year-old William Austin Townsend provided an alternative.[44]

William Austin ("Austin" to his family, "W. A." to his business associates) was Osborne's mother Winney's eldest son, the only surviving child of hers who hadn't been fathered by Samuel Townsend.[45] He and Osborne, then, were half-brothers on their mother's side. Unlike his half-brothers by Samuel, however, Osborne did make a distinction between himself and Austin. In 1871, when listing his living family members on a bank application, Osborne named "3 brothers"—Thomas, Wesley, and Willis—leaving Austin out entirely.[46] Like Wesley and Woodson, Osborne seemed to have inherited some of his father's elitism. But Austin, too, looked after his little brother. Sometime during the war, he had struck out west for distant Colorado Territory. Perhaps he had heard stories of the Rockies from Woodson, who may have traveled as far west as Colorado Territory on his freighting routes as a teamster. Ensconced as a barber in a small mining town in the Rocky Mountains, Austin was comfortable enough to offer his brother assistance.[47] "He promises to lend me some money to go to school," Osborne wrote Cabaniss from Leavenworth. So in August 1866, twenty-three-year-old Osborne Townsend determined to head "a cross the Plains to Central City Colorado to see Austin."[48]

Though the railroad hadn't made it to the Rockies yet, travel "a cross the Plains" had massively improved since large numbers of would-be gold miners first set their sights on Colorado in the late 1850s. By 1866, the six-hundred-odd-mile journey from Leavenworth to Denver took a mere week or less by stagecoach, though $125 was a stiff price for most migrants.[49] Colorado's gold rush hadn't panned out for most prospectors, but silver mines were booming and Osborne would have still seen the white canvas canopies of wagon trains painted with optimistic mottos: "Bound for the Peak," or "On to the Promised Land."[50] Like Alabama in the 1820s and Kansas in the 1850s, Colorado Territory was the western frontier, accompanied by all the same boosterism and grandiose claims as its predecessors. Promotional literature proclaimed the territory a new "El Dorado," in raptures over "the magic potency of untold mineral wealth" to be found in its mountains. This was a land for pioneers of "great daring and energy," it said, "the most adventurous and enterprising individuals from all communities."[51] Back in 1831, French diplomat Alexis de Tocqueville had written that the "gradual and continuous progress of the European races towards the Rocky Mountains, has the solemnity of a providential event," that American migrants were "driven onward by the hand of God."[52] Decades later, with "Manifest Destiny" a byword among Anglo-Americans, western boosters emblazoned de Tocqueville's words on the opening pages of their guidebooks.[53] Osborne didn't expect to make his fortune mining silver when he left Leavenworth in 1866; he didn't plan on staying long at all. But Austin Townsend likely had believed in the frontier's promise. Without Osborne's $16,000 inheritance to look forward to, Austin joined the latest wave of daring, desperate, or delusional migrants bound for Colorado. He was one of the few Black men among them.

In the aftermath of the Civil War, white Americans liked to picture the Far West as a world apart from the racial tensions and violent conflict that had characterized North and South for so long.[54] Once again there was virgin land to the west—but this time, not merely to be conquered. Untouched by sectional strife, this west took on a special place in the national imagination. In the Rocky Mountains, amid a landscape one tourist called "all grandeur" and "almost terror," filled with "the glory of unprofaned works of God," white Americans need not be reminded of slavery or the war it had caused.[55] Nor need they interact much with African Americans, with so few living in the region. In 1860, the entirety of Colorado Territory counted only forty-six Black residents. By 1870, that number had increased, but only to 456, still just .01 percent of the total population.[56] In contemporary descriptions of the region, boosters erased even these small numbers. The *Rocky Mountain Directory and Colorado Gazetteer* for 1871 boasted a population comprised of "all nations," though in this case they only mentioned Americans, Englishmen, and Cornishmen.[57]

Yet at the time, the West was the most ethnically diverse region of the United States—a place where white Americans mixed with Mexican miners, Chinese migrants, and the Indian nations that had held the land for centuries before their arrival. The Rocky Mountains were home to the Ute peoples, whose ancestral domain stretched across the Great Basin through present-day

Utah and Colorado. At mid-century, approximately five thousand Utes lived in Colorado Territory, nomadic bands hunting buffalo, sending trade expeditions as far south as northern Mexico, and expertly raiding enemy tribes on horseback like their rivals among the Plains Indians.[58] But to the white migrants who settled along the Front Range mining and farming, the Utes were "savages," undeserving of the rich land they occupied.[59] Either the Utes would be removed to reservations, one Colorado newspaper predicted in 1865, "or the white man must abandon the mountains, with their inexhaustible stores of mineral wealth"—and Anglo-Americans had never yet returned native land once they had claimed it.[60] No use being a "goody-goody" and wasting tears on the Utes, one particularly plainspoken congressman from Colorado told his colleagues in the capital; Indian removal was what Americans had always done. "Our fathers robbed and plundered the Indians," he declared, "and now gentlemen [I] stand here in the name of God and humanity" and "say the time has come when these Indians should be treated by this Government as other Indians have been treated." After all, even the Cherokees had been removed from Georgia, and they had been "civilized." His speech, the congressional record noted, was met with "Laughter and applause."[61]

As it had during the earlier rush to Alabama and emigration to Kansas, settlers' success in the region depended on the dispossession of native peoples. In the South, military and government officials struggled to determine how freedpeople and former rebels could be knit back into the fabric of a nation torn apart by war. Westerners, meanwhile, grappled with the question of how to incorporate another region characterized by racial and ethnic conflict into their more perfect union.[62] Yet many settlers farming, mining, building towns, and raising families in Colorado and other western territories believed that Native Americans did not, and could never, belong. A century before, Native Americans in the trans-Mississippi West had held immense social and economic power. No European could have hoped to find success in trade or politics without forging deep relationships with indigenous communities.[63] This latest wave of white migrants, however, didn't want to trade. They wanted land free from the land's original inhabitants. Native Americans were no longer power brokers in the West; they were an obstacle to settlers' ambitions, pushed off their land and relegated to the bottom of the region's racial hierarchy. Ironically, white settlers' contempt for native peoples opened a space for African American settlers. Black migrants were Christians, farmers, and miners, with a shared culture if not the culture's favored skin color, and they arrived in such small, unthreatening numbers. In Colorado and across the Far

West, white Americans decided that African Americans were more like them than the Utes and other Native Americans in the region. The catastrophic situation was, for men like Osborne and Austin Townsend, an opportunity.[64]

Indeed, Black migrants were some of the most famous figures in Colorado's gold and silver rushes. John Frazier, who named his mine "Black Prince," hit a massive lode of gold ore in the 1850s. An ex-slave named Jim was offered $100,000 for his rich silver vein by "wealthy capitalists" "dining, wining, and carriage-riding" him around the silver mining camp of Georgetown in 1880.[65] "Professor" Lorenzo Bowman, an old hand at lead mining in Missouri, pioneered gold and silver smelting techniques in Colorado, forming an all–African American mining company with the country's most famous escaped slave and abolitionist, Frederick Douglass, as a shareholder.[66] In 1870, Bowman sold one of his silver lodes for the massive sum of $25,000. But few Black migrants were as legendary as "Aunt" Clara Brown, who purchased her freedom in the 1850s, worked her way to Colorado in 1859 as the cook and washerwoman for a wagon train, and invested her hard-earned savings in mining and real estate, donating to charity all the while. By 1866, she had amassed a fortune of $10,000. She used the funds to reunite dozens of relatives separated by slavery and the Civil War, including a daughter sold away from her as a child, and bring them west to Denver. In the 1870s, Clara Brown became one of the first African Americans, and the first woman, to be elected a member of the Colorado Pioneer Association.[67]

These successes, however, hardly meant that African Americans faced no prejudice in Colorado. Black leaders in Denver, home to the most densely concentrated and politically organized African American community in the territory, faced strong resistance from white residents when they pushed for their civil rights. When the territorial legislature approved a new constitution denying Black men the vote in 1865, William Jefferson Hardin—a mixed-race barber in Denver—led the opposition.[68] Hardin organized a petition to Congress, demanding that the federal government reject statehood for Colorado until there was universal male suffrage. Local whites were shocked. The protest was "treachery and ingratitude," one newspaper declared, seeing as most Colorado voters had supported the Union in the recent war. Of course Colorado whites supported "the advancement of the colored race," the paper continued. Hadn't they freed "the poor, despised and downtrodden slave in the swamps of Alabama"? But suffrage was too much, too soon; Colorado's Black residents should have been happy with what they had. The editorialist seemed most perplexed that Hardin, of all men, should lead the charge. Hardin was an "octoroon," the writer calculated, with "seven-eighth

Anglo-Saxon origin" and only one great-grandparent of African descent. He was wealthy, too, with personal assets worth $1,500 (the average Black Denver resident had only $90), and local whites had "never seen anything 'nigger' about him."[69]

White Coloradans' color and class prejudices may have benefited Austin Townsend when he arrived in the territory in the mid-1860s. Though not one of Samuel's sons, Austin was considered a "mulatto," undoubtedly because his mother Winney had mixed-race ancestry herself.[70] So did Henry Townsend, son of the late planter's probable concubine Emily, who died before she could be emancipated. Henry made the trek to Colorado around the same time as Austin, and by 1870 he was working as a cook in a hotel, with real estate worth $600.[71] Austin owned even more—$700 in real estate and $1,000 in personal property—having taken up the skilled profession of barbering.[72] In 1870, Black barbers in Denver alone accounted for 65 percent of all the barbers in Colorado Territory.[73] But the Townsend men hadn't found their success in Denver. They had instead chosen a small mining town called Central City.

When Osborne met Austin there in 1866, he wasn't impressed. Denver's population numbered nearly five thousand in 1870, with a little under two hundred Black residents. Central City had fewer than six hundred residents total, and only sixty African Americans lived in the entire surrounding county.[74] Central City's economy worried Osborne too. For a mining town, not much mining seemed to be going on. "Work of every kind is shutting down," Osborne wrote in 1867, with prospectors plagued by "bad machinery and New York speculation."[75] The town's financial troubles may have impacted Austin's trade, which relied on a steady influx of customers willing to spend money on a shave and a haircut. As a result, Osborne found himself in Central City for longer than he had anticipated. Though he had left Kansas "hoping that fortune will favor me and my request will be granted," Austin couldn't lend him the money for school after all, and Osborne settled in to join his half-brother in barbering.[76] It was "the poorest business a man can get into in this country," he told Cabaniss, though he may have exaggerated in an attempt to convince the attorney to fund his education. He still inquired "whether or not to expect any thing from down to Huntsville so I can come back to the states," but the attorney was having trouble collecting debts from southern planters bankrupted by the Civil War and couldn't provide much assistance. Compared to Osborne's hoped-for future, working as a barber in a roughshod mining town held little appeal. "I undertook to learn a trade & am still working at it," he wrote. "How long I can continue," however, "I don't know."[77]

Yet Central City had at least one advantage over Xenia and Leavenworth: for the first time, local whites weren't trying to run the Townsends off. Even on the controversial question of Black suffrage, white residents limited their opposition to rhetoric, eschewing the mob violence the Townsends had witnessed in Ohio and Kansas. In 1867, when Congress passed the Territorial Suffrage Act—prohibiting race-based voting restrictions in US territories— Colorado's white population accepted the legislation without a fight. "So far as this question of negro suffrage affects us," one Democratic newspaper printed, "it is quite plain how the case stands." Though they "could never be induced to vote for it," the matter was settled, and "we have nothing further to say against it!"[78] In Central City, white residents heard the news with a shrug. Western boosters asserted that "the white inhabitants of Colorado" possessed a particular "spirit of progress and liberality"—and while this certainly wasn't true with regard to the Utes, and while white "liberality" had its limits even in nearby Denver, smaller communities like Central City seemed to bear out the boosters' claim. Denver's city directories would have placed a mark beside the Townsend men's names: "col," for "colored."[79] But Central City didn't distinguish between its Black and white residents in print, an encouraging sign of local whites' attitudes about race more generally, and Henry Townsend would choose to make his home there until at least the 1880s.[80] In December 1867, however, Austin and Osborne decided to move to a more promising location: a silver boomtown eight thousand feet up in the Rocky Mountains. There, they would find an even more egalitarian community, and Osborne Townsend would never go back.

Georgetown, Colorado, was a virtual ghost town when prospectors hit pay dirt in the winter of 1864.[81] After the gold rush of 1859 seemed to empty the vicinity of ore, the little mining community carried on "in a desultory manner without profit" for years, most residents leaving in hope of better luck elsewhere. But news of the Belmont silver lode—one of the largest finds in the territory—brought settlers back in record numbers. As one Colorado historian would write in 1889: "Reports of this and other discoveries spread with the usual rapidity, and various colors of exaggeration to the uttermost parts, bringing a multitude."[82] Georgetown, filling the role of supply station and central hub for the surrounding mines, quickly became more prominent than it had ever been during the gold rush years, its population increasing from around eight hundred people in 1870 to five thousand by 1876.[83] In the first year of the silver strikes, Clear Creek County (Georgetown's mining district) produced only $500 in silver bullion. One year later, its output jumped to $400,000. The annual totals only continued to rise, and Georgetown was christened the "Silver Queen" of the Rockies. Between 1859 and 1868, Clear Creek County had mined roughly $2.5 million in gold. Miners produced nearly that much money in silver in 1874 alone.[84] At the county's height in 1879, the annual total for silver was $4.5 million.[85]

When Austin and Osborne Townsend arrived in 1868 or 1869, the future looked promising from Georgetown. Unlike Central City, where Osborne had described a decline in activity, Georgetown saw new buildings going up on every corner—boarding houses, banks, churches, schools, and saloons. General stores proudly advertised the best California wines "direct from San Francisco."[86] The streets were narrow but at least they were level, paved with river pebbles and kept clear of mud as residents planted trees along new sidewalks.[87] A daily coach service and express wagon brought mail and passengers the eighteen miles from Central City—a four-hour journey up the steep Clear Creek canyons—crowded alongside droves of pack mules carrying ore and supplies.[88] Water wheels powered lumber mills, forges, smelters, and all the necessities of mines dug deep into the mountains around the town. "There was mining everywhere," a British tourist wrote in 1873, "with all its destruction and devastation, its digging, burrowing, gulching, and sluicing" filling the district with "noise, hubbub, and smoke by night and day."[89]

Of all the mining towns in Colorado Territory, Georgetown most impressed visitors. John Codman, an easterner who published a travelogue titled *The Round Trip* in 1879, found fault in nearly every western town he saw. Denver's feted dry climate was too dusty, the dirt and dust "inhaled by the throat and lungs till the mucous membrane became like sandpaper and the voice between sneezes was like the caw of a raven." Neither did Idaho Springs, about fifteen miles east of Georgetown, satisfy Codman. Though he acknowledged that "the village's mineral springs, hot and cold, of iron and soda, are said to be wonderfully efficacious," Codman doubted that Idaho Springs would ever become the "watering-place and sanitarium" it aspired to be. "There is no order or beauty" in the village of five hundred, he wrote. "The buildings . . . straggle about in the uniformity of ugliness, still preserving the wretched characteristics of a mining camp." Codman criticized Central City for similar reasons. "Here where gold has been scooped up by the handfuls no use has been made of it to make life comfortable or anything other than endurable," and "the town is one vast mining gulch, with shapeless houses dumped here and there among the excavations, and clinging to the side hills."

The mining towns on Codman's "round trip" lacked the picturesque beauty he seemed to desire from Rocky Mountain communities.[90]

Georgetown was different. Surrounded by mountains on three sides—their peaks towering two thousand feet above the valley floor where the town lay—the Silver Queen's landscape took travelers' breath away. Naturalist Isabella Bird, author of the bestselling *A Lady's Life in the Rocky Mountains*, wrote that Georgetown occupied "as remarkable a gorge as was ever selected for the site of a town." The wooden houses with their gable-ended roofs, "perched here and there" on the steep hillsides, reminded her of Swiss villages in the Alps. Above, precipitous mountains loomed, dusted with snow and dotted with pines and cedars warped by the gusting winds that swept through the canyons. Frozen waterfalls sparkled among them as creeks rushed "impetuously" down the mountains to the town. "Sometimes the walls of the abyss seemed to meet overhead," Bird wrote. One moment they would be "dark with shadow" and the next glowing with "the most brilliant coloring." She described a dawn over Georgetown where "mountains which reflect the yet unrisen sun have the purple light of amethysts."[91] This, truly, was the sublime.

Elevated by such natural splendor, Georgetown seemed somehow distinctive from the typical rowdy mining town. Part of that was due to the nature of silver mining. Unlike gold, silver couldn't be found by "placer" mining—sifting sand and gravel for easily accessible surface deposits in the beds of lakes or rivers. Silver was "hard rock mining," requiring laborers to tunnel into nearly impenetrable granite before hitting ore. Even then, smelting and refining silver was a complicated and labor-intensive project. Miners needed expensive equipment (such as the steam-powered drill, which made its first debut in Georgetown in 1870), technical knowledge, and plenty of outside capital if they wanted to succeed.[92] As a result, Georgetown's silver rush brought investors, inventors, chemists, and skilled experts—"soft-handed gentlemen," the locals called them—along with the usual throngs of hopeful independent prospectors. In September 1866, Georgetown's *Daily Mining Journal* reported that "nearly all the known lodes of the district" had "passed into the hands of Eastern men." The newcomers gave Georgetown a reputation as a surprisingly genteel mining community. As one writer quipped in later years: "If you decide to settle in the 'Silver Queen' you will find both a boiled shirt and a dress suit a stern necessity."[93]

Along with eastern capitalists, Georgetown attracted migrants from a variety of regions and nations. Englishmen like Robert Old came representing overseas mining companies; Italian families opened groceries and restaurants, as did Frenchman Louis DuPoy; and Irish immigrant Frank DeLamar founded a local chapter of the Fenian Brotherhood.[94] Chinese immigrants opened laundries and worked in town, while Mexican miners brought centuries-old *arrastra* techniques for milling ore and smelted their silver in adobe furnaces.[95] Three fourths of Georgetown's residents were native-born Americans from across the United States, and most of the southerners were African Americans. Nelson Johnson from Virginia, Hiram Sanders and his wife Maria from Missouri, and even the famous "Professor" Lorenzo Bowman were all neighbors of Alabama-born Austin and Osborne Townsend.[96]

Georgetown's Black residents were vastly outnumbered, fifteen in a town of eight hundred in 1870.[97] In such a small community, each of these men and women would have been known to one another and to every other white resident. Interactions between white and Black residents were generally friendly. They played baseball together, with the white *Colorado Miner* editor cheering on Gabriel "Power of the Press" Saunders, the Black South Carolina man who operated the newspaper's printing press.[98] Englishman Robert Old gave a speech on Emancipation Day in 1873, joining Georgetown's African Americans in a parade, dinner, and dance as they celebrated the anniversary of the abolition of slavery in the British West Indies.[99] Austin Townsend won a local government contract to erect telegraph poles in town.[100] Elsewhere in Colorado Territory, white miners used violence and intimidation to push African Americans out of their camps. In some places, local ordinances prohibited Black prospectors from owning property, forcing them to find white men willing to file mining claims on their behalf—and increasing the risk that these claims would be "jumped" by the person who legally held title to them.[101] This was precisely what happened to Barney Ford, a former slave living in Central City, in 1859. After having his mines seized by armed white men at least three times, Ford ultimately gave up on gold and set up shop in Denver as a barber. But just eighteen miles away, at the clerk's office in Georgetown, African Americans registered claims and took out deeds under their own names with little fear, as did women, both Black and white.[102]

In a place like this, Osborne Townsend believed that he could find economic opportunity and social status—though by then he wasn't Osborne anymore. Nearly a decade before, at Wilberforce University, Samuel Townsend's fourth son had told his teachers that his name was Charles. "Osborne" might have been what his father called him, but to his closest family members and to himself he had long been "Charley."[103] S. D. Cabaniss quickly put an end to that, writing R. S. Rust that, since "he is known in all the Judicial proceedings here" as Osborne, "I think it best for him to retain that name."[104] As a soldier he had been Osborne too, not bothering to tell the Union Army lieutenant who filled out his enlistment paperwork that he preferred a different name. But in Georgetown, he was Charles to everyone—signing his letters and advertising his business ventures as "C. O. Townsend," for Charles Osborne. He made other changes too. Georgetown's largely Republican white population respected him as a Union Army veteran, and he played up his military service, telling locals he had enlisted at just age seventeen. He allowed them to call him a "graduate" of Wilberforce University, though he had attended for two years at most.[105] These were minor revisions to his personal history, but they gave Charles Osborne the opportunity to shape his own identity without white authority figures like Cabaniss to stop him. Few archetypes held the power of the "self-made man" in the nineteenth-century United States, and few places seemed better suited to such a man than the American West. It was a myth that caught Charles Osborne's imagination and gave him permission to seize control of his future.

He started by building a reputation as an entrepreneur. In 1869, Charles Osborne partnered with John McMurdy, a white lawyer from Ohio, to open a "business house" on Taos Street.[106] At the center of Georgetown's district for boarding houses, it was the perfect location for a barbershop. In a mere two years Charles Osborne was a Georgetown "celebrity," better known than Austin.[107] Local papers praised "Charley Townsend, the 'Boss' Barber" of Georgetown—"one of the best barbers that ever handled a razor in this city"— and in 1871, a traveling soap saleswoman used him in a publicity stunt.[108] The *Daily Register Call* reported that "the lady who has been circulating freely among our colored population selling soap, which she recommends as being superior for the complexion, has taken on Townsend, of tonsorial celebrity, as an advertisement, and proposes to operate on him. Admission free."[109] One wonders whether the "fair complexion" noted on his Union Army enlistment record had something to do with the woman's choice. Charles Osborne's relationship with McMurdy certainly played a role in his success. The lawyer was one of Georgetown's richest residents, with $25,000 in real estate and an additional $10,000 in personal property.[110] His ability to bankroll the Taos Street shop allowed Charles Osborne to attract wealthier clients and quickly become the most distinguished practitioner in town. With name recognition and a prime location, Charles Osborne felt little need to advertise his business in the local papers. Austin's ads—promising a smooth shave and shampoo "that will make you feel as bright as a newly coined dollar looks"—appeared often.[111] The only time he received free publicity was when a man was stabbed to death across the street from his shop in 1877.[112]

FIGURE 5.1 Stereograph of Taos Street in Georgetown, Colorado, 1875–1885. The striped barber's pole on the right side of the street marks the location of Charles Osborne Townsend's barber shop. Christine Bradley Collection, Clear Creek County Library District Archives.

Charles Osborne's skin color, military service, education, and connections to white residents may have raised his profile in town. But unlike Woodson in Leavenworth or Wesley in New Richmond, he didn't reject the local Black community. In 1871, a middle-aged Black barber named William Randolph gave Charles Osborne power of attorney, authorizing him to "sell and convey" property on his behalf.[113] Randolph, who had never learned to read or write, had been born in New York to a Missourian father and a mother from the West Indies; Charles Osborne, trusted and admired in town, must have seemed like a natural choice to manage his affairs.[114] A decade later, another man named Matthew Brown would do the same.[115] Then, in 1873, Osborne married into African American pioneer royalty. In an all-day affair that started at the Methodist church and ended at a friend's house where the wedding guests "danced until daylight," he took Josephine Smith—niece of the famous Clara Brown—as his bride. Charles Osborne was a "thriving barber" and "respectable citizen of Georgetown," and locals considered him a good match for Josephine, an Oberlin-educated woman who brought property in town to the marriage as well as her relationship to Colorado's most celebrated Black migrant.[116] The *Daily Colorado Miner*'s glowing coverage of the wedding pointed out that "the colored people were out in force of course, but the white folks crowded the house."[117] George O'Connor, the white town marshal, attended the festivities, and the party's host, Charles Yates, was a white Kentucky-born barber who lived two doors down from Austin Townsend.[118]

When John Armstrong Townsend, half-brother to Samuel's son Thomas, joined the other Townsends in Georgetown in 1875, he quickly integrated himself into local society as well.[119] John worked as a laborer in town, first as a porter and then a janitor for the courthouse, but his own nuptials indicate that he too became a prominent member of the local community—"one of the leading colored citizens of this place, and a most excellent young man," according to one paper.[120] Three years after settling in Georgetown, John married Hannah A. Clark, a woman from his old home of Leavenworth. "The affair came off with great *éclat* in the Presbyterian church," the *Colorado Miner* reported, the venue standing room only with "at least 300 persons present." The majority of the guests, considering Georgetown's small Black population, would have been local whites. "Most of the spectators came out of respect for the bridegroom," the *Miner* said, "a young gentleman who, during his residence here has, by his industry and general deportment, made hosts of friends." John chose Austin as his best man. Though they weren't related by blood, the two had grown up together and called themselves cousins. Charles Osborne, however, remained the most distinguished guest mentioned in the article. He also gave the most extravagant wedding present: a "silver castor" for sprinkling spices or sugar.[121]

Charles Osborne, Austin, John, and Henry Townsend kept in touch with their relatives in Kansas, and their accounts of life in Colorado drew other members of the family west. By 1877, Henry's twenty-four-year-old brother Amos had moved to Del Norte, Colorado, with his wife Fannie; by 1880 they had settled in Cañon City, a gold and silver mining town as well as the site of the first commercial oil well west of the Mississippi River.[122] Just a child when the Townsends were emancipated in 1860, Amos had been a bellboy in Leavenworth since he was a teenager, living with John Armstrong before John moved to Georgetown. In Cañon City, he found a job as a hotel waiter before heading southeast to Texas and Oklahoma City.[123] Around 1878, Henry and Amos's brother Wade joined the rest of the Townsends in Georgetown. When he was arrested that year for purportedly stealing a diamond ring in Leavenworth, the local paper expressed doubt: "he has borne a fair character while here, and we hope he may prove himself honest."[124] Apparently he did, as Wade was welcomed back to Georgetown shortly after, working alongside John as a porter and eventually saving enough to purchase a one-story cottage on the southern edge of town.[125] Sometime around 1882, William Townsend—the son of Martha, one of the legatees of the second class—headed west as well. Unlike the Colorado Townsends, William didn't stay in contact with his family, but they believed he ended up somewhere in Arizona, which had experienced its own silver boom in the late 1870s.[126]

Disbursements from the estate in Alabama made much of this possible, giving the Townsends a level of financial security most migrants did not benefit from as they began their new lives in Colorado Territory. Cabaniss had finally succeeded in collecting some debts from planters who had purchased land or slaves from Samuel Townsend's executors before the Civil War, and throughout the 1860s and '70s he was able to distribute it piecemeal to the late planter's legatees. In 1866, Henry and Austin were two of the first Townsends to receive their $200 inheritances, money that allowed them to establish themselves in Central City before any of their relatives arrived. The $200 would have helped Austin equip his barbershop with supplies and accouterments: "three (3) barber chairs, three (3) large looking glasses, one sink, Five common chairs, One Box stove, One Hat Rack, One stand, Two spittoons, Two dozen Razors . . . Three Bath Tubs, One Boiler & Two Tanks," and more.[127] John and Amos, each paid out in 1872, likely used the disbursements to fund their travel west as well. Wade, who moved to Georgetown the year before he received his inheritance in 1879, probably put some of the money into purchasing his cottage. All of the Colorado Townsends invested in silver, too—buying and selling shares in mines with encouraging names (the Sweepstakes Lode) and glamorous connotations (the Sarah Bernhardt Lode, after a famous French actress).[128] None of them put as much into silver mining as Charles Osborne, however, who received $375 from his father's estate in 1871 alone and expected more as a member of Samuel Townsend's "first class." In 1866, he had reluctantly followed Austin to the Rocky Mountains, but Georgetown's boomtown optimism was contagious. Just six years later Charles Osborne had quit his day job, shuttered his successful barbershop, and devoted himself entirely to Colorado's most important industry. "I am not doing any business in town now," he wrote his brothers Thomas and Wesley in December 1872. "I think I have a very good mine now and I hope as soon as I get a little deeper to make it pay."[129]

Charles Osborne never took up a pickaxe or shovel himself. He was careful to note that although he and the other "Townsend boys" in Colorado were involved in mining, they "do not do the work themselves but are in-terested"—meaning, they invested.[130] Charles Osborne's correspondence with Thomas in the 1870s and '80s suggests that he felt the need to compete with his brother, who had moved back to Alabama and was making a name for himself as a cotton planter and community leader in the Huntsville area. Charles Osborne compared his mining to Thomas's farming: "I suppose you are looking out for an immense cotton crop this year same as we are going for the silver crop just now." He boasted that if one of his mines eventually paid out, "you can make more money in a month than you can make in a life time raising cotton." In his letters, Charles Osborne framed himself as a property owner and elite like Thomas—more of a class with the capitalists who came from New York and London than the laborers driving and blasting hundred-foot tunnels into the mountains on his behalf.[131] He acknowledged that his silver mines were "of a very uncertain value" and that "it may be worth thousands and it may not be worth much of anything," but Georgetown was a flourishing community in which residents, even African Americans, amassed great amounts of wealth every year. "Five men made 40,000 dollars this year hear in Georgetown and are now spreading themselves back east," Charles Osborne wrote in 1882. "You must know two of them, Poyner and Jerry Lee. Lee is Mrs. Gwines son of Leavenworth."[132] Not only were Poyner and Lee Black men, they were men from back home, friends and neighbors of the Townsends in Kansas. Jeremiah Lee and Austin Townsend had even been in business together in Georgetown for a time.[133] If they could strike it rich, why shouldn't he?

Throughout the 1870s and '80s, "C. O. Townsend" visited Georgetown's clerk at least twenty-six times to buy or sell property, most of it related to mining.[134] In 1870, he sold his interest in one mine for $100, and just days later used the money to purchase another from Lorenzo Bowman—which he sold for $200 the next year. In 1876, when Austin's friend and fellow barber Washington Ready fell into debt, Charles Osborne snapped up Ready's pro-perty in town at bargain prices. He made a tidy $470 profit selling his shares in the Sarah Bernhardt Lode to E. S. Martin, an investor from Chicago. He built a house for his family—"a comfortable house as could be built in town for $1300"—and purchased a ranch in Hammond Gulch a couple miles southeast of Central City, where he grazed cows, heifers, and bulls.[135] Charles Osborne wrote Thomas that he had "a lot of Texas land stock land located near Fort Worth," too, though the life of a cowboy didn't suit him. "I don't believe it is worth 10 cents an acre," he said, and "I wouldn't live on it if it was worth ten millions."[136] For now, Charles Osborne put his hopes into silver mining. "All the Townsends hear are engaged in mining," he told Thomas in 1882, and "I predict before one year goes over our head some one of us will have it good."[137] But boomtown bluster alone couldn't make Charles Osborne's mines pay, and on multiple occasions he was forced to mortgage his cattle and ranch land to pay debts or fund his investments.[138] There was a reason that corporations with eastern or foreign backers dominated silver mining in Clear Creek County: hard-rock mining required more equipment, capital, and labor than even Charles Osborne, with his disbursements from the Townsend estate, could provide. The meager amounts of silver his mines generated were "not enough to keep up the heavy ecspensive working neces-sary," he wrote Thomas. He used the descriptive term common to experienced miners but perhaps unfamiliar to his planter brother: "dead work."[139] Though he attempted to offset these costs by organizing a mining company comprised of the "loose negroes" in Georgetown—as Lorenzo Bowman, Jeremiah Lee, and Clara Brown had partnered to mine gold in the early 1860s—he appar-ently didn't succeed in that endeavor either.[140] Though he tried to persuade his wealthier brother Thomas to invest money in one of his mines, Charles Osborne didn't exaggerate his prospects. "If you have any spare cash this is a good envestment," he said, but on the other hand, "if you need all your money to carry on your cropping perhaps you have better not go in as we may strike it in a barron place."[141] Years of experience and disappointment were making Charles Osborne more realistic about his chance of hitting a bonanza.

Personal losses also shook his confidence. Back in 1872, he had told Thomas and Wesley that he was "almost forced to marry just now," suggesting that something had hastened his wedding to Josephine Smith.[142] But the *Daily Colorado Miner* was right when they predicted that Josephine would "make Charlie happy and not half try."[143] When she died in childbirth in 1876, Charles Osborne called it "the saddest event of my life." He wrote his brothers in despair: "I think all the powers that be are against me. I feel some-times like seccoming to whatever fate awaits me."[144] Yet their infant child had survived, and the widower couldn't give himself over to grief. He remarried, a young woman named Margaret ("Maggie") Hall who gave her husband five more boys in time.[145] After two decades in Colorado, Charles Osborne Townsend realized he needed a more stable source of income to support his growing family, and in 1877 he re-opened his barbershop.[146] After all, he wrote Thomas, "it is no use to kill yourself trying to get rich."[147]

Yet even as Charles Osborne's fortunes sank, Thomas Townsend was rising ever higher in Alabama. He bought stock in the *Huntsville Gazette*, an African American newspaper that elected him to its board of directors.

He invested in the Nashville and North Alabama Railroad Company. He served as a juror in state and county courts. He was a local representative for the Freedman's Bank. He assisted Black Civil War veterans attempting to get pensions from the federal government. After years of comparing himself to Thomas, Charles Osborne had to know that "tonsorial celebrity" in the small mining community of Georgetown couldn't compare to his brother's status in Alabama. When Thomas married in 1888, Charles Osborne only learned the news when he saw the social page of the *Huntsville Gazette*. It was the best way to keep up with events in Alabama, as Thomas neglected to answer many of his letters. "Well I know how it is when a fellow is busy," Osborne excused his brother.[148] The *Gazette* lavished attention on Thomas and his young wife Tamar's wedding, the "different kinds of fruits composing the two immense pyramids built upon the table, the different kinds of meats, cakes" at the invitation-only event.[149] Charles Osborne probably read the article to his family with a mixture of pride and sadness. His wife Maggie, he wrote Thomas, "has at least a hundred guesses about your wife," that Tamar was "pretty, accomplished, lovely, bewitching and the very picture of an angel and you gallant kind and the very embodiment of a gentleman in everything." Charles Osborne, Maggie, and their children could only guess, however, as they hadn't made the guest list. "You didn't know whether we were too poor to attend or not," Charles Osborne supposed, "but you guess aright."[150]

Charles Osborne wasn't going to be the next Lorenzo Bowman or Jeremiah Lee, and measuring himself against his brother only left him melancholy. But in the 1880s and '90s, as southern whites re-took control of state and local governments across the South, Charles Osborne came to value his community for more than its silver mines. He may not have had Thomas's wealth or position, but he appreciated the social and political equality Georgetown afforded him compared to the rest of the country. "Down there" in Alabama, life was dangerous and precarious for African Americans, even for elites like Thomas. "Out here," Charles Osborne believed, the situation was different— and he wouldn't trade places for anything.[151]

———◆———

"I read gloomy reports of the condition of the colored man in the South," Charles Osborne wrote Thomas in 1889.[152] Family members sent him copies of his brother's newspaper, allowing the Coloradan to follow Alabama politics from his home 1,300 miles away. Like many Black publications, the *Huntsville Gazette* reported on violence and injustice across the country, tallying lynchings, arson, and economic exploitation with outrage and exhaustion. Perhaps it reminded Charles Osborne of his year in Vicksburg—the guerilla attacks from ex-Confederates who never really surrendered when their army did, the failure of the Freedmen's Bureau to support African Americans' desire for land and independence. Even Black soldiers seemed to have been forgotten by the country they had served.[153] "I think the Journal had better taken up the subject of Government given pensions to colored soldiers the same as to whites," Charles Osborne suggested to Thomas. He had never received a cent himself and didn't know "but 8 men out of my regiment" who had.[154] Not to mention the daily indignities African Americans faced even outside the South. Charles Osborne had been humiliated when he was forced to ride second-class on the Kansas Pacific Railroad and was denied service at a restaurant during a visit to his family in Leavenworth in 1871.[155] The experience stuck with him. "I never expect to come South again untill I can travel like other people," he swore. "I mean any body."[156]

In Georgetown, Charles Osborne believed he had joined a community untroubled by violence and discrimination, a conviction he used to distinguish his world from Thomas's as African Americans faced increasing hostility after Reconstruction. Here, the old idea that the West stood apart from the rest of the country's racial problems seemed to hold some truth. When Charles Osborne wrote a letter to the *Colorado Miner* describing his ordeal on the Kansas Pacific, Georgetown's whites were furious on his behalf. "If corporations sell first-class tickets," the paper declared, "the holders thereof are entitled to first-class fare"—especially when the ticket holder was a "worthy barber" like C. O. Townsend.[157] But the support and acceptance Charles Osborne found as an African American man in Georgetown came at a price for the small mining community's other non-white members: Native Americans and Chinese immigrants.[158]

Chinese migrants had engaged in mining in the American West since the California Gold Rush, arriving in huge numbers during the 1850s. By the end of the decade, Chinese men comprised a quarter of the state's miners. During the following years, immigrant communities would spread into Oregon, Idaho, Montana, and finally Colorado's Rocky Mountains.[159] Chinese migrants never settled in Colorado in large numbers: in 1870 there were only seven in the entire territory, and while 1,408 Asian immigrants were counted in the state's 1890 census, they still comprised a mere 0.3 percent of the total population, less even than African Americans.[160] Yet they faced virulent xenophobia, with white and Black Coloradans alike troubled by their foreign customs and fearful of labor competition—even though most of the Chinese in the region worked in laundries, not mines, and therefore posed little economic threat. Native-born Americans and European immigrants harassed and assaulted Chinese workers in Colorado, and in 1880 a mob of three thousand people rioted in Denver, destroying nearly every home in the city's Chinese neighborhood and beating a laundryman to death.[161] Bowing to anti-immigration sentiment in the West, Congress passed the Chinese Exclusion Act in 1882, banning the entry of any Chinese person into the United States.[162] Here, author Mark Twain wrote, "a Chinaman had no rights that any man was bound to respect."[163]

In Colorado, Chinese residents faced prejudice, threats, and violence with no hope of protection from local law enforcement—a hostile climate that consistently characterized Georgetown and nearby mining communities throughout the last third of the nineteenth century. When "William Young, colored" physically assaulted a Chinese resident of Central City in 1872, both men received the same $5 fine. The "Heathen Chinee" man's "abusive language" was "unbecoming a Chinee and a washerman," and "terribly offensive" to William Young, Georgetown's *Daily Colorado Miner* reported; Young wouldn't stand for insolence from an inferior.[164] Again, African Americans in Colorado gained status from the marginalization of a seemingly more alien group. The Chinese were inassimilable, local whites said in 1880, "an extraneous ingredient" in the melting pot of America who showed "no affinity for our customs."[165] That same year, a council of miners in Summit, Colorado, unanimously voted "that no Chinaman be employed in any capacity, or allowed to remain" in their mining district.[166] In 1887, when the body of a Chinese migrant was found dead and frozen in a snowdrift just below Georgetown—"bruised about the head, body and hands"—locals chose not to hold an inquest. It was "unnecessary," they said, assuming he had simply fallen from a height.[167] Three miles away, Silver Plume's newspaper proudly approved of the gang of "boys with a rope" who drove a Chinese man out of their mining camp a mere fifteen minutes after his arrival in 1894.[168] When Charles Gow, a Chinese restaurant proprietor, kept his pit bull beside him when he rode into Georgetown in the early twentieth century, it may have been for more than companionship.[169]

Anti-Indian sentiment, too, bound Black and white Coloradans in common cause.[170] When soldiers with the Colorado U.S. Volunteer Cavalry massacred a village of Cheyenne and Arapaho men, women, and children at Sand Creek in 1864, much of the country reacted with shock.[171] A congressional committee declared the attack "brutal and cowardly," the men responsible having "disgraced the government."[172] Georgetown disagreed, issuing a public resolution denouncing the "misplaced sympathy now being uttered in the east."[173] Easterners simply didn't understand what life was like in Colorado, locals said, describing graphic scenes of "smoke arising from innocent blood, shed by merciless savages" across the territory.[174] Sarah Rowe Corbett, a Georgetown resident, remembered the peaceful Utes who passed through in the summers of her childhood in the 1870s, mothers carrying "papooses" on their backs as men traded in town.[175] Sarah's own mother would hand the women food through the house's open windows. But Sarah and her brother still hid under their beds, terrified that the Native Americans would scalp them. Perhaps they had heard adults parroting the local papers— that native peoples could be "held in check by fear" alone, and "extermination" might be the only path to peace on the plains.[176]

Like the Chinese, Colorado's Native American population showed little interest in westernizing, and miners and settlers resented their refusal to conform to their ideas of "civilized" behavior. The Utes occupied "the finest agricultural lands in the west," one Georgetown man grumbled, and yet they refused to cultivate them, choosing instead to "roam at will over the country" during the summer and return to reservations in the winter, where they could live "without an effort" on government largesse.[177] In 1879, the *Colorado Miner* expressed the settlers' viewpoint in an excerpt from an imaginary children's history book set in the year 1900. Once upon a time, the author began, "wicked savages" controlled the beautiful lands of western Colorado:

> This land was good for farming and raising stock, and on some portion of it there were very rich mines. This land was set apart to these savages, who were called Utes, and white people were not allowed to hunt game or look for gold on it. The Utes did not farm it, or dig for gold . . . they would neither use it themselves nor let others do so. They were very lazy, and would have starved to death only the government gave them flour and beef and clothing and guns.

The story ended happily, for the miners and farmers, at least, with the Utes removed from the state and politicians and philanthropists leaving issues "they did not know much about" for westerners to manage.[178]

That year, an attack on the White River reservation gave Colorado settlers an excuse to make their fairytale real. Forced to abandon their traditional lifestyle and take up farming, and already facing threats of extermination from white soldiers and civilians alike, a group of White River Utes killed federal Indian Agent Nathan Meeker and ten of his employees in September

1879.[179] "There never was a more fatherly and honest Indian Agent than N. C. Meeker," the *Colorado Miner* lamented, suddenly supportive of an easterner charged with looking after "the welfare of the Utes."[180] Locals demanded that the government remove the Utes from White River, certain that the reservation would otherwise become "the permanent rendezvous for all the renegade Indians in the West." And again: "What the people of Colorado want is that the Utes should go . . . and the people of this section are the most desirous."[181] By 1881, Ute removal from Colorado to Utah was complete. "They have been moved several hundred miles South west of us," Charles Osborne wrote when Thomas asked if he could send Native American moccasins and a buffalo robe to Huntsville in 1882. "Several years ago when we had a chance to trade with the Utes we had plenty such things," he added, but those days were over.[182]

Charles Osborne probably didn't miss them. The *Colorado Miner* promoted Indian removal by arguing that the federal government had a responsibility to "protect its law abiding white subjects"—but Black Coloradans like Charles Osborne shared many of their white neighbors' beliefs and prejudices. In one letter expressing his disgust that the Townsends had not yet received the full inheritance they expected from their father's estate, he commented that the matter would even "make a breech clout ute indian sick."[183] He didn't care much for Jewish people either, seeming to believe anti-Semitic conspiracy theories about a "hooked nose Fraturnity" controlling world finances. "Mr. D. E. Rothschilds will mistake the temper of the American people one of these days," Charles Osborne wrote—referring to a Jewish banking family with the largest private fortune in the world at the time—and hinted at violence.[184] By the 1880s, Charles Osborne no longer aspired to be one of Georgetown's "soft-handed gentlemen." Instead he had adopted a deep distrust of outsiders, particularly eastern politicians and financiers, whom he and many Coloradans considered out of touch with the average westerner. Like Chinese exclusion and Indian removal, economic issues united Black and white settlers in Colorado, and in the last decades of the nineteenth century, the all-consuming "money question" was chief among them.[185]

Miners in the western United States had been experiencing a long period of economic decline since the "Panic of 1873," a world financial crisis that resulted in a sharp decrease in the value of silver. In 1871, the German Empire had stopped minting silver coins—a decision that rippled across the Atlantic and influenced American legislators to change their monetary policy, placing the country on a "gold standard" and halting coinage of their own silver dollars.[186] The decision devastated Coloradans, whose regional economy depended heavily on silver production. Georgetown's residents responded furiously: the legislation was "swindling, humbugging and dishonesty" on the part of the federal government.[187] Paper money, too, was losing value in the country. During the Civil War, the federal government had issued "greenbacks" as an emergency currency backed by nothing but the promise that they were legal tender. In an attempt to reduce inflation after the war, however, the government refused to exchange this paper money for gold and moved to reduce the number of greenbacks in circulation, resulting in a dramatic decrease in the amount of currency available throughout the country.[188] The government was contracting the money supply even as population and commerce expanded, and farmers and laborers revolted. A new independent political party, the Greenback-Labor Party, emerged in 1876, demanding—among other things—a return to free and unlimited silver coinage.[189] It was a platform that strongly appealed to Coloradans like Charles Osborne.

"Times are hard and money is hard to secure," he wrote Thomas and Wesley in 1876, and the situation only worsened with time.[190] As Charles Osborne's mining prospects waned throughout the late 1870s and '80s, sickness and death plagued the Townsends. His wife Maggie was ill, and in 1882 Osborne sent her to Iowa to spend the winter in a milder climate.[191] By spring, she still hadn't recovered and they spent several weeks in Denver, where Maggie could receive better medical treatment than in Georgetown.[192] Two years later the twenty-eight-year-old woman gave birth to a "stout healthy" boy, but the pregnancy weakened her and Charles Osborne reported that Maggie "has been sick ever since and at times at death's door"—a situation Osborne called "near unbearable."[193] At some point after 1880, his and Maggie's son Willis died, followed in 1888 by their son Lony; months later, Charles Osborne wrote that "I have not been good since."[194] By 1890, he was nearly lame from rheumatism. "Since I had the grippe," he wrote Thomas, "it seems as though as fast as one thing leaves me another takes hold."[195] In 1892 he lost his youngest son, "little Roy," after which he settled Maggie and their two surviving children—Charles Osborne Jr. and Thomas Clarence—in Denver permanently while he continued to work in Georgetown with Austin and Wade.[196] In 1896, Maggie was struck again by an unspecified disease that required her to stay at a hospital for six months after doctors "performed surgical operations on her."[197] She survived, but the long series of sicknesses, losses, and medical treatments put financial pressure on Charles Osborne and his family. "If I ever could get the settlement" from Samuel Townsend's estate "I would not feel so straighten," he said. With that money, "I could float myself several months."[198] But decades after their father's death, Samuel's children had received only one third of what they were owed, around $5,000 for each legatee of the first class.

There wouldn't be much more. In 1879, the estate retained a little over $13,000 in assets but owed nearly $24,000 in debts.[199] Wesley and Thomas hired a new lawyer, a white Alabama man named D. D. Shelby, to take Cabaniss to court over the settlement, but the process was slow. Meanwhile, financial policy at the national level only aggravated Charles Osborne's circumstances. "Let me know any new move of D. D. Shelby makes in our favor," he reminded Thomas. "I certainly need my part for the price of silver and lead has about killed this country."[200]

Without his long-promised, long-undelivered inheritance to look forward to, Charles Osborne found himself at the mercy of the same economic forces battering miners across the state and began to see himself as more politically aligned with them than any other interest group. By the late 1870s, he had left the Republican Party—"the republican swindle," he called it— and threw himself into local Greenbacker and "Free Silver" movements. He was fervent ("I tell you Thomas the people will yet come to the principle of the Greenbacks") and furious ("we produce two millions of silver every year but the government takes all the profit in it").[201] In 1878, Charles Osborne attended Clear Creek County's "Greenback Convention" as a delegate for Georgetown, alongside English mining agent Robert Old, French miner Peter Bourquin, Irish carpenter and saloonkeeper James Sherry, and Irish laborer Frank DeLamar.[202] Here was another place where Charles Osborne could participate in local politics as an equal with white Coloradans. It's not difficult to imagine the kind of speech Charles Osborne might have given at the convention, if his letters to Thomas were any indication. The country's troubles were "all on account of the Ignorance of the East on the silver question," he wrote his brother in one, "backed by the administration that don't seem to know a thing about Finances, manufacturing, agriculture, extent of our country or anything else." The price of silver in Clear Creek County was plummeting, a "calamity" non-westerners couldn't begin to understand. "Yesterday I was worth something and today I am worth nothing," he spat, "penniless and a family to support."[203] Charles Osborne's story clearly resonated with his neighbors and fellow miners. Out of the five Georgetown men, the county convention elected C. O. Townsend, the only African American delegate, as their candidate for state legislature. The vote, the *Georgetown Courier* reported, was unanimous.[204]

Charles Osborne never reached the state legislature, but he remained committed to populist politics throughout his life, increasingly identifying himself with "the people of the West."[205] During the pivotal presidential election of 1896, when Republican William McKinley faced off against Democrat and

thundering "Free Silver" advocate William Jennings Bryan, Osborne felt no
shame telling his brother "well yes we are for Bryan."[206] Massively popular in
western states, Bryan was seen as a hero of the common man. His assertion
that "the miners who go 1,000 feet into the earth . . . are as much businessmen
as the few financial magnates who in a back room corner the money of the
world" certainly would have buoyed Coloradans' pride and self-worth.[207]
Charles Osborne's support for Bryan in 1896 reveals just how deeply his sense
of self had become tied to his region after thirty years in Colorado. Though he
lamented the "gloomy" circumstances African Americans faced in the South,
he chose to insulate himself from the challenges they faced—content to live
in a community where skin color seemed to matter less than solidarity with
the economic interests of white miners and homesteaders. It was a departure
from the racial uplift ideology of his teachers at Wilberforce, who had taught
him that individual advancement was inextricably tied to the elevation of all
African Americans. Unlike William Jefferson Hardin, the mixed-race barber
whose civil rights activism had provoked white Denver residents' ire in the
1860s, Osborne limited his attention to the "affairs in the West" and was
rewarded with full inclusion in Georgetown's white society. Outsiders were
the enemy: Chinese migrants, Native Americans, Jews, government officials,
bankers, and even Thomas, sometimes, when the *Huntsville Gazette* advocated positions Osborne considered contrary to western interests. "I have
remonstrated with you about the unfavorable course of the Gazette towards
silver but it kept on blaiting about something it knew nothing about (the
silver question) until it has helped wall street . . . to ruin thousand and thousand of people in the west," Charles Osborne fumed in 1893. "If the Gazette
don't know anything about a subject," he added, disdain dripping from his
pen, "it is very strong in comment unfavorable about it."[208]

Charles Osborne wanted what all the Townsends wanted after their emancipation: social mobility, economic opportunity, and equality. But he had a
different sense of how—and, more importantly, where—he could best achieve
those goals. As a young man, Charles Osborne had thrown himself into
African Americans' struggle for freedom when he joined the Union Army
in 1865. Decades in Georgetown, however, with its remarkable harmony between Black and white residents, if not other ethnic groups, had given him
the luxury to think in terms of region and class rather than race—a worldview
he used to distinguish himself from family members like his brother Thomas.
To Charles Osborne's mind, Thomas was a southerner; Charles Osborne was
a westerner. Thomas lived in a segregated world; he lived in a community
where white and Black residents could work together for common interests.

Thomas was a member of the Black elite; he was an everyman, and proud of it. Sometimes he fell prey to nostalgia about his childhood in Alabama. "Wade and Austin and I sit around Sundays and talk over things that happened twenty five years ago in the South," he wrote Thomas in one letter.[209] Yet even when Georgetown lost its title of "Silver Queen," along with most of its residents, in the 1880s and '90s, it remained his home. Charles Osborne may not have wished to move to Colorado in 1866, but in the end he never left—and he never stopped believing in its promise. In 1896, in the midst of a nationwide depression, C. O. Townsend was back at the Georgetown clerk's office buying shares in silver mines.[210] He still owned a house and barbershop in his haven in the Rocky Mountains in 1910, years after his wife's death left him a widower and his sons left home for Montana and Seattle.[211]

To Charles Osborne, Georgetown seemed like one of the few safe places left.[212] Jim Crow reigned across the South, where African Americans didn't have the option to ignore the violence and dangers they faced from white Americans determined to prevent them gaining any modicum of influence or independence. And Thomas Townsend—back where everything had started in Madison County, Alabama—needed to develop a different strategy to achieve the status and success the family had been seeking since 1860.

6

Who Hasn't Yearned to Be Home?

ON SEPTEMBER 15, 1865, Septimus Douglas Cabaniss received his official presidential pardon, a printed form signed by Secretary of State William Seward, bound with a purple ribbon and stamped in red with the Great Seal of the United States.[1] As a high-level ex-Confederate with more than $20,000 in personal property, Cabaniss had been excluded from President Andrew Johnson's policy of "general amnesty," which simply required an oath of allegiance to the laws and proclamations of the United States. But after submitting his request for a special pardon, claiming that he hadn't voluntarily sought his position as a financial agent of the Confederate Congress and that after paying his own debts he wouldn't really be worth $20,000, Cabaniss too was forgiven.[2] Perhaps William Seward recognized the name of the Huntsville lawyer who had written him three years earlier to ask for advice on the best place to settle a colony of forty-five manumitted slaves. More likely, Cabaniss was just another former rebel rubberstamped during the federal government's remarkably lenient treatment of ex-Confederates.

In any case, by the autumn of 1865 S. D. Cabaniss was once again a loyal citizen of the United States—and almost immediately back at work as the executor of the late Samuel Townsend's estate. He wasn't happy about it. If settling the estate had seemed complicated in 1860, the case was nearly unsalvageable now. On the eve of the Civil War, more than 900,000 people had lived in Alabama, nearly half of them enslaved.[3] When the Thirteenth Amendment abolished slavery and freed those 435,000 men, women, and children (along with nearly 4 million more across the South), the nation's white planter class lost a fortune in human property.[4] "Nearly all the people in this country who were once well off are ruined in fortune," Cabaniss wrote in 1866, and when he attempted to collect money owed to the estate he found

Samuel Townsend's debtors unwilling to pay.[5] After writing what he considered a "polite note" to one of these men, Cabaniss received a typical reply: the man declared that the lawyer "wished to take the bread out of the mouths of his children."[6] In 1860 and 1861, Cabaniss had sold Samuel's property for a total of $220,000—much of it on credit—and by 1866 he calculated that more than $150,000 of the money owed might never be collected.[7] Cabaniss had refused to accept payments in Confederate currency during the war, so he believed that the Townsend estate had "fared better than almost any other in this part of the state."[8] Still, he confided to a colleague, "I entertain no doubt but that the estate will not be worth as much by one half as it was estimated at before the war."[9]

The reason, in a particularly ironic twist of fate, was emancipation. Five years before, when auctioning off Samuel's property, Cabaniss had noted that "the lands sold low" while "the negroes sold high"—meaning that most of the money owed to the estate, and therefore owed to Samuel's children and their relatives, had come from the sale of other enslaved people, men and women without the dubious privilege of being the old planter's blood relations.[10] Cabaniss could seek a court order to resell Samuel's lands if the buyers couldn't pay their debts after the Civil War, but debts for slaves were a different matter. "Nearly all of those who owe for slaves . . . refuse to pay and will do all they can to evade payment," he wrote, "on the ground that the property for which their bonds were given was taken from them by the government."[11] Alabama's new Republican government sided with the ruined planters. At constitutional conventions across the South, former slaveholders, former abolitionists, and former slaves alike found common cause on the issue of debt relief—albeit for vastly different reasons. Black and white Republicans declared that enforcing debts for slave purchases was immoral, a latter-day justification of slavery. As one delegate to South Carolina's constitutional convention asked, and numerous others echoed: "Shall we now, after having succeeded in getting free from this terrible curse, still continue to recognize its legality in any shape or form?" Meanwhile, the once-wealthy southerners bankrupted by the war also stood to benefit if slave debts were wiped away; for them, it was a form of "reparations" for their lost human property. The sellers would bear the loss now, but as far as the debtors were concerned, they deserved it. Many of those who had offloaded property in slaves early in the war had been betting that the Confederacy would fail. In a sense, debt nullification rewarded buyers for their faith in the rebellion. So with freedpeople and white planters in rare agreement, six southern states—including Alabama—passed constitutions or ordinances annulling all debts for the purchase of slaves.[12]

By December 1866, Cabaniss had filed lawsuits against all of the estate's debtors, legal action that pressured some to agree to "compromises" whereby Cabaniss would discharge the full debt if they paid a smaller amount immediately.[13] The new laws threatened to undo all his hard work. Cabaniss suspected that the Alabama convention's ordinance was unconstitutional (and in 1870, the Alabama Supreme Court would rule this way), but in the meantime his hands were tied. "If these compromises are 'repealed,' " he wrote Major General John Pope, commander of the Union Army's occupation of Alabama, "it would seem to follow that I may be compelled to refund the moneys received."[14] Cabaniss may have hoped he could persuade Pope to exercise some influence on his behalf—after all, he added pointedly, the money was intended for the benefit of former slaves—but his letter seemed to have no effect. To make matters worse, even debts owed for land, livestock, or other property couldn't be collected until 1869, according to additional relief measures passed as incentives for struggling white Alabamians to ratify the new constitution.[15] The word "impossible" began to appear more frequently in Cabaniss's papers.[16]

It wasn't a word the Townsends wanted to hear.

Ten years after their father's death, Samuel's legatees were still waiting on the full value of the life-changing inheritance they had been promised. Unable to write to Cabaniss or receive payments from the estate during the war, they had been left to fend for themselves in Kansas and Ohio, but by 1865 lines of communication had reopened and the Townsends made sure the lawyer heard them loud and clear. It was a different world now for former slave owners, and the Townsends knew it. "The new state of affairs gives us the power to enforce remedies and we shall do it," Elvira Townsend wrote Cabaniss in 1865, demanding a "full, exact statement, of the condition of the estate."[17] Elvira had always been a shrewd judge of risks and opportunities. In March 1861, perhaps concerned that mounting political turmoil across the country would put her inheritance in danger, she had told Cabaniss's agent in Kansas that she needed immediate title to the land he was supposed to purchase for her: it was "now or never."[18] One month later, Confederate forces fired on Fort Sumter. But at the same time the Civil War delayed disbursements from Samuel's estate, it also gave the Townsends unanticipated leverage over Cabaniss, who would never again dictate their decisions as absolutely as he had before the war. "Either through the Military Commanders, or the Freedmans Bureau, we can obtain our full rights," Elvira reminded the lawyer. As citizens with the support of the federal government, the Townsends would "call any and all partner to a strict account."[19]

Frustrated with Cabaniss's lack of progress with the estate and suspicious that he might attempt to cheat them out of their inheritance, some of the Townsends vented their anger more freely than they would have dared when they were first manumitted. "I think very hard of it that you men call yourselfs so good and can not even lend me as much as a hundred dollars to keep me from suffring," Willis wrote Cabaniss in September 1866.[20] "A poor man has a hard time in this country," he would lament the next year; "it would be better if he were not borne."[21] Willis insinuated that Cabaniss, in distant Alabama with the entirety of the estate "under your controll," might be enriching himself.[22] According to the terms of Samuel's will, Cabaniss would receive a salary of $3,000 for each year he served as executor. To the Townsends, that seemed like a strong incentive to drag out the process as long as possible.[23] Cabaniss was not, in fact, cheating them. He wasn't even collecting a salary at that point, and when he died in 1889 the lawyer would be owed more than $18,000 in back pay.[24] But with only his word as guarantee, members of the Townsend family continued to suspect Cabaniss's motives. "I am not yet lost faith and hope in you," Wesley claimed in October—"alltho," he added, "we are told by a great many that you will never settle the State of Samuel Townsend with us as long as you live."[25] In December 1866, Edmund's daughter Lizzie sent her husband to Huntsville to determine, in person, precisely what was happening with the estate.[26] In 1867, Willis once again expressed what much of the family may have been thinking: "It is hardly worth while to ask you to send any money," he wrote Cabaniss, "because if you was to do it you would do something you never did do yet."[27]

The Townsends' accusations exasperated the lawyer. "She must think that I can squeeze money out of the debtors of the Estate whether they are willing to pay or not," Cabaniss fumed after an especially "ill-natured" letter from Edmund's daughter Jennie.[28] It was an affront to his honor as a southern gentleman—and to his sense of racial superiority. A former slaveholder who had once suggested that the legatees might return to Alabama and have him for their master, Cabaniss was accustomed to deference from those he considered his inferiors. Before the war, he had scoffed at the idea that former slaves could be permitted to "do as you please" with Samuel's fortune, and he had threatened to withhold payments if they failed to conduct themselves with the "propriety" he expected.[29] Those days were over. In December 1866, Wesley initiated a lawsuit against S. D. Cabaniss, calling the executor to account just as Elvira had threatened the family would do. With his brothers Willis, Thomas, and Charles Osborne, his sister Milcha and her husband, and his cousins Lizzie and Jennie signing onto the lawsuit, Wesley forced

Cabaniss to stand before the Chancery Court of Madison County and justify his actions as the estate's administrator.[30] Cabaniss's associates in Alabama were not inclined to sympathize. "Mr. Townsends will was very unpopular in the community," the lawyer wrote that same month, and as executor he had been obligated to collect debts from men who were once his "warm friends" but who now resented him for the "active part" he took in the case.[31] When he swore to Elvira that he was "exceedingly anxious to get the Estate wound up & be relieved from any further trouble with it," he wasn't dissembling.[32] As Cabaniss told a former law partner, if he had known back in 1853 what he knew now about being Samuel Townsend's executor, "I would have rejected the office at once and I have regretted often that I did not reject it."[33]

With the onset of Reconstruction in the South, the balance of power between S. D. Cabaniss and the Townsends had shifted. The legatees weren't pleading for financial assistance anymore; they were demanding action. Cabaniss was the one looking for an ally this time, someone to intercede for him with the newly empowered, increasingly assertive members of the Townsend family. In 1860, he had hoped that Samuel's eldest son Wesley might step into the role of supervising the legatees' money, keeping the lawyer updated on their lives and work, and effectively acting as the new Townsend patriarch. But six years later, Wesley was spearheading legal proceedings against Cabaniss; Woodson was in prison; Willis wanted nothing to do with him; Charles Osborne would soon head west for Colorado Territory; and young Bradford was dead. Unable to imagine a woman managing the Townsend estate, Cabaniss saw just one option left: Thomas, Samuel Townsend's third son. Twenty-five years old at the time, Thomas was a schoolteacher in Kansas with a head for business. He owned a house in Leavenworth City worth $100 (though he bragged he'd only paid $85) and a mule for working his small farm, with the substantial sum of $150 left over "to speculate with."[34] As Cabaniss remarked—perhaps with a sigh of relief—he was the only member of the Townsend family who had "not at any time shown any disposition to complain of me."[35] Thomas was exactly what Cabaniss needed in an agent.

And Cabaniss's trust was exactly what Thomas needed to get ahead.

———◆———

Thomas Townsend began his teaching career sometime during the Civil War. Relocating to Leavenworth after Wilberforce University closed in 1862, the young man found himself at the center of Union Army mobilization in Kansas. Between 1864 and 1865 alone, more than two hundred Black soldiers enlisted at the Leavenworth recruitment center, and "soldiering" was the most common occupation for African American men across the state.[36] Advertisements in city papers touted military service as a moral duty, a means of advancement, a way for free Black people and former slaves to prove their worth to a bigoted nation—and, in the words of a local Black leader, an opportunity to "thrash" the white southerners who sought to keep them down.[37] "NO COMPROMISE WITH TRAITORS," the Leavenworth *Daily Conservative* blasted in block letters: "FREEDOM FOR ALL."[38] Back in Xenia, Thomas's half-brother Charles Osborne took up the cause and joined the Union Army in 1865. A year before, General Townsend, brother of Wesley's first wife Jane, had taken advantage of wartime chaos to flee enslavement on the Mullens Place plantation to Union-occupied Huntsville, where he enlisted as an infantry soldier.[39] Thomas, however, had a different idea of how to serve his community.

Thomas had only spent a year and a half at Wilberforce, but he could read and write; he had studied "mental arithmetic, written arithmetic," geography, American history, world history, grammar, and composition; he had read speeches by Cicero, George Washington, and Napoleon.[40] It was more than enough to satisfy the former slaves who flocked to Kansas during and after the Civil War, eager for an education. So Thomas peddled his literacy and elocution from town to town, an itinerant teacher in high demand. One year after the war ended, he was nearly overwhelmed by requests to establish schools for Black communities in eastern Kansas as freedpeople in Atchison, Leavenworth, and Washena all clamored for his services.[41] "I am called on very often by the constituents to constitute a school," he told Cabaniss, though a lingering case of pneumonia made the work difficult.[42] He also faced a new source of competition: "Yankee teachers" and reformers who had flooded the region, causing "wages to dwindle to little or nothing."[43] By 1868, Thomas had grown disillusioned with the life of a schoolteacher. Perhaps he could have accepted the low pay and unpleasant working conditions, but he found tedium of teaching "augmented tenfold by the stupid pupils."[44] Or at least, that's what he told Cabaniss.

Reading, writing, and arithmetic weren't the only subjects Thomas had studied in the years since his emancipation. He had seen how Wesley lost the lawyer's good opinion, drinking, gambling, "borrowing" Jane's, Martha's, and his mother's money and running off with another woman.[45] He had witnessed his cousin Woodson thrown in jail for a crime he didn't commit, abandoned by a local Black community that resented his contempt for them and by Cabaniss for his "offensive" and "insulting" letters.[46] He remembered, viscerally, the fear and anxiety the Townsends had felt when the outbreak of war cut them off from the inheritance they had been counting on to survive. "My Dear Sir, to be turned out in the cold and friendless world without a penny to gain a livelihood," he remarked in a letter to Cabaniss, "is far from being pleasant to anyone."[47] The federal government's apparent commitment to freedpeople's rights after the Civil War had emboldened Thomas's family to openly challenge Cabaniss, both in their correspondence and in court. But Cabaniss was still executor and in control of Samuel Townsend's estate. Prudent and perceptive, Thomas recognized that gaining, and keeping, the lawyer's confidence was essential to his future success. If Cabaniss was telling the truth about the estate—that it might be entangled in lawsuits for years, worth only a fraction of its pre-war value—the white ex-Confederate's good opinion might be the most valuable asset Thomas possessed. The shrewd Kansas schoolteacher knew exactly how to get it, too.

"Now Mr Cabaniss I have <u>never</u> doubted your integrity, your ability to transact the most difficult matters pertaining to Law or the estate; never doubted <u>once</u> that you have acted otherwise than a perfect gentleman or a skillful administrator," Thomas wrote in 1867.[48] Appealing to Cabaniss's sense of honor and duty had served other members of the Townsend family well. In her letters from New Richmond, Susanna's requests for financial assistance followed praise for Cabaniss having "favored me like a gentleman."[49] Samuel's daughter Milcha, who had taken part in religious revivals at Wilberforce, wrote Cabaniss that "I thank the all mighty God for employing such an honest man as you are for our agent"—although waiting for her inheritance required "patience like Job."[50] Martha Townsend, one of the legatees of the second class, conjured up the ghost of the late Samuel Townsend as a model for Cabaniss. "I do hope that you will not disappoint me," she wrote the former slave-owner. After all, "Old master would not have permitted it, and <u>he</u> trusted you, and the gentleman of the South do not betray a trust."[51]

With elegant penmanship and an expressive vocabulary, Thomas—unlike Willis and Elvira—soothed Cabaniss's bruised ego. He also played on the lawyer's prejudices, ridiculing white northerners alongside his own "stupid" free Black students. Discussing his landholdings in Leavenworth, Thomas commented that he'd like to purchase some additional property in the city, "if I can stuff any Reason in the Yankees cranium."[52] He even seemed to empathize with white Alabama planters' financial difficulties and resentment of northern "carpetbaggers" setting up shop in the occupied South. As Thomas wryly observed: "I am aware of the injury in some element that war has done property Holders in the South," and, accordingly, "the blessing it has bestowed

upon the North—on Northern property-holders."[53] He was a reliable correspondent, sending Cabaniss detailed letters about members of the Townsend
family: who had married whom, who lived where, who was sick or dead or
"hard-up" for money.[54] And he never failed to promote himself as a man just a
cut above the great mass of freedpeople. They were "honest and industrious,"
true, but also "indigent"—not like Thomas, the teacher and landowner.[55] He
was a respectable citizen, a sympathetic ear. He could be trusted with information about the estate.

For his part, Cabaniss agreed. "I will be glad to hear from you frequently,"
the lawyer wrote Thomas in 1866.[56] Cabaniss quickly made him his go-between, pleading with him to talk to "those of your family who are inclined to
indulge in such illiberal suspicions and who seem determined not to believe
what I have taken so much pains to explain touching the condition of the
Estate."[57] On at least one occasion, the lawyer referred colleagues in Kansas to
Thomas when they needed assistance dealing with the Townsends. "I believe
you know Dan Stone," Cabaniss said, referring to Caroline's husband. "Please
tell him to get Thomas Townsend to call & see you."[58] Cabaniss wanted Thomas
to tell his agents "which of the legatees are in the most imminent danger of
suffering" so that he knew whose disbursements to prioritize. Thomas, always
a useful source of information, could get the job done—and, most important, be relied upon "not to mention" his purpose to his relatives. Trusting
Thomas's judgment and discretion, Cabaniss sent him financial details about
the estate that he had never shared with another Townsend. "On <u>one</u> day I received notice of the bankruptcy of parties who owed the Estate about fifty
thousand dollars," he wrote in 1868, "and since then many other debtors have
taken the benefit of the law." Cabaniss's letters to Thomas lacked the condescension so evident in his correspondence with other Townsends. He wrote
the young, mixed-race schoolteacher with the same matter-of-factness that he
wrote his white business partners and, as with his white colleagues, shared the
same complaints about Alabama's financial troubles and "dense and ignorant
colored population."[59] If the ex-Confederate, ex-slaveholder Cabaniss was capable of seeing any African American man as his equal, Thomas Townsend
was that man.

Thomas took full advantage of the lawyer's trust. He was the only Townsend
who dared offer advice about the estate, and Cabaniss quickly realized that
Thomas's insight could be profitable. After the Civil War, R. S. Rust—the
former president of Wilberforce University—claimed that the Townsend estate still owed around $1,500 for the children's room, board, and tuition in
Ohio.[60] To Thomas, the number seemed outrageously high. "Every scholar

from the South had to work," he told Cabaniss. He, Willis, and Charles
Osborne had all chopped wood and tended cornfields to purchase clothes
and offset their expenses, a fact that he said "can be substantiated by every
student of Wilberforce." The Yankee Rust, Thomas hinted, was taking advantage of Cabaniss. "R. S. Rust indeed ceased to be a friend to us shortly after
funds ceased arriving from South," he noted, and "now that the war is over
he presents some larger bill without thinking." Thomas believed Rust's claim
was "too large by a third," and indeed, Cabaniss ultimately settled the bill for
$941.26.[61] Thomas had ideas for how to deal with the estate's other creditors
too. Perhaps, he proposed, Cabaniss could divide Samuel's land among the
legatees rather than attempt to resell it for cash. The estate's remaining debts
didn't deter him; Thomas felt confident that "each man or heir" would be able
to pay back whatever money was owed once they had farmland of their own.
Or at least, Thomas felt confident that he could. When he recommended that
Cabaniss "let all who are of age and capable of managing their business take
immediate possession of the land assigned them," there's no doubt he meant
himself.[62]

But Thomas acted as an advocate for his family just as often. The Townsends
trusted him to present their needs to the lawyer in Alabama and respected his
opinion. Often, they simply wanted information. Samuel Townsend had freed
a specific group of forty-five enslaved people: his concubines, his children,
their half-siblings, his children's sexual partners, and his brother Edmund's
daughters. Each of those forty-five left friends and family members behind
in Alabama—more than one hundred other enslaved people to be sold and
separated with the rest of Samuel's property. Lizzie, Jennie, and Woodson's
brother Armstead hadn't been freed with his siblings; Wesley's first wife Jane
had left her elderly parents, three brothers, and two sisters; Dick's daughter
Frances was still in Alabama, as was Martha's daughter Emeline and Peggy's
son Barney. With the end of slavery, the Townsends wanted to know what
had happened to the family they left behind. Thomas sent their inquiries and
carried Cabaniss's messages back, the bearer of good, bad, and bittersweet
news. Armstead was in Whitesburg, Alabama, working for a Mr. Hobbs.[63]
Frances was still living in Madison County, a mother of several children.[64]
Willis had family he hadn't known existed—a "very good looking child" who
"favors the Townsend family very much," by a woman named Leana who
had lived on a neighboring plantation.[65] Emeline was living with Mr. and
Mrs. Higginbotham, a white couple who had overseen the Home Place after
Samuel's death. The girl was "in fine health," "happy & contented," the lawyer
said; she had been so young in 1860 that Cabaniss believed she had forgotten

her mother entirely.[66] Lizzy Perryman—the mother of Edmund's two daughters, sold away from her children in 1850—was alive in west Tennessee.[67] And Barney, Peggy learned, was dead.[68]

Holding both Cabaniss's and his relatives' trust, Thomas had become the family ambassador and clearinghouse for information from Alabama. But maintaining this position was a balancing act, and Thomas remained ever careful to present himself to Cabaniss as a man worthy of trust, a paragon of industry and moral rectitude. He praised Milcha's efforts to elevate herself by marrying "a very industrious carpenter, destitute of bad habits, in short a respectable citizen" who was "a step above poverty."[69] Of all his siblings, Milcha seemed most committed to the racial uplift ideology inculcated at Wilberforce, enjoining Cabaniss to "tell the collored people" she'd known in Alabama "to strive to do right and work and try to live as people ought to."[70] Thomas mourned the death of his half-brother Bradford, who had been "a pious Christian, ever faithful to the precepts of God and the admonitions of teachers and friends."[71] Other members of the Townsend family, however, failed to live up to these respectable norms. Parthenia had "got to cutting up and running with bad girls" during the war, and had become "so completely recless and destitute of consistency, that she has gone with strangers (probably to have a better access to her malicious designs) rather than remain with her Aunt Rainey" in Leavenworth.[72] She could be "reserved from ruin," Thomas supposed, but only if "placed under a proper jurisdiction." Ironically, Thomas had begun to exert the same kind of paternalistic control over the Townsend women that Cabaniss had once exercised over all the legatees. His concern, however, was less for Parthenia's well-being than for the opinion of Cabaniss. "All these dark actions," Thomas wrote, "of course cast gloomy reflection upon her Relatives."[73]

Yet Thomas did have a soft spot for his sister Elvira. Most of Samuel Townsend's children seemed closer to each other than to their half-siblings on their mothers' sides—Charles Osborne considered Willis, Thomas, and Wesley more his brothers than his mother's son William Austin, and Milcha bonded most with Bradford, born just a few months before her. But Thomas loved Elvira best. Four or five years older than her half-brother, Elvira was Hannah's eldest living child, the daughter of one of Samuel's concubines and may have been his concubine herself by age seventeen. To Wesley she was a "torment," challenging his authority and demanding control of her own inheritance. To Cabaniss's agent Lakin she was a troublemaker like her husband Woodson, "stubborn," passionate, and irritatingly assertive.[74] Elvira never conformed to the decorous behavior that Cabaniss—and later

Thomas—expected from the Townsend women. After divorcing Woodson, she married a man named William Clay, a laborer who worked as a coal miner in Memphis for a time before moving to St. Louis, Missouri.[75] Clay wasn't a "respectable" tradesman like Milcha's husband, and when Elvira fell seriously ill in July 1867 he abandoned her. Elvira claimed Clay had died, but as Thomas remarked, "it would not astound me to cross him some day."[76] Yet Thomas protected Elvira's reputation, never criticizing her in his letters to Cabaniss. When Parthenia began associating with "bad girls," Thomas lambasted her behavior and advised that the lawyer only send her money "a little at a time." When Elvira conceived a child out of wedlock in 1866, however, Thomas described her condition delicately ("she will be sick" soon) and passed along her request for financial assistance without comment.[77] Then, the next year, when he heard the news about Elvira's illness and questionably "deceased husband," he relocated to St. Louis.

Thomas spared no expense, employing five or more physicians who spent months "trying or experimenting their physical skill" on his sister. "But alas!" he mourned, "who can arrest the Grim monster death who has never been known to falter in the discharge of apparently relentless duties?"[78] He marked the hour of Elvira's death: just past four in the afternoon, February 22, 1868. He told Cabaniss that he didn't know the cause of Elvira's illness, "deeming it unbecoming to enquire further"—but after six months and five doctors, he must have had some sense of how his favorite sister died. More likely, he was guarding her reputation again. Elvira's out-of-wedlock pregnancy in 1866 had ended in miscarriage after a series of complications; perhaps she had conceived William Clay's child before he left her and suffered similar complications, this time fatal.[79] Whatever the cause, this was information Cabaniss didn't need to know, and, just once, Thomas bent his exacting standards. Perhaps he believed Elvira had suffered more under slavery than his other sisters. He may have seen her abused by his own father when she was a teenager. Thomas couldn't do anything for Elvira then, but he could at least give her dignity in death.

Thomas returned to Leavenworth with Elvira's daughters Sarah and Elizabeth in March 1868, placing them in their grandmother Hannah's care.[80] "Who has not earnestly yearned to be at home after an absence?" he wrote Cabaniss.[81] But with Elvira gone, and the life of a schoolteacher wearing on him, Kansas didn't feel like home anymore. Like Charles Osborne, who had struck out for Colorado Territory two years earlier, Thomas was ready to move on—and he knew exactly where he wanted to go. In 1866, Cabaniss had suggested to Thomas that the Townsends appoint "some intelligent and honest man to visit Huntsville" and report back on the estate, seeing as so many members of the family had clearly lost faith in him. "Would you ask them," the lawyer wrote, "whom they would like to have in my place"?[82] Considering Cabaniss's opinions of freedpeople's intelligence and honesty, he probably expected the Townsends to select another white man as their agent. But Thomas saw himself as the "intelligent and honest man" the family needed to look after their interests. He had convinced Cabaniss of it. In Alabama, he would convince the rest of Madison County too.

———

The men on horseback wore disguises: black and red gowns that brushed their toes, conical paper hats eighteen inches tall, and cloth masks with holes for the eyes.[83] Some of them displayed black devils' horns on their foreheads; others spoke through mouthpieces that distorted their voices. "They said they came from hell," one witness reported, "that they died at Shiloh fight and Bull Run."[84] Looking diabolical in their robes and masks, the lost souls usually visited around midnight, circling their victims' houses and whistling for them to come out or, if that failed, firing a pistol through the window. In Madison County, they raided Black families' homes for weapons and cash, taking "old blunderbusses," revolvers, and whatever money the freedpeople had managed to save.[85] They often targeted Black soldiers, men who had fought on the Union side and "talked too much."[86] Other times, the victims simply had something they wanted—like Joseph Gill, a farm laborer with a horse they considered too good for a former slave. "They said they wanted him for a charger to ride to hell," Gill said, but he knew better than that.[87] This was no host of damned Confederate martyrs. This was Madison County's Ku Klux Klan, and when they left Gill with two hundred lashes on his back and a bullet in his dog one night in 1868, they didn't ride to the underworld. They took the old Fayetteville road to Parks Townsend's farm in Hazel Green.

Men like Edmund and Samuel Townsend had once ruled northern Alabama, their wealth and influence placing them at the top of the social order—and granting them power to brutalize the enslaved population with impunity. Parks Townsend's father had been present the day in 1848 when Edmund led a posse to a neighboring plantation and ordered an enslaved man whipped to the bone.[88] Two decades later, "Young Park," as the locals called him, rode at the head of mob of his own, twenty-odd masked men terrorizing the former slaves who had made his family's fortune. Joseph Gill, born a slave, had labored on Parks and his mother's farm just the year before.[89] A new form of the old slave patrols, Klansmen across the South broke up freedpeople's election meetings and attacked Black schools and churches. They threatened, beat, and murdered—anything to disrupt the mobilization or empowerment of Black communities. They targeted Union veterans, Freedmen's Bureau agents, Republican officeholders, farmers, teachers, tenants, or any African American with a modicum of self-sufficiency. Like Parks, they were the sons of once-great slaveholders, soured by the planter aristocracy's fall; they were bankrupted white farmers, resentful of competition from a free Black labor force; they were ex-Confederate soldiers, enraged by the sight of Black men at the polls. In central Alabama's Black Belt and other regions where freedpeople made up large majorities and could better defend themselves, vigilante attacks were less common. But in northern Alabama, with its smaller, more dispersed Black population, the Ku Klux Klan waged a war of violence and terror without restraint.[90]

Peyton Lipscomb, a Black Union Army veteran, was whipped and shot in the arm for playing his banjo at a white family's house. "They said the laws of the country didn't allow Black and white to mix together," Lipscomb recalled. They had targeted him at his last home in Tennessee as well, whipping him for voting: "They said I had voted on the North side," and "if I could not vote on the other side, I must not vote at all." Lipscomb hadn't cast a ballot since, and when asked if any other freedpeople in his Madison County neighborhood voted he said no, "none of them."[91] James M. Moss, a landowner who considered it a point of pride to be the only white Republican in his precinct, faced death threats from local Klan members. "There is that old Yankee Moss that voted for Grant out in Meridian," he heard a man say once, "and he won't live more than six weeks." The Klan targeted Moss's farm laborers too, looping a noose around one freedman's neck, tossing the rope over a tree branch, and threatening to hang him if he voted anything but the Democratic ticket.[92] Joseph Gill fled to Arkansas after Young Parks and his gang of horse thieves visited his house. "They told me if I didn't leave they would take my life." Nevertheless, Gill was defiant. Despite the violence against freedpeople like himself, he said "a great many voted" Republican anyway.[93] But overall, Madison County's Klan was emboldened, and other victims weren't so lucky. As James Moss reported, Parks Townsend and his friends "had a little more spite against negroes who had been in the Union Army" than even other Klan members. On Parks Townsend's farm in 1868, he recalled, "they killed three in open daylight."[94]

If the climate of racial violence in Madison County frightened Thomas when he planned his move in December 1868, he never let on. Nor did Cabaniss seem to think he would encounter any trouble when he arrived.

The lawyer's letters were straightforward, businesslike, addressing the logistics of travel and possible employment opportunities in Huntsville. "I don't think you will find much difficulty in getting into business of some kind here," he wrote, and "you will have no trouble finding the way from Memphis." Cabaniss's letters exuded confidence in the young teacher's abilities, and he was quick to offer help should Thomas need it. Before Thomas even boarded the steamboat for St. Louis—and from there another steamer to Memphis, and finally the twelve-hour train to Huntsville—Cabaniss had already made arrangements with the owner of a "grocery establishment" half a mile from his office "to give you such employment as will pay your expenses until you can look around and see what will be best for you to do." The lawyer also had connections at the Freedman's Savings Bank in Huntsville, with a line on a position for Thomas as a clerk. "I dont think you will have any difficulty in getting employment as a teacher" in the long term, Cabaniss wrote, "and you can doubtless get better wages here for teaching than you could in Kansas," but there was no harm in finding temporary work while he considered his options.[95]

Little wonder Thomas didn't quaver at the thought of returning to the dangerous, violence-ridden state his brother Charles Osborne swore he would never set foot in again. Thomas had S. D. Cabaniss, a respected attorney from one of Huntsville's founding families, vouching for him to friends and colleagues. He had leveraged the lawyer's good will into access to the highest echelons of Madison County society—but that wasn't the only reason he had chosen Madison County. "Townsend" was still a recognizable name in northern Alabama. Samuel C. Townsend's widow Virginia owned several thousand acres in the county, with a farm worth $15,000 even after the war.[96] Her brother-in-law Parks S. Townsend and his wife lived nearby on another large, equally valuable farm.[97] Virginia's son Young Parks, of course, was notorious as a local Klan leader. As the "old Yankee" James Moss noted, Madison County was a place where family ties were close and family memory was long. "You see the people have lived a long time together and married in together, and you can hardly say 'booh!' to a man anywhere but you are talking to some of his relatives," he explained—"and of course they have a great many grudges, grudges between old residents."[98] Here, Thomas Townsend's ancestry and history would have been known to everyone. Perhaps that was part of the appeal. The news would spread quickly: Samuel Townsend's mixed-race son, the enslaved boy who had inherited a piece of the fortune all his white relatives had coveted, was back. Some, like the younger Parks (Thomas's first cousin once removed), would probably be furious. But by the way he presented himself, the work he practiced, and the connections he cultivated, Thomas could ensure his position among the eminent men of the county. By the time he was done, no one would call Thomas Townsend Samuel's slave. He would be rightly known as Samuel's heir.

He started modestly, with forty-eight acres of farmland in Limestone County, about twenty miles east of Huntsville. He grew corn primarily but raised livestock as well: two oxen for plowing the fields, one horse, one mule, one milk cow, and a small herd of twelve hogs. In 1870, he calculated the farm was worth $500 and the livestock $700—nothing special for the state, where farm sizes still averaged more than two hundred acres, but a fortune compared to most freedpeople's finances.[99] One Greensboro newspaper speculated that would-be farmers needed at least $100 in capital to make a successful start, but in 1870, only 20 percent of Alabama's Black households could muster even $50. Though land ownership had been a top priority for Black southerners since the end of the Civil War, just 4 percent of African American families in Alabama owned any real estate whatsoever.[100] The majority of freedpeople worked as tenant farmers and sharecroppers, laboring on rented lands in exchange for a portion of the final crop. The system was far from ideal—and increasingly left tenants severely indebted to landlords for supplies—but Black families largely preferred sharecropping to working directly under white overseers, as they had while enslaved.[101] Impoverished planters benefited too. In postwar Alabama, where many landowners lacked sufficient currency to pay laborers in cash or coin, sharecropping stabilized the agricultural economy without the need for traditional wages.[102] Thomas Townsend, however, broke the mold. With money saved from earlier disbursements from his father's estate, he had purchased a farm of his own. After one year in Alabama, he had increased his net worth to more than $1,200. When Thomas paid his laborers their wages at the end of the year, he paid in cash.[103]

In early 1871, Thomas returned to Madison County and the plantations where he and his family had been enslaved. Empowered by new court orders allowing him to resell Samuel Townsend's lands, Cabaniss was putting the long-dead cotton king's plantations up for auction again. Cabaniss's son Charles and the executor's ex-law firm partner L. P. Walker purchased some property, as did James Robinson, the lawyer Edmund Townsend had once hired to defend his son Woodson against a criminal charge. Thomas Townsend joined the leading lights of the Huntsville bar at the courthouse auction, and his money was as good as theirs. With $270 in hand, Thomas purchased one-third interest in the plantation his father had called the "Aminett" or "Ammoneth" Place, formerly the home of thirteen slaves who had been sold for nearly $10,000 after Samuel's death. He hadn't made the purchase for himself. General Townsend and his younger brother Shadrach wanted the Ammoneth Place, and while they couldn't have afforded 270 acres of prime farming land alone, Thomas had the capital to assist them. The three men went in on the purchase together—General and Shadrach each paying half of their portion of the asking price, and Thomas the full $270 for his third. Then, Thomas signed over his share to the brothers. "Shadrach and General Townsend are men of industrious habits," Cabaniss wrote to justify the sale to the Chancery Court, and "the lands purchased by them constitute an ample security for the balance of the purchase money due upon them."[104] Thomas vouching for them couldn't have hurt either. The purchase was symbolically significant, putting a piece of Samuel Townsend's land in the hands of his ex-slaves for the first time. It was also tragically ironic: the money from his inheritance that Thomas used to purchase the land derived largely from the pre-war sale of other enslaved people who had lived and worked on that plantation. Land ownership—the unfulfilled dream of so many freedpeople in the South—was possible for the Townsends because their father had owned human property. Nevertheless, the purchase gave General and Shadrach some of the economic security that Thomas and his siblings enjoyed as Samuel's beneficiaries. Shadrach (or "Mr. Shach Townsend," as he would be known by the 1890s) would go on to own 225 acres in Hazel Green and provide, as one local newspaper noted, "a worthy example" to other Black farmers.[105] In addition, the transaction signaled Thomas's willingness to use his money, good name, and links to local white elites to support Madison County's freedpeople.

Thomas had all the traits of a typical Black community leader of the Reconstruction era. Though "mulattoes" comprised less than 10 percent of Alabama's total Black population at the time, nearly half of the state's leading African American activists and elected officials during Reconstruction had mixed-race ancestry.[106] More than one third had either been born free or manumitted before the Civil War. Teachers, preachers, business owners, and skilled tradesmen filled their ranks. Thomas—an educated, mixed-race landowner freed in 1860—met every requirement. In 1869, with funding from the Freedmen's Bureau, he established a school for African American children in rural northern Alabama.[107] Along with one assistant, he taught a class of one hundred to 160 pupils for five and a half hours each day. He served as an agent of Huntsville's branch of the Freedman's Savings and Trust Company Bank, chartered by Congress in 1865, and convinced General, Shadrach, and their brother Spencer, along with his own half-brothers Wesley and Charles Osborne Townsend, to deposit their savings in order to finance mortgages and buy land.[108] When the bank collapsed in 1874, losing $57 million in freedpeople's deposits, he volunteered as an accountant and representative for Huntsville's "industrious laborers who lost their little earnings" in seeking relief from Congress.[109] He continued to purchase property in Madison County, once even from the younger Parks Townsend's mother, Virginia Townsend.[110] In the 1870s, Thomas became something of a community banker, buying mortgages from hard-pressed Black farmers and business owners in need of a loan, giving them better terms than they would have gotten elsewhere.[111] He favored strivers like himself: a "mulatto" gardener named Alfred Clay and the middle-aged blacksmith Ivey Beard, for example, struggling members of what one historian has called the Black "aspiring class."[112] It does not appear that Thomas ever received formal legal training, but he had spent years studying the litigation over his own inheritance, and he knew how to maneuver in white society. Employing this acquired knowledge as well as his own shrewd business insights, he administered the estates of Black Huntsville residents looking to buy or sell property, and he assisted some Civil War veterans to claim pensions from the federal government.[113]

As a community leader, Thomas preached industry, morality, and hard work—the middle-class values he believed would earn African Americans the respect and acceptance of white society. The *Huntsville Gazette*, a newspaper he helped establish in 1879, provided an outlet for these racial uplift ideals.[114] Distributed throughout Alabama, Tennessee, and even distant Niagara Falls, "The People's Paper" declared its commitment to "equal rights and fair play for all men in the race of life."[115] Its staff—including Thomas, who served as a writer, treasurer, and member of the paper's board of directors—would advocate "civil and political rights" not as a favor granted by whites, but as "a simple act of justice."[116] They would promote "an equal chance" for African Americans in "the world of science, literature, art, commerce, and the affairs of life generally" as their "high Christian duty." Someday, they declared, "broadened and enlightened opinion shall completely liberate the Negro from the wrongs inflicted by prejudices."[117] But until then, they would have to prove their merit if they wanted to rise in the world, advising "The road of work; the path of virtue."[118]

The *Gazette* championed education as a key strategy for advancement, but good schools were hard to find in 1880s Alabama. The state's 1875 constitution had established a public school system—one of Black Alabamians' chief victories during Reconstruction—and though the law prescribed a segregated educational system, it also mandated equal funding for Black and white schools. Nevertheless, state funding was rarely enough. Northern states provided five times more money for public schools than southern states, and local school districts didn't always adhere to the law.[119] Only 10 percent of Black children attended school in Alabama, compared to more than 30 percent of white children.[120] African American teachers earned smaller salaries, with Black women earning the least of all, and as a result of inadequate funding Black schools often ran for significantly shorter terms.[121] As the *Gazette* lamented: "What is needed by the people is a public school system which will give the poor children nine months schooling in a year instead of three."[122] The US Congress's "Blair Bill," which would have distributed federal funds to state schools based on each state's illiteracy rate, seemed like a promising solution to the *Gazette,* as well as to Black and white teachers across the South. But southern politicians—suspicious of centralized government power and contemptuous of federal aid to African Americans—defeated the legislation four times between 1881 and 1890. It was yet another form of "the old hallucination, 'fifty acres and a mule,'" one former slaveholder remarked and, in the end, just as empty a promise.[123]

In response, Huntsville's Black leaders pushed for vocational training instead of a traditional liberal arts education. In 1882, Thomas Townsend sat on a committee "for the purposes of establishing an industrial College in or near the city of Huntsville, for the benefit of our rising youth."[124] Support for industrial education was in the air. Booker T. Washington—the African American educator who would become the most famous exponent of a vision of racial progress through economic advancement—founded his Tuskegee Institute in southern Alabama that same year. Like Tuskegee, which instructed students in "farm work, brick making, carpentry, printing, and sewing," the proposed industrial school in Huntsville would train tradesmen, not teachers and preachers.[125] In the past, the *Gazette* noted, African American students could follow two narrow paths after graduation: "the teachers' desk or the pulpit," or "a menial position or farming." With vocational training, graduates could enter new fields, earning higher wages as skilled laborers while decreasing the competition for aspiring teachers and clergymen. "Comfortable homes" and "ease of mind" would flow from this increased prosperity.[126] For the *Gazette*, economic advancement was just as important as the moral and intellectual kind.

In an 1882 editorial, William H. Gaston, a clergyman and teacher who sat on the industrial college committee with Thomas Townsend, asked Huntsville's Black residents "what have we in North Alabama, done for ourselves?"[127] Yes, "there has been a great deal done to promote the elevation, education, and moral culture of our people," he said, but money mattered too. According to Gaston, Alabama's Black population had "nearly as many among us who own real estate as in any other State, in the South," and Huntsville could lead the way putting that wealth to use. "Let us develop a prosperity among ourselves," he declared.[128] After all, as the *Gazette* stated, "It does not appear that anything is so much needed now among us as monied men and institutions."[129] With more of these "monied men," Huntsville's Black community could establish schools and other institutions without needing to depend on government agencies or white philanthropists—and their self-sufficiency would earn respect from Huntsville's "better class of people."[130] For the *Gazette*, Thomas Townsend embodied this combination of success and social consciousness; he was a man who demonstrated all that wealthy African Americans could contribute to the city. When he purchased stock in the Nashville and North Alabama Railroad Company, it was more than a personal financial decision: Thomas was demonstrating African Americans' "willingness to aid in any enterprise for the upbuilding of the country."[131] Once the spokesman and representative for his family to S. D. Cabaniss, Thomas—"one of our leading business men and property holders"—had become a representative of Huntsville's Black community to the white power structure.[132] In 1880, he decided to make it official.

T. W. Townsend, as he was known in professional circles, chose a peculiar time to run for political office. In 1880, when he and mixed-race plasterer Nelson Hendley were elected Huntsville's first African American city aldermen, Alabama's state government had already been under the control of white Democrats for six years.[133] Although the end of Reconstruction is often marked by President Rutherford B. Hayes's withdrawal of US Army troops from southern states in 1877, Alabama's Reconstruction period actually ended three years earlier, in 1874.[134] After a federal investigation into Klan violence in 1871 and 1872, Congress had authorized then-president Ulysses S. Grant to declare martial law and quell the violence.[135] As a result, the Ku Klux Klan disbanded and Black voters—protected by federal troops at the polls—swept Republicans into state office in 1872. Determined to "redeem" their state, white Democrats regrouped. So when Wall Street crashed in 1873, when heavy flooding in the Black Belt drowned entire farms, when Alabama and the nation plunged into financial crisis, they blamed the disasters on Reconstruction.[136] In 1874, many of Alabama's white Republicans voted alongside ex-Confederates to reinstate white rule.[137] Over the next several years, every state in the former Confederacy would be "redeemed" by conservative Democratic governments. The new leaders called themselves "Bourbons," a reference to the Bourbon kings of the French monarchy; overthrown during the French Revolution, they had returned to power after the fall of Napoleon. In the American South of the 1870s, the planter aristocracy ruled once more.

African Americans knew exactly what this meant. "The democratic party is nothing more than a secret society to keep down the Negroes," Atlanta's *Weekly Defiance*, quoted in the Huntsville *Gazette*, would later seethe, "and the passwords are, never let the nigger rise."[138] Alabama Democrats had learned from their interregnum. Back in power, they adopted a subtler strategy than the outright racist terrorism of the late 1860s. They gerrymandered congressional districts to break up Black majorities, brought in white supporters from along the Georgia border to pad the ballot box with Democratic votes, and bought up voter registration certificates from African American men for a tempting $2 each.[139] *Gazette* contributors did what they could to warn Black voters against white southerners' machinations. "They will advise you not to vote at all," a correspondent wrote in a letter to the editor. "You will be offered work on election day with promise of double pay, to keep you away from the polls and cheat you out of your vote." They might even "threaten to refuse to rent land" to any who voted against the Democrats. He ended on a dire note: "If I had ever been a slave, I should hate the name of Bourbon Democrat."[140] But no letter to the editor, however passionate, could circumvent Alabama's 1879 election law. Under the guise of preventing election fraud, the state legislature established strict criteria for what constituted a valid ballot: "a plain piece of white paper, without any figures, marks, rulings, characters or embellishment thereon, not less than two nor more than two and one-half inches wide, and not less than five nor more than seven inches long."[141] Under the law, white officials at polling places could throw out any ballot cast for a Republican candidate—they only had to claim it didn't conform to the state's new requirements.

To maintain a foothold in politics and avoid total disenfranchisement, Black leaders practiced pragmatism. In 1874, Alabama Republicans triaged their fight for "social equality enforced by law," accepting instead a platform that favored segregation in schools and public facilities.[142] Others abandoned the party of Lincoln altogether. Former slave William Hooper Councill—Alabama's most prominent African American educator at the time—endorsed the 1874 Democratic candidate for governor in exchange for a position as the head of Huntsville's new public school.[143] "Coalition" became the byword of the 1880s, as African Americans formed shifting biracial partnerships with white Independents, Greenbackers, and the occasional disaffected Democrat.[144] Northern Alabama's hill country, home to a large number of poor and working-class whites who had long resented the wealthy planter class, had been the state's Unionist stronghold during the war.[145] In the 1880s, they were the most likely white Alabamians to vote a "fusion" or independent ticket. These fragile alliances focused on issues with broad working-class appeal: better schools, fair election laws, and an end to the state's notorious convict leasing program, which hired out prisoners to factories and coal mining companies. Convict leasing, which provided large corporations with an unpaid labor force that couldn't strike or unionize, was just as unpopular among white laborers as among African Americans.[146] White Greenbacker David D. Shelby, son of a former slave owner and attorney for the Townsends in their lawsuit against S. D. Cabaniss, made direct appeals to Black voters in the pages of the *Gazette*.[147] Running for state senator in 1882, he promised to fight for "liberal appropriations for the public schools," condemned the state's violation of "the sacred and constitutional right of suffrage," and denounced convict leasing, "which, for trifling misdemeanors, imposes a slavery worse than death."[148] The strategy worked. Shelby won his senate seat in an election that flipped fourteen northern Alabama counties, including Madison, from Democrat to Independent. In Huntsville, the *Gazette* declared "VICTORY" in bold block letters.[149] Though Huntsville's sole Black newspaper still called itself the "leading Republican journal in Alabama," its editors added a caveat: though they would always adhere to "Republican principles," they couldn't ignore "the political conditions in Alabama."[150] These days, the paper declared, "no party need take as a matter of course the Negro will vote the Republican ticket."[151]

The message was clear: Alabama whites could use the state's large Black population for votes in exchange for certain limited reforms. As for the diehard Republicans who refused to join the coalition, they would just have to "join in holy wedlock" with white Independents if Huntsville's Black citizens were to retain any influence whatsoever.[152] Forging successful alliances across the color line in post-Reconstruction Alabama, however, was never easy. It took a particular type of Black man to court white elites—someone white and Black Americans alike would come to call the "Best Man."[153] The Best Man was educated, successful, and moral; he accepted mainstream, bourgeois ideals of hard work, self-improvement, and propriety; and, if he wanted to hold political office, he needed to be willing to work with local whites.[154] It was a virtually impossible set of criteria to fulfill, designed to give the illusion of a merit-based society. Not every man considered a Best

Man by his communities embraced the burden the role carried. In 1883, the *Gazette* described an Alabama clergyman nominated to a district convention as "the best man" for the job. Hesitant to accept the title, he said "he did not wish too much to be expected of him."[155] But in a state dominated by white leaders who, even if they weren't Democrats, shared the same racial prejudices, striving to meet the standards of the irreproachable Best Man was one of the only ways for African Americans to exercise political power. Thomas Townsend, who possessed a net worth of $4,000 in 1880 as well as a priceless rapport with some of the city's principal white men, joined a minuscule number of Black Huntsville leaders who fit the bill. When he took his seat on the board of aldermen in 1880, Huntsville's mayor appointed him to the committees on weights and measures, the fire department, and education. Huntsville was willing to have an African American man on the city board, but it was Thomas's "high moral character and intelligence" that won him their acceptance, one local historian wrote.[156] Retaining it, however, was a never-ending challenge.

Take Nelson Hendley, the alderman for Huntsville's Fourth Ward. At a rowdy assembly in 1882, attendees—a "miscellaneous" crowd "thoroughly mixed in shades of opinion and shades of skin"—clashed over the independent ticket's candidates for the upcoming municipal election. Tongue in cheek, a *Gazette* reporter present at the meeting compared this "opening skirmish" in the election cycle to the battle of Bull Run. Voters had gathered at the city courthouse to discuss "the fitness of the selection of some of the proposed candidates"— Hendley in particular. In a move that drew anger and "vigorous" criticism from the alderman's friends, coalition leaders had removed the incumbent alderman Hendley's name from the ticket that year.[157] Perhaps when they questioned his "fitness" they meant his race, bowing to pressure from local whites who objected to a Black man's presence on the ballot. (When one attendee suggested adding "a third colored Alderman" to the ticket, the proposal gained little traction.) Perhaps it was a matter of social status. Hendley was a tradesman who may not have been able to read or write, and he lived in the working-class Fourth Ward, at times maligned by whites as the home of the city's most "ignorant negroes."[158] Somehow, for the smallest reason or no reason at all, Hendley had lost favor. Meanwhile, Thomas Townsend's place on the ballot was never in question. An educated property owner whose constituents lived in the more comfortably middle-class Third Ward, Thomas remained popular, and his name appeared on no fewer than three coalition slates that year: the ticket proposed at the courthouse meeting (without Hendley) as well as the competing "Municipal Ticket" and "People's Ticket" (with Hendley).[159] In the end, both men won reelection, with Thomas beating his white opponents by more than two hundred votes.[160] The *Gazette* considered it a sign of "the liberal progressive tendency of the times" that "over three hundred white men—Republicans and Democrats—cheerfully cast their ballots for the colored candidates."[161]

Unfortunately, those liberal times were nearly over.

The year 1882 marked the height of Thomas's influence in Huntsville politics. A city alderman popular among white and Black voters alike, he had successfully made himself the best-known Townsend in Madison County. To the *Gazette* correspondent who praised Thomas as one of Huntsville's most "intelligent and leading colored men," he was simply "Townsend"—no first name necessary.[162] Some constituents envisioned even greater heights for Thomas to scale: federal office, perhaps. But Thomas's position had always depended on the goodwill of Huntsville's white elites, and in late nineteenth-century Alabama that was a shaky foundation for a political career. In the decade after the end of Reconstruction in Alabama, but before it solidified as a Jim Crow state, white leaders were willing to overlook Thomas's race because he had the money, connections, and "high moral character" of a Black paragon.[163] As Alabama's color line hardened throughout the 1880s and '90s, neither money nor social capital would be enough to protect Samuel Townsend's son from the resentment and deep-seated racial prejudice of the city's power brokers.

In 1883, one year after Thomas's triumphant reelection to the city board, white Huntsville legislators devised a plan to make the popular African American alderman's second term his last. "There was a petition," one Black Huntsville resident recalled, "quietly circulated among the elect . . . to have the boundaries of certain wards changed."[164] As a result, the state legislature passed a bill amending Huntsville's city charter. Voting districts were gerrymandered, redrawn to place the vast majority of Black citizens in the Fourth Ward. Unlike the previous charter, which permitted residents to vote on the entire slate of city aldermen, the new bill prohibited anyone from voting for candidates who represented districts in which they didn't live. Legislators claimed that the Ward Bill was simply "carrying out the principle of local self-government," allowing each ward "to select its own Aldermen, instead of electing all of them on one ticket."[165] But in practice, it limited the Black community's voting influence, giving Black voters a voice in one ward only, the Fourth Ward. If local residents were to be believed, Huntsville's white leaders had conspired with the Alabama state legislature for a single reason: "to prevent a colored man being elected Alderman from the 3rd ward."[166] That man was T. W. Townsend. Although the newly gerrymandered districts placed most Black residents in the Fourth Ward, Thomas's house remained in the Third, meaning few of his former constituents could vote for him.[167] Former Confederate officer A. S. Fletcher and Mayor Edward Mastin were the alleged architects of the bill; Mastin was well liked among Huntsville's Black residents for his support of public education, but he and Fletcher may have considered Thomas's popularity a threat to their own political ambitions.[168] With Thomas separated from his constituents and deprived of votes, Fletcher would become the new alderman for the Third Ward.[169] "Grin and Endure It," the *Gazette* counseled.[170]

Thomas didn't give up so easily. Though he couldn't win in the now predominantly white Third Ward, he could still run for county office. In 1884, Thomas campaigned for a seat on the all-white Madison County Commissioners' Board.[171] Once again he ran on the "fusion or people's ticket," alongside Black farmer and schoolteacher W. H. Blankenship, a candidate for the state legislature.[172] The *Gazette* appealed to Black voters' racial solidarity, stating that "a colored representative is needed on the Commissioners' Board," but Thomas's supporters attempted to drum up votes among white independents as well.[173] The fusion ticket, "without exception, is made up of property owners of the county," the *Gazette* reported—men of means that voters could trust to be "fully identified with its interests and welfare."[174] This time, however, class status failed to overcome race prejudice, and Thomas lost the election. He wouldn't run for public office again.

Across the country, white Republicans had begun to join their Democratic adversaries in pushing African American men out of the public political sphere—as when a "delegation of colored Alabamians" met with Republican president Benjamin Harrison in 1889, and he told them "that office was not the thing they needed most."[175] Huntsville's white leaders followed suit, further restricting African Americans' electoral influence throughout the 1880s and '90s. In 1888, another new city charter stripped residents of the right to elect the mayor by direct vote. The board of alderman, already gerrymandered to give Black voters one or two representatives at most, would instead choose Huntsville's mayor.[176] "It is a game of choke and the sentiment of the people is almost solidly against it," a Black Huntsville resident wrote, incredulous. "No such measure should have been undertaken without consulting the people."[177] But Alabama's white legislators, in full control of all branches of state and local government, didn't need to consult the people—or at least not the Black population. Vigilante violence surged across the rural South once again in the mid-1880s and '90s, lynch mobs silencing critics and enforcing white supremacy. The brief era of biracial coalitions was, by and large, at its end.[178]

Under threat of violence and racist terrorism, many southern Black communities turned inward—pursuing self-sufficiency, strengthening families and local institutions, and seeking economic opportunities not as a means of earning white leaders' respect but as a matter of survival. Thomas Townsend turned his attention to his family too. Sixteen years before, in 1872, he had married Mary Mastin, a devout Christian known to Huntsville's Black community as a "noble cultured woman" committed to "encouraging and uplifting" the race—a perfect match for Thomas.[179] Within two years, Mary Mastin would die, leaving Thomas a widower. He married again in 1874, to a woman named Mary Ann Scruggs, who would also die sometime before 1880.[180] A widower twice over with no children, Thomas had spent the last decade consumed by work. Pushed out of politics, he married a third time.[181] In 1888, the forty-seven-year-old newlywed and his wife Tamar C. Tate—the woman Charles Osborne and his wife imagined as "the very picture of an angel"—moved into a "new and cosy cottage on Adams Avenue" in Huntsville.[182] They had two children, Thomas Jr. and Inez, both of whom pursued higher education in the early 1900s: Inez at the State Normal College in Nashville and Thomas at Wilberforce, Howard University, and Fisk.[183] Thomas Townsend, now Thomas Sr., continued to look after his extended family's affairs from afar—sending letters back and forth to Kansas, Ohio, and Colorado about the litigation over their father's estate.[184] In the end, their legal and financial affairs wouldn't be settled until 1890, one year after S. D. Cabaniss's death, with the Townsend legatees having received less than one third of what they were owed. But the family still admired Thomas, the Townsend who had returned to Alabama and made a name for himself. Wesley and Ada, who left New Richmond for Huntsville for a time before relocating to Mississippi, kept in close contact with Thomas. Wesley was a witness at his brother's first wedding, and he gave Thomas the honor of naming one of his and Ada's daughters. The girl, Carrie Leontee, would write to her uncle as a teenager, sharing news of her accomplishments: "uncle I am not bragging but you ought to see me play the piano," she wrote in 1890. "I tell you I make ours ring."[185] Thomas's stamp of approval still meant something, at least to the Townsends.

Huntsville's white elites may have cast him out of politics, and Thomas may have accommodated himself to the new status quo, but Samuel Townsend's son never let them forget what he was capable of. As an administrator for local Black residents' estates, he appeared regularly at the Madison County courthouse to settle bills and pay legal fees. When he did, he paid in gold.[186]

"Wealthy Negro Dies," the *Huntsville Mercury-Banner* printed on August 31, 1916, announcing the death of "one of the best known colored citizens of North Alabama."[187] "He owned considerable property and was quite wealthy," the *Chicago Defender* echoed in September, with the *Philadelphia Tribune* picking up the story in nearly the same words a week later.[188] Perhaps it seemed like a contradiction to their readers, the words "wealthy" and "negro" side by side. But the deceased man's success had been hard won, and "wealthy negro" was the least his obituary could say to commemorate a life of shrewd calculations and precarious alliances.

Thomas W. Townsend, 75, dead of natural causes.

He was a lawyer, the papers said, a property owner in Huntsville and Hazel Green whose funeral drew mourners "from miles around" in the sweltering Alabama summer.[189] They remembered him as a community leader who "always took part in affairs that tend toward the uplift of his people."[190] They remembered how he had done it, too.

From the *Defender*: "He held office for years and was held in high esteem by both Races."

From the *Tribune*: "Despite the fact that he held State office at a critical time, Townsend was generally esteemed by the white people."

And from the *Banner*: "He was once a legislator during the reconstruction period, but conducted himself so that he was respected and esteemed by white citizens as well as colored."

After a lifetime striving for wealth and respect, perhaps Thomas Townsend's most remarkable feat was to retain Madison County's goodwill in death. His political history, a mark of distinction and leadership in Huntsville's Black community during the 1880s, could have easily become a liability in later years, when Jim Crow reigned supreme in Alabama. Thomas, however, had long been a diplomat—an advocate for his family and community, and all the while assuring white elites that he was a man they could trust. The balancing act was exhausting, unending. But it won Thomas and his family a reprieve from the violence and hardship African Americans across the South suffered and would continue to suffer in the twentieth century. It won them a home of their own, a cottage on Adams Avenue where Thomas died of old age, surrounded by friends and family.

In his time, in that place, this alone was an accomplishment.

Epilogue

SO MUCH FOR FREEDOM

"ABOUT A MONTH ago we left the South in search of a parent whom we had not seen for twenty-five years," William Bolden Townsend wrote in July 1889.[1] Manumitted at age six with the legatees of the second class, William Bolden—or "Bolling," as Samuel Townsend called him as a boy—had spent most of his life in Leavenworth.[2] He had grown up in a large extended family, the tight-knit community of emigrant Townsends who had remained in Leavenworth after their emancipation. Some, like his cousin Joseph, one or two years younger than William Bolden, would have barely remembered slavery in Alabama. Others, like his mother Peggy, born in Virginia and sold to Samuel Townsend as a young girl, would have remembered it all too well.[3] For Peggy, freedom was a mixed blessing: she herself had been freed because she was the sister of Lucy, one of Samuel's former concubines, but she had been compelled to leave her son Barney behind in Alabama when S. D. Cabaniss moved the legatees to Kansas in 1860.[4] William Bolden, meanwhile, escaped his brother's fate only because he was the child of Samuel's eldest son, Wesley. Yet after nearly thirty years in Kansas, he scarcely knew his father. Wesley Townsend had considered the enslaved woman Jane his wife back in Alabama, not Peggy. Once freed, he left Jane for Adelaide, whom he had met in Ohio. Now William Bolden had learned that Wesley was living with Adelaide and their seven children, half-siblings he had never met, in Mississippi.[5] So the thirty-six-year-old newspaper editor decided to revisit the South for the first time since his emancipation—searching for his estranged father and, in the process, bearing witness to the life he might have led if he hadn't shared his wealthy white master's blood.

FIGURE E.1 Sketch of William Bolden Townsend published in
The Afro-American Press by I. Garland Penn in 1891. kansasmemory.
org, Kansas Historical Society.

William Bolden published a detailed account of his month-long tour of
the South when he returned home at the end of July. It was the inverse of a
trip his father had taken three decades earlier, when Wesley joined Cabaniss's
agent William Chadick on a tour of Ohio. In 1858, Reverend Chadick had
gone north with Wesley, visiting communities across the state to determine
where African American migrants might safely settle.[6] In 1889, William
Bolden canvassed Kentucky, Tennessee, Mississippi, and Louisiana, all the
while "inquiring and observing the real condition of our people there."[7] What
he witnessed was the establishment of Jim Crow America. Racial prejudice
reared its head as soon as William Bolden's journey began, when he boarded a
train departing St. Louis. Despite having purchased a first-class ticket, he was
quickly "driven by a rough and insulting brakeman from the first class coach"
to a segregated train car.[8] Ironically, as the only African American passenger
on the train, William Bolden had the entire coach to himself for twelve hours.
He told his readers not to bother spending their money on first-class tickets
when they traveled south; they would be "compelled to ride in what is known

as the 'coon car'" regardless. Then, when they arrived at the train depot, they would be sent to segregated waiting rooms, behind doors marked by humiliating signs reading: "For colored people."[9]

The situation didn't improve when William Bolden reached his destination. "We do not hesitate to say," he wrote in the Leavenworth *Advocate*, "that during our short stay in the South we saw and heard more from the lips of our down trodden and helpless people, concerning the impositions, the wrongs, trials and vicisitudes heapened upon them by the whites than the people of the North are willing to believe." The Black southerner was a willing, hardworking laborer, he said, but "on nine plantations out of ten, he is working the white man's plantation where he was formerly held as a slave," alongside a wife who should have been at home and children who should have been in school. Virtually none had farms of their own, and those who managed to "rent a few acres of that poor blood red land" often faced crippling debt. Sharecropping, which had once seemed like a path toward independent land ownership, had become a trap for tenant farmers: landowners and storekeepers who furnished seed, livestock, equipment, and supplies took "cut-throat" mortgages on Black tenants' share of the final crops. Sometimes, William Bolden heard, "when the crop is about matured and promises a big yield," landlords conspired with white vigilantes to "come at midnight and shoot and kill some of the poor colored men" and drive off the others. If the laborers dared to return and seek payment for their share, they were told that because they had run off they had broken their contract and were thus entitled to nothing. "From a stand-point of labor," William Bolden concluded, the circumstances were akin to slavery. African Americans in the South were "free" in name only.[10]

Yet William Bolden, a journalist and civil rights activist in Leavenworth, knew that Kansas was no paradise either. Though white residents congratulated themselves on the state's antislavery history, African Americans faced heightened violence and repression throughout the 1880s and '90s.[11] The catalyst was the arrival of the "Exodusters," a mass movement of Black migrants to Kansas in the mid- to late 1870s, pushed by violence and economic exploitation in the South and pulled by Kansas's free state mythology.[12] When the Townsend legatees arrived in Leavenworth in 1860, Wesley had described "the Whit people" harassing Cabaniss's agent "for bringing them Neggrows here"—and the Townsends had only been thirty-six in number, with considerable money in hand.[13] Exodusters arrived in the thousands, most of them destitute, and white Kansans, who had never been as welcoming of African Americans as they claimed, responded by enforcing white supremacy through legal and extralegal means. In 1879, at the height of the Exodus, state legislators passed a new law segregating the public school system: school boards in the state's largest cities, where 90 percent of the state's African American population lived, would be permitted to establish separate elementary schools for Black and white children.[14] As in the South, Kansas's Black schools received fewer resources and operated under challenging conditions. As one resident observed ten years after the education bill passed, one of Leavenworth's schools for Black children was a mere "hut" beside a foul-smelling creek, "with a railroad running almost directly over the building."[15] In smaller cities and rural areas, where separate schools were not permitted, local white leaders found loopholes to exclude African Americans—requiring Black students to take special entrance exams, for example—or simply ignored the law altogether.[16]

Over the course of the next two decades, as white Kansans drew and enforced an increasingly rigid color line, African Americans would be segregated or excluded from hotels, restaurants, theaters, and residential neighborhoods across the state. They would be arrested, convicted, and imprisoned disproportionately.[17] They would be stereotyped in the press as dangerous, degraded, and innately criminal.[18] And they would live under the constant threat of violence—assault, arson, police brutality, rape, murder, and lynching—from white Kansans.[19] The most dramatic incident in Kansas occurred in 1901, when a mob of Leavenworth whites burned a Black man named Fred Alexander alive for the alleged attempted rape of a white woman and murder of another. A crowd of eight thousand people watched him die, calling for his mother and professing his innocence to the end. When the fire burned down, white spectators took pieces of flesh, fragments of bone, and scraps of the chain that had bound the victim as "souveniers."[20] The lynching of Fred Alexander was as gruesome and sadistic a murder as any in Alabama or Mississippi, and it haunted Black residents—demonstrating in brutal fashion that white supremacy reigned outside the South as well. "Times have changed for the Negroes in Kansas," William Bolden Townsend would write two years later. "Instead of that state, the home of John Brown, being the haven of rest for Negroes it is a veritable hell, for there they burn Negroes alive, and when they are not burning them, they are being proscribed and denied their rights."[21]

"So much for freedom," he remarked.[22]

The deteriorating situation in Kansas in the last decades of the nineteenth century reflected white Americans' nationwide retreat from protecting Black citizens' rights. In 1883, the US Supreme Court repealed the Reconstruction-era Civil Rights Act, which had mandated equal treatment in public accommodations and transportation. Private businesses and individuals would be legally permitted to discriminate on the basis of race.[23] In 1889, William Bolden pleaded with Kansas congressman Harrison Kelley—a man he had campaigned for among Black voters—to "hold up the bloody flag" and remind his colleagues that white southerners were "lawless ex rebels" while African Americans were "patriots" who had given their lives to defend the Union. "If all the Republican Congress men would speak out and denounce those unrepented rebels there would be a very different state of affairs in the South," he wrote.[24] Across the country, white Republicans, wearied by conflict and pressured by northern businessmen eager to spend their money industrializing the region, had largely abandoned civil rights activism in the interest of reconciling North and South.[25] In 1896, the Supreme Court's *Plessy v. Ferguson* decision codified the "separate but equal" standard of racial segregation that would stand until the 1950s. African Americans' liberties, and their very lives, were not a priority.

William Bolden fought back. Unlike his father Wesley, who'd disdained the fugitive slaves seeking refuge in Ohio, or Woodson, who Leavenworth's Black leaders said had "always considered himself a white man," William Bolden Townsend didn't hold himself apart from his local Black community because of his mixed-race ancestry.[26] Unlike Charles Osborne, he didn't expect his inheritance or politics to earn him social equality with white neighbors. And unlike Thomas, he largely rejected the notion that alliances with elite whites based on class status and respectability would end racial prejudice. For decades, Samuel and Edmund Townsend's children had occupied a middle ground between slavery and freedom, white and Black—benefiting from the planter brothers' conviction that they were different somehow, better than other slaves and freedpeople. The course of the freed Townsends' lives had been shaped by the possibility that their skin color and class status might win them privileges and opportunities unavailable to other African Americans. By the end of the nineteenth century, the nebulous racial spectrum the Townsends once occupied had hardened into a solid color line. In politics and education, at train depots and hotels, and in the minds of white Americans bent on violence, neither money nor mixed-race ancestry set families like the Townsends apart. William Bolden, Samuel Townsend's eldest grandson, scorned the idea that his fate wasn't tied to that of the rest of the country's Black population.

William Bolden had long identified himself with Leavenworth's larger Black community, influenced perhaps by his place among Samuel Townsend's legatees of the "second class." Though entitled to an inheritance of $200 when he turned twenty-one, William Bolden quickly learned that his needs weren't a priority to Cabaniss. Wesley and his siblings could at least expect a response from the executor when they wrote asking for news of the estate, even if the news was rarely good; William Bolden's letters often went unanswered.[27] Throughout the 1870s, he regularly wrote Cabaniss about his family's need for money—to complete his education, to pay doctor's bills, even just to bury his cousin Joseph when he died suddenly in 1877.[28] William Bolden worked as a laborer and hotel waiter to raise money between school terms, but that wasn't enough to cover books and tuition.[29] "I have a willing mind," he told Cabaniss; all he needed to succeed was "a little encouragement."[30] He wouldn't receive it from his grandfather's estate. Instead, William Bolden credited his mother Peggy with putting him through school. Peggy had married a carpenter named George Armistead sometime in the 1860s. By 1870, Armistead was working as a grocery store clerk and owned a tidy $700 in real estate and $100 in personal property.[31] But William Bolden claimed that his stepfather "dont do anything but to indulge in strong drink all of which as you know is a mighty obstacle to education."[32] Though the young man managed to stay in school, he did so "only through the kindness of my Mother," who "helps me all that she can."[33] When William Bolden graduated and became a teacher in 1876, he repaid the favor and had Peggy, either widowed or separated from her husband, move in with him.[34] When she died in 1887, William Bolden, Peggy's last living child, arranged to have a stone monument erected "in loving memory" over her grave.[35]

Throughout the 1870s and '80s, William Bolden's career in Kansas seemed to mirror his uncle Thomas's in Alabama: from teacher to journalist to political leader.[36] He held several appointed government positions, city weighmaster and mail carrier in the 1880s and assistant prosecutor for Leavenworth in the 1890s.[37] In 1898 he reportedly "came within a few votes" of becoming the Republican nominee for state auditor, and twice he was elected a delegate to the national Republican Party convention.[38] During campaign years, he earned a reputation as a "Republican spellbinder" when he stumped for candidates across the state.[39] His accomplished yet "modest and retiring" wife Martha was active in charitable endeavors and attended women's suffrage meetings in Leavenworth.[40] A model of Black middle-class domesticity, Martha was said to preside over "one of the handsomest city homes owned by colored men in Kansas."[41] With his well-groomed mustache, "smart" tailored clothes, and genteel family life, William Bolden Townsend looked every bit the part of a respectable Black community leader.[42] Unfortunately for Martha, who shied from "notoriety," her husband had little interest in respectability.[43]

William Bolden used the Leavenworth *Advocate* to champion civil and political rights far more outspokenly than his uncle in Huntsville.[44] His stance was militant, uncompromising, and he seemed to relish confrontation. Supporters called him "a true and radical race man" who "never fails to pick up the gauntlet thrown down by any one who would abridge the rights of his people."[45] But William Bolden threw down the gauntlet just as often, and even his friends confessed that if the man had any fault, it was that "he allows his earnestness and zeal" to make him "viciously savage" in his attacks.[46] When white Kansas Republicans expelled Black members from their organizations and meetings—"for fear," William Bolden scoffed, "that our color may stain you"—the journalist asserted that he and his allies "will do our utmost to snow them under."[47] When locals spread rumors that the *Advocate* was a Democratic paper in disguise, he offered his readers a reward to "find out the names of these traitors" so he could answer their slander.[48] He lambasted southern whites for their many crimes ("infamy, ruffianism, treachery, bloodthirstiness, mendacity, cowardice, ingratitude and vengeance toward the Negroes," just to name a few), warning readers that white Democrats would never give up their cherished "lost cause" to join hands with African Americans.[49] "They are insane on one subject," he wrote, "that this should be a white man's government and that they alone must rule it."[50] As for "colored Democrats"—they were traitors to their own people. African Americans who believed they could ever trust Democratic candidates were "swallowing a dynamite bomb," he said. For his part, William Bolden hoped it would "explode at the roof of their mouths and blow the tops of their heads 'off.'"[51] When violence threatened, as it increasingly did, he dared his opponents to do their worst. "Who is going to lynch us?" he demanded in 1889. "Trot out the fellows that are to do the job, we would like to form their acquaintance."[52]

This was no empty bluster. William Bolden graduated from law school at the University of Kansas in 1891, and as a practicing attorney he earned a statewide reputation for defending Black men accused of rape and assault—charges that often led to threats of lynching for the accused and their lawyer alike.[53] In 1892, when Black farmer Noah Ashby was imprisoned in Tonganoxie, Kansas, for allegedly raping a white woman, William Bolden announced that he would represent the man in court. Local whites promised violence if the Leavenworth lawyer came to town, but as one newspaper remarked: "You all know that they have to do more than threaten Townsend." William Bolden arrived on the next train, along with "25 of the bravest black boys in Kansas," all carrying weapons and ready for a fight. An additional 125 armed Black men met him at the station and camped around the jail all night, successfully preventing white vigilantes from seizing Ashby.[54] William

Bolden's activism earned him many Black Kansans' admiration—"true-hearted Townsend," they called him, a "brave hero" and "fearless defender of human rights"—but his militancy alienated Leavenworth's Black community leaders.[55] These were men similar to Thomas Townsend, who saw propriety, diplomacy, and alliances with elite whites as key to eroding prejudice and up-lifting the race. In the face of political ostracism, they championed economic progress and individual advancement. In the face of violence and repression, they sought compromise. To William Bolden, they were dangerously mis-guided. "Let those who will submit," he wrote, "but for me I never will."[56] To them, William Bolden was a liability whose actions could bring retribution upon the entire Black community. So when he spoke up at a public meeting in 1901 to condemn the burning of Fred Alexander, and local whites responded by burning his home, Leavenworth's Black elites looked the other way.[57]

William Bolden and his wife fled to Topeka in late January, saying they expected to return to Leavenworth once the city "cools off."[58] It didn't. With William Bolden's life still in danger, they left Kansas for good and settled in Colorado, where he practiced law.[59] Surprisingly, William Bolden didn't blame hostile whites for his exile; he had never expected any better from them. But he did blame Leavenworth's Black elites for their silence. "When Alexander was burned," he told a reporter in Topeka, they turned their heads aside and said "don't say anything." When he himself was driven from the state, they did the same. "When will they say anything?" he asked. "Will they wait until the insult . . . and injury comes to their own doors?" He was furious and incredulous. "My God," he demanded, "when will they say an-ything about the wrongs imposed upon the race?" Across the country, he observed, "would-be leaders" were "hunting popularity with white folks at the expense of the rights of my people."[60] They traded votes for a pittance "to maintain a 'Jim Crow' Negro school" when, he believed, they should have demanded equality.[61] They pursued individual wealth and status instead of "organization and concert of action."[62] For William Bolden, collective ac-tion—bringing "the colored to stand together and demand fair treatment from the police"—was how African Americans would advance.[63] Perhaps "now and then one of us may be able to overcome the storm of combined op-pression and opposition and fight his or her way to the stars," he told a forum in Pueblo, Colorado, "but he or she is an exception to the rule." For the rest of the ("dare I say defenseless") race, solidarity was the best protection against the virulent racism and discrimination that pervaded turn-of-the-century America.[64] To William Bolden, Black leaders who held themselves apart from the mass of African Americans, who failed to speak out against injustice, or who disdained the poor and working class because they didn't adhere to their middle-class values, were no leaders at all.

William Bolden Townsend understood full well the challenges that African Americans would continue face in Jim Crow America, and his commitment to solidarity and collective action would characterize civil rights activism throughout the twentieth century—from the coalition of labor unions and radical political groups that would form during the Great Depression, to the grassroots organizing and mass movements for civil rights in the 1950s and '60s.[65] It was a departure from the racial uplift ideals his aunts and uncles had learned at Wilberforce University, which taught students to hold themselves up as examples for less educated, less elevated African Americans. It was certainly a far cry from his grandfather Samuel's sense that a white man's blood should confer special status and privilege. In Jim Crow America—governed by a "one-drop rule" that placed any person with the slightest African ancestry on the "black" side of a rigid color line—a lighter skin tone was of less concrete benefit to the next generation of Townsends than it had been for the family in the nineteenth century.

Wesley Townsend, William Bolden's father, once told S. D. Cabaniss that he would not suffer any man to "make a negro of him."[66] He wanted autonomy, full control of his inheritance, and the social status to which he believed his wealth and mixed-race ancestry entitled him. Similar to his cousin Woodson—whom neighbors accused of having "always considered himself a white man"—Wesley set himself apart from his local Black community, holding to his belief that Samuel Townsend's ancestry and money put him in a special class. Over the years, Wesley would inherit a total of $5,380.15 from his father's estate—not the $16,000 he had expected as Samuel's son, but enough to provide a home and education for his children.[67] In 1880, Wesley, his wife Adelaide, and their seven children aged five to twenty years old were living together in the town of Brookhaven, Mississippi, where Wesley managed a restaurant.[68] Ada was deeply involved in the community as a schoolteacher, as was her eighteen-year-old daughter Ida. Ida, as Ada would later write to her brother-in-law Thomas with a hint of pride, was a particularly "fine scholar."[69] Over the course of the next decade, another daughter, Carrie Leontee, would also pursue further education, attending New Orleans University.[70] When William Bolden headed south to seek out his estranged father in 1889—just one year before Wesley's death—he didn't find a destitute household. But prosperity and ambition were dangerous in rural Mississippi at the turn of the century. In 1903, a gang of white farmers fired shots into the home of Eli Hilson, an African American man with a farm several miles outside Brookhaven, hoping to force him off his property. When Hilson refused to abandon his hard-won land, they murdered him.[71] The Townsends in Brookhaven certainly would have heard about the lynching; they may even have known Hilson personally. His murder was hardly the last such incident they would witness as terror and violence swept the South in the age of Jim Crow. To many white Americans of their time, Wesley Townsend's children were only "negroes," and neither money, nor education, nor skin color could protect them.

Charles Osborne Townsend, a Union Army veteran who swore he would never set foot in the South again, was certain he would find his fortune in the West. "Some one of us will have it good," he told his brothers, filled with boomtown optimism. In the end, Charles Osborne would receive more money from Samuel Townsend's estate than he ever made mining in Colorado. By 1879, he had inherited a total of $5,299.79, including the portion that had gone to his education at Wilberforce.[72] But he found something more precious than silver in the Rocky Mountains: acceptance and respect in his community as a social and political equal. Both of Charles Osborne's surviving children followed their father's example and headed west when they left home. Thomas Clarence Townsend first struck out for Montana but had trouble finding work.[73] In 1920—a full century after their grandfather Samuel Townsend arrived with his brothers in Alabama—Thomas Clarence and his elder brother Charles Osborne Jr. were living together in Seattle, Washington, on the Pacific coast, about as far west as a man could go. Neither son expected to make a fortune, as their father once thought he would in Colorado. Neither would be praised or celebrated in local papers. Instead, they took the best jobs they could find—as janitors at an auto garage or washing windows at the Navy yard.[74] For Thomas Clarence, it was enough to support his wife and son and purchase a house in the city, but it hardly earned him or his brother the social status their father once enjoyed.[75] In 1865, Charles Osborne Townsend Sr. had served as a quartermaster sergeant for the Union Army in Vicksburg. In 1940, his son Thomas Clarence worked as a menial at the US Quartermaster Depot in Seattle.[76]

Thomas Townsend returned to Alabama in 1869 to reclaim his father's elite position in Madison County. He rose to social and political heights, becoming one of Huntsville's first two African American aldermen before being cast down by local white politicians who resented his success. Thomas inherited $4,753.12 from his father's estate and husbanded the money carefully. Both his son and daughter received a college education, and when he died in 1916 Thomas was able to leave them the family home on Adams

Avenue, where Thomas Townsend Jr. would live for the next fifty years. While his sister Inez taught school, married a doctor, and made a new life in Cincinnati, Thomas Jr. supported himself and his mother as a farmer.[77] An educated property owner with a comfortable home, Thomas Jr. might have been one of Huntsville's "Best Men" had he come of age in the 1870s or '80s. In Jim Crow Alabama, however, the idea that the son of a former slave might rise any higher than this was unthinkable. He lived to see the passage of the Civil Rights Act of 1964—the most significant civil rights legislation in the United States since Reconstruction—and died in 1968, at the age of seventy-six.[78]

None of Samuel or Edmund Townsend's children would ever receive all of the money that their late master had promised them. Samuel's will had stipulated that his twelve legatees of the first class should share equally in a trust fund worth approximately $200,000. Due to the difficulties S. D. Cabaniss faced trying to collect debts from bankrupt planters after the Civil War, the legatees ultimately received less than a third of what they were owed. Cabaniss managed to pay out the bulk of the Townsends' inheritances before 1879; by then, Samuel and Edmund's surviving children had received roughly $5,000 each.[79] Less than they had hoped for, the money was still a fortune compared to the finances of the vast majority of freedpeople in the United States. It allowed the Townsends to experience a level of security they may not have been able to achieve in a nation where African Americans across the country were being systematically blocked from education, high-paying work, home ownership, and other avenues for social and economic mobility. Even the $200 that each legatee of the second class inherited could change a life. When she died in Leavenworth in 1898, Martha Townsend—"Aunt Martha" to locals—had parlayed her inheritance into a house on a small plot of land and an additional $535. A devout Catholic, Martha left $530 plus the proceeds of the sale of her household goods and property to local Catholic charities; the remaining $5 went to her estranged son William, who had gone west sixteen years earlier and never returned.[80] William Townsend may not have benefited from his mother's care with her money, but other members of the Townsend family, like Thomas and his children, were able to start building generational wealth with their disbursements from the old cotton planter's estate. It was a foundation for a more stable life as other markers of status— mixed-race ancestry, for example—failed to pay dividends in the age of the one-drop rule.

Samuel Townsend's paternity freed his children, and the inheritance he left the family enabled the Townsends to start new lives for themselves across the country. As they crisscrossed the United States in the years after

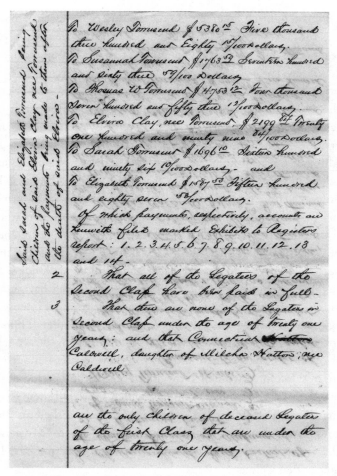

FIGURE E.2 Page from S. D. Cabaniss's report on the settlement of Samuel Townsend's estate, noting the money paid out to each of the Townsend legatees as of April 1879. University of Alabama Libraries Special Collections.

their emancipation, the Townsends used their mixed-race ancestry, money, and connections to prominent whites like S. D. Cabaniss to seek social and economic mobility in a changing nation. They found that perceptions of their race and status could shift depending on their region, state, and local community. Living through one of the most transformative periods in American history, the Townsends struggled—and sometimes succeeded—in transforming their own identities as free men and women. Throughout the second half of the nineteenth century, the privileges that money and mixed-race ancestry brought the Townsends made their new lives possible. But for

William Bolden, fighting for civil rights at the turn of the twentieth century, the legacies his father's generation had relied on to advance themselves were no privileges at all. His lighter skin color wasn't a mark of superiority: it was a reminder of slavery.

In November 1901, William Bolden addressed a Republican meeting at the Protho Hotel in Bessemer, Colorado. Throughout the speech he held the audience "spell bound with his eloquence," his listeners "now in tears with his pathos, now shouting in the enthusiasm of his scintillating oratory, now laughing at his keen humor and satire." He discussed politics and political leaders, like President Theodore Roosevelt, who had invited Booker T. Washington to dine with him at the White House just the month before. The dinner caused an uproar among white Americans shocked that a sitting president would share a meal with a Black man. In response, one Democratic politician, Senator Ben Tillman of South Carolina, had joked that the president must be "preparing to have mulatto grandchildren." William Bolden wasn't laughing. "There is no danger of President Roosevelt having mulatto grandchildren," he told his audience in Bessemer ("in tones of intense scorn," according to the local paper), "but it is not unlikely that Ben Tillman may have them." William Bolden Townsend—the son of a mixed-race man, the grandson of an enslaved woman and a white slave owner—mourned "the conditions of the colored women in the South during their period of slavery." He spoke openly of "the frightful bondage which subjected them to the lust of their masters," with a "bitterness and sorrow" that astonished his audience. "Who is responsible for my color?" William Bolden asked. "My master," he answered. "Through the web of consanguinity I can trace my blood to the same source as Ben Tillman."[81]

The intensity of his words, the pain in his voice, and the expression on his face made clear that this lineage was no source of pride for William Bolden Townsend. He looked out at his audience. One hundred fifty faces—Black and white and every shade in between—gazed up at him, rapt. "The most intense silence prevailed for a moment" as his words sank in. An "overpowering quiet" descended over his listeners. Then the spell broke, and the quiet lifted, and they applauded until the rafters shook.[82]

Note on Methodology

ALONG WITH REAMS of legal documents, financial records, and personal materials, the Septimus D. Cabaniss Papers include a collection of more than seven hundred empty envelopes. The sheer number of envelopes testifies to the success of Huntsville attorney S. D. Cabaniss's nineteenth-century legal practice. He was a busy man, with daily letters to write and respond to, and a significant portion of it concerned the Townsend family. Envelopes from the Townsends bear postmarks from across the country—Alabama, Ohio, Kansas, Colorado—all of the places where Cabaniss's most time-consuming correspondents settled in the years after their emancipation. Scribbled calculations mark the front and back of some, the lawyer's notes to himself on money paid and owed to Samuel Townsend's legatees. They are physical remnants of the Townsends' resolve, small but significant markers of their insistence on their inheritance and rights as free men and women.

The letters themselves have also survived, donated to the University of Alabama in 1952 and stored elsewhere in the archive.[1] These traces of the Townsends, left in fading ink on yellowed paper, are a rare and remarkable collection, a cache of nearly two hundred first-person narratives written by a family of former slaves in their own words. Throughout the nineteenth century, Americans of all classes and backgrounds wrote to each other frequently. When friends and family were separated by great distances, as the Townsends were in their migrations across the country, letter-writing was one of the few ways to maintain relationships and social networks. Yet most families likely wouldn't have considered such messages valuable to anyone beyond their friends and close kin.[2] This would have been true for a family of freedpeople like the Townsends, living in a society where they may have felt that few cared about them or their needs. Why bother saving letters for years or decades? Who else would be interested in their daily lives? The extant Townsend letters were preserved only because they were written to S. D. Cabaniss, a wealthy white lawyer who needed them for his work as Samuel Townsend's executor. The countless missives members of the family would have written to each other over the decades are largely lost.

It's so tempting to imagine the Townsends' letters as a window into their innermost thoughts and feelings. The reality is, of course, more complicated. In the words of anthropologist Michel-Rolph Trouillot, "the production of traces"—or primary sources—"is always also the creation of silences."[3] Historical sources and the archives and narratives built from them are shaped by complex power dynamics. When the Townsends took pen in hand to write, they didn't set down their unfiltered thoughts. Their letters weren't private diary entries; they were carefully crafted documents written for a specific purpose. In many cases, that purpose was to get money out of Samuel Townsend's estate. So they took what they knew about their intended audience, S. D. Cabaniss, and presented themselves and their requests accordingly. The Townsends knew they were writing to a powerful authority figure; Jacob Hatton, Milcha Townsend's second husband, addressed one letter simply to "Mr. Lawyer Cabaniss."[4] Power dynamics are further evident in the name of the collection that houses the Townsends' letters: the Estate of Samuel Townsend Subseries of the Septimus D. Cabaniss Papers. Samuel and Cabaniss's race, class, and status guaranteed that their names and traces of their lives would survive into the present day. Traces of the freed Townsend family, however, survive only incidentally—not because their voices were considered meaningful to their contemporaries in their own right but because they happened to mean something to these elite white men. Samuel and Cabaniss's power influenced the words the Townsends wrote, the pieces of their lives that were preserved, and, in turn, the stories that we can tell about them today.

The interpretive challenges that the Cabaniss papers present mean that the Townsends' letters need to be read closely for what they hide as well as what they reveal. Examining the letters written between family members hints at what the Townsends excluded from the ones directed to the lawyer. Only a handful of the Townsends' extant letters are addressed to someone other than Cabaniss; these are letters Samuel's son Charles Osborne Townsend and other relatives sent to Thomas Townsend over the years. Unlike the other letters in the collection, these exist as typewritten transcripts, not manuscripts, likely copied from the originals by historian Frances Cabaniss Roberts when she interviewed Thomas's son Thomas Townsend Jr. as research for her 1940 master's thesis.[5] Thomas, himself an elite within Huntsville's African

American community, would have saved his correspondence for much the same reason Cabaniss had: to keep track of business and family obligations. Less formal than the Townsends' letters to the lawyer, Charles Osborne's epistles from Colorado are filled with emotional personal updates and outspoken political commentary. They are the only letters in the collection in which the Townsends reminisce about their family's past. Charles Osborne asks Thomas to visit "our father" and "Uncle Edmund's" graves to copy down the inscriptions on their tombstones.[6] He inquires whether Thomas's wife Tamar descended from "the family of Tates that lived adjoining us" back in Madison County—the old farmer and his wife who had "caught us kids one Sunday morning going chestnut hunting" on his property. "Wade and Austin and I sit around Sundays and talk over things that happened twenty-five years ago in the South," he tells his brother.[7] Letters like these are artifacts of private conversations otherwise lost to time, but they are few and far between. When writing to S. D. Cabaniss, none of the Townsends shared stories from their lives as slaves.

These issues aren't exclusive to the Townsends' letters: every source and archive obscures as much as it reveals, resulting in imbalances in whose story can be told. Such imbalances are particularly marked in histories of enslaved people. The Townsends' words may require close reading and careful

FIGURE N.1 Graves of Edmund and Samuel Townsend in Hazel Green, Madison County, Alabama. Photograph by author, April 2021.

interpretation to parse, but the vast majority of enslaved people left no such sources whatsoever. In the case of this story, the Townsend women were considerably more difficult to trace than their male relatives. Certain pieces of evidence hint at their determination and force of will: on the steamer to Kansas in 1860, Cabaniss's agent David Lakin wrote that had had "the greatest trouble with the women," suggesting that the newly freed Townsend women were not afraid to speak their minds in person.[8] But most of the letters in the Cabaniss papers were written by men, namely, Samuel and Edmund's sons and their half-brothers. Wesley Townsend wrote thirty-eight extant letters to Cabaniss after his emancipation. Susanna, the lawyer's most regular correspondent among Samuel's daughters, wrote nine. Samuel's eldest daughter Caroline seems not to have sent Cabaniss any letters at all; a twenty-four-year-old mother when she was freed, Caroline did not attend Wilberforce University with her half-sisters and, at least up to 1870, remained unable to read or write.[9]

The Townsend children's mothers proved even more elusive. Numerous historians have discussed the challenges of writing about enslaved women, who generally appear in the historical record only fleetingly: a first name on a bill of sale, an anonymous tally mark on the manifest of a slave ship. To the creators of these sources the women were property, not people with thoughts and experiences that someone might wish to uncover one day. Reconstructing their lives requires scholars "to read documents against the grain," asking new questions of old sources and mining them for information they weren't intended to record.[10] Consider Samuel and Edmund's former concubines. Unsurprisingly, the Cabaniss papers do not include a comprehensive accounting of the planter brothers' sexual encounters with enslaved women they owned. The collection does hold, however, an "inventory and appraisement" of Samuel's property, made in the years after his death. The purpose of the inventory was to calculate the monetary value of the deceased man's children and other slaves, in the event that Cabaniss fail to uphold his will in court. To that end, the lawyer and Samuel's nephew Samuel C. Townsend took down the name of every enslaved person on the Townsend plantations. They noted age, injuries, and illness—as each individual's health and vigor would, of course, factor into how much they could be sold for on the open market. Neither man would have intended this information to be used to reverse-engineer a timeline of Samuel Townsend's sexual history. But by moving backward from Samuel's children's ages (as noted on the inventory and later census records), to their birth years, to their conceptions, we can arrive at an approximate time

period for when each of their mothers was subjected to her master's attention. We can see, from the ages of their mothers' other children by enslaved
men, how Samuel separated these women from the partners they had chosen.
If we look closely, we can even catch a glimpse of what the women may have
hoped might come from their circumstances. Rainey, notably, named one of
her young sons "Freeman."[11]

These sources, however, only reveal the enslaved concubines with whom
Samuel Townsend fathered children. Samuel may have sexually abused and
exploited other enslaved women who never had children by him or whose
children didn't survive to 1853, when the planter began writing his will. Elvira
Townsend was likely one of these women. Although Elvira had no children
by Samuel, meaning that sexual contact between her and her master cannot
be definitively confirmed, Samuel's wills and other archival materials provide
strong circumstantial evidence to support the idea that she too was one of his
concubines. In Cabaniss's notes on the Townsend family, the lawyer identified Elvira as "a favorite & [Samuel's] housekeeper," and as historian Brenda
Stevenson has written, the term "housekeeper" was a common euphemism
used to encompass "enslaved women's physical, sexual, and emotional labor as
their master's consorts."[12] Furthermore, Samuel singled out Elvira as a particular "favorite" in multiple drafts of his will.[13] Samuel freed all of his children,
their mothers, and their mothers' children by enslaved men; as the half-sister
of Samuel's son Thomas, Elvira would have been freed even if she had not been
one of Samuel's concubines. This would have made her one of the "legatees of
the second class," with an inheritance of $200. Yet in his 1853 will, Samuel gave
Elvira an equal share in his estate alongside his children and nieces, as well as a
separate legacy of $5,000 exclusively for her use. By including her in the "first
class" of legatees in his final 1856 will, along with attempting to leave her additional money in earlier versions, Samuel left evidence of Elvira's status on the
Home Place in the last years of his life. Because she was not one of Samuel's
children—as noted in Cabaniss's legal papers—the most plausible explanation for this unrestrained show of favoritism is that Elvira had had sexual contact with Samuel, perhaps during the period he was writing his will.[14] But as
complete certainty is impossible in this case, I describe Elvira as a "likely" or
"possible" concubine throughout this book.

Much about the Townsends' lives—especially their inner lives, thoughts,
and motivations—remains unknown or uncertain. No one today can truly
know what it was like to live in the nineteenth century, to be a slave owner,
an enslaved person, or a freedman or woman. As the oft-quoted L. P. Hartley

line goes: "The past is a foreign country: they do things differently there."[15] At its core, the study of history is an exercise in empathy and imagination, an attempt to catch a glimpse of that country. This is not the imagination of the novelist, playwright, or artist—historians are still bound by facts and sources. But historical scholarship is as much an act of creation as discovery. Stories don't emerge fully formed in libraries and archives but must be pieced together from fragments, incomplete evidence, and biased sources. Historians are "creative synthesizers" who construct narratives by analyzing and reinterpreting what the archive does hold, and when we find gaps, we use our research findings to offer grounded speculation.[16] Where specificity is impossible, we provide context, incorporating what we know from other sources about the world our historical actors lived in and the lives of people similar to them. Wesley Townsend didn't write at length about what he felt in 1858, when he left his pregnant wife Jane enslaved in Alabama to start his new life as a free man in Ohio. The escaped slave Henry Bibb, however, did describe the pain of separation from his wife and his sense of guilt that he couldn't free her too. His story fills some of the holes in Wesley's, offering insight into what Samuel Townsend's eldest son may have experienced in his first years of freedom. Along with historical context and comparison, we also use what we know about human beings in general. Although some of the Townsends' experiences were radically different from those of a modern reader, other experiences—love, loss, grief, hope, and fear—haven't changed all that much over the centuries. Using what can be gleaned from the historical record as well as what is known about human behavior, it's not such a leap to speculate that Woodson resented his cousins; that Thomas loved his sister Elvira; that Rainey dreamed of freedom for her children.

Other scholars might interpret these complicated sources differently, bringing new perspectives and piecing them together into alternate narratives. I, after all, disagree with many of Frances Cabaniss Roberts's conclusions about the Townsends' character and motivations, and we were working from the same cache of archival material. The gaps and silences that riddle the historical record make disagreements and reinterpretations inevitable. As Wendy Warren wrote in an article about an unnamed woman's rape and enslavement: "This is not *the* story, not the *only* story."[17] Like any historian, I have to hope that the people I write about would recognize themselves and their times in this version of their story, but perhaps it's a mercy not to know. Historian Natalie Zemon Davis imagined a conversation with the subjects of one of her books, who turn on her, demanding: "You have a lot of explaining to do."[18] Even with the most meticulous study, the most careful interpretation, and the most voluminous footnotes, some pieces of the story can never be told with certainty.

This uncertainty doesn't make the effort any less vital. The Townsends' story is, in some ways, a small one. Their actions didn't steer the course of the nation. For the most part, the influence they did exert during their lives wouldn't have extended far beyond their families and local communities. Like many people then and now, they worked hard to make a living, striving to advance their social and economic positions in the world. Sometimes they succeeded; often, they met resistance in a society that considered their efforts offensive or contemptible. They were ordinary Americans, but their story can provide new insights into the times and places that they lived. In *Ties That Bind,* her book about an Afro-Cherokee family in the nineteenth century, historian Tiya Miles references anthropologist Raymond Fogelson, framing her story as one of Fogelson's "epitomizing events," a narrative that can "condense, encapsulate, and dramatize longer-term historical processes."[19] Family stories can have incredible interpretive power because, in Miles's words, they serve as "a barometer for the society" in which the family lived.[20] Over the centuries, US federal, state, and local governments have attempted to define and regulate the American family according to the values and standards of the age. The laws of slavery that delegitimized Samuel and Edmund Townsend's mixed-race children and denied their mothers the right to marry provide one example. Another can be seen in the fact that Madison County and the state of Alabama considered the presence of the mixed-race Townsends, legitimized by their father's will after years of legal debate, so unacceptable that they were forced to leave their home and birthplace altogether. But social norms differed radically from community to community. More than a thousand miles west, Georgetown, Colorado, welcomed Charles Osborne and his relatives as equals with white residents. How the Townsends were perceived, integrated or excluded, and treated in their communities reflected the values of their specific place and time. These insights can only come from close attention to the fine-grained details of an individual's or family's lived experiences—from the small stories.

Yet the Townsends are important as more than vehicles for historical argumentation. They were real people with hopes and fears, dreams and ambitions, and deep inner lives. Simply recognizing the Townsends' dignity and worth as human beings may not sound radical, but in their time, the family's race and enslaved status would have made this a revolutionary proposition. Writing the Townsends' story—one of many stories that could be told about them—is an attempt to correct an imbalance in the historical record, whose biases and silences have often worked to erase the experiences of women, people of color, and enslaved people. By an accident of the archives, the names and voices of a formerly enslaved family were preserved. This book is my inevitably imperfect effort to share their words and render their experiences with empathy and nuance as well as scholarly rigor. The Townsends deserve to be heard.

Acknowledgments

I FIRST ENCOUNTERED the Townsend family in the W. S. Hoole Special Collections Library at the University of Alabama in 2011, never expecting that I would spend the next ten years researching them and writing about their lives. As my work has developed and evolved over the past decade—from undergraduate research paper to doctoral dissertation to this book—I have benefited from the generosity and assistance of family, friends, professors, advisers, archivists, and numerous others. I owe a special debt of gratitude to the descendants of the Townsend family with whom I have had the pleasure of corresponding and speaking over the years: Antoinette Broussard, Kay Brumbaugh, Briauna Johnson, Mary Johnson, Mi-Ling Stone Poole, and Joe Ross. I deeply appreciate the time they have taken to converse with me and share their stories. To all of the Townsends' descendants: I am honored and humbled to tell this small part of your family history.

I have been fortunate to learn from some truly remarkable scholars while working on this project. I couldn't possibly thank Martha Sandweiss enough for her guidance, advice, and belief in me. As my dissertation adviser at Princeton University, her thoughtful and incisive comments enormously improved my work; as a mentor, she helped me begin my career in public history; and her own books, the seminars she taught, and her leadership of the Princeton & Slavery Project have provided a model for the kind of history I hope to write and practice. She also introduced me to my fantastic editor at Oxford University Press, Susan Ferber, whose keen insights have helped to shape this into a much sharper book. I offer my sincerest thanks to the members of my dissertation committee—Tera Hunter, Hendrik Hartog, and Karl Jacoby—whose research and books have inspired me as a writer and historian. Princeton University Archivist Dan Linke deserves acknowledgment for his support and advice throughout my graduate career. The faculty of the history department at the University of Alabama were also instrumental in my development as a researcher, particularly Jenny Shaw, who advised my undergraduate honors thesis and taught the research seminar where I first heard the names Townsend and Cabaniss. Many thanks as well to my undergraduate academic adviser Margaret Abruzzo; to Steven Bunker, who taught my first-ever research seminar; and to George McClure, whose courses inspired me to become a history major. I am appreciative too of my early teachers, particularly Jan Callender, whose enthusiasm for my "stories" I have never forgotten.

I received valuable assistance from researchers at cultural and historical institutions across the country, especially Mary Ann Brown at the Leavenworth County Historical Society, who has been generous in providing information about members of the Townsend family who lived in the Leavenworth area. I have also benefited from the expertise of staff at the University of Alabama's Division of Special Collections; the Madison County Records Center; the Alabama Department of Archives and History; the Clear Creek County Department of Archives and Records; the History Colorado Center; the Denver Public Library; the Leavenworth County Historical Society; the DePaul Library at the University of St. Mary; the Kansas Historical Society; the Richard Allen Cultural Center; Northern Kentucky University; Historic New Richmond; the Ohio State Archives; and the Amon Carter Museum of American Art.

I am, as always, thankful to my family for their encouragement. My mother Sara was the first person to foster my interest in writing; she and my sisters Gabriela and Carolina have been reading my work, for better or worse, since I was five years old; and my father Joe inspired the first story I ever "published."

Finally, I thank my husband Charles for his unfailing love, kindness, and support.

Enslaved Townsends
Manumitted in 1858 and 1860

LEGATEES OF THE FIRST CLASS

Children of Samuel Townsend
Wesley Townsend
Caroline Townsend Stone
Willis Townsend
Thomas Townsend
Charles Osborne Townsend
Parthenia Townsend McCarty
Milcha Townsend Caldwell Hatton
Joseph Bradford Townsend
Susanna Townsend

Children of Edmund Townsend
Elizabeth "Lizzie" Mariah Townsend Yerger Checks
Virginia "Jennie" Townsend Meuer

Other
Elvira Townsend Clay

LEGATEES OF THE SECOND CLASS

Mothers of Samuel Townsend's Children
Hannah Townsend
Lucy Townsend Roy
Rainey Townsend

Relatives of First Class Legatees

Albert Milton Townsend

Elizabeth "Annie" Townsend Chambers (daughter of Caroline)

Elizabeth Townsend (daughter of Elvira and Woodson)

Elizabeth Townsend (daughter of Jane and Wesley)

Freeman Townsend

Harrington Townsend

Jane Townsend Robinson Biggs (wife of Wesley)

Jane Sales (daughter of Rachel)

Jane Townsend (daughter of Rainey)

John Armstrong Townsend

Joseph Townsend

Malinda Prince

Margaret "Peggy" Townsend Armistead

Mary Eddings

Mildred Ann Green

Rachel Townsend

Sam Townsend

Warner Townsend

Wesley Townsend Jr.

William Austin Townsend

William Bolden Townsend

Woodson Townsend

Other

Amos Townsend

Dick Townsend

Henry Townsend

Martin "Wade" Townsend

Martha Townsend

Roxanna Elizabeth Townsend

Sylvanus Townsend

William Turner Townsend

Families of the Legatees of the First Class After Emancipation

<u>Underlined</u> - Children of Edmund Townsend
Bold - Children of Samuel Townsend
= Indicates an unmarried union
+ Indicates a marriage under slavery
m. Indicates a legal marriage

<u>Woodson Townsend</u>

> \+ **Caroline Townsend Stone**
>
> m. Elvira Townsend Clay
>
> > ┬── Elizabeth Townsend (b. 1857)
> > ├── Sarah Townsend (b. 1862)
> > └── Julia Townsend (b. 1864)

<u>Elizabeth "Lizzie" Mariah Townsend Yerger Checks</u>

> m. John Nelson Yerger
>
> m. John W. Checks

<u>Virginia "Jennie" Townsend Meuer</u>

> m. Peter Meuer
>
> > └── George Meuer (b. before 1866)

Wesley Townsend

    = Margaret "Peggy" Townsend Armistead

          └──── William Bolden Townsend (b. ~1853)

          m. Martha Craig Townsend

             └─ Nola Townsend (b. 1897)

    + Jane Townsend Robinson Biggs

        ├──── Elizabeth Townsend (b. ~1856)

        └──── Wesley Townsend Jr. (b. 1858)

    m. Adelaide "Ada" Townsend

        ├──── Hattie Townsend (b. 1860)

        ├──── Ida May Townsend (b. 1862)

        ├──── Ella Townsend (b. 1867)

        ├──── Osborne Townsend (b. 1868)

        ├──── Carrie Leontee Townsend (b. 1873)

        ├──── Farma Townsend (b. 1874)

        └──── Page Townsend (b. 1875)

Caroline Townsend Stone

    + Woodson Townsend

    = *Enslaved man*

          └──── Elizabeth "Annie" Townsend Chambers (b. ~1859)

    m. Daniel Stone

        ├──── Samuel Stone (b. 1862)

        ├──── Sophia Stone (b. 1866)

        ├──── William Stone (b. 1868)

        └──── Harry Stone (b. 1869–70)

Willis Townsend

= Leana Noblin

  └── *Unknown child*

m. Eliza Townsend

  ├── Alice Townsend (b. 1873)
  ├── Harry Townsend (b. ~1874)
  └── Perlie Townsend (b. 1877)

Thomas Townsend

m. Mary Mastin Townsend

m. Mary Ann Scruggs Townsend

m. Tamar Tate Noblin Townsend

  ├── Thomas W. Townsend Jr. (b. 1892)
  └── Inez P. Townsend (b. 1897)

Charles Osborne Townsend

m. Josephine Smith Townsend

  └── *Unknown child* (b. 1876)

m. Margaret "Maggie" Hall Townsend

  ├── Charles Osborne Townsend Jr. (b. 1878)
  ├── Willis A. Townsend (b. 1879-80)
  ├── Lony Townsend
  └── Roy Townsend

Parthenia Townsend McCarty

m. James McCarty

  ├── Samuel McCarty (b. ~1867)
  ├── Thomas M. McCarty (b. ~1868)
  ├── Alice Townsend McCarty (b. ~1870)
  └── Clara McCarty (b. ~1873)

Milcha Townsend Caldwell Hatton

m. John Caldwell

└─ Connecticut "Nettie" Caldwell (b. 1868)

m. Jacob L. Hatton

Susanna Townsend

= *Unknown man*

└─ *Unknown child* (b. 1868)

Notes

1. S. D. Cabaniss to C. D. Lindley, letter dated 15 May 1858, Septimus D. Cabaniss Papers, University Libraries Division of Special Collections, University of Alabama (hereafter Septimus D. Cabaniss Papers). The collection has been fully digitized and is available on the University of Alabama Libraries Special Collections website at www.digitalcollections.libraries.ua.edu. Throughout this book, some footnotes for materials from the Cabaniss Papers include an "item" number; this number corresponds to the organization of the digital collection.

2. Throughout this book, I have chosen to use the term "concubine" as a descriptive category for the enslaved women with whom Samuel and Edmund Townsend had sexual contact and, in a number of cases, fathered children. Historians generally agree that phrases such as "mistress" or "slave mistress" are offensive and inappropriate, as they connote willingness on the women's part and ultimately serve to obscure the inherently exploitative nature of sexual contact between white slave-owning men and enslaved women. As an alternative, "concubine" and "concubinage" emphasize the systematic nature of the rape and sexual abuse of enslaved women, as well as the power differences between the parties both in social custom and as enshrined by law. On concubinage in the antebellum South, see in particular Brenda E. Stevenson, "What's Love Got to Do with It? Concubinage and Enslaved Women and Girls in the Antebellum South," *Journal of African American History* 98, no. 1, Special Issue: "Women, Slavery, and the Atlantic World" (Winter 2013). For the debate over "slave mistress," see Emily Owens, "On the Use of 'Slave Mistress,'" *Black Perspectives* (African American Intellectual History Society; AAIHS), 21 August 2015, https://www.aaihs.org/on-the-use-of-slave-mistress/; Martha S. Jones, "Julian Bond's Great-Grandmother a 'Slave Mistress?' How the New York Times Got It Wrong," History News Network, 26 August 2015, http://historynewsnetwork.org/article/160451.

3. Henry Campbell Black, *A Dictionary of Law* (St. Paul, MN: West Publishing, 1891), 243.

4. Stevenson, "What's Love Got to Do with It?" See also Alexandra J. Finley, *An Intimate Economy: Enslaved Women, Work, and America's Domestic Slave Trade* (Chapel Hill: University of North Carolina Press, 2020).

5. Frederick Douglass, *Narrative of the Life of Frederick Douglass, An American Slave, Written by Himself* (Boston: 1845), 4, accessed at docsouth.unc.edu.

6. Annette Gordon-Reed, *The Hemingses of Monticello: An American Family* (New York: W. W. Norton, 2008), 106–107.

7. Discussions of sex across the color line raise complicated questions about enslaved women's agency and the impossibility of consent under slavery. On the difficulties of describing sexual contact between enslaved women and their masters, see, for example, Adrienne D. Davis, "The Private Law of Race and Sex: An Antebellum Perspective," *Stanford Law* Review 51 (1998–99): 221–288; Marisa J. Fuentes, "Power and Historical Figuring: Rachael Pringle Polgreen's Troubled Archive," *Gender and History* 223 (2010): 564–584; Gordon-Reed, *The Hemingses of Monticello*, 106–107; Saidiya Hartman, *Scenes of Subjection: Terror, Slavery, and Self-Making in Nineteenth-Century America* (New York: Oxford University Press, 1997); Saidiya Hartman, "Venus in Two Acts," *Small Axe* 26, no. 2 (June 2008): 1–14; Stevenson, "What's Love Got to Do with It?"; Deborah Gray White, *Ar'n't I a Woman? Female Slaves in the Plantation South* (New York: W. W. Norton, 1985).

8. This quote derives from a 1938 Works Progress Administration (WPA) interview with former slave Sarah Fitzpatrick. As scholars have discussed since the narratives' publication, WPA ex-slave narratives are problematic sources: the interviewers were primarily white, creating a complicated power dynamic between interviewer and interview subject that could lead to biases both in how questions were asked and how they were answered. Like many other WPA interviewers, the interviewer Thomas Campbell transcribed Fitzpatrick's narrative in a stereotypical African American "dialect." I have standardized the spelling here so that the racial bias inherent in the interviewer's transcription choices does not detract from the power of Sarah's words. The original quote reads: "Co'se back in de days when I come 'long us wimmen couldn't hep'it ef a white man wanted to take up time wid us." John W. Blassingame, ed., *Slave Testimony: Two Centuries of Letters, Speeches, Interviews, and Autobiographies* (Baton Rouge: Louisiana State University Press, 1977), 639. On historical approaches to the WPA ex-slave narratives, see John W. Blassingame, "Using the Testimony of Ex-Slaves: Approaches and Problems," *Journal of Southern History* 41 (November 1975): 473–492; Lynda M. Hill, "Ex-Slave Narratives: The WPA Federal Writers' Project Reappraised," *Oral History* 26, no. 1 (Spring 1998): 64–72; Steven Hahn, *A Nation Under Our Feet: Black Political Struggles in the Rural South from Slavery to the Great Migration* (Cambridge, MA: Belknap Press of Harvard University Press, 2003), 10.

9. Blassingame, *Slave Testimony*, 533.

10. Item 1, Will of Samuel Townsend dated 10 September 1853, Wills, Septimus D. Cabaniss Papers.
11. From Frederick Jackson Turner's 1893 essay, "The Significance of the Frontier in American History," to popular culture in the present day, Americans have often interpreted westward expansion as a driving force in the nation's history and national character. Westerners and frontier settlers in general have been portrayed as especially individualistic and self-reliant, despite the numerous ways federal government policy shaped the development of the region. Henry Nash Smith, *Virgin Land: The American West as Symbol and Myth* (Cambridge, MA: Harvard University Press, 1950, 1978). For critiques of the Turner thesis, see in particular Patricia Nelson Limerick, *The Legacy of Conquest: The Unbroken Past of the American West* (New York: W. W. Norton, 1988). For the influence of government policy in the American West after the Civil War, see Heather Cox Richardson, *West from Appomattox: The Reconstruction of America after the Civil War* (New Haven, CT: Yale University Press, 2007).
12. D. L. Lakin to S. D. Cabaniss, letter dated 29 February 1860, Septimus D. Cabaniss Papers.
13. D. L. Lakin to S. D. Cabaniss, letter dated 19 March 1860, Septimus D. Cabaniss Papers.
14. Bernie D. Jones, *Fathers of Conscience: Mixed-Race Inheritance in the Antebellum South* (Athens: University of Georgia Press, 2009), 7.
15. "Nigger in the Wood Pile," *The Xenia Torchlight* (Xenia, OH), 28 July 1858, State Archives, Ohio History Connection, Columbus, OH.
16. Barbara J. Fields, "Ideology and Race in American History," in *Region, Race, and Reconstruction: Essays in Honor of C. Van Woodward*, ed. J. Morgan Kousser and James McPherson (New York: Oxford University Press, 1982), 152. See also Martha Hodes, "Fractions and Fictions in the United States Census of 1890"; Martha Hodes, "The Mercurial Nature and Abiding Power of Race: A Transnational Family Story," *American Historical Review* 108, no. 1 (1 February 2003): 84–118; Thomas C. Holt, "Marking: Race, Race-making, and the Writing of History," *American Historical Review* 100, no. 1 (February 1995): 1–20.
17. Economist Howard Bodenhorn's *The Color Factor* provides valuable statistical data on the ways that mixed-race ancestry could result in advantageous outcomes for individual families in employment, finances, health, and access to freedom, as compared to African Americans without mixed-race ancestry. Howard Bodenhorn, *The Color Factor: The Economics of African-American Well-Being in the Nineteenth Century South* (New York: Oxford University Press, 2015)
18. S. D. Cabaniss to C. C. Clay, letter dated 21 January 1858; E. Tefft to O. O. Howard, letter dated 17 April 1867, Septimus D. Cabaniss Papers.
19. Hodes, "Fractions and Fictions in the United States Census of 1890," 244, 254.

20. "Belden Townsend," 1870 United States Federal Census, Kansas, Leavenworth, Leavenworth Ward 4; "Balden Townsend," Leavenworth, Kansas, City Directory, 1874, accessed 15 January 2018, www.ancestry.com.

21. *Wichita Reflector* (Wichita, KS), 9 October 1897, in Kansas Scrap-Book Biography, Theis-Tyler, Clippings, T, Volume 2, State Archives, Kansas Historical Society; "Hon. W. B. Townsend," *Topeka Plaindealer* (Topeka, KS), 27 September 1901, p. 1, America's Historical Newspapers. The Amon Carter Museum of American Art in Fort Worth, Texas, also holds four photographs of Leila Townsend, taken over the course of several years in Leavenworth, Kansas. Leila, born free in Kansas in 1885, was the daughter of Freeman Townsend, the half-brother of Samuel Townsend's children by Rainey Townsend, Wesley and Caroline. Special thanks to John Rohrbach at the Amon Carter Museum for his assistance in identifying the photographs of Leila Townsend.

22. In the antebellum South, mixed-race ancestry could be a predictor of whether or not an enslaved person might expect to be emancipated at some point in their lives. In Alabama alone, approximately 73 percent of free people of color were categorized as "mulattoes." Enslaved people with lighter skin also often held skilled positions on plantations or worked in the master's home, though this was not always an advantage. Historians have explored how close proximity to a white master or his family—living or working in the same house—gave enslaved people less physical and psychological distance than those who worked and lived outside the plantation house. See Nancy Rohr, "Free People of Color in Madison County, Alabama," accessed 24 January 2014, www.huntsvillehistorycollection.org; Ira Berlin, *Slaves Without Masters: The Free Negro in the Antebellum South* (New York: Pantheon Books, 1974); Thavolia Glymph, *Out of the House of Bondage: The Transformation of the Plantation Household* (Cambridge: Cambridge University Press, 2008).

23. Four more were the sons of a predeceased woman named Emily, whose children's manumission hints that she may have been a possible concubine of Samuel Townsend. Another three were a woman named Martha and two of her three children; Martha may have been a concubine of Samuel or perhaps the sexual partner of one of Samuel or Edmund's sons. This would account for the emancipation of only two of her three children, if these two were Samuel's grandchildren or otherwise related to him by blood. A woman named Peggy, for example, was freed as the mother of Wesley Townsend's son William Bolden; her other son Barney, fathered by an unknown enslaved man who was not related to Samuel Townsend, was not freed along with Peggy and William Bolden. The forty-fifth manumitted person was Dick, the enslaved husband of Samuel's concubine Hannah.

24. Colonial-era Virginia provides a notable example of the hardening of racial lines in the early eighteenth century, when lawmakers in 1705 first codified "blackness" as the state of having more than one-eighth African ancestry. See Kathleen M. Brown, *Good Wives, Nasty Wenches, and Anxious Patriarchs: Gender, Race and Power in Colonial Virginia* (Chapel Hill: University of North Carolina Press, 1996);

Winthrop D. Jordan, *White over Black: American Attitudes Toward the Negro, 1550–1812* (Chapel Hill: University of North Carolina Press, 1968).

25. Elliot West discusses the fluidity of racial lines in the second half of the nineteenth century in "Reconstructing Race," noting: "In the years after the Civil War, all America was a kind of borderland where racial edges and meanings were shifty and blurred." Elliott West, "Reconstructing Race," *Western Historical Quarterly* 34, no. 1 (Spring 2003): 15. Historian Anne Hyde similarly explores how changing racial definitions altered the lived experience of the mixed-race children of Native Americans and Europeans in the nineteenth-century American West. Anne F. Hyde, *Empires, Nations, and Families: A New History of the North American West, 1800–1860* (New York: Harper Collins, 2011).

26. For racial regimes in the Caribbean, see Edward E. Baptist and Stephanie M. H. Camp, *New Studies in the History of American Slavery* (Athens: University of Georgia Press, 2006); Jerome S. Handler, *The Unappropriated People: Freedmen in the Slave Society of Barbados* (Baltimore, MD: Johns Hopkins University Press, 1974); Gad J. Heuman, *Between Black and White: Race, Politics, and the Free Coloreds in Jamaica, 1792–1865* (Westport, CN.: Greenwood, 1981); Gad J. Heuman, "White Over Brown Over Black: The Free Coloureds in Jamaican Society During Slavery and After Emancipation," *Journal of Caribbean History* (May 1, 1981): 46–69; Hodes, "The Mercurial Nature and Abiding Power of Race"; Martha Hodes, *The Sea Captain's Wife: A True Story of Love, Race, and War in the Nineteenth Century* (New York: W.W. Norton, 2006); Matthew D. O'Hara and Andrew B. Fisher, eds., *Imperial Subjects: Race and Identity in Colonial Latin America* (Durham, NC: Duke University Press, 2009); Kimberly S. Hanger, *Bounded Lives, Bounded Places: Free Black Society in Colonial New Orleans, 1769–1803* (Durham, NC: Duke University Press, 1997); Arnold A. Sio, "Marginality and Free Coloured Identity in Caribbean Slave Society," *Slavery & Abolition* 8, no. 2 (1987): 166–182; Peter Wade, *Race and Ethnicity in Latin America* (New York: Pluto Press, 2010).

27. Hodes, "The Mercurial Nature and Abiding Power of Race," 105.

28. James Oliver Horton and Stacy Flaherty, "Black Leadership in Antebellum Cincinnati," in *Race and the City: Work, Community, and Protest in Cincinnati, 1820-1970*, ed. Henry Louis Taylor Jr. (Urbana: University of Illinois Press, 1993), 83.

29. *The Wilberforce Annual: A Comprehensive Review of the Origin, Development and Present Status of Wilberforce University*, ed. B. W. Arnett and S. T. Mitchell (Xenia, OH: 1885), 17–18.

30. For Black political activism and war mobilization in Kansas, see Brent M. S. Campney, *This Is Not Dixie: Racist Violence in Kansas, 1861–1927* (Urbana: University of Illinois Press, 2015); Noah Andre Trudeau, *Like Men of War: Black Troops in the Civil War, 1862–1865* (New York: Little, Brown, 1998).

31. "Belden Townsend," 1870 Federal Census, Kansas, Leavenworth, accessed 15 January 2018, www.ancestry.com; "Balden Townsend," Leavenworth, Kansas, City Directory, 1874, accessed 15 January 2018; www.ancestry.com; "Elvira Townsand,"

Leavenworth City Directory and Business Mirror, 1865–66 (St. Louis, MO: James Sutherland, 1866), Leavenworth County Historical Society at the Carroll Mansion Museum, Leavenworth, KS (hereafter LCHS).

32. *Leavenworth Daily Conservative,* 20 January 1864, State Archives, Kansas Historical Society, Topeka, KS (hereafter KHS).

33. See Quintard Taylor, *In Search of the Racial Frontier: African Americans in the American West, 1528–1990* (New York: W.W. Norton, 1998), 104.

34. See Liston E. Leyendecker, Christine A. Bradley, and Duane A. Smith, *The Rise of the Silver Queen: Georgetown, Colorado, 1859–1896* (Boulder: University Press of Colorado, 2005).

35. *Daily Register Call,* 29 September 1871, p. 4, Colorado Historic Newspapers Collection, Colorado State Library, www.coloradohistoricnewspapers.org.

36. Transcription of "Wealthy Negro Dies," *Huntsville Mercury-Banner,* 31 August 1916, Septimus D. Cabaniss Papers.

37. Frances Cabaniss Roberts, "An Experiment in Emancipation of Slaves by an Alabama Planter" (MA thesis, University of Alabama, 1940).

38. Citing Black feminist theorist Patricia Hill Collins and anthropologist Raymond Fogelson, Tiya Miles has written that family histories possess an "epitomizing" power that can provide insight into the ways in which race, gender, class, and communities are formed within the larger society. As families are often associated with the health and interests of the nation, the ways in which families are formed "illuminate the values and dictates of the communities in which families live." Tiya Miles, *Ties That Bind: The Story of an Afro-Cherokee Family in Slavery and Freedom* (Berkeley: University of California Press, 2005). For other works in which historians have examined the lives of individuals and families to explore specific ways in which racial lines were challenged or crossed, see W. Ralph Eubanks, *The House at the End of the Road: The Story of Three Generations of an Interracial Family in the American South* (New York: Harper Collins, 2009); Gordon-Reed, *The Hemingses of Monticello*; Hodes, *The Sea Captain's Wife*; Karl Jacoby, *The Strange Career of William Ellis: The Texas Slave Who Became a Mexican Millionaire* (New York: W.W. Norton, 2016); Martha A. Sandweiss, *Passing Strange: A Gilded Age Tale of Love and Deception Across the Color Line* (New York: Penguin Press, 2009); Daniel J. Sharfstein, *The Invisible Line: Three American Families and the Secret Journey from Black to White* (New York: Penguin Press, 2011). Like microhistorical studies, comparative work can also prove useful in highlighting distinctions and differences between regions at a fine-grained level. See Jeff Forret and Christine E. Sears, eds., *New Directions in Slavery Studies: Commodification, Community, and Comparison* (Baton Rouge: Louisiana State University Press, 2015).

39. Susanna Townsend to S. D. Cabaniss, letter dated 4 June 1868, Septimus D. Cabaniss Papers.

40. John W. Checks and Elizabeth Yerger, Alabama, Select Marriages; John W. Checks, U.S. Returns from Regular Army Infantry, 1821–1916; Elizabeth Cheeks, 1870

United States Federal Census, North Carolina, Raleigh, accessed 22 June 2016, www.ancestry.com.

41. For an in-depth study of the myths and realities of racial passing in the United States, see Allyson Hobbs, *A Chosen Exile: A History of Racial Passing in American Life* (Cambridge, MA: Harvard University Press, 2014).

42. In many ways, the shrinking of a middle space for mixed-race African Americans in the late nineteenth century paralleled the experiences of mixed-race descendants of European fur traders and Native American women in the early nineteenth-century West. See, for example, Hyde, *Empires, Nations, and Families*; Miles, *Ties That Bind*; Claudio Saunt, *Black, White, and Indian: Race and the Unmaking of an American Family* (New York: Oxford University Press, 2005).

43. Liston E. Leyendecker et al., *The Rise of the Silver Queen*, 88–89; Charles Osborne Townsend to Thomas Townsend, letter dated 14 February 1888, Septimus D. Cabaniss Papers.

44. "Whites Don't Know the Negro!," *Topeka Plaindealer* (Topeka, KS), 7 April 1905, p. 1, America's Historical Newspapers.

45. For analyses of the ways in which power dynamics shape historical archives, particularly with regard to the history of slavery and enslaved people, see Michel-Rolph Trouillot, *Silencing the Past: Power and the Production of History* (Boston: Beacon Press, 1995); Wendy Anne Warren, "'The Cause of Her Grief': The Rape of a Slave in Early New England," *Journal of American History* 93, no. 4 (March 2007): 1031–1049; Fuentes, "Power and Historical Figuring: Rachael Pringle Polgreen's Troubled Archive."

46. Roberts, "An Experiment in Emancipation of Slaves by an Alabama Planter." Roberts's 1940 thesis was the first account to examine the Townsend family in detail. Samuel Townsend's will is also briefly mentioned in Joel Williamson's studies of race in the American South. See Joel Williamson, *The Crucible of Race: Black/White Relations in the American South Since Emancipation* (New York: Oxford University Press, 1984), 41–42; Joel Williamson, *A Rage for Order: Black/White Relations in the American South Since Emancipation* (New York: Oxford University Press, 1986). More recently, historian Sharony Green devoted a chapter to the Townsend family in her monograph *Remember Me to Miss Louisa*. Sharony Green, *Remember Me to Miss Louisa: Hidden Black-White Intimacies in Antebellum America* (Dekalb: Northern Illinois University Press, 2015).

47. Roberts, "An Experiment in Emancipation of Slaves by an Alabama Planter," 85.

48. Roberts, "An Experiment in Emancipation of Slaves by an Alabama Planter," 85, 75.

49. Roberts, "An Experiment in Emancipation of Slaves by an Alabama Planter," 3–4.

50. For critical analyses of early slavery, Civil War, and Reconstruction historiography, see David W. Blight, *Race and Reunion: The Civil War in American Memory* (Cambridge, MA: Harvard University Press, 2001); W. E. B. Du Bois, *Black Reconstruction: An Essay Toward a History of the Part Which Black Played in the Attempt to Reconstruct Democracy in America, 1860–1880* (New York: Harcourt,

Brace, 1935); Eric Foner, *Forever Free: The Story of Emancipation & Reconstruction* (New York: Vintage Books, 2006); James Oliver Horton and Lois E. Horton, *Slavery and the Making of America* (New York: Oxford University Press, 2006).

CHAPTER 1

1. Depositions of Julia E. Bayne, Parks Ashworth, Mary J Wood, Robert Branch and William Lewis, T. J. Redmond vs. Thomas Townsend et al., Chancery Court files, Madison County Records Center, Huntsville, AL (hereafter MCRC).

2. Item 4, deposition of Archer and Elizabeth Townsend, Townsend vs. Townsend, Answers, Septimus D. Cabaniss Papers.

3. Will of Edmund Townsend dated 25 February 1850, Estate of Edmund Townsend, Probate Court of Madison County; T. J. Redmond vs. Thomas Townsend et al., MCRC. Numbers regarding average farm sizes in free and slave states from Clayton E. Jewett and John O. Allen, *Slavery in the South: A State-by-State History* (Westport, CT.: Greenwood Press, 2004), 287.

4. See Lawrence H. Officer and Samuel H. Williamson, "Explaining the Measures of Worth," accessed 23 June 2020, www.measuringworth.com.

5. Item 4, deposition of Archer and Elizabeth Townsend, Townsend vs. Townsend, Answers, Septimus D. Cabaniss Papers. Details on Edmund Townsend's real estate and personal property from Will of Edmund Townsend dated 25 February 1850, Probate Court of Madison County, MCRC.

6. John Locke, *Two Treatises of Government*, Book II, Sect. 87 (London: 1688).

7. See Frederika Teute Schmidt and Barbara Ripel Wilhem, "Early Proslavery Petitions in Virginia," *William and Mary Quarterly* 30, no. 1 (January 1973): 133–146.

8. For an extensive study of tobacco cultivation and slave communities in the Chesapeake up to the turn of the nineteenth century, see Allan Kulikoff, *Tobacco and Slaves: The Development of Southern Cultures in the Chesapeake, 1680–1800* (Chapel Hill: University of North Carolina Press, 1986).

9. A number of factors make it difficult to know much for certain about Edmund and his siblings' parents. The names William and Elizabeth were very common; a large number of Townsends lived in Lunenburg County at the end of the eighteenth century; and there is a lack of consistent census information from the colonial period and early Republic. Family trees created by present-day descendants tend to favor the birth and death years 1760 or 1766 to 1815 for William and 1764 to 1810 for Elizabeth (whom a number identify as Elizabeth Cousins of Henrico, Virginia), though other biographical details are lacking. The father may have been the William Townsend who enlisted as a private in the Revolutionary War and was injured at the Battle of Brandywine; he may also have been the William Townsend whom the 1810 United States Federal Census recorded as owning five slaves. For family genealogies, see RATownsend Family Tree, Stone Shellman Families, Townsend Family Tree, CARL AUGUST TIMMEL, and Rhodemans of Kansas,

accessed 1 February 2019, www.ancestry.com. See also US Revolutionary War Rolls 1775–1783, accessed 1 December 2015, www.ancestry.com; John Frederick Dorman, *Adventures of Purse and Person, Virginia, 1608–1624/5: Families G-P* (Baltimore, MD: Genealogical Publishing, 2004), 155, fn. 276.

10. Thomas Jefferson, "Answers to de Meusnier Questions, 1786," *The Works of Thomas Jefferson*, vol. 5, ed. Paul Leicester Ford (New York: G. P. Putnam's Sons, 1905); Thomas Jefferson, "Q.XIX, 1782" in *Notes on the State of Virginia* (Philadelphia: Prichard and Hall, 1788), accessed 1 February 2019, https://docsouth.unc.edu.

11. See Sven Beckert, *Empire of Cotton: A New History of Global Capitalism* (New York: Alfred A. Knopf, 2014); Joyce E. Chaplin, "Creating a Cotton South in Georgia and South Carolina," *Journal of Southern History* 57, no. 2 (May 1991): 171–200; Steven Deyle, *Carry Me Back: The Domestic Slave Trade in American Life* (New York: Oxford University Press, 2005); Daniel Walker Howe, *What Hath God Wrought: The Transformation of America, 1815–1848* (New York: Oxford University Press, 2007); Walter Johnson, *Soul by Soul: Life Inside the Antebellum Slave Market* (Cambridge, MA: Harvard University Press, 1999); Angela Lakwete, *Inventing the Cotton Gin: Machine and Myth in Antebellum America* (Baltimore, MD: Johns Hopkins University Press, 2003).

12. Smith, *Virgin Land*.

13. Daniel S. Dupre, *Transforming the Cotton Frontier: Madison County, Alabama, 1800–1840* (Baton Rouge: Louisiana State University Press, 1997), 16.

14. William Warren Rogers et al., *Alabama: The History of a Deep South State* (Tuscaloosa: University of Alabama Press, 2010); Adam Rothman, *Slave Country: American Expansion and the Origins of the Deep South* (Cambridge, MA: Harvard University Press, 2005); Gregory A. Waselkov, *A Conquering Spirit: Fort Mims and the Redstick War of 1813–14* (Tuscaloosa: University of Alabama Press, 2006); Karl Davis, "'Remember Fort Mims': Reinterpreting the Origins of the Creek War," *Journal of the Early Republic* 22, no. 4 (Winter 2002): 611–636.

15. Andrew Jackson as quoted in Rothman, *Slave Country*, 138.

16. Andrew Jackson, "On Indian Removal" (1830), accessed 1 December 2015, www.ourdocuments.gov.

17. Rogers et al., *Alabama: The History of a Deep South State*, 54, 139.

18. Andrew Jackson as quoted in Rothman, *Slave Country*, 139.

19. Thomas Jefferson to George Rogers Clark, letter dated 25 December 1780, Papers of Thomas Jefferson, accessed 1 December 2015, http://founders.archives.gov.

20. See Smith, *Virgin Land*; Judge Thomas Jones Taylor, *A History of Madison County and Incidentally of North Alabama, 1732–1840*, ed. W. Stanley Hoole and Addie S. Hoole (Tuscaloosa, AL: Confederate Publishing, 1976), 49.

21. Dupre, *Transforming the Cotton Frontier*, 43; Taylor, *A History of Madison County*, 48.

22. Dupre, *Transforming the Cotton Frontier*, 38, 42; Taylor, *A History of Madison County*, 45.

23. Taylor, *A History of Madison County*, 49.

24. As quoted in Rothman, *Slave Country*, 171.

25. Taylor, *A History of Madison County*, 45.

26. Dupre, *Transforming the Cotton Frontier*, 70–73.

27. Dates derive from the headstones of Samuel and Edmund Townsend at their gravesite in Madison County, Alabama, as well as Roberts, "An Experiment in Emancipation of Slaves by an Alabama Planter." Large planters already dominated Madison County's best land by the 1820s, while smaller farmers were concentrated in the more mountainous regions of northern Alabama. One of Edmund Townsend's plantations, which he called the Mullens Place, was situated on the Mullens "flat lands"— described as a "fine body of lands" that sold for an average of $30 per acre, second only to the Patton and Stevens plots, which sold for approximately $50 an acre. Taylor, *A History of Madison County*, 45.

28. Items 16 and 17, Notes on conversations with Anthony Perryman, Mrs. Prentis, and Captain Godden dated June 1860, Legal notes/strategy/depositions, Septimus D. Cabaniss Papers.

29. P. Brown, "The Leonid Meteor Shower: Historical Visual Observations," *Icarus* 138, no. 2 (1 April 1999): 287–308. For contemporary accounts in nineteenth-century scientific journals, see D. Olmstead, "Observations of the Meteors of November 13, 1833," *American Journal of Science* 25 and 26 (1834).

30. "Phenomenon; People; Country; Advocations; Increased," *Evening Post* (New York), 13 November 1833, accessed 1 February 2019, Newspapers.com.

31. Revelation 6:13, 6:17, *King James Version*.

32. Donald W. Olson and Laurie E. Jasinski, "Abe Lincoln and the Leonids," *Sky & Telescope* (November 1999): 34–35. The anecdote regarding Lincoln comes from an essay by Walt Whitman titled "A Lincoln Reminiscence," published in the 1882 volume *Specimen Days & Collect*.

33. On the role of territorial expansion in the spread of cotton cultivation and slave labor, see Ira Berlin, *Generations of Captivity: A History of African-American Slaves* (Cambridge, MA: Harvard University Press, 2003); Deyle, *Carry Me Back*; Jewett and Allen, *Slavery in the South*; Edmund S. Morgan, *American Slavery, American Freedom* (New York: W.W. Norton, 1975); Rothman, *Slave Country*.

34. Rogers et al., *Alabama: The History of a Deep South State*, 55.

35. Dupre, *Transforming the Cotton Frontier*, 126.

36. Sellers, *Slavery in Alabama*, 141.

37. Item 1, receipts dated 1827–1847, Samuel Townsend slave receipts, Septimus D. Cabaniss Papers.

38. Will of Stith Townsend dated 8 September 1828, Probate Court of Madison County, MCRC.

39. Items 1–18, Slave receipts dated 1827–1847, Samuel Townsend slave receipts, Septimus D. Cabaniss Papers.
40. Sellers, *Slavery in Alabama*, 142.
41. The number of enslaved people sold in the domestic slave trade exceeded the number of enslaved people transported to North America in the international slave trade—one of the reasons historians call the mass forced removal of enslaved people west and south in the nineteenth century the "Second Middle Passage." See Berlin, *Generations of Captivity*; Deyle, *Carry Me Back*; Johnson, *Soul by Soul*.
42. Blassingame, *Slave Testimony*, 222.
43. Blassingame, *Slave Testimony*, 421.
44. Lewis Hayden as quoted in Blassingame, *Slave Testimony*, 697. Hayden's description of sale as equivalent to death provides another example of the similarities of enslaved people's experience of the Atlantic slave trade and African American slaves' forced migration west in the domestic slave trade. Both involved the extreme alienation that historical sociologist Orlando Patterson has described as "social death"—although some scholars have pushed back against "social death" as a too-abstract framework and have complicated the concept with more detailed studies of lived experiences of enslavement and the Middle Passage. See Orlando Patterson, *Slavery and Social Death: A Comparative Study* (Cambridge, MA: Harvard University Press, 1982); Vincent Brown, "Social Death and Political Life in the Study of Slavery," *American Historical Review* 114, no. 5 (December 2009): 1233.
45. Slave traders increasingly sent enslaved people south on steamboats and railroads in the 1850s, but early settlers did not have this option. While steamboats were used extensively in the 1820s and '30s to transport enslaved people to port cities such as New Orleans, and Mobile in Alabama, a destination in northern Alabama required overland travel. Sellers, *Slavery in Alabama*, 151–153.
46. Taylor, *A History of Madison County*, 49.
47. Sellers, *Slavery in Alabama*, 151.
48. Berlin, *Generations of* Captivity; Steven F. Miller, "Plantation Labor Organization and Slave Life on the Cotton Frontier: The Alabama-Mississippi Black Belt, 1815–1840," in *Cultivation and Culture: Labor and the Shaping of Slave Life in the Americas,* ed. Ira Berlin and Philip D. Morgan (Charlottesville: University of Virginia Press, 1993), 156.
49. James A. Tait as quoted in Sellers, *Slavery in Alabama*, 33.
50. See Miller, "Plantation Labor Organization and Slave Life on the Cotton Frontier"; Berlin, *Generations of Captivity*; Jewett and Allen, *Slavery in the South*; Kulikoff, *Tobacco and Slaves*; Philip D. Morgan, *Slave Counterpoint: Black Culture in the Eighteenth-Century Chesapeake and Lowcountry* (Chapel Hill: University of North Carolina Press, 1998).
51. For further discussions of the "negotiations" that took place between masters and slaves over terms of labor and customary practices, see Ira Berlin, *Many*

Thousands Gone: The First Two Centuries of Slavery in North America (Cambridge, MA: Belknap Press of Harvard University Press, 1998); Hahn, *A Nation Under Our Feet,* 31; Hilary McD. Beckles, "An Economic Life of Their Own: Slaves as Commodity Producers and Distributors in Barbados" in *Caribbean Slavery in the Atlantic World: A Student Reader,* ed. Verne Shepherd and Hilarly McD. Beckles (Kingston, Jamaica: Ian Randle, 2000), 732–742.

52. James A. Tait as quoted in Sellers, *Slavery in Alabama,* 67.

53. Item 2, 1858 and 1860 inventory of slaves inherited by Samuel C. Townsend, Cabaniss v. Townsend exhibits; Item 35, "Negroes at E. Townsends," Miscellaneous file notes, Septimus D. Cabaniss Papers.

54. Sellers, *Slavery in Alabama,* 51; Item 2, Receipt for payment to E. G. Townsend dated 8 January 1852, Edmund Townsend receipts, Septimus D. Cabaniss Papers.

55. See Morgan, *American Slavery, American Freedom;* Ariela J. Gross, *Double Character: Slavery and Mastery in the Antebellum Southern Courtroom* (Athens: University of Georgia Press, 2006), 49.

56. Sellers, *Slavery in Alabama,* 45.

57. Hahn, *A Nation Under Our Feet,* 30. See also Stephanie M. H. Camp, *Closer to Freedom: Enslaved Women and Everyday Resistance in the Plantation South* (Chapel Hill: University of North Carolina Press, 2004).

58. Edmund Townsend to James Robinson, letter dated 18 April 1850, Septimus D. Cabaniss Papers.

59. Bradley Wilson to Edmund Townsend, incoming correspondence dated 1849–1853, Septimus D. Cabaniss Papers.

60. Edmund Townsend to James Robinson, letter dated 18 April 1850, Septimus D. Cabaniss Papers.

61. Item 1, Wilborn G. Barton vs. Henry King & Others, Complaints/petitions dated 1828–1861, Septimus D. Cabaniss Papers.

62. Samuel Townsend et al. v. Elisabeth Routt Adm'r, Madison County Circuit Court records, Alabama Department of Archives and History, Montgomery, AL.

63. Edmund Townsend to James Robinson, letter dated 18 April 1850, Septimus D. Cabaniss Papers.

64. Sellers, *Slavery in Alabama,* 141.

65. Receipts dated 1834–1859, Samuel Townsend receipts, Septimus D. Cabaniss Papers.

66. Rohr, "Free People of Color in Madison County, Alabama"; Sellers, *Slavery in Alabama,* 362.

67. Slave pass dated 7 July 1856, Samuel Townsend outgoing correspondence, Septimus D. Cabaniss Papers.

68. Rohr, "Free People of Color in Madison County, Alabama"; Sellers, *Slavery in Alabama,* 362.

69. Samuel Townsend to J. E. Townsend, letter dated 13 July 1856, Septimus D. Cabaniss Papers.

70. Jewett and Allen, *Slavery in the South*, 2; Rohr, "Free People of Color in Madison County, Alabama." Rohr quotes a letter from a Madison County militia colonel to the Alabama governor in 1831, requesting one hundred muskets with bayonets to arm the white population. Without support, he feared, if thousands of "able bodied Negro men" revolted "the Town might be destroyed and many of our people slain or ruined." This and the Madison County patrol law were direct responses to news of Nat Turner's rebellion in 1831.

71. Edmund Townsend to James Robinson, letter dated 18 April 1850, Septimus D. Cabaniss Papers.

72. In *Many Thousands Gone* and *Generations of Captivity*, Ira Berlin defines a "slave society" as one in which slavery was at the center of economic production and the master-slave relationship served as the model for all social relations, as opposed to "societies with slaves," in which slavery was marginal to economic production and only one form of coercive labor among others. For an in-depth study of the plantation complex in the nineteenth-century South, see also Walter Johnson, *River of Dark Dreams: Slavery and Empire in the Cotton Kingdom* (Cambridge, MA: Belknap Press of Harvard University Press, 2013).

73. Sellers, *Slavery in Alabama*, 42.

74. Edmund Townsend, Alabama, Civil Appointments, 1818–1939, accessed 25 March 2020, www.ancestry.com; James Record, *A Dream Come True: The Story of Madison County and Incidentally of Alabama and the United States* (Huntsville, AL: John Hicklin Printing, 1970), 235.

75. The account of Edmund Townsend and his men's assault on the enslaved man Lewis derives from Adam Dale's testimony before the Circuit Court of Madison County in August 1848. The clerk who took Dale's deposition transcribed the testimony as Dale spoke it, in first person with multiple direct quotes from Dale, Edmund Townsend, Harrison Curry, and Dale's wife Mary. Quotations are presented without alteration. Deposition of Adam Dale, Saml Townsend et al. v. Elisabeth Routt Adm'r, MCRC.

76. See "Adam Dale" and "Elizabeth Evans Hall Dale," Huntsville History Collection, accessed 25 March 2020, www.huntsvillehistorycollection.org. William Jeffries was the son of Elizabeth and her third husband, Alexander Jeffries. At the time of Edmund Townsend and his posse's arrival at the Routt plantation in 1848, Elizabeth and her sixth husband Willis Routt were away from home on their honeymoon. Elizabeth had six husbands over the course of her life, some of whom reportedly died under mysterious circumstances.

77. Appeals in the Routt case continued at least until 1854, after Edmund and Parks Townsend had both died, eventually moving from the county circuit court to the Alabama Supreme Court. Edmund's brother Samuel Townsend, who had not been present at the assault, became the defendant as the executor of Edmund's will. Ariela Gross discusses this case as an example of "unmasterly" conduct on the part of a slave owner—who, according to paternalist ideology, was supposed to be firm

but not impassioned and to respect other slave owners' property. Edmund did not demonstrate restraint in either respect. Gross, *Double Character*, 118–120.

78. Items 16 and 17, Legal notes/strategy/depositions; S. D. Cabaniss to Macfarland and Roberts, letter dated 5 March 1859; S. D. Cabaniss to Macfarland and Roberts, letter dated 11 August 1859, Septimus D. Cabaniss Papers.

79. S. D. Cabaniss to Macfarland and Roberts, letter dated 11 August 1859, Septimus D. Cabaniss Papers.

80. See Hodes, *White Women, Black Men*.

81. S. D. Cabaniss to Macfarland and Roberts, letter dated 11 August 1859, Septimus D. Cabaniss Papers.

82. S. D. Cabaniss hired investigators to look into Lizzy's origins in 1858 and 1859, when Edmund Townsend and Lizzy's daughters filed a suit for freedom based on the assertion that their mother was a free woman sold into slavery illegally. As the daughters were by then the property of Samuel Townsend's estate, and Cabaniss was Samuel's executor, Cabaniss was responsible for disproving their claims. During this process, Cabaniss discovered that Edmund Townsend's bills of sale from this period had been destroyed in a fire, meaning the exact date of Lizzy's purchase and the amount paid remain unknown. S. D. Cabaniss to Macfarland and Roberts, letter dated 5 March 1859; S. D. Cabaniss to George W. Cook, letter dated 12 August 1859, Septimus D. Cabaniss Papers.

83. Johnson, *Soul by Soul*, 113; Stevenson, "What's Love Got to Do with It?," 105.

84. Deyle, *Carry Me Back*, 56.

85. Johnson, *Soul by Soul*, 113.

86. Stevenson, "What's Love Got to Do with It?," 101.

87. Item 3, "Inventory and Appraisement" dated February–March 1858, Inventories, Septimus D. Cabaniss Papers.

88. Items 3 and 4, Petitions of Virginia Townsend and Eliza M. Townsend filed 4 June 1859, Cabaniss v. Townsend, Complaints/petitions, Septimus D. Cabaniss Papers. The description of Lizzy as Edmund Townsend's "wife" echoes other cases in the antebellum South, where wealthy planters or slave traders kept enslaved concubines for long periods of time. Alexandra Finley examines the case of slave trader Silas Omohundro's longtime concubine Corrina, who performed both sexual and domestic labor in his household and business and who signed her name "Mrs. Corinna Omohundro." Finley argues that through concubinage, white men gained the benefits of a wife without owing the enslaved woman any reciprocal legal or economic support or protection. Alexandra Finley, "'Cash to Corinna': Domestic Labor and Sexual Economy in the 'Fancy Trade,'" *Journal of American History* 104, no. 2 (September 2017): 410–430.

89. Harriet Jacobs, *Incidents in the Life of a Slave Girl, Written by Herself*, ed. L. Maria Child (Boston: 1861), 44.

90. Jacobs, *Incidents in the Life of a Slave Girl,* 45.

91. Item 3, "Inventory and Appraisement" dated February-March 1858, Inventories; Petitions of Virginia Townsend and Eliza M Townsend filed 4 June 1859, Septimus D. Cabaniss Papers.

92. On manumissions of and testamentary transfers of property to enslaved concubines and their children, see Jeffory A. Clymer, *Family Money: Property, Race, and Literature in the Nineteenth Century* (New York: Oxford University Press, 2013); Davis, "The Private Law of Race and Sex: An Antebellum Perspective"; Jones, *Fathers of Conscience.*

93. For clothing purchases made on behalf of Edmund's daughters, see receipts dated 1860, Legatee accounts, Septimus D. Cabaniss Papers. Regarding anti-literacy laws in Alabama: the state's 1833 slave codes imposed a fine of $250 to $500 on any person who attempted to teach an enslaved person or free person of color to read or write. See John G. Akin, *A Digest of the Laws of the State of Alabama* (Philadelphia: Alexander Towar, 1833), 397.

94. S. D. Cabaniss to Macfarland and Roberts, letter dated 17 January 1859, Septimus D. Cabaniss Papers. In correspondence with his investigators, Cabaniss described the strategy of Lizzy and Jennie's supporters in their suit for freedom: that they would attempt to "create a belief [in] the public mind that the negroes are entitled to be free — & that they will produce [men] to swear" to this, one of them being the overseer Daniel Curry, who claimed to have been present when Edmund Townsend spoke with the two men from Virginia. Cabaniss assumed that these witnesses would lie under oath or employ other "unfair means." He seemed confident that a jury would not believe Curry on account of his "bad character," but feared that Lizzy's testimony would be convincing, writing "there would be too much risk . . . for us to make a witness of her." The idea that Curry or the other witnesses deposed in Virginia lied under oath cannot be substantiated, and aside from Lizzy none of them stood to benefit (financially or otherwise) if Edmund's daughters were declared free. Nor did Cabaniss or his investigators ever prove that Lizzy was not Fanny Perryman's daughter. To the contrary, various white witnesses including Fanny's own niece insisted that she was. For Cabaniss's notes and comments on the freedom suit, see S. D. Cabaniss to Wesley Townsend, letters dated 11 December 1858, 21 December 1858, 18 November 1859; S. D. Cabaniss to Mcfarland and Roberts, letters dated 17 January 1859, 21 February 1859, 18 February 1859, 5 March 1859, 11 August 1859, 30 September 1859; S. D. Cabaniss to George W. Cook, letter dated 12 August 1859, Septimus D. Cabaniss Papers.

95. Items 3 and 4, Petitions of Virginia Townsend and Eliza M Townsend filed 4 June 1859, Cabaniss v. Townsend, Complaints/petitions, Septimus D. Cabaniss Papers.

96. Deposition of Robert Branch and William Lewis, T. J. Redmond v. Thomas Townsend et al., MCRC.

CHAPTER 2

1. Will of Edmund Townsend dated 25 February 1850, Madison County Probate Court records, MCRC.
2. Will of Edmund Townsend dated 25 February 1850, Madison County Probate Court records, MCRC.
3. Item 4, deposition of Archer and Elizabeth Townsend, Townsend vs. Townsend, Answers, Septimus D. Cabaniss Papers.
4. Sellers, *Slavery in Alabama*, 230.
5. Notes on Edmund Townsend's will, filed 26 September 1853 and deposition of Robert Branch and William Lewis, both in T. J. Redmond v. Thomas Townsend, et al., MCRC.
6. Item 4, deposition of Archer and Elizabeth Townsend, Townsend vs. Townsend, Answers, Septimus D. Cabaniss Papers.
7. For examinations of the lives and habits of slave traders in this period, as well as their reputation for unscrupulousness, see Deyle, *Carry Me Back* and Johnson, *Soul by Soul*.
8. Item 4, deposition of Archer and Elizabeth Townsend, Townsend vs. Townsend, Answers, Septimus D. Cabaniss Papers.
9. Item 6, deposition of Jones D. Crow and Rushia Crow, Townsend v. Townsend, Answers, Septimus D. Cabaniss Papers.
10. Deposition of Robert Branch and William Lewis, T.J. Redmond v. Thomas Townsend, et al., MCRC.
11. Item 2, deposition of Upton and Jane Crow, Townsend v. Townsend, Answers, Septimus D. Cabaniss Papers. Emphasis in original.
12. Item 6, deposition of Jones D. Crow and Rushia Crow, Townsend v. Townsend, Answers, Septimus D. Cabaniss Papers.
13. Item 4, deposition of Archer and Elizabeth Townsend, Townsend vs. Townsend, Answers, Septimus D. Cabaniss Papers.
14. Redmond's fraudulent contracts with the Townsends were ultimately overturned, and Edmund's relatives in Virginia inherited approximately $5,000 per married couple. See Case #392, T. J. Redmond vs. Thomas Townsend et al., Chancery Court Files, MCRC.
15. For more on the "transformative possibilities" of slave ownership that white southerners imagined in the antebellum period, see Johnson, *Soul by Soul*, particularly chapter 3, "Making a World Out of Slaves."
16. Item 1, deposition of Elias Wellborn dated 29 August 1857, Legal notes/ strategy/ depositions, Septimus D. Cabaniss Papers.
17. Ira Berlin, *Slaves Without Masters*.
18. Rohr, "Free People of Color in Madison County"; Sellers, *Slavery in Alabama*, 362.
19. The *Southern Advocate* as quoted in Dupre, *Transforming the Cotton Frontier*, 212. The article Dupre excerpts was published on 12 November 1831, illustrating the

impact of the Nat Turner rebellion on white Madison County residents' opinions about free Black people.

20. Rohr, "Free People of Color in Madison County"; Sellers, *Slavery in Alabama*, 384.

21. Sellers, *Slavery in* Alabama, 176, 368.

22. See "Alabama Supreme Court Decisions on Manumission: Trotter v. Blocker, 6 Porter 269 (1838)" and "Manumission by Last Will in Antebellum Alabama," Auburn University Archives and Manuscripts Department, accessed 1 April 2016, http://www.lib.auburn.edu/archive/aghy/manumission/trotter.htm and https://www.lib.auburn.edu/archive/aghy/manumission/manu-txt.htm.

23. "Alabama Supreme Court Decisions on Manumission: Trotter v. Blocker, 6 Porter 269 (1838)" and "Manumission by Last Will in Antebellum Alabama."

24. 26 October 1859 article in the *Southern Advocate* as quoted in Sellers, *Slavery in Alabama,* 368.

25. Sellers, *Slavery in Alabama,* 368, 378.

26. Item 4, deposition of Archer and Elizabeth Townsend, Townsend vs. Townsend, Answers, Septimus D. Cabaniss Papers.

27. Notes on Edmund Townsend's will filed 26 September 1853, T.J. Redmond vs. Thomas Townsend et. al., MCRC.

28. In the November 1854 draft of his will, Samuel Townsend described the mother of his son Joseph Bradford and daughter Susanna as "a woman named Celia of dark complexion." The fact that she was distinguished from the other mothers of Samuel's children by her "dark complexion" suggests that the other women, like their children, were lighter-skinned. When listed in federal census records after their emancipation, some of Samuel's former concubines (as well as their children by enslaved men) were also classified as "mulattoes." In addition, Cabaniss discussed the light skin color of the Townsend women and children who were not Samuel's descendants in an 1853 letter to a colleague. In total, these sources indicate that the Townsends' mixed-race ancestry did not begin with Samuel's children's generation. See in particular S. D. Cabaniss to C.C. Clay letter dated 21 January 1858, Septimus D. Cabaniss Papers.

29. For more on the development of this timeline of Samuel Townsend's sexual contact with enslaved women on his plantations, see "Note on Methodology." Sources used to determine these dates include Item 1, will of Samuel Townsend dated 10 September 1853, Wills; Item 2, will of Samuel Townsend (November 1854 draft), Wills; Item 3, will of Samuel Townsend dated 6 September and 15 October 1853, Wills; Items 4 and 5, will of Samuel Townsend dated 6 September 1856, Wills; Item 3, "Inventory and Appraisement" dated February-March 1858, Inventories, Septimus D. Cabaniss Papers.

30. Antebellum plantation mistress Mary Chesnut described slave owners living "like the patriarchs of old . . . all in one house with their wives & their concubines." Mary Boykin Chesnut and C. Vann Woodward, ed., *Mary Chesnut's Civil War* (New Haven, CT: Yale University Press, 1981), 29.

31. Item 1, will of Samuel Townsend dated 10 September 1853, Wills, Septimus D. Cabaniss Papers.

32. See "Note on Methodology" for the process of identifying Elvira as a possible concubine of Samuel Townsend. For Elvira's anomalous status in Samuel's household, see in particular Item 1, deposition of S. D. Cabaniss, Depositions, 1859 and undated; Item 10, notes of Samuel Townsend's wills, Legal notes/ strategy/ depositions; Item 1, will of Samuel Townsend dated 10 September 1853, Wills; Item 2, will of Samuel Townsend dated November 1854; Items 4 and 5, wills of Samuel Townsend dated 6 September and 15 October 1856.

33. Item 3, "Inventory and Appraisement" dated February–March 1858, Inventories, Septimus D. Cabaniss Papers.

34. Item 8, notes on John E. Townsend by S. D. Cabaniss, Legal notes/ strategy/ depositions, Septimus D. Cabaniss Papers.

35. Will of Stith Townsend dated 8 September 1828, Madison County Probate Court records, MCRC.

36. Sellers, *Slavery in Alabama*, 28; Samuel Townsend, 1850 United States Federal Census, accessed 1 April 2016, www.ancestry.com.

37. Observation from the author's visits to the Townsend brothers' gravesite in July 2015 and April 2021. See also Item 1, Bill of Revision dated 12 March 1860, Cabaniss v. Townsend, Septimus D. Cabaniss Papers.

38. Petition for Probate of Edmund Townsend's will, dated after 25 January 1853, MCRC.

39. "Died," *Southern Advocate*, 27 April 1853. "Consumption" was a historical term used to describe wasting diseases in general but most often referred to tuberculosis.

40. Item 1, will of Samuel Townsend dated 10 September 1853, Wills; Item 2, depositions of Busby, Holloway and Others, Legal notes/ strategy/ depositions, Septimus D. Cabaniss Papers. Samuel also made a similar remark to his friend Elias Wellborn in virtually the same words. Item 1, deposition of Elias Wellborn dated 29 August 1857, Legal notes/ strategy/ depositions, Septimus D. Cabaniss Papers.

41. Item 1, Farm Book, 1856–1858, Septimus D. Cabaniss Papers; Roberts, "An Experiment in Emancipation of Slaves by an Alabama Planter," 5.

42. Roberts, "An Experiment in Emancipation of Slaves by an Alabama Planter," 8.

43. Item 2, Inventory of Samuel Townsend's personal property sold at public auction, dated 20 March 1858, Inventories, Septimus D. Cabaniss Papers. Further descriptions of Samuel Townsend's plantation are drawn from excerpts from Mildred E. Carlisle, *Early History of North Central Madison County, 1819–1859, Hazel Green Area, Madison County, Alabama*, as published online, accessed 1 December 2015, www.findagrave.com.

44. Carlisle, *Early History of North Central Madison County,* accessed 1 December 2015, www.findagrave.com.

45. See Joshua D. Rothman, *Notorious in the Neighborhood: Sex and Families across the Color Line in Virginia, 1787–1861* (Chapel Hill: University of North Carolina

Press, 2003); Josephine Boyd Bradley and Kent Anderson Leslie, "White Pain Pollen: An Elite Biracial Daughter's Quandary," in *Sex, Love, Race: Crossing Boundaries in North American History*, ed. Martha Hodes (New York: New York University Press, 1999); Gross, *Double Character*. Rothman, Bradley and Leslie, and Gross each examine the relationship between the slave South's ideology of racial difference and community norms regarding interracial sex. In their discussion of Amanda Dickson, the mixed-race daughter of a wealthy white planter, Bradley and Leslie suggest that it was "public sentiment, not abstract ideology" that "controlled the amount of miscegenation that took place in the nineteenth-century South." Similarly, Gross looks at court cases as a window into "triumphs of custom over law, in which social practices overwhelm formal legal rules."

46. Blassingame, *Slave Testimony*, 421.

47. See Gordon-Reed, *The Hemingses of Monticello*; Hodes, *White Women, Black Men*; Jones, *Fathers of Conscience*; Novkov, *Racial Union*. In her extensive study of the Hemings family, Annette Gordon-Reed comments on the consequences of American slavery following the condition of the mother. Because it was the mother's status, whether enslaved or free, that determined a child's legal status, "the private conduct of men would have no serious impact on the emerging slave society as a whole," and white men could have mixed-race children who didn't pose a threat to the maintenance of the racial and social order. Martha Hodes focuses on the children of white women and Black men, who—because their mothers were white—would be born free; she argues that "it was the presence of free children that precipitated a local crisis." A similar argument could be made for mixed-race children whose white fathers manumitted them. Bernie Jones's study of these cases demonstrates that the opposition of white relatives to the emancipation or inheritance of enslaved children was the cause of most conflict. Julie Novkov cites Edmund Townsend's will as an example of the consequences of planters being "too extravagant" in their favored treatment of enslaved children or concubines, people who were "extremely subordinated by their race and gender in the social system" despite their relationship with their master.

48. Chesnut and Woodward, *Mary Chesnut's Civil War*, 29.

49. Item 1, deposition of Elias Wellborn dated 29 August 1857, Legal notes/ strategy/ depositions; Petitions of Elizabeth and Virginia Townsend filed 4 June 1860, Septimus D. Cabaniss Papers. In 1859–60, Elizabeth and Virginia pursued their emancipation and their original inheritance from Edmund Townsend's estate through the judicial system. Because they were legally slaves, Elizabeth and Virginia had no standing in court; George W. Carmichael, a former Madison County sheriff, served as their "next friend" and sued on their behalf. Edmund's daughters dropped the suit when Samuel Townsend's will was successfully probated in 1860 and they were emancipated. On similar lawsuits in the antebellum South, see Ariela J. Gross, "Litigating Whiteness: Trials of Racial Determination in the Nineteenth-Century South," *Yale Law Journal* 108 (October 1998): 109–188.

50. Hannah (Elvira and Thomas Townsend's mother) was described as having her "hand crippled"; Rainey's twenty-eight-year-old daughter Jane was described as "sickly"; a teenaged girl named Nancy had "defective eyes"; and one woman named Jane was missing an eye. Other hand and wrist injuries were noted, and multiple women were described simply as "sickly" with no further explanation. See Item 3, "Inventory and Appraisement" dated February–March 1858, Inventories, Septimus D. Cabaniss Papers.

51. Item 3, will of Samuel Townsend dated 10 September 1853, Wills; Items 4 and 5, will of Samuel Townsend dated 6 September and 15 October 1856, Wills, Wills; E. Tefft to O.O. Howard, letter dated 17 April 1867, Septimus D. Cabaniss Papers.

52. Item 2, depositions of Busby, Holloway and Others, Legal notes/ strategy/ depositions; S. D. Cabaniss to Osborne Townsend, letter dated 30 March 1866, Septimus D. Cabaniss Papers.

53. Enlistment record for Osborne Townsend, Company Descriptive Book, 5th Heavy Artillery U.S.C.T., Civil War Soldiers, Union, Colored Troops Artillery, accessed 9 August 2018, www.fold3.com.

54. Item 1, deposition of S. D. Cabaniss, Depositions, 1859 and undated, Septimus D. Cabaniss Papers. See also Stevenson, "What's Love Got to Do with It?," 107; Bradley and Leslie, "White Pain Pollen: An Elite Biracial Daughter's Quandary."

55. "Elvira Townsend," Kansas State Census Collection, 1855–1925, accessed 30 March 2020, www.ancestry.com; "Townsand, Alvira," *Leavenworth City Directory and Business Mirror, 1865-66* (St. Louis, MO: James Sutherland, 1866).

56. "Elvira Townsend," Kansas State Census Collection, 1855–1925, accessed 30 March 2020, www.ancestry.com; "Townsand, Alvira," *Leavenworth City Directory and Business Mirror, 1865–66* (St. Louis, MO: James Sutherland, 1866); "Mrs. Hannah Townsend," *Edwin Green's City Directory for 1878-9*, LHCS.

57. At the same time, close proximity to a white master or his family—living or working in the same house—gave certain enslaved people less physical and psychological distance than those who lived and worked outside the plantation house. White slave owners' preference for interacting with mixed-race people was far from always being a benefit. See Glymph, *Out of the House of Bondage.*

58. Berlin, *Slaves without Masters*; Rohr, "Free People of Color in Madison County."

59. Item 2, will of Samuel Townsend (November 1854 draft), Wills, Septimus D. Cabaniss Papers.

60. Item 1, will of Samuel Townsend dated 10 September 1853, Wills, Septimus D. Cabaniss Papers.

61. Item 1, Inventory of debts owed to the estate of Samuel Townsend, dated 24 March 1858, Inventories, Septimus D. Cabaniss Papers.

62. S. D. Cabaniss to Wesley Townsend, letters dated 29 April 1858 and 29 June 1858, Septimus D. Cabaniss Papers.

63. Charles Osborne Townsend to Thomas Townsend, letter dated 14 February 1888, Septimus D. Cabaniss Papers.

64. Abner Tate was a large planter and migrant from South Carolina around the same age as Samuel. S. D. Cabaniss listed him in his notes as someone who would be able to confirm details of Samuel Townsend's life and his children's parentage. Abner Tate, 1860 United States Federal Census; Abner Tate, United States Federal Census Non-Population Schedules, 1860, accessed 1 April 2015, www.ancestry.com.

65. Charles Osborne Townsend to Thomas Townsend, letter dated 14 February 1888, Septimus D. Cabaniss Papers.

66. Edmund Townsend to James Robinson, letter dated 18 April 1850, Septimus D. Cabaniss Papers.

67. Item 1, deposition of S. D. Cabaniss, Depositions, 1859 and undated, Septimus D. Cabaniss Papers.

68. Notes on Edmund Townsend's will filed 26 September 1853, T.J. Redmond vs. Thomas Townsend et al., MCRC.

69. Petition for Probate of Edmund Townsend's will, dated after 25 January 1853, MCRC.

70. Item 1, deposition of S. D. Cabaniss, Depositions, 1859 and undated, Septimus D. Cabaniss Papers.

71. Items 9 and 10, notes on Samuel Townsend's will by S. D. Cabaniss, Legal notes/ strategy/ depositions; Item 1, will of Samuel Townsend dated 10 September 1853, Wills, Septimus D. Cabaniss Papers.

72. Item 1, will of Samuel Townsend dated 6 September 1856, Wills; Item 3, "Inventory and Appraisement" dated February–March 1858, Inventories, Septimus D. Cabaniss Papers.

73. Wesley Townsend to S. D. Cabaniss, letter dated 22 March 1858, Septimus D. Cabaniss Papers.

74. Tera Hunter explores enslaved people's relationships in her extensive study of marriages and partnerships created by African Americans in the nineteenth century. Though slave owners could force enslaved people "into playing the role of a spouse," their control over private relationships was limited. Even under coercion "slaves bestowed their affections selectively" and could refuse to recognize the man or woman a master chose for them as their partner. Tera W. Hunter, *Bound in Wedlock: Slave and Free Black Marriage in the Nineteenth Century* (Cambridge, MA: Harvard University Press, 2017).

75. Item 1, will of Samuel Townsend dated 10 September 1853, Wills, Septimus D. Cabaniss Papers.

76. S. D. Cabaniss to W. D. Chadick, letter dated 2 March 1858, Septimus D. Cabaniss Papers.

77. Item 3, "Inventory and Appraisement" dated February–March 1858, Inventories, Septimus D. Cabaniss Papers.

78. Item 3, "Inventory and Appraisement" dated February–March 1858, Inventories, Septimus D. Cabaniss Papers.

79. Item 3, "Inventory and Appraisement" dated February–March 1858, Inventories, Septimus D. Cabaniss Papers.
80. Item 2, depositions of Busby, Holloway and Others, Legal notes/ strategy/ depositions, Septimus D. Cabaniss Papers.
81. "Septimus Douglass Cabaniss," Huntsville History Collection, accessed 1 April 2016, www.huntsvillehistorycollection.org.
82. Item 1, deposition of S. D. Cabaniss, Depositions, 1859 and undated, Septimus D. Cabaniss Papers.
83. "Septimus Douglass Cabaniss," Huntsville History Collection, accessed 1 April 2016, www.huntsvillehistorycollection.org.
84. "Inhabitants: Petition," Lunenburg County, VA, 1785, Legislative Petitions Digital Collection, Virginia Memory, accessed 30 January 2020, http://www.vir giniamemory.com/collections/petitions. See also Schmidt and Wilhelm, "Early Proslavery Petitions in Virginia, *The William and Mary Quarterly*, 140–143.
85. "Septimus Douglass Cabaniss," Huntsville History Collection, accessed 1 April 2016, www.huntsvillehistorycollection.org.
86. Item 1, Farm Book, 1856–1858, Septimus D. Cabaniss Papers; Sellers, *Slavery in Alabama*, 46.
87. Item 1, deposition of S. D. Cabaniss, Depositions, 1859 and undated, Septimus D. Cabaniss Papers.
88. Item 1, deposition of S. D. Cabaniss, Depositions, 1859 and undated, Septimus D. Cabaniss Papers.
89. Item 2, depositions of Busby, Holloway and Others, Legal notes/ strategy/ depositions, Septimus D. Cabaniss Papers.
90. Item 1, deposition of S. D. Cabaniss, Depositions, 1859 and undated, Septimus D. Cabaniss Papers.
91. Item 1, will of Samuel Townsend dated 10 September 1853, Wills, Septimus D. Cabaniss Papers.
92. Item 1, will of Samuel Townsend dated 10 September 1853, Wills, Septimus D. Cabaniss Papers.
93. After the restrictive anti-immigration and seizure acts passed by the state legislature in the 1830s, the proportion of free people of color in Madison County dropped by more than half—from a height of 0.5 percent in 1830 to 0.2 percent in 1860. Rohr, "Free People of Color in Madison County, Alabama."
94. At a Probate Court hearing on 6 January 1857, John E. Townsend and the other complainants argued that "the persons named in the said paper writings" (Samuel Townsend's will) had exercised "undue influence" over him—essentially casting Samuel's concubines in the role of the manipulative "Jezebel," a racial stereotype Deborah Gray White explores in her book *Ar'n't I a Woman?*. There were, however, nineteenth-century cases in which southern courts rejected "undue influence" claims leveled against enslaved legatees. In the 1844 case *O'Neall v. Farr*,

the South Carolina Court of Appeals upheld the will of J. B. O'Neall, who had attempted to free "a negro woman named Fan" (O'Neall's concubine) as well as another enslaved man named Henry, dividing his estate between the two of them. O'Neall's white relatives had claimed that Fan procured O'Neall's property by undue influence, but the court declared the will valid because Fan had not committed any fraud, nor had she engaged in "threats" or "menaces" against O'Neall. Ironically, Fan's enslavement actually worked to her benefit in this case, as the court stated that "Fan's conduct was as submissive to his will as could well be expected from one in her condition," making her unable to threaten or exploit him. See Ronald J. Scalise Jr., "Undue Influence and the Law of Wills: A Comparative Analysis," *Duke Journal of Comparative & International Law* 19, no. 1 (Fall 2008): 41–106; Nathan Abbott, *A Selection of Authorities on Descent, Wills, and Administration* (St. Paul, MN: West Publishing, 1894), 337–340.

95. Item 2, will of Samuel Townsend (November 1854 draft), Wills, Septimus D. Cabaniss Papers. The $12,000 figure appears in the notes from Samuel to Cabaniss regarding a draft written between the first and second published wills, and again in the November 1854 draft. See Items 7 and 8, undated draft of Samuel Townsend's will; Item 2, will of Samuel Townsend (November 1854 draft), Wills, Septimus D. Cabaniss Papers.

96. Items 4 and 5, will of Samuel Townsend dated 6 September 1856, Wills, Septimus D. Cabaniss Papers.

97. Item 1, deposition of S. D. Cabaniss, Depositions, 1859 and undated, Septimus D. Cabaniss Papers. Emphasis in original.

98. Item 2, will of Samuel Townsend (November 1854 draft), Wills, Septimus D. Cabaniss Papers.

99. Items 9 and 10, notes on Samuel Townsend's will by S. D. Cabaniss, Legal notes/ strategy/ depositions; Item 18, notes on Edmund Townsend's will by S. D. Cabaniss, Legal notes/ strategy/ depositions; Item 1, inventory of debts owed to the estate of Samuel Townsend, dated 24 March 1858, Inventories, Septimus D. Cabaniss Papers.

100. Item 8, notes on John E. Townsend by S. D. Cabaniss, Legal notes/ strategy/ depositions, Septimus D. Cabaniss Papers.

101. Item 18, Notes on Edmund Townsend's will and John E. Townsend by S. D. Cabaniss, Legal notes/ strategy/ depositions, Septimus D. Cabaniss Papers.

102. Item 8, notes on John E. Townsend by S. D. Cabaniss, Legal notes/ strategy/ depositions, Septimus D. Cabaniss Papers. Emphasis in original.

103. Headstones of Martha J. Townsend, Sarah A. T. Townsend, and Parkes M. Townsend at Townsend family gravesite in Madison County, Alabama.

104. Item 1, deposition of Elias Wellborn dated 29 August 1857, Legal notes/ strategy/ depositions; Item 18, notes on Edmund Townsend's will by S. D. Cabaniss, Legal notes/ strategy/ depositions Septimus D. Cabaniss Papers.

105. Item 1, deposition of Elias Wellborn dated 29 August 1857, Legal notes/ strategy/ depositions; Item 2, depositions of Busby, Holloway and Others, Legal notes/ strategy/ depositions, Septimus D. Cabaniss Papers.

106. Items 9 and 10, notes on Samuel Townsend's will by S. D. Cabaniss, Legal notes/ strategy/ depositions, Septimus D. Cabaniss Papers.

107. Items 4 and 5, will of Samuel Townsend dated 6 September 1856, Wills, Septimus D. Cabaniss Papers.

108. Cabaniss introduced another clause intended to discourage Samuel C. from challenging the will. Item 27 of the 10 September 1856 will preemptively disqualified and disinherited executors who opposed Samuel's will: "It is my will, that no person shall be permitted to qualify as Executor of my will, who shall oppose the probate thereof, or who shall oppose the emancipation of any slaves, that are therein directed to be emancipated. Nor do I wish or intend, that any person shall take any thing under my will, who shall oppose the probate thereof, or the emancipation of said slaves or any of them."

109. Item 2, petition for probate of Samuel Townsend will, Probate Court minutes dated 6 January 1857, Cabaniss v. Townsend, Reports to court (1), 1866–1871; Item 5, Probate Court minutes dated 15 November 1856, Wills, Septimus D. Cabaniss Papers.

110. Item 3, "Inventory and Appraisement" dated February–March 1858, Inventories, Septimus D. Cabaniss Papers.

111. Item 5, Probate Court minutes, 20 January 1857 to 20 January 1858, Wills, Septimus D. Cabaniss Papers.

CHAPTER 3

1. Item 2, depositions of Busby, Holloway and Others, Legal notes/ strategy/ depositions, Septimus D. Cabaniss Papers.

2. Item 2, will of Samuel Townsend dated November 1854, Wills, Septimus D. Cabaniss Papers.

3. For a history of the Mexican-American War that pays particular attention to the Jacksonian white supremacist ideas that influenced the decision to invade Mexico, see Peter Guardino, *The Dead March: A History of the Mexican-American War* (Cambridge, MA: Harvard University Press, 2017).

4. See Andrew K. Diemer, *The Politics of Black Citizenship: Free African Americans in the Mid-Atlantic Borderland, 1817–1863* (Athens: University of Georgia Press, 2016); Lorenzo Johnson Greene, *The Negro in Colonial New England, 1620-1776* (New York: Columbia University Press, 1962); Leslie M. Harris, *In the Shadow of Slavery: African Americans in New York City, 1626–1863* (Chicago: University of Chicago Press, 2003); Leon Litwack, *North of Slavery: The Negro in the Free States, 1790–1860* (Chicago: University of Chicago Press, 1961); Joanne Pope Melish, *Disowning Slavery: Gradual Emancipation and "Race" in New*

England, 1780–1860 (Ithaca, NY: Cornell University Press, 1998); Gary B. Nash, *Forging Freedom: The Formation of Philadelphia's Black Community, 1720–1840* (Cambridge, MA: Harvard University Press, 1988); Julie Winch, *Between Slavery and Freedom: Free People of Color in America from Settlement to the Civil War* (Lanham, MD: Rowman & Littlefield, 2014).

5. See James Oliver Horton and Lois E. Horton, "A Federal Assault: African Americans and the Impact of the Fugitive Slave Law of 1850," *Chicago-Kent Law Review* 68, no. 3 (1993): 1179–1198; Thomas D. Morris, *Free Men All: The Personal Liberty Laws of the North, 1780–1861* (Union, NJ: Lawbook Exchange, 2001).

6. See R. J. M. Blackett, *Making Freedom: The Underground Railroad and the Politics of Slavery* (Chapel Hill: University of North Carolina Press, 2013); Eric Foner, *Gateway to Freedom: The Hidden History of the Underground Railroad* (New York: W. W. Norton and Company, 2015); Cheryl Janifer LaRoche, *Free Black Communities and the Underground Railroad: The Geography of Resistance* (Urbana: University of Illinois Press, 2014).

7. Blassingame, *Slave Testimony*, 401.

8. Nikki Taylor, *Frontiers of Freedom: Cincinnati's Black Community, 1802–1868* (Athens: Ohio University Press, 2005), 154–155.

9. Dred Scott was an African American man born into slavery in Virginia. In the 1830s his master moved to Illinois, a free state, and then Wisconsin Territory, in which slavery was prohibited by the Missouri Compromise. Scott sued for freedom in 1846 on the basis that he had been a resident of free territories. Scott ultimately appealed up to the United States Supreme Court, which ruled that Scott's African ancestry disqualified him from American citizenship and therefore he had no legal standing to sue. For details on the case as well as its legal and historical context, see Austin Allen, *Origins of the Dred Scott Case: Jacksonian Jurisprudence and the Supreme Court, 1837–1857* (Athens: University of Georgia Press, 2006); Daniel A. Farber, "A Fatal Loss of Balance: *Dred Scott* Revisited," *Pepperdine Law Review* 39, no. 1 (2011): 13–48; Lea VanderVede, "The *Dred Scott* Case in Context," *Journal of Supreme Court History* 40, no. 3 (November 2015): 263–281.

10. Items 4 and 5, will of Samuel Townsend dated 6 September 1856, Wills, Septimus D. Cabaniss Papers.

11. For the ACS and colonizationist thought more broadly, see Douglas R. Egerton, "'Its Origin Is Not a Little Curious': A New Look at the American Colonization Society," *Journal of the Early Republic* 5, no. 4 (Winter 1985): 463–480; Nicholas Guyatt, "The Outskirts of Our Happiness": Race and the Lure of Colonization in the Early Republic," *Journal of American History* 95, no. 4 (March 2009): 986–1011; Samantha Seeley, "Beyond the American Colonization Society," *History Compass* 14, no. 3 (March 2016): 93–104.

12. Item 3, codicil to will of Samuel Townsend, dated 31 October 1856, Wills, Septimus D. Cabaniss Papers.

13. S. D. Cabaniss to D. L. Lakin, letter dated 6 November 1860, Septimus D. Cabaniss Papers.

14. Item 3, codicil to will of Samuel Townsend, dated 31 October 1856, Wills, Septimus D. Cabaniss Papers. The codicil's reference to "North America" also left open the possibility of Canada, an increasingly common choice for free Black people in the North who feared that the 1850 Fugitive Slave Act put their freedom at risk in the United States.

15. S. D. Cabaniss to Stephen Douglas, letter dated 21 January 1858, Septimus D. Cabaniss Papers.

16. S. D. Cabaniss to C. C. Clay, letter dated 22 January 1862, Septimus D. Cabaniss Papers. Emphasis in original.

17. S. D. Cabaniss to Stephen Douglas, letter dated 21 January 1858, Septimus D. Cabaniss Papers.

18. Karl Jacoby's book *The Strange Career of William Ellis* explores a case with some parallels: the life of former slave William Ellis, who reinvented himself as "Guillermo Eliseo." Born and raised along the Mexican border in Texas, Ellis was fluent in Spanish and knowledgeable about Mexican culture; these skills, along with his light skin, allowed Ellis to "pass" across the color line in Gilded Age New York—not as a white man, but as a wealthy Mexican businessman.

19. S. D. Cabaniss to C. C. Clay letter dated 21 January 1858, Septimus D. Cabaniss Papers.

20. S. D. Cabaniss to Taft and Perry, letter dated 16 July 1860, Septimus D. Cabaniss Papers.

21. Cabaniss states this explicitly in a letter to a colleague in Virginia at the start of the Civil War, when he was prohibited from sending the emancipated Townsends disbursements out of Samuel Townsend's estate: "I am satisfied now that they would have been much happier in a state of slavery." S. D. Cabaniss to William Chilton, letter dated 23 January 1862, Septimus D. Cabaniss Papers.

22. S. D. Cabaniss to D. L. Lakin, letter dated 8 November 1860, Septimus D. Cabaniss Papers.

23. S. D. Cabaniss to C. C. Clay, letter dated 22 January 1862, Septimus D. Cabaniss Papers.

24. S. D. Cabaniss to C. C. Clay, letter dated 22 January 1862, Septimus D. Cabaniss Papers. Emphasis in original.

25. David A. Gerber, *Black Ohio and the Color Line, 1860–1915* (Urbana: University of Illinois Press, 1976), 26, 31.

26. See, in particular, Paul Finkelman, "The Strange Career of Race Discrimination in Antebellum Ohio," *Case Western Reserve Law Review* 55, no. 1 (Fall 2004): 374; James Oliver Horton and Stacy Flaherty, "Black Leadership in Antebellum Cincinnati," in *Race and the City: Work, Community, and Protest in Cincinnati, 1820–1970,* ed. Henry Louis Taylor Jr. (Urbana: University of Illinois Press, 1993), 83.

27. Historical wealth and occupational patterns in Cincinnati show that in Ohio— as in other northern communities as well as free Black communities in southern cities such as New Orleans—mixed-race heritage was tied to class status. In 1860, "mulattoes" in Cincinnati held 75 percent of the Black community's wealth and were more likely to be educated. Although white Ohioans preferred to hire white laborers for skilled jobs, and 80 percent of mixed-race Cincinnatians were engaged in unskilled labor, a larger percentage of mixed-race workers held skilled positions than workers without mixed-race ancestry: 20 percent versus 10 percent in 1860. See Taylor, *Frontiers of Freedom,* 136; Horton and Flaherty, "Black Leadership in Cincinnati," 87.

28. S. D. Cabaniss to Wesley Townsend, letter dated 12 December 1860, Septimus D. Cabaniss Papers.

29. W. D. Chadick to S. D. Cabaniss, letter titled "Mission to Ohio," Septimus D. Cabaniss Papers.

30. Writers Program of the Works Project Administration in the State of Ohio, *Cincinnati: A Guide to the Queen City and Its Neighbors* (Cincinnati, OH: Wiesen-Hart Press, 1943).

31. See Taylor, *Frontiers of Freedom.*

32. "Population of the 100 Largest Urban Places: 1860," 15 June 1998, U.S. Bureau of the Census, accessed 1 February 2019, www.census.gov; Taylor, *Frontiers of Freedom,* 2.

33. W. D. Chadick to S. D. Cabaniss, letter dated 18 February 1856, Series 1, Subseries B, Box 22, Folder 1, Frances Cabaniss Roberts Collection, Dept. of Archives/Special Collections, M. Louis Salmon Library, University of Alabama in Huntsville, Huntsville, AL.

34. Taylor, *Frontiers of Freedom,* 118.

35. W. D. Chadick to S. D. Cabaniss, letter dated 18 February 1856, Series 1, Subseries B, Box 22, Folder 1, Frances Cabaniss Roberts Collection, Dept. of Archives/Special Collections, M. Louis Salmon Library, University of Alabama in Huntsville, Huntsville, AL.

36. W. D. Chadick to S. D. Cabaniss, itemized list of expenses dated 10 January 1858 to 13 March 1858, Septimus D. Cabaniss Papers; Writers Program of the Works Project Administration in the State of Ohio, *Cincinnati: A Guide to the Queen City and its Neighbors,* 156–157, 151.

37. W. D. Chadick to S. D. Cabaniss, letter dated 18 February 1856, Series 1, Subseries B, Box 22, Folder 1, Frances Cabaniss Roberts Collection, Dept. of Archives/Special Collections, M. Louis Salmon Library, University of Alabama in Huntsville, Huntsville, AL.

38. S. D. Cabaniss to Wesley Townsend, letter dated 26 March 1858, Septimus D. Cabaniss Papers.

39. W. D. Chadick to S. D. Cabaniss, letter dated 22 February 1858, Septimus D. Cabaniss Papers.

40. W. D. Chadick to S. D. Cabaniss, letter titled "Mission to Ohio," Septimus D. Cabaniss Papers.

41. W. D. Chadick to S. D. Cabaniss, letter titled "Mission to Ohio," Septimus D. Cabaniss Papers.

42. Gerber, *Black Ohio and the Color Line,* 9. See also Thomas King, "Black Settlement in Xenia, Ohio, 1850–1880: An Historical Geography" (M.A. thesis, University of Colorado, 1983).

43. Caleb Atwater's 1838 *History of the State of Ohio,* as quoted in Daniel J. Ryan, *History of Ohio: The Rise and Progress of an American State,* vol. 4 (New York: Century History Company, 1912), 119.

44. The legal repression Ohio's Black population faced in the early nineteenth century was in some ways similar to (and contemporaneous with) the regime of gradual emancipation in the northeast. In *The Trouble with Minna,* historian Hendrik Hartog challenges "neo-abolitionist" ideas of a strict dividing line between slavery and freedom, a binary that ignores "the legal culture, neither 'slave' nor 'free'" that he examines in the context of New Jersey's gradual emancipation period. Hartog's effort "to reconstruct core features of everyday life" within a particular legal system provides a useful model for examining lived experiences in diverse communities across the United States. Hendrik Hartog, *The Trouble with Minna: A Case of Slavery and Emancipation in the Antebellum North* (Chapel Hill: University of North Carolina Press, 2018). On Ohio's "Black Codes" from statehood through the antebellum period, see Ellen Eslinger, "The Evolution of Racial Politics in Early Ohio," in *The Center of a Great Empire: The Ohio Country in the Early American Republic,* ed. Andrew R. L. Cayton and Stuart D. Hobbs (Athens: Ohio University Press, 2005); Gerber, *Black Ohio and the Color Line;* Horton and Flaherty, "Black Leadership in Antebellum Cincinnati"; Frederick Alphonso McGinnis, *The Education of Negroes in Ohio* (Wilberforce, OH: Frederick A. McGinnis, 1962); Stephen Middleton, *The Black Laws: Race and the Legal Process in Early Ohio* (Athens: Ohio University Press, 2005); Taylor, *Frontiers of Freedom.*

45. Gerber, *Black Ohio and the Color Line,* 8.

46. Horton and Flaherty, "Black Leadership in Antebellum Cincinnati," 75.

47. W. D. Chadick to S. D. Cabaniss, letter titled "Mission to Ohio," Septimus D. Cabaniss Papers.

48. Gerber, *Black Ohio and the Color Line,* 57.

49. For an account of the 1829 riots and the emigration that followed, as well as other outbreaks of violence against Black Ohioans, see Taylor, *Frontiers of Freedom.*

50. Henry Bibb, *Narrative of the Life and Adventures of Henry Bibb, An American Slave* (New York: 1849), 29.

51. *Uncle Tom's Cabin* sold 300,000 copies in the United States in its first year of publication, and more than 1 million copies in England. It would become the best-selling novel of the nineteenth century. See Christopher G. Diller, "Introduction,"

Harriett Beecher Stowe, *Uncle Tom's Cabin; or, Life Among the Lowly* (1852), ed. Christopher G. Diller (Buffalo, NY: Broadview Press, 2009), 12.

52. Ryan, *History of Ohio*, 130.

53. Taylor, *Frontiers of Freedom*, 176; Gerber, *Black Ohio and the Color Line*, 57; Ryan, *History of Ohio*, 124–126.

54. Historians have explored Ohio's marginal cultural and political status, putting particular emphasis on Cincinnati as a border city in a border state. Henry Louis Taylor Jr. characterizes antebellum Cincinnati as having a "dual personality" with "two cultures, two unreconciled strivings; two warring ideals in a single city." In her book on Black activism in Cincinnati, Nikki Taylor counters this viewpoint and argues that rather than a city "at war with itself," Cincinnati's multiple identities fused into a culture that was uniquely hostile to African Americans: "It was a crossroad of the worst aspects of northern, southern, and western culture," including "northern segregation and discrimination, a southern racial code, and western frontier mob violence." See Henry Louis Taylor Jr., ed., Race and the City: Work, Community, and Protest in Cincinnati, 1820–1970 (Urbana: University of Illinois Press, 1993); Taylor, *Frontiers of Freedom*.

55. W. D. Chadick to S. D. Cabaniss, letter titled "Mission to Ohio," Septimus D. Cabaniss Papers.

56. W. D. Chadick to S. D. Cabaniss, letter dated 22 February 1858, Septimus D. Cabaniss Papers.

57. W. D. Chadick to S. D. Cabaniss, letter titled "Mission to Ohio," Septimus D. Cabaniss Papers.

58. W. D. Chadick to S. D. Cabaniss, letter dated 8 March 1858; W. D. Chadick to S. D. Cabaniss, letter titled "Mission to Ohio," Septimus D. Cabaniss Papers.

59. Wesley Townsend to S. D. Cabaniss, letter dated 10 July 1858, Septimus D. Cabaniss Papers.

60. W. D. Chadick to S. D. Cabaniss, letter dated 18 February 1856, Series 1, Subseries B, Box 22, Folder 1, Frances Cabaniss Roberts Collection, Dept. of Archives/Special Collections, M. Louis Salmon Library, University of Alabama in Huntsville, Huntsville, AL.

61. W. D. Chadick to S. D. Cabaniss, letter titled "Mission to Ohio," Septimus D. Cabaniss Papers.

62. W. D. Chadick to S. D. Cabaniss, letter titled "Mission to Ohio," Septimus D. Cabaniss Papers.

63. W. D. Chadick to S. D. Cabaniss, letter dated 22 February 1858; W. D. Chadick to S. D. Cabaniss, letter titled "Mission to Ohio," Septimus D. Cabaniss Papers.

64. W. D. Chadick to S. D. Cabaniss, letter dated 8 March 1858, Septimus D. Cabaniss Papers.

65. Ivan M. Tribe, *Albany, Ohio: The First Fifty Years of a Rural Midwestern Community* (Athens, OH: Athens County Historical Society and Museum, 1985), 39, 45.

66. W. D. Chadick to S. D. Cabaniss, letter dated 8 March 1858, Septimus D. Cabaniss Papers.

67. S. D. Cabaniss to W. D. Chadick, letter dated 10 March 1858, Septimus D. Cabaniss Papers.

68. S. D. Cabaniss to Captain D. B. Turner, letter dated 2 March 1858; S. D. Cabaniss to W. D. Chadick, letter dated 6 March 1858, Septimus D. Cabaniss Papers.

69. "Bill of Revision" filed 6 March 1860, Cabaniss v. Townsend; S. D. Cabaniss to W. D. Chadick, letter dated 9 March 1858, Septimus D. Cabaniss Papers.

70. S. D. Cabaniss to W. D. Chadick, letter dated 9 March 1858, Septimus D. Cabaniss Papers. Emphasis in original.

71. S. D. Cabaniss to W. D. Chadick, letter dated 9 March 1858, Septimus D. Cabaniss Papers.

72. Wesley Townsend to S. D. Cabaniss, letter dated 22 March 1858, Septimus D. Cabaniss Papers.

73. Wesley Townsend to S. D. Cabaniss, letter dated 21 June 1858, Septimus D. Cabaniss Papers.

74. Wesley Townsend to S. D. Cabaniss, letter dated 10 July 1858, Septimus D. Cabaniss Papers.

75. Roberts, "An Experiment in Emancipation of Slaves by an Alabama Planter," 17.

76. Wesley Townsend to S. D. Cabaniss, letter dated 2 June 1858, Septimus D. Cabaniss Papers.

77. Wesley Townsend to S. D. Cabaniss, letter dated 21 June 1858, Septimus D. Cabaniss Papers.

78. Wesley Townsend to S. D. Cabaniss, letter dated 2 June 1858, Septimus D. Cabaniss Papers.

79. Wesley Townsend to S. D. Cabaniss, letter dated 21 June 1858, Septimus D. Cabaniss Papers.

80. Wesley Townsend to S. D. Cabaniss, letter dated 10 July 1858, Septimus D. Cabaniss Papers.

81. Wesley Townsend to S. D. Cabaniss, letter dated 16 August 1858, Septimus D. Cabaniss Papers.

82. S. D. Cabaniss to Wesley Townsend, letter dated 29 April 1858, Septimus D. Cabaniss Papers.

83. S. D. Cabaniss to Wesley Townsend, letter dated 29 June 1858, Septimus D. Cabaniss Papers.

84. S. D. Cabaniss to Wesley Townsend, letter dated September 1858, Septimus D. Cabaniss Papers. In a letter to Samuel C. Townsend written the next year, Cabaniss asked his co-executor to "ascertain the names of Wesleys children by Jane." See S. D. Cabaniss to S. C. Townsend, letter dated 30 December 1859, Septimus D. Cabaniss Papers.

85. Wesley Townsend to S. D. Cabaniss, letter dated 1 November 1858, Septimus D. Cabaniss Papers.

86. Wesley Townsend to S. D. Cabaniss, letter dated 14 December 1858, Septimus D. Cabaniss Papers.

87. Bibb, *Narrative of the Life and Adventures of Henry Bibb*, 47, 80.

88. S. D. Cabaniss to Wesley Townsend, letter dated 23 March 1859, Septimus D. Cabaniss Papers.

89. On private education in Ohio, see King, "Black Settlement in Xenia, Ohio"; Kabria Baumgartner, "Building the Future: White Women, Black Education, and Civic Inclusion in Antebellum Ohio," *Journal of the Early Republic* 37, no. 1 (Spring 2017): 117–145; Taylor, *Frontiers of Freedom*.

90. Tribe, *Albany, Ohio,* 87. On Oberlin and its antislavery politics, see Nat Brandt, *The Town that Started the Civil War* (Syracuse, NY: Syracuse University Press, 1990); Brent Morris, *Oberlin, Hotbed of Abolitionism: College, Community, and the Fight for Freedom and Equality in Antebellum America* (Chapel Hill: University of North Carolina Press, 2014).

91. W. D. Chadick to S. D. Cabaniss, letter dated 22 February 1858, Septimus D. Cabaniss Papers.

92. Tribe, *Albany, Ohio,* 87, 91.

93. W. D. Chadick to S. D. Cabaniss, letter titled "Mission to Ohio," Septimus D. Cabaniss Papers.

94. Tribe, *Albany, Ohio,* 75–76, 90, 64.

95. Wesley Townsend to S. D. Cabaniss, letter dated 8 February 1859, Septimus D. Cabaniss Papers.

96. S. D. Cabaniss to Wesley Townsend, letter dated 11 December 1858, Septimus D. Cabaniss Papers.

97. W. D. Chadick to S. D. Cabaniss, letter titled "Mission to Ohio," Septimus D. Cabaniss Papers.

98. Wesley Townsend to S. D. Cabaniss, letter dated 7 February 1860, Septimus D. Cabaniss Papers.

99. Wesley Townsend to S. D. Cabaniss, letter dated 1 November 1858; S. D. Cabaniss to Wesley Townsend, letter dated 13 November 1858, Septimus D. Cabaniss Papers.

100. Wesley Townsend to S. D. Cabaniss, letter dated 1 November 1858, Septimus D. Cabaniss Papers.

101. Wesley Townsend to S. D. Cabaniss, letter dated 8 February 1859, Septimus D. Cabaniss Papers.

102. S. D. Cabaniss to Wesley Townsend, letter dated 26 March 1858, Septimus D. Cabaniss Papers.

103. S. D. Cabaniss to C. D. Lindley, letter dated 15 May 1858, Septimus D. Cabaniss Papers.

104. Roberts, "An Experiment in Emancipation of Slaves by an Alabama Planter," 17.

105. Wesley Townsend to S. D. Cabaniss, letter dated 16 August 1858, Septimus D. Cabaniss Papers.

106. The rumors about Wesley's gambling and drinking in Albany did not reach Cabaniss until 1860, after Wesley had already moved to Kansas with the "legatees of the second class." Cabaniss and members of the Townsend family addressed the rumors and reality of Wesley's activities in Ohio and Kansas in multiple letters from 1858 to 1860, including S. D. Cabaniss to Wesley Townsend, letters dated September 1858, 26 January 1860, 27 January 1860, 13 February 1860; Elvira Townsend and Jane Townsend to S. D. Cabaniss, letter dated 31 January 1860; S. D. Cabaniss to Elvira Townsend, letter dated 8 February 1860.

107. S. D. Cabaniss to Wesley Townsend, letter dated 12 December 1859, Septimus D. Cabaniss Papers.

108. S. D. Cabaniss to C. C. Clay, letter dated 21 January 1858, Septimus D. Cabaniss Papers.

109. S. D. Cabaniss to Wesley Townsend, letter dated 12 December 1859, Septimus D. Cabaniss Papers.

110. S. D. Cabaniss to Wesley Townsend, letter dated 30 December 1859, Septimus D. Cabaniss Papers.

111. Roberts, "An Experiment in Emancipation of Slaves by an Alabama Planter," 20.

112. S. D. Cabaniss to Wesley Townsend, letter dated 12 December 1859, Septimus D. Cabaniss Papers.

113. S. D. Cabaniss to Wesley Townsend, letter dated 12 December 1859, Septimus D. Cabaniss Papers.

114. *The Xenia Torchlight* reported a population of 5,000 on 2 July 1860. Thomas King calculated the population to be 6,055 in 1860 in his 1983 thesis. King, "Black Settlement in Xenia, Ohio," 145.

115. "How Xenia Impresses a New England Doctor of Divinity," *Xenia Torchlight* (Xenia, OH), 2 July 1860, State Archives, Ohio History Connection.

116. King, "Black Settlement in Xenia, Ohio," 90.

117. "Benevolent Societies" and "Church Directory," *Xenia Torchlight* (Xenia, OH), 30 June 1858, State Archives, Ohio History Connection.

118. "Woman's Rights!" *Xenia Torchlight* (Xenia, OH), 13 February 1856; "Frederick Douglass," *Xenia Torchlight* Xenia, OH), 27 February 1856, State Archives, Ohio History Connection.

119. "Mr. Lincoln Here, To-Day, for Five Minutes Only!" *Xenia Torchlight* (Xenia, OH), 13 February 1861, State Archives, Ohio History Connection.

120. "Items of Local News," *Xenia Torchlight* (Xenia, OH), 11 January 1860, State Archives, Ohio History Connection.

121. "Polygamy," *Xenia Torchlight* (Xenia, OH), 11 April 1860; "Horrid Affair in Maysville—Negro Burned to Death," *Xenia Torchlight* (Xenia, OH), 16 January 1856; "Local Department," *Xenia Torchlight* (Xenia, OH), 20 February 1856, State Archives, Ohio History Connection.

122. "Negrophobia," *Xenia Torchlight* (Xenia, OH), 28 July 1858, State Archives, Ohio History Connection.

123. "Nigger in the Wood Pile," *Xenia Torchlight* (Xenia, OH), 28 July 1858, State Archives, Ohio History Connection.

124. "Columbus Items," *Xenia Torchlight* (Xenia, OH), 25 January 1858, State Archives, Ohio History Connection.

125. "Where Shall the Free Negro Go?," *Xenia Torchlight* (Xenia, OH), 15 February 1860, State Archives, Ohio History Connection.

126. "Notice," *Xenia Torchlight* (Xenia, OH), 22 August 1860, State Archives, Ohio History Connection.

127. "Colonization Meeting," *Xenia Torchlight* (Xenia, OH), 29 August 1860, State Archives, Ohio History Connection.

128. "The Black Republic of Hayti," *Xenia Torchlight* (Xenia, OH), 5 December 1860, State Archives, Ohio History Connection.

129. Editor's response to "The Wilberforce University—Why it was located in Greene County, and the effect of such Location," *Xenia Torchlight* (Xenia, OH), 4 August 1858, State Archives, Ohio History Connection.

130. For examples, see King, "Black Settlement in Xenia, Ohio," 145; "The Xenia Memorial and the Answer of the Cincinnati Conference," *Xenia Torchlight* (Xenia, OH), 6 October 1858, State Archives, Ohio History Connection.

131. King, "Black Settlement in Xenia, Ohio, 1850–1880," 75.

132. "The Xenia Memorial and Answer of Conference—Again," *Xenia Torchlight* (Xenia, OH), 13 October 1858; "Negrophobia," *Xenia Torchlight* (Xenia, OH), 28 July 858, State Archives, Ohio History Connection.

133. Fannie Parker Currier, unpublished document titled "Reminiscences of My Childhood," Parker Family papers, Northern Kentucky University, Highland Heights, KY; *The Wilberforce Annual: A Comprehensive Review of the Origin, Development and Present Status of Wilberforce University*, ed. B. W. Arnett and S. T. Mitchell (Xenia, OH: 1885), 6; Wilhelmena Robinson, "The Negro in the Village of Yellow Springs, Ohio," *Negro History Bulletin* 29, no. 5 (1 February 1966), 104.

134. Hallie Q. Brown, *Pen Pictures of Pioneers of Wilberforce* (Xenia, OH: Aldine Publishing, 1937), 34–38.

135. Article from the *Cincinnati Commercial* as quoted in Robinson, "The Negro in the Village of Yellow Springs, Ohio," 104. See also Frederick Alphonso McGinnis, *A History and An Interpretation of Wilberforce University* (Blanchester, OH: Brown Publishing, 1941).

136. *The Wilberforce Annual*, 17–18; Brown, *Pen Pictures of Pioneers of Wilberforce*, 89.

137. W. D. Chadick to S. D. Cabaniss, letter titled "Mission to Ohio," Septimus D. Cabaniss Papers.

138. W. D. Chadick to S. D. Cabaniss, letter dated 22 February 1858.

139. Brown, *Pen Pictures of Pioneers of Wilberforce*, 89.

140. Wesley Townsend to S. D. Cabaniss, letter dated 18 January 1860, Septimus D. Cabaniss Papers.

141. Willis Townsend to S. D. Cabaniss, letter dated 12 March 1860, Septimus D. Cabaniss Papers.
142. Willis Townsend to S. D. Cabaniss, letter dated 8 April 1860, Septimus D. Cabaniss Papers.
143. Willis Townsend to S. D. Cabaniss, letter dated 12 March 1860; Wesley Townsend to S. D. Cabaniss, letter dated 18 January 1860, Septimus D. Cabaniss Papers.
144. S. D. Cabaniss to Samuel C. Townsend, letter dated 16 July 1860, Septimus D. Cabaniss Papers.
145. S. D. Cabaniss to R. S. Rust, letter dated 12 June 1860, Septimus D. Cabaniss Papers.
146. Thomas Jefferson, "Query XIV" in *Notes on the State of Virginia,* accessed 1 February 2019, https://docsouth.unc.edu.
147. John S. Rock, "I Will Sink or Swim With My Race," in *Lift Every Voice: African American Oratory, 1787–1900,* ed. Philip S. Foner and Robert James Branham (Tuscaloosa: University of Alabama, 1998), 318.
148. Most modern studies of racial uplift ideology focus on the Jim Crow period of the late nineteenth and early twentieth centuries. On an early reformer (and Wilberforce graduate), see Albert G. Miller, *Elevating the Race: Theophilus G. Steward, Black Theology, and the Making of an African American Civil Society, 1865–1924* (Knoxville: University of Tennessee Press, 2003).
149. *Catalogue of the Wilberforce University. 1859–60. Xenia, Ohio* (Cincinnati, OH: Methodist Book Concern, 1860), 25, 16, 14, 16–17. Emphases in original.
150. S. D. Cabaniss to R. S. Rust, letter dated 14 December 1860, Septimus D. Cabaniss Papers.
151. S. D. Cabaniss to R. S. Rust, letter dated 14 December 1860, Septimus D. Cabaniss Papers.
152. Elizabeth Townsend to Armstead Townsend, letter dated 18 March 1861, Septimus D. Cabaniss Papers.
153. Willis Townsend to S. D. Cabaniss, letter dated 8 May 1860, Septimus D. Cabaniss Papers.
154. "Greeley at Yellow Springs," *Xenia Torchlight* (Xenia, OH), 13 February 1861, State Archives, Ohio History Connection.
155. In September 1858, three hundred white Xenians signed a petition to the Cincinnati Methodist Episcopal Conference demanding that Wilberforce University be moved out of Greene County. The petition was debated at length in the *Torchlight* from September through October, with the paper's editor firmly on the side of the petitioners. The petition appeared to have been sparked by a series of articles printed in late July and early August blaming Wilberforce for an influx of free black immigrants; only one letter to the editor noted that black immigration into the town and surrounding county had begun some years before the school was founded. The first article on the subject was "Negrophobia," *Xenia Torchlight* (Xenia, OH) 28 July 1858, State Archives, Ohio History Connection.

156. The teacher who resigned, a white woman and Oberlin graduate, was replaced by Sarah J. Woodson, a Black Oberlin graduate and one of the earliest African American women to become a college faculty member. Woodson was the daughter and sister of prominent African Methodist Episcopal (AME) ministers and was strongly influenced by her family's commitment to moral reform movements. She was the superintendent of the Colored Division of the Women's Christian Temperance Union from 1888 to 1892, as well as the spokesperson for Tennessee's Prohibition Party. Ellen NicKenzie Lawson and Marlene D. Merrill, *The Three Sarahs: Documents of Antebellum Black College Women* (New York: Edwin Mellen Press, 1984), 158.

157. Currier, "Reminiscences of My Childhood," Parker Family papers, Northern Kentucky University.

158. Willis Townsend to S. D. Cabaniss, letter dated 26 March 1860, Septimus D. Cabaniss Papers.

CHAPTER 4

1. D. L. Lakin to S. D. Cabaniss, letter dated 29 February 1860, Septimus D. Cabaniss Papers; Item 3, "Inventory and Appraisement" dated February–March 1858, Inventories, Septimus D. Cabaniss Papers. According to the inventory conducted by S. D. Cabaniss and Samuel C. Townsend in 1858, the "second class" legatees had an estimated monetary value of $29,225 total. For biographical details on Lakin, see David L. Lakin, 1850 United States Federal Census; David L. Lakin, 1859 Kansas State Census, accessed 31 June 2017, www.ancestry.com.

2. See Items 4 and 5, will of Samuel Townsend dated 6 September 1856, Wills; Item 3, "Inventory and Appraisement" dated February–March 1858, Inventories, Septimus D. Cabaniss Papers.

3. S. D. Cabaniss to Wesley Townsend, letter dated 27 February 1860; "Shewing moneys furnished David L. Lakin for the removal, emancipation and maintenance of slaves and for payment of legacies to adult legatees of second class," undated document, Septimus D. Cabaniss Papers.

4. D. L. Lakin to S. D. Cabaniss, letter dated 29 February 1860, Septimus D. Cabaniss Papers. Emphasis in original.

5. On western expansion and the development of federal Indian policy throughout the nineteenth century, see Ned Blackhawk, *Violence over the Land: Indians and Empires in the Early American West* (Cambridge, MA: Harvard University Press, 2008); Nancy Carol Carter, "U.S. Federal Indian Policy: An Essay and Annotated Bibliography," *Legal Reference Services Quarterly* 30, no. 3 (2011): 210–230; Deborah A. Rosen, *American Indians and State Law: Sovereignty, Race, and Citizenship, 1790–1880* (Lincoln: Nebraska University Press, 2007); Bernard W. Sheehan, *Seeds of Extinction: Jeffersonian Philanthropy and the American Indian* (Chapel Hill: University of North Carolina Press, 1973); Anthony F. C. Wallace,

The Long, Bitter Trail: Andrew Jackson and the Indians (New York: Hill and Wang, 1993); West, *The Contested Plains: Indians, Goldseekers, and the Rush to Colorado* (Lawrence: University Press of Kansas, 1998).

6. *The Expeditions of Zebulon Montgomery Pike*, ed. Elliott Coues (New York: Francis P. Harper, 1895), vol. 2, 525.

7. Robert R. Crifasi, *A Land Made from Water: Appropriation and the Evolution of Colorado's Landscape, Ditches, and Water Institutions* (Boulder: University Press of Colorado, 2015), 12, 15.

8. Crifasi, *A Land Made from Water,* 12, 15.

9. William S. Burke and J. L. Rock, *The History of Leavenworth, the Metropolis of Kansas, and the Chief Commercial Center West of the Missouri River* (Leavenworth, KS: Leavenworth Times Book and Job Printing Establishment, 1880), 8. Burke and Rock's account exemplifies the contempt with which white Kansas responded to Native American claims to the land: "There was a fierce opposition to the enterprise from its inception, by . . . certain Government officials, who pretended such sincere devotion to the poor Indian, who in their vivid imagination was being robbed by the avarice of the squatters."

10. Burke and Rock, *The History of Leavenworth,* 8.

11. Walter B. Sloan, *History and Map of Kansas & Nebraska: Describing Soil, Climate, Rivers, Prairies, Mounds, Forests, Minerals* (Chicago: R. Fergus, 1855), 18.

12. Sloan, *History and Map of Kansas & Nebraska,* 18; Sutherland & McEvoy, *Leavenworth City Directory, and Business Mirror for 1859–60, Containing the Name and Residence of Every Male Citizen, a Business Mirror, and an Appendix of Much Useful Information* (St. Louis, MO: Sutherland & McEvoy, 1859), Carroll Mansion of Leavenworth, Leavenworth County Historical Society; West, *The Contested Plains,* 8.

13. Sutherland & McEvoy, *Leavenworth City Directory, and Business Mirror for 1859–60,* 25, Carroll Mansion of Leavenworth, Leavenworth County Historical Society; William P. Tomlinson, *Kansas in Eighteen Fifty-Eight, Being Chiefly a History of the Recent Troubles in the Territory* (New York: H. Dayton, 1859), 26.

14. Sutherland & McEvoy, *Leavenworth City Directory, and Business Mirror for 1859–60,* xiii, Carroll Mansion of Leavenworth, Leavenworth County Historical Society.

15. "THE WEST," *Leavenworth Daily Conservative* (Leavenworth, KS), 27 February 1864, KHS.

16. Tomlinson, *Kansas in Eighteen Fifty-Eight, Being Chiefly a History of the Recent Troubles in the Territory,* 301–302.

17. Henry Tanner, *Directory & Shippers' Guide of Kansas & Nebraska* (Leavenworth City, KS: T. A. Holland & Co., 1866).

18. Tomlinson, *Kansas in Eighteen Fifty-Eight, Being Chiefly a History of the Recent Troubles in the Territory,* 300; Tanner, *Directory & Shippers' Guide of Kansas & Nebraska,* 62.

19. Tanner, *Directory & Shippers' Guide of Kansas & Nebraska*, 62, 61.

20. Sutherland & McEvoy, *Leavenworth City Directory, and Business Mirror for 1859-60*, xiii, Carroll Mansion of Leavenworth, Leavenworth Historical Society; Tomlinson, *Kansas in Eighteen Fifty-Eight, Being Chiefly a History of the Recent Troubles in the Territory*, 299.

21. Elliot West notes that the greatest amount of literature promoting Kansas settlement was published in the winter of 1858–59. This was precisely the period when Cabaniss was writing letters of inquiry to prominent men across the country, asking for advice on where to send the Townsends when they were emancipated. Considering the timing, Cabaniss would have likely come across promotional materials as he conducted his own research. West, *The Contested Plains*, 132.

22. S. D. Cabaniss to Wesley Townsend, letter dated 1 February 1860, Septimus D. Cabaniss Papers.

23. "THE WEST," *Leavenworth Daily Conservative* (Leavenworth, KS), 27 February 1864, KHS.

24. Charles Sumner, *The Crime Against Kansas. The Apologies for the Crime. The True Remedy. Speech of Hon. Charles Sumner, in the Senate of the United States, 19th and 20th May, 1856* (Boston: John P. Jewett & Company, 1856), 3.

25. Public perception of the "virgin" American West transformed during the antebellum period largely as a result of the spread of plantation agriculture across the American South during the first decades of the nineteenth century. Henry Nash Smith argues that by the 1830s, two mutually exclusive visions of the country's agrarian future had developed: the first following from the late eighteenth-century ideal of a country of independent yeoman farmers, and the second of an expanding plantation complex made possible by slave labor. In this interpretation, the battle for Kansas Territory's future in the 1850s was a conflict over the public imagination as well as political power and influence. Smith, *Virgin Land*.

26. See Nicole Etcheson, *Bleeding Kansas: Contested Liberty in the Civil War Era* (Lawrence: University Press of Kansas, 2004), 23–25; Pearl T. Ponce, *To Govern the Devil in Hell: The Political Crisis in Territorial Kansas* (DeKalb: Northern Illinois University Press, 2014). 43–47.

27. On public perception and fears of a "Slave Power" conspiracy, see John Craig Hammond, *Slavery, Freedom, and Expansion in the Early American West* (Charlottesville: University of Virginia Press, 2007); Howe, *What Hath God Wrought: The Transformation of America, 1815-1848*; Sean Wilentz, *The Rise of American Democracy: Jefferson to Lincoln* (New York: W.W. Norton, 2005).

28. The New England Emigrant Aid Society (NEEAC), founded in 1854, was the most prominent emigration organization to involve itself in Kansas. Lawrence (a NEEAC town) achieved a reputation as a haven for fugitive slaves and hub for Underground Railroad activity in Kansas. Lawrence was also a stronghold for free-soilers during the territorial conflict: as an example, during the November 1854 election to choose a delegate to Congress, Lawrence was the only city in Kansas

Territory in which the proslavery candidate did not receive the majority of votes. This does not, however, indicate that it was the only town where free-soilers made up the majority of residents. A congressional delegation discovered afterward that over 1,700 of the votes cast in the 1854 delegate election were fraudulent or cast by non-residents. This was repeated, to a larger extent, in March 1855, when 6,000 votes were cast (5,427 of them for a proslavery candidate) despite the territorial census having counted only 2,905 permanent settlers to be eligible voters. See Etcheson, *Bleeding Kansas: Contested Liberty in the Civil War Era*, 36, 53–59.

29. "Letter, J. A. Davies to Dear Friend [Thomas Wentworth] Higginson," Territorial Kansas Online, accessed June 23, 2017, www.territorialkansasonline.org.

30. Taylor, *In Search of the Racial Frontier*, 95; Richard B. Sheridan, "From Slavery in Missouri to Freedom in Kansas: The Influx of Black Fugitives and Contrabands into Kansas," *Kansas History* 12, no. 1 (Spring 1989): 28–47.

31. Sheridan, "From Slavery in Missouri to Freedom in Kansas," 30.

32. H. C. Bruce, *The New Man. Twenty-Nine Years a Slave. Twenty-Nine Years a Free Man* (New York: Negro Universities Press, [1895] 1969), 99.

33. James B. Abbott, an early Kansas settler who migrated to the territory with a NEEAC party in 1854, coined Lawrence's nickname as "the best-advertised antislavery town in the world." Abbott fought alongside John Brown during the territorial conflict and later held political offices in Kansas, as well as served as a government agent for the Shawnee Indians in De Soto, Kansas. See Francis W. Blackmar, ed., "Abbott, James B.," *Kansas: A Cyclopedia of State History* (Chicago, IL: 1912).

34. Sheridan, "From Slavery in Missouri to Freedom in Kansas," 31; Taylor, *In Search of the Racial Frontier*, 95.

35. Bruce, *The New Man*, 109.

36. Wesley Townsend to S. D. Cabaniss, letter dated 14 February 1860, Septimus D. Cabaniss Papers.

37. "Excitement in Southern Kansas," *Xenia Torchlight* (Xenia, OH), 29 November 1860, State Archives, Ohio History Connection.

38. S. D. Cabaniss to Wesley Townsend, letter dated 17 February 1860, Septimus D. Cabaniss Papers.

39. Items 4 and 5, will of Samuel Townsend dated 6 September 1856, Wills, Septimus D. Cabaniss Papers.

40. D. L. Lakin to S. D. Cabaniss, telegram dated 13 March 1860, Septimus D. Cabaniss Papers.

41. Wesley Townsend to S. D. Cabaniss, letter dated 4 March 1860; "Bill of Revision," filed 12 March 1860, Cabaniss v. Townsend, Septimus D. Cabaniss Papers.

42. S. D. Cabaniss to John B. Brandon and Thomas W. Brandon, letter dated 11 February 1860, Septimus D. Cabaniss Papers.

43. "Population of the United States in 1860," Census of Population and Housing, accessed 30 June 2017, www.census.gov; Sutherland & McEvoy, *Leavenworth City Directory, and Business Mirror for 1859–60*, xii–xiii, Carroll Mansion of

Leavenworth, Leavenworth Historical Society; Kansas State Historical Society Historic Sites Survey, *Black Historic Sites: A Beginning Point* (Topeka: Kansas State Historical Society, 1977), 8.

44. Wesley Townsend to S. D. Cabaniss, letter dated 15 March 1860, Septimus D. Cabaniss Papers.

45. Sheridan, "From Slavery in Missouri to Freedom in Kansas," 40.

46. Wesley Townsend to S. D. Cabaniss, letter dated 4 March 1860, Septimus D. Cabaniss Papers.

47. Woodson Townsend to S. D. Cabaniss, letter dated 27 March 1860, Septimus D. Cabaniss Papers.

48. S. D. Cabaniss to W. D. Chadick, letter dated 2 March 1858, Septimus D. Cabaniss Papers.

49. Item 1, will of Samuel Townsend dated 10 September 1853, Wills, Septimus D. Cabaniss Papers.

50. Wesley Townsend to S. D. Cabaniss, letter dated 18 January 1860, Septimus D. Cabaniss Papers.

51. Wesley Townsend to S. D. Cabaniss, letter dated 14 February 1860, Septimus D. Cabaniss Papers.

52. W. D. Chadick to S. D. Cabaniss, letter dated 18 February 1856, Series 1, Subseries B, Box 22, Folder 1, Frances Cabaniss Roberts Collection, Dept. of Archives/Special Collections, M. Louis Salmon Library, University of Alabama in Huntsville, Huntsville, AL.

53. Wesley Townsend to S. D. Cabaniss, letter dated 18 January 1860, Septimus D. Cabaniss Papers.

54. S. D. Cabaniss to Wesley Townsend, letter dated 8 February 1860, Septimus D. Cabaniss Papers.

55. Edmund Townsend to James Robinson, letter dated 18 April 1850, Septimus D. Cabaniss Papers.

56. W. D. Chadick to S. D. Cabaniss, letter dated 18 February 1856, Series 1, Subseries B, Box 22, Folder 1, Frances Cabaniss Roberts Collection, Dept. of Archives/Special Collections, M. Louis Salmon Library, University of Alabama in Huntsville, Huntsville, AL.

57. Woodson Townsend to S. D. Cabaniss, letter dated 16 February 1866, Septimus D. Cabaniss Papers.

58. Item 3, "Inventory and Appraisement" dated February–March 1858, Inventories, Septimus D. Cabaniss Papers.

59. Wesley Townsend to S. D. Cabaniss, letter dated 18 January 1860, Septimus D. Cabaniss Papers.

60. Elvira Townsend and Jane Townsend to S. D. Cabaniss, letter dated 31 January 1860, Septimus D. Cabaniss Papers.

61. S. D. Cabaniss to Elvira Townsend, letter dated 8 February 1860; S. D. Cabaniss to D. L. Lakin, letter dated 16 October 1860, Septimus D. Cabaniss Papers.

62. Elvira Townsend and Jane Townsend to S. D. Cabaniss, letter dated 31 January 1860, Septimus D. Cabaniss Papers.

63. See S. D. Cabaniss to Wesley Townsend, letters dated September 1858, 26 January 1860, 27 January 1860, 13 February 1860; Elvira Townsend and Jane Townsend to S. D. Cabaniss, letter dated 31 January 1860; S. D. Cabaniss to Elvira Townsend, letter dated 8 February 1860.

64. Wesley Townsend to S. D. Cabaniss, letter dated 8 February 1860, Septimus D. Cabaniss Papers.

65. Wesley Townsend to S. D. Cabaniss, letter dated 14 February 1860, Septimus D. Cabaniss Papers.

66. Woodson Townsend to S. D. Cabaniss, letter dated 27 March 1860, Septimus D. Cabaniss Papers.

67. Willis Townsend to S. D. Cabaniss, letter dated 8 May 1860, Septimus D. Cabaniss Papers.

68. Wesley Townsend to S. D. Cabaniss, letter dated 15 March 1860, Septimus D. Cabaniss Papers.

69. Woodson Townsend to S. D. Cabaniss, letter dated 27 March 1860, Septimus D. Cabaniss Papers.

70. D. L. Lakin to S. D. Cabaniss, letter dated 24 April 1860; Item 3, "Inventory and Appraisement" dated February–March 1858, Inventories, Septimus D. Cabaniss Papers.

71. D. L. Lakin to S. D. Cabaniss, letters dated 7 March 1860 and 24 April 1860, Septimus D. Cabaniss Papers.

72. D. L. Lakin to S. D. Cabaniss, letter dated 24 April 1860, Septimus D. Cabaniss Papers.

73. West, *The Contested Plains,* 327; Cutler, *History of the State of Kansas.* When describing the weather and agriculture of the state in the 1860s, Cutler's history calls 1860 simply the year of "the great drouth."

74. "The Famine in Kansas" and "Help for Starving Kansas," *Xenia Torchlight* (Xenia, OH), 14 November 1860, State Archives, Ohio History Connection.

75. "The Famine in Kansas, *Xenia Torchlight* (Xenia, OH), 14 November 1860, State Archives, Ohio History Connection.

76. "Help for Starving Kansas," *Xenia Torchlight* (Xenia, OH), 14 November 1860, State Archives, Ohio History Connection.

77. S. D. Cabaniss to Wesley Townsend, letter dated 13 November 1858; "Bill of Revision," filed 12 March 1860, Cabaniss v. Townsend, Septimus D. Cabaniss Papers.

78. S. D. Cabaniss to Dr. John S. Payne, letter dated 14 July 1859, Septimus D. Cabaniss Papers.

79. S. D. Cabaniss to R. S. Rust, letter dated 5 March 1861, Septimus D. Cabaniss Papers.

80. Elizabeth Townsend to Armstead Townsend, letter dated 18 May 1861, Septimus D. Cabaniss Papers.

81. S. D. Cabaniss to R. S. Rust, letter dated 5 March 1861, Septimus D. Cabaniss Papers.

82. Woodson Townsend to S. D. Cabaniss, letter dated 16 February 1866, Septimus D. Cabaniss Papers.

83. S. D. Cabaniss to W.W. Walker, letter dated 30 November 1858, Septimus D. Cabaniss Papers.

84. Item 1, Bill of Revision filed 12 March 1866, Cabaniss vs. Townsend, Septimus D. Cabaniss Papers.

85. "Shewing moneys furnished David L. Lakin for the removal, emancipation and maintenance of slaves and for payment of legacies to adult legatees of second class," undated document, Septimus D. Cabaniss Papers.

86. For an examination of black domestic servants' conceptions of autonomy within and outside the workplace, see Tera W. Hunter, *To 'Joy My Freedom: Southern Black Women's Lives and Labors after the Civil War* (Cambridge, MA: Harvard University Press, 1997).

87. "Bill of Revision," filed 12 March 1860, Cabaniss v. Townsend, Septimus D. Cabaniss Papers.

88. D. L. Lakin to S. D. Cabaniss, letter dated 24 April 1860, Septimus D. Cabaniss Papers. Emphasis in original.

89. Item 1, deposition of S. D. Cabaniss, Depositions, 1859 and undated, Septimus D. Cabaniss Papers.

90. S. D. Cabaniss to R. S. Rust, letter dated 12 July 1860, Septimus D. Cabaniss Papers.

91. S. D. Cabaniss to R. S. Rust, letter dated 5 March 1861, Septimus D. Cabaniss Papers.

92. S. D. Cabaniss to Willis Townsend, letter dated 14 February 1860, Septimus D. Cabaniss Papers.

93. S. D. Cabaniss to Wesley Townsend, letter dated 27 January 1860, Septimus D. Cabaniss Papers.

94. S. D. Cabaniss to Wesley Townsend, letter dated 17 February 1860, Septimus D. Cabaniss Papers. Emphasis in original.

95. S. D. Cabaniss to R. S. Rust, letter dated 27 February 1860, Septimus D. Cabaniss Papers.

96. Wesley Townsend to S. D. Cabaniss, letter dated 16 August 1858, Septimus D. Cabaniss Papers.

97. S. D. Cabaniss to Elvira Townsend, letter dated 31 January 1860, Septimus D. Cabaniss Papers.

98. D. L. Lakin to S. D. Cabaniss, letter dated 19 March 1861, Septimus D. Cabaniss Papers.

99. J. H. Johnson III, *Early Leavenworth and Fort Leavenworth: A Photographic History* (Leavenworth, KS: J. H. Johnson III, 1977), 26–27; Tomlinson, *Kansas*

in Eighteen Fifty-Eight, Being Chiefly a History of the Recent Troubles in the Territory, 25.

100. The Planters' House (anecdotally) hired two bartenders during the territorial period: one to serve proslavery men and one to serve free-soil men, in order to keep violent fights over political issues from breaking out in the hotel. Johnson, *Early Leavenworth and Fort Leavenworth: A Photographic History*, 26–27.

101. D. L. Lakin to S. D. Cabaniss, letter dated 19 March 1861, Septimus D. Cabaniss Papers. Emphasis in original.

102. D. L. Lakin to S. D. Cabaniss, letter dated 19 March 1861, Septimus D. Cabaniss Papers.

103. D. L. Lakin to S. D. Cabaniss, letter dated 29 March 1861, Septimus D. Cabaniss Papers.

104. David L. Lakin, 1859 Kansas State Census, 1860 United States Federal Census Non-Population Schedules, 1860 and 1880 United States Federal Censuses, accessed 30 June 2017, www.ancestry.com. The 1860 and 1880 federal censuses provide conflicting information on Lakin's birthplace, stating variously Virginia and Alabama. Either state, however, would account for his prior acquaintance with Cabaniss, whose family moved from Virginia to Alabama shortly before the Townsends did. Lakin went on to have a long, successful career as a businessman and land speculator in Kansas after the Civil War. Namesake of the present-day town of Lakin, Kansas, he served as the treasurer and first land commissioner of the Atchison, Topeka and Santa Fe Railway beginning in 1864. Between 1866 and 1868, the trustees of Lincoln College, now Washburn University, considered purchasing a tract of land Lakin owned in Topeka on which to establish the college. In a letter to Cabaniss, Lakin referred to the buyers as "the Lincoln (nigger) College," but his politics did not prevent him from attempting to make the sale—though the trustees ultimately chose a different location. See Joseph W. Snell and Don W. Wilson, "The Birth of the Atchison, Topeka and Santa Fe," *Kansas History* 34, no. 2 (Summer 1968); Russell K. Hickman, "Lincoln College, Forerunner of Washburn University: Part Two: Later History and Change of Name—Concluded," in *Kansas Historical Quarterly* 18, no. 2 (May 1950), 177 fn 149; D. L. Lakin to S. D. Cabaniss, letter dated 22 May 1866, Septimus D. Cabaniss Papers.

105. D. L. Lakin to S. D. Cabaniss, letter dated 29 March 1861, Septimus D. Cabaniss Papers. Emphasis in original.

106. S. D. Cabaniss to Wesley Townsend, letter dated 8 February 1860; S. D. Cabaniss to D.L. Lakin, letter dated 22 March 1860, Septimus D. Cabaniss Papers. Emphasis in original.

107. D. L. Lakin to S. D. Cabaniss, letter dated 19 March 1861, Septimus D. Cabaniss Papers.

108. D. L. Lakin to S. D. Cabaniss, letter dated 29 March 1861, Septimus D. Cabaniss Papers.

109. D. L. Lakin to S. D. Cabaniss, letters dated 19 March 1861 and 29 March 1861, Septimus D. Cabaniss Papers. Emphasis in original.

110. S. D. Cabaniss to D. L. Lakin, letter dated 4 April 1861; S. D. Cabaniss to Woodson Townsend, letter dated 3 April 1861.

111. S. D. Cabaniss to Woodson Townsend, letter dated 3 April 1861, Septimus D. Cabaniss Papers.

112. Cabaniss and Lakin were especially determined not to purchase land with extensive timber grounds as they believed the Townsends would attempt to sell the timber for lumber and live on the profits rather than farm the tillable land themselves. See in particular S. D. Cabaniss to D. L. Lakin, letter dated 28 June 1860, Septimus D. Cabaniss Papers.

113. S. D. Cabaniss to Willis Townsend, letter dated 16 March 1860, Septimus D. Cabaniss Papers.

114. D. L. Lakin to S. D. Cabaniss, letter dated 19 March 1860, Septimus D. Cabaniss Papers.

115. S. D. Cabaniss to D. L. Lakin, letter dated 8 November 1860, Septimus D. Cabaniss Papers.

116. S. D. Cabaniss to D. L. Lakin, letter dated 22 March 1860, Septimus D. Cabaniss Papers.

117. D. L. Lakin to S. D. Cabaniss, letter dated 29 March 1861, Septimus D. Cabaniss Papers.

118. S. D. Cabaniss to D. L. Lakin, letter dated 9 July 1860, Septimus D. Cabaniss Papers.

119. D. L. Lakin to S. D. Cabaniss, letter dated 22 August 1860, Septimus D. Cabaniss Papers.

120. S. D. Cabaniss to R. S. Rust, letter dated 5 March 1861, Septimus D. Cabaniss Papers.

121. S. D. Cabaniss to R. S. Rust, letter dated 5 March 1861, Septimus D. Cabaniss Papers.

122. S. D. Cabaniss to unnamed recipient in Natchez, MS, letter dated 9 November 1860, Septimus D. Cabaniss Papers.

123. S. D. Cabaniss to D. L. Lakin, letter dated 8 November 1860, Septimus D. Cabaniss Papers.

124. D. L. Lakin to S. D. Cabaniss, letter dated 19 March 1861, Septimus D. Cabaniss Papers. Emphasis in original.

125. The Confederate States Congress passed a "Sequestration Act" on August 30, 1861, which authorized the Confederate government to seize the property of "alien enemies" in the United States. The Townsends, as free men and women living outside of the South, fell under that category, though Cabaniss did not believe there was any danger of Samuel Townsend's estate being "permanently confiscated" during the war. Looking for a "peculiarity" (or loophole) in the Townsend legatees' case, Cabaniss petitioned the Madison County Chancery Court for permission

to transfer funds specifically to the Townsends under the age of twenty-one as he argued that they would be unable to support themselves otherwise, but his request was refused. Because communications with the Townsends were cut off during the war, Cabaniss was not fully informed about whether they were still living in Ohio or Kansas and seemed to be under the impression that at least some of the Townsends had moved to Canada. If this were the case, they would have been non-citizens of the United States and therefore able to receive funds, but this legal argument also failed. S. D. Cabaniss to R. S. Rust, letter dated July 15 1861; S. D. Cabaniss to "Brevt Brg Gen; J.B. Callis, Sub Assr Comm'r," letter dated 8 May 1867, Septimus D. Cabaniss Papers; *Sequestration Act, Passed by The Congress of the Confederate States* (Richmond, VA: Tyler, Wise and Allegre: 1861).

126. S. D. Cabaniss to R. S. Rust, letter dated 15 July 1861, Septimus D. Cabaniss Papers.

127. S. D. Cabaniss to William Chilton, letter dated 23 January 1862, Septimus D. Cabaniss Papers.

128. See McGinnis, *A History and an Interpretation of Wilberforce University,* 37; Robinson, "The Negro in the Village of Yellow Springs, Ohio," 104; *The Wilberforce Annual: A Comprehensive Review of the Origin, Development and Present Status of Wilberforce University,* 6.

129. S. D. Cabaniss to R. S. Rust, letter dated 15 July 1861, Septimus D. Cabaniss Papers.

130. Thomas Townsend to S. D. Cabaniss, letter dated 21 February 1866, Septimus D. Cabaniss Papers.

131. Wesley Townsend to S. D. Cabaniss, letter dated 13 October 1865, Septimus D. Cabaniss Papers; Wesley Townsend to S. D. Cabaniss, letter dated 25 January 1866, Septimus D. Cabaniss Papers.

132. Thomas Townsend to S. D. Cabaniss, letter dated 21 February 1866, Septimus D. Cabaniss Papers.

133. Wesley Townsend to S. D. Cabaniss, letter dated 13 October 1865, Septimus D. Cabaniss Papers.

134. Wesley Townsend to S. D. Cabaniss, letter dated 13 October 1865, Septimus D. Cabaniss Papers.

135. "Westley Townsend" and "Ada Townsend," 1880 Federal Census, accessed 10 June 2020, www.ancestry.com.

136. Wesley Townsend to S. D. Cabaniss, letter dated 13 October 1865, Septimus D. Cabaniss Papers; "Wesley Townsend," Co. D, 100 Reg't U.S. Col'd Inf., Company Descriptive Book, accessed 15 August 2018, www.fold3.com.

137. On laundresses and other common occupations for Black women in the nineteenth century, see Hunter, *To Joy My Freedom.*

138. In her book *Righteous Propagation,* historian Michele Mitchell explores Black reformers' concern with "respectability" during the late nineteenth and early twentieth centuries, a concern that emerged from earlier generations' politics of racial uplift. Reformers focused particular attention on Black women's bodies and sexual purity, which had been compromised by white men's practices of rape and

concubinage under slavery. Mitchell argues that reformers focused on purity as a means of countering racist assumptions of Black men's lasciviousness and Black women's immorality—stereotypes that had serious, real-world consequences. See Michele Mitchell, *Righteous Propagation: African Americans and the Politics of Racial Destiny after Reconstruction* (Chapel Hill: University of North Carolina Press, 2004).

139. Wesley Townsend to S. D. Cabaniss, letter dated 13 October 1865, Septimus D. Cabaniss Papers.

140. Item 4 (1), Deposition of Willis Townsend, dated 21 May 1872, Cabaniss v. Townsend, Depositions, 1866–1873, Septimus D. Cabaniss Papers.

141. Item 4 (2), Deposition of Thomas Wood, dated 21 May 1872, Cabaniss v. Townsend, Depositions, 1866–1873, Septimus D. Cabaniss Papers.

142. Item 4 (1), Deposition of Willis Townsend, dated 21 May 1872, Cabaniss v. Townsend, Depositions, 1866–1873, Septimus D. Cabaniss Papers.

143. Item 4 (2), Deposition of Thomas Wood, dated 21 May 1872, Cabaniss v. Townsend, Depositions, 1866–1873, Septimus D. Cabaniss Papers.

144. Susanna Townsend to S. D. Cabaniss, letter dated 1 January 1866, Septimus D. Cabaniss Papers.

145. Wesley Townsend to S. D. Cabaniss, letter dated 13 October 1865, Septimus D. Cabaniss Papers.

146. Wesley Townsend to S. D. Cabaniss, letter dated 25 January 1866, Septimus D. Cabaniss Papers.

147. Susanna Townsend to S. D. Cabaniss, letter dated 28 March 1866,

148. Susanna Townsend to S. D. Cabaniss, letter dated 1 January 1866, Septimus D. Cabaniss Papers.

149. *Historical Sketches of the Higher Educational Institutions and also of Benevolent and Reformatory Institutions of the State of Ohio* (Philadelphia: 1876), 78, 81.

150. Susanna Townsend to S. D. Cabaniss, letter dated 16 April 1866, Septimus D. Cabaniss Papers.

151. Susanna Townsend to S. D. Cabaniss, letter dated 8 August 1866, Septimus D. Cabaniss Papers.

152. S. D. Cabaniss to Osborne Townsend, letter dated 30 March 1866, Septimus D. Cabaniss Papers.

153. S. D. Cabaniss to R. S. Rust, letter dated 2 April 1866, Septimus D. Cabaniss Papers.

154. S. D. Cabaniss to Susanna Townsend, letter dated 7 April 1866, Septimus D. Cabaniss Papers.

155. Susanna Townsend to S. D. Cabaniss, letter dated 16 April 1866, Septimus D. Cabaniss Papers;

156. Susanna Townsend to S. D. Cabaniss, letter dated 27 March 1867, Septimus D. Cabaniss Papers.

157. Wesley Townsend to S. D. Cabaniss, letter dated 8 February 1860, Septimus D. Cabaniss Papers.

158. Wesley Townsend to S. D. Cabaniss, letter dated 14 July 1868, Septimus D. Cabaniss Papers.

159. Item 4 (2), Deposition of Thomas Wood, dated 21 May 1872, Cabaniss v. Townsend, Depositions, 1866–1873; Wesley Townsend to S. D. Cabaniss, letter dated 28 October 1866, Septimus D. Cabaniss Papers.

160. Susanna Townsend to S. D. Cabaniss, letter dated 24 May 1866, Septimus D. Cabaniss Papers.

161. Wesley Townsend to S. D. Cabaniss, letter dated 14 May 1866; Susanna Townsend to S. D. Cabaniss, letter dated 1 January 1866, Septimus D. Cabaniss Papers.

162. Susanna Townsend to S. D. Cabaniss, letter dated 8 August 1866, Septimus D. Cabaniss Papers.

163. Susanna Townsend to S. D. Cabaniss, letter dated 12 September 1866, Septimus D. Cabaniss Papers.

164. Susanna Townsend to S. D. Cabaniss, letter dated 12 September 1866; S. D. Cabaniss to Elizabeth Yerger, letter dated 31 January 1866, Septimus D. Cabaniss Papers.

165. Wesley Townsend to S. D. Cabaniss, letter dated 28 October 1866, Septimus D. Cabaniss Papers.

166. Wesley Townsend to S. D. Cabaniss, letters dated 4 December 1866 and 27 December 1866, Septimus D. Cabaniss Papers.

167. S. D. Cabaniss to Brevet Brigadier General J. B. Callis, letter dated 8 May 1867, Septimus D. Cabaniss Papers.

168. Susanna Townsend to S. D. Cabaniss, letter dated 4 June 1868, Septimus D. Cabaniss Papers.

169. Susanna Townsend to S. D. Cabaniss, letters dated 16 April 1866 and 1 January 1866, Septimus D. Cabaniss Papers.

170. It was also a role white society usually denied enslaved, African, and African American women, who for centuries had been stereotyped as immoral, un-feminine, and even monstrous. Jennifer Morgan's *Laboring Women* explores the long history of stereotypes about Black women's bodies and supposed sexual immorality, dating to Europeans' earliest contact with Africans. See Jennifer Morgan, Laboring Women: Reproduction and Gender in New World Slavery (Philadelphia: University of Pennsylvania Press, 2004).

171. Susanna Townsend to S. D. Cabaniss, letter dated 4 June 1868, Septimus D. Cabaniss Papers.

172. Marriage record for John W. Checks and Elizabeth Yerger, Alabama, Select Marriages, accessed 22 June 2016, www.ancestry.com; military service record for John W. Checks, U.S. Returns from Regular Army Infantry, 1821–1916, accessed 22 June 2016, www.ancestry.com; Elizabeth Cheeks, 1870 United States Federal Census, North Carolina, Raleigh, accessed 22 June 2016, www.ancestry.com.

173. For an in-depth study of "miscegenation" law in the United States, see Peggy Pascoe, *What Comes Naturally: Miscegenation Law and the Making of Race in America* (New York: Oxford University Press, 2009).

174. Susanna Townsend to S. D. Cabaniss, letter dated 4 June 1868, Septimus D. Cabaniss Papers.

175. S. D. Cabaniss to Wesley Townsend, letter dated 1868, Septimus D. Cabaniss Papers.

176. Wesley Townsend to S. D. Cabaniss, letter dated 14 July 1869, Septimus D. Cabaniss Papers.

177. S. D. Cabaniss to Wesley Townsend, letter dated 25 January 1869.

178. Wesley Townsend to S. D. Cabaniss, letter dated 14 July 1869, Septimus D. Cabaniss Papers.

179. Wesley Townsend to S. D. Cabaniss, letter dated 1 January 1869, Septimus D. Cabaniss Papers.

180. Adelaide Townsend to S. D. Cabaniss, letter dated 10 May 1869, Septimus D. Cabaniss Papers.

181. Wesley Townsend to S. D. Cabaniss, letter dated 1 January 1869, Septimus D. Cabaniss Papers.

182. Wesley Townsend to S. D. Cabaniss, letter dated 3 May 1869, Septimus D. Cabaniss Papers.

183. According to Wesley's wife Ada, Susanna's last request was to be buried in Ada's plot with one of Ada's predeceased children. Adelaide Townsend to S. D. Cabaniss, letter dated 10 May 1869, Septimus D. Cabaniss Papers.

184. Burke and Rock, *The History of Leavenworth, the Metropolis of Kansas, and the Chief Commercial Center West of the Missouri River*.

185. Tomlinson, *Kansas in Eighteen Fifty-Eight, Being Chiefly aHistory of the Recent Troubles in the Territory*, 26.

186. Diane Mutti Burke, "Scattered People: The Long History of Forced Evictions in the Kansas-Missouri Borderlands," in *Civil War Wests: Testing the Limits of the United States,* ed. Adam Arenson and Andrew R. Graybill (Berkeley: University of California Press, 2015), 79–80; Roger D. Cunningham, "Douglas's Battery at Fort Leavenworth," *Kansas History* 23, no. 4 (Winter 2000-2001): 200-217; Sheridan, "From Slavery in Missouri to Freedom in Kansas."

187. Sheridan, "From Slavery in Missouri to Freedom in Kansas," 37.

188. 1865 Kansas State Census, accessed 30 June 2017, www.ancestry.com.

189. 1862 Leavenworth editorial as quoted in Sheridan, "From Slavery in Missouri to Freedom in Kansas," 41.

190. Campney, "'Light Is Bursting Upon the World!': White Supremacy and Racist Violence against Blacks in Reconstruction Kansas," 94; Taylor, *In Search of the Racial Frontier: African Americans in the American West, 1528–1990,* 136. On state-building efforts in the West, see Karl Jacoby, *Shadows at Dawn: An Apache Massacre and the Violence of History* (New York: Penguin Press, 2008);

Ari Kelman, *A Misplaced Massacre: Struggling over the Memory of Sand Creek* (Cambridge, MA: Harvard University Press, 2013); Richardson, *West from Appomattox*; Richard White, *Railroaded: The Transcontinentals and the Making of Modern America* (New York: W. W. Norton, 2011).

191. William G. Cutler, *History of the State of Kansas* (Chicago: A.T. Andreas, 1883); Roger D. Cunningham, "Douglas's Battery at Fort Leavenworth," *Kansas History* 23, no. 4 (Winter 2000-2001), 204; Taylor, *In Search of the Racial Frontier*, 98.

192. As quoted in Campney, "'Light Is Bursting Upon the World!': White Supremacy and Racist Violence against Blacks in Reconstruction Kansas," 86.

193. *The Wilberforce Annual*, 17–18.

194. Noah Andre Trudeau, *Like Men of War: Black Troops in the Civil War, 1862–1865* (New York: Little, Brown, 1998), 11–14.

195. "Bill of Revision" filed 12 March 1860, Cabaniss v. Townsend, Septimus D. Cabaniss Papers; Caroline Stone, 1875 Kansas State Census and 1880 Federal Census, accessed 30 June 2017, www.ancestry.com.

196. Mildred Green and Henry Green, 1870 Federal Census, accessed 11 June 2020, www.ancestry.com.

197. Thomas Townsend to S. D. Cabaniss, letter dated 20 March 1866, Septimus D. Cabaniss Papers.

198. Freeman Townsend, 1895 Kansas State Census; Freeman Townsend, Leavenworth, Kansas, City Directory, 1891 and 1900, accessed 31 July 2021, www.ancestry.com.

199. James Sutherland, *Leavenworth City Directory and Business Mirror, 1863–64* (Leavenworth, KS: James Sutherland, 1864), Carroll Mansion of Leavenworth, Leavenworth Historical Society. See also Hunter, *To 'Joy My Freedom*.

200. Sutherland, *Leavenworth City Directory and Business Mirror, 186--64,* Carroll Mansion of Leavenworth, Leavenworth Historical Society.

201. Jesse A. Hall and LeRoy T. Hand, *History of Leavenworth County, Kansas* (Topeka, KS: Historical Publishing Company, 1921), 125.

202. Charles Collins, *Leavenworth City Directory and Business Mirror, June 1866* (Leavenworth, KS: Charles Collins, 1866), Carroll Mansion of Leavenworth, Leavenworth Historical Society; Martha Townsend to S. D. Cabaniss, letter dated 12 December 1881, Septimus D. Cabaniss Papers.

203. West, *The Contested Plains,* 224.

204. Sutherland, *Leavenworth City Directory and Business Mirror, 1863–64,* Carroll Mansion of Leavenworth, Leavenworth Historical Society.

205. Collins, *Leavenworth City Directory and Business Mirror, June 1866,* Carroll Mansion of Leavenworth, Leavenworth Historical Society; Thomas Townsend to S. D. Cabaniss, letter dated 20 March 1866, Septimus D. Cabaniss Papers.

206. Osborne Townsend, Company Descriptive Book, 5th Heavy Artillery U.S.C.T., Civil War Soldiers, Union, Colored Troops Artillery, accessed 9 August 2018, www.fold3.com.

207. Henry Jarvis as quoted in Hahn, *A Nation Under Our Feet,* 70. Emphasis in original.

208. Trudeau, *Like Men of War*, 13.

209. Cunningham, "Douglas's Battery at Fort Leavenworth," 204.

210. Cunningham, "Douglas's Battery at Fort Leavenworth," 204.

211. "Capt. W. D. Matthews," Mary Everhard Collection, 1888, Amon Carter Museum of American Art, Fort Worth, Texas, accessed 1 February 2019, https://www.carte rmuseum.org/.

212. Cunningham, "Douglas's Battery at Fort Leavenworth," 206, 215. On nineteenth-century Leavenworth's relative lack of discrimination in local government positions such as police officers, see Randall B. Woods, "Integration, Exclusion, or Segregation? The 'Color Line' in Kansas, 1878–1900," in *African Americans on the Western Frontier*, ed. Monroe Lee Billington and Roger D. Hardaway (Boulder: University Press of Colorado, 1998).

213. Cunningham, "Douglas's Battery at Fort Leavenworth," 215.

214. W. D. Matthews's efforts to encourage military service both reflected and contributed to a broader sense among African Americans that courage in battle would allow Black men to prove themselves the equals of white Americans and demonstrate their worthiness for citizenship—another early form of "racial uplift" ideology. It paralleled the strain of self-help thought among Wilberforce University founders that education would serve a similar purpose in demonstrating the abilities of African Americans. See Hahn, *A Nation Under Our Feet*; Mitchell, *Righteous Propagation*; Trudeau, *Like Men of War*. The U.S. Colored Light Artillery (also called the Independent Battery, or Douglas's Battery) especially appealed to Black Kansans on account of its specific structure and the compensation it offered. Not only was the battery commanded by Black commissioned officers, but pay and bounty for enlistment was equal for Black and white recruits: privates earned $16 a month, and were eligible for a $300 bounty after three years with $100 paid up front. Cunningham, "Douglas's Battery at Fort Leavenworth," 207.

215. Cunningham, "Douglas's Battery at Fort Leavenworth," 205.

216. *Leavenworth Daily Conservative* (Leavenworth, KS), 20 January 1864, KHS.

217. *The Leavenworth Daily Times* (Leavenworth, KS), 20 January 1864, KHS.

218. *The Leavenworth Daily Times* (Leavenworth, KS), 20 January 1864, KHS; Taylor Turner, 1870 United States Federal Census, accessed 30 June 2017, www.ancestry. com.

219. C. H. Chase, Untitled, *The Leavenworth Daily Times* (Leavenworth, KS), 25 February 1864, KHS.

220. C. H. Chase, Untitled, *The Leavenworth Daily Times* (Leavenworth, KS), 25 February 1864, KHS. In *Stories of Scottsboro*—his book on the infamous Alabama trial of nine Black teenagers for the alleged rape of two white women on a train in 1931—historian James Goodman considers what may have motivated the women,

Ruby Bates and Victoria Price, to lie about what happened on the train. Both Bates and Price, poor working-class white women, lived among African Americans in a Black neighborhood; because of this, "their lives mocked the white South's most sacred ideal," that of an inviolable separation between races. While voluntary association with African Americans clouded their reputations before the alleged assault, afterward white Alabama residents "treated them as white southern women, poor but virtuous, for the first time in their lives." The accusations they made against the "Scottsboro Boys" inspired sympathy and consideration from white men and women who would have previously condemned them for lifestyles that did not adhere to conventions of "white womanhood." Elizabeth McFarland bears certain similarities to Bates and Price in that she too was a white woman whose voluntary association with Black men and women reduced her social status among whites. The fact that she did not inspire much sympathy from local whites (including the all-white jury at the trial) may have to do with the early date of this case. In 1864, Jim Crow-era ideologies of white womanhood and Black male sexuality had not yet fully developed. In the late nineteenth and early twentieth centuries, white Americans would increasingly use forms of control such as lynching, mobbing, and unjust trials such as that of the "Scottsboro Boys" to regulate interracial relationships and enforce white supremacy. See James Goodman, *Stories of Scottsboro* (New York: Vintage Books, 1995), 20–21; Novkov, *Racial Union*; Pascoe, *What Comes Naturally*.

221. C. H. Chase, Untitled, *The Leavenworth Daily Times* (Leavenworth, KS), 25 February 1864, KHS.

222. *The Leavenworth Daily Times* (Leavenworth, KS), 20 January 1864, KHS.

223. C. H. Chase, Untitled, *The Leavenworth Daily Times* (Leavenworth, KS), 25 February 1864, KHS.

224. In his study of racist violence in Kansas from the Civil War into the Jim Crow period, Brent Campney attributes the relative lack of violence against the state's fugitive slave population during the Civil War—as well as white Kansans' deprecation of slave hunters and kidnappers—to white citizens' understanding that they benefited from the military service and manual labor that Black men and women performed during the period. With the end of the war, however, a sense of white "racial solidarity" in upholding white supremacy re-emerged, leading to increasing violence in the forms of lynchings, race riots, mobbings, and police brutality. Ultimately, at the same time that white Kansans developed and propounded a triumphal narrative of free-soil activism in the state, strong anti-Black sentiment resulted in suppression of the Black population. See Brent M. S. Campney, *This Is Not Dixie: Racist Violence in Kansas, 1861-1927* (Urbana: University of Illinois Press, 2015); Campney, "'Light Is Bursting Upon the World!': White Supremacy and Racist Violence against Blacks in Reconstruction Kansas."

225. Woodson's distrust of Cabaniss had led him to seek out other legal firms in Leavenworth for advice—another reason he would have been known to the

city's legal profession. In November 1860, the firm of Brewer & Pierce wrote to Cabaniss's co-executor Samuel C. Townsend, saying that Woodson "calls on us frequently for advice as to what course he shall pursue to obtain the property which he says was willed to himself & wife by two relatives of yours." Brewer & Pierce to Samuel C. Townsend, letter dated 5 November 1860, Septimus D. Cabaniss Papers.

226. S. D. Cabaniss to the Jail of Leavenworth Co., letter dated 16 May 1866, Septimus D. Cabaniss Papers.

227. *Leavenworth Daily Conservative* (Leavenworth, KS), 20 January 1864, KHS.

228. Woodson Townsend to S. D. Cabaniss, letter dated 16 February 1866, Septimus D. Cabaniss Papers.

229. Milcha Townsend to S. D. Cabaniss, letter dated 21 January 1866, Septimus D. Cabaniss Papers; *Leavenworth Daily Times* (Leavenworth, KS), January 1864, KHS.

230. Woodson Townsend to S. D. Cabaniss, letter dated 16 February 1866, Septimus D. Cabaniss Papers.

231. S. D. Cabaniss to Elvira Townsend, letter dated 28 March 1867, Septimus D. Cabaniss Papers.

232. Woodson Townsend to S. D. Cabaniss, letter dated 16 February 1866, Septimus D. Cabaniss Papers.

233. Woodson Townsend to S. D. Cabaniss, letter dated 16 February 1866, Septimus D. Cabaniss Papers.

234. S. D. Cabaniss to the Jail of Leavenworth Co., letter dated 16 May 1866; S. D. Cabaniss to Woodson Townsend, letter dated 16 May 1866, Septimus D. Cabaniss Papers.

235. Woodson Townsend to S. D. Cabaniss, letter dated 16 February 1866, Septimus D. Cabaniss Papers.

CHAPTER 5

1. Robert W. Fogel, Stanley L. Engerman, and James Trussel, "Exploring the Uses of Data on Height: The Analysis of Long-Term Trends in Nutrition, Labor Welfare, and Labor Productivity," *Social Science History* 6, no. 4 (Autumn 1982): 401–421.

2. Enlistment record for Osborne Townsend, Company Descriptive Book, 5th Heavy Artillery U.S.C.T., Civil War Soldiers, Union, Colored Troops Artillery, accessed 9 August 2018, www.fold3.com; "Declaration of Recruit" and "Volunteer Enlistment" documents for Osborne Townsend in "Compiled Military Service Records of Volunteer Union Soldiers Who Served the United States Colored Troops: Miscellaneous Personal Papers," accessed 9 August 2018, www.fold3.com.

3. *The Wilberforce Annual*, 14; Osborne Townsend to S. D. Cabaniss, letter dated 27 March 1866, Septimus D. Cabaniss Papers.

4. Osborne Townsend to S. D. Cabaniss, letter dated 27 March 1866, Septimus D. Cabaniss Papers; Roberts, "An Experiment in Emancipation of Slaves by an Alabama Planter" 38–39.

5. *The Wilberforce Annual,* 18–20; Brown, *Pen Pictures of Pioneers of Wilberforce,* 82–84.

6. Item 2, deposition of Richard S. Rust filed 5 July 1871, Cabaniss v. Townsend, Depositions, 1866–1873, Septimus D. Cabaniss Papers.

7. Thomas Townsend to S. D. Cabaniss, letter dated 21 February 1866, Septimus D. Cabaniss Papers.

8. Item 2, deposition of Richard S. Rust filed 5 July 1871, Cabaniss v. Townsend, Depositions, 1866–1873, Septimus D. Cabaniss Papers.

9. Osborne Townsend to S. D. Cabaniss, letter dated 27 March 1866, Septimus D. Cabaniss Papers.

10. Osborne Townsend to S. D. Cabaniss, letters dated 2 May 1866 and 6 August 1866, Septimus D. Cabaniss Papers.

11. In the thirteen extant letters from Osborne to Thomas, Wesley, and Willis Townsend, he opens with the greetings "Dear Bro," "Dear Bros," "My Dear Brother," and "Dear Brother," and closes with "I am your brother" or "Your Bro." In contrast, Osborne refers to John Armstrong—his cousin and Thomas's half-brother by his mother Hannah as "your half brother." C. O. Townsend to Thomas Townsend, Wesley Townsend, and Willis Townsend, letters dated 1872 to 1896, Septimus D. Cabaniss Papers.

12. Trudeau, *Like Men of War,* 8.

13. Richard Albert Folk, "Black Man's Burden in Ohio, 1849–1863" (PhD diss., University of Ohio, 1972), 358.

14. "Osborn Townsend," Muster and Descriptive Roll, Civil War Soldiers, Union, Colored Troops Artillery, accessed 15 August 2018, www.fold3.com.

15. Wesley Townsend to S. D. Cabaniss, letter dated 13 October 1865, Septimus D. Cabaniss Papers; Wesley Townsend, Co. D, 100 Reg't U.S. Col'd Inf., Company Descriptive Book, accessed 15 August 2018, www.fold3.com.

16. It is unlikely that Wesley was formally drafted into the Union Army, and military records describe him as a "volunteer." However, he may easily have felt coerced to enlist by local whites. In Cincinnati, while white residents initially rejected Black men's attempts to enlist, by August and September of 1862, local whites fearing a Confederate invasion from Kentucky rounded up African American men and forced them to build fortifications and provide labor for the war effort. Wesley was not living in Cincinnati at the time and would not have been among these men, but white Ohioans twenty miles downriver in New Richmond may have exerted similar pressures. Having already experienced hostility from white neighbors in Albany and Xenia, military service out of state may have seemed like the safest option. For the political climate and forced labor in Cincinnati during the Civil War, see Taylor, *Frontiers of Freedom,* 180. For Wesley Townsend's military records,

see Wesley Townsend, Co. D, 100 Reg't U.S. Col'd Inf., Carded Records Showing Military Service of Soldiers Who Fought in Volunteer Organizations During the American Civil War, accessed 5 September 2018, www.fold3.com.

17. Wesley Townsend to S. D. Cabaniss, letter dated 30 December 1866, Septimus D. Cabaniss Papers.

18. Wesley Townsend to S. D. Cabaniss, letter dated 25 January 1866, Septimus D. Cabaniss Papers

19. Wesley Townsend to S. D. Cabaniss, letter dated 30 December 1866, Septimus D. Cabaniss Papers.

20. Osborne's regiment underwent several name changes before 1865. Originally the 9th Louisiana Infantry (African Descent), it was re-designated the 1st Mississippi Heavy Artillery and then the 4th U.S. Colored Heavy Artillery before becoming the 5th U.S. Colored Heavy Artillery in April 1864. See Frederick H. Dyer, *A Compendium of the War of the Rebellion*, vol. 1 (Des Moines, IA: Dyer Publishing Company, 1908), accessed 5 September 2018, https://archive.org/details/08697 590.3359.emory.edu.

21. Bradley R. Campitt, *Occupied Vicksburg* (Baton Rouge: Louisiana State University Press, 2016), 1–3.

22. Campitt, *Occupied Vicksburg,* 120–125; Mississippi, Freedmen's Department (Pre-Bureau Records), 1863–1866, accessed 16 August 2018, www.familysearch.org.

23. Mississippi, Freedmen's Department (Pre-Bureau Records), 1863–1866, accessed 16 August 2018, www.familysearch.org.

24. Campitt, *Occupied Vicksburg,* 150, 156; Trudeau, *Like Men of War,* 466.

25. Osborne Townsend, Company Muster Roll, May and June 1865, Civil War Soldiers, Union, Colored Troops Artillery, accessed 16 August 2018, www.fold3.com.

26. Campitt, *Occupied Vicksburg,* 134–136.

27. Mississippi, Freedmen's Department (Pre-Bureau Records), 1863–1866, accessed 16 August 2018, www.familysearch.org; Campitt, *Occupied Vicksburg,* 125.

28. Samuel Thomas, 19 January 1865, Register of Letters Received, Mississippi, Freedmen's Department (Pre-Bureau Records), 1863–1866, accessed 16 August 2018, www.familysearch.org.

29. Osborne Townsend, Company Muster Roll, July and August 1865; Osborne Townsend, Detachment Muster-out Roll, 22 February 1866, Civil War Soldiers, Union, Colored Troops Artillery, accessed 16 August 2018, www.fold3.com.

30. Osborne Townsend, Returns, Civil War Soldiers, Union, Colored Troops Artillery, accessed 16 August 2018, www.fold3.com.

31. Osborne Townsend, Company Muster Roll, January and February 1866; Osborne Townsend, Company Muster Roll, March and April 1865, Civil War Soldiers, Union, Colored Troops Artillery, accessed 16 August 2018, www.fold3.com; Thomas Townsend to S. D. Cabaniss, letter dated 20 April 1866, Septimus D. Cabaniss Papers.

32. Osborne Townsend, Company Muster Roll, January and February 1866, Civil War Soldiers, Union, Colored Troops Artillery, accessed 16 August 2018, www.fold3. com.

33. Campitt, *Occupied Vicksburg,* 175.

34. Richardson, *West from Appomattox,* 42.

35. In an exception to the general rule, Samuel Thomas, the Provost Marshal for Vicksburg, was considered particularly sympathetic to freedpeople's needs during his term of office. Chaplain John Eaton and others agreed that Thomas would "devote himself with willingness to the Negro cause," and civilian missionaries and teachers praised him for his dedication to educating former slaves—as compared to Freedmen's Bureau officials elsewhere in the South, who were often accused of fraud and/or indifference. While a treasury agent writing to Brigadier General W. S. Smith in 1865 expressed sympathy for white plantation owners, calling it "an act of justice and right" to return the land to its original owners, Samuel Thomas favored leasing confiscated property to Black farmers over white southerners. In issuing instructions to the new Provost Marshal of Freedmen for a district under his jurisdiction, he ordered that the appointee should "encourage industry among the Freedmen and protect them in the exercise of their rights and privileges." See Campitt, *Occupied Vicksburg,* 134, 144; Mississippi, Freedmen's Department (Pre-Bureau Records), 1863–1866, accessed 16 August 2018, www.familysearch.org.

36. "Committee of Freedmen on Edisto Island, South Carolina, to the Freedmen's Bureau Commissioner," 20 or 21 October 1865, as quoted in Hahn, *A Nation Under Our Feet,* 144.

37. For more extensive analyses of land redistribution efforts (and their ultimate failure) during and after the Civil War, see Eric Foner, *A Short History of Reconstruction, 1863–1877* (New York: Harper & Row, 1990); Hahn, *A Nation Under Our Feet*; Julie Saville, *The Work of Reconstruction: From Slave to Wage Labor in South Carolina, 1860–1870* (New York: Cambridge University Press, 1996).

38. See, for example, Howard Pashman, "The People's Property Law: A Step Toward Building a New Legal Order in Revolutionary New York," *Law and History Review* 31, no. 3 (August 2013): 587–626.

39. Historian Amy Dru Stanley's book *From Bondage to Contract,* details the ways in which the Freedmen's Bureau was complicit in establishing and enforcing the contract—rather than land ownership, which freedpeople largely preferred—as "the very symbol of freedom" during Reconstruction. Freedpeople often saw contracts as a means of returning them to economic dependence on whites. Freedmen's Bureau officials, however, defined freedom not as economic independence but rather the right to sell one's labor as a free market commodity. In this view, land redistribution was at best unnecessary and, at worst, equivalent to charity, which would undermine freedpeople's work ethic. Amy Dru Stanley, *From Bondage to Contract: Wage Labor, Marriage, and the Market in the Age of Slave Emancipation*

(Chicago: University of Chicago Press, 1998). See also Saville, *The Work of Reconstruction*.

40. Osborne Townsend to S. D. Cabaniss, letter dated 2 May 1866, Septimus D. Cabaniss Papers.

41. Osborne Townsend to S. D. Cabaniss, letters dated 27 March 1866 and 6 August 1866, Septimus D. Cabaniss Papers.

42. Thomas Townsend to S. D. Cabaniss, letters dated 20 January 1866, 20 March 1866, 20 April 1866, 9 March 1868, Septimus D. Cabaniss Papers. See also Heather Andrea Williams, *Self-taught: African American Education in Slavery and Freedom* (Chapel Hill: University of North Carolina Press, 2005). For schools and Black teachers in Kansas specifically, see Nell Irvin Painter, *Exodusters: Black Migration to Kansas after Reconstruction* (New York: W.W. Norton, 1976).

43. Wesley Townsend to S. D. Cabaniss, letter dated 15 January 1866, Septimus D. Cabaniss Papers.

44. Thomas Townsend to S. D. Cabaniss, letter dated 21 February 1866, Septimus D. Cabaniss Papers.

45. Items 4 and 5, will of Samuel Townsend dated 6 September 1856, Wills; Item 3, "Inventory and Appraisement" dated February–March 1858, Inventories, Septimus D. Cabaniss Papers.

46. Osborne Townsend, Freedman's Bank Records, 1865–1874, accessed 7 June 2016, www.familysearch.org. In a letter to Thomas, Osborne refers to John Armstrong as "your half brother." See C. O. Townsend to Thomas and Wesley Townsend, letter dated 19 January 1876, Septimus D. Cabaniss Papers.

47. The absence of letters written by William Austin and the general lack of communication between any of the Townsends and S. D. Cabaniss during the Civil War make it difficult to determine with certainty when he left Kansas for Colorado. However, since he was already well established in Central City in the summer of 1866, it seems likely that he made the journey in the years prior.

48. Osborne Townsend to S. D. Cabaniss, letter dated 6 August 1866, Septimus D. Cabaniss Papers.

49. West, *The Contested Plains*, 213–215.

50. West, *The Contested Plains*, 148.

51. *The Rocky Mountain Directory and Colorado Gazetteer, for 1871* (Denver, CO: S. S. Wallihan and Company, 1871), 111, 112, accessed 24 August 2018, https://archive.org/details/rockymountaindiroowall.

52. Alexis de Tocqueville, *Democracy in America*, vol. 1, part 7, trans. Henry Reeve, accessed 24 August 2018, https://www.gutenberg.org/files/815/815-h/815-h.htm.

53. *The Rocky Mountain Directory and Colorado Gazetteer, for 1871*. While arguments in favor of Anglo-American expansion westward across the North American continent can be dated to before the founding of the Republic, the use of "Manifest Destiny" (as both a common phrase and justification for territorial expansion) dates particularly to the annexation of Texas and Mexican-American War in the 1840s.

Nash, *Virgin Land*. See also Martha Sandweiss's *Print the Legend* for examples of the ways art and photography were used to promote and reinforce the doctrine in American popular culture throughout the century. Martha A. Sandweiss, *Print the Legend: Photography and the American West* (New Haven, CT: Yale University Press, 2002).

54. Richardson, *West from Appomattox*.

55. Isabella L. Bird, *A Lady's Life in the Rocky Mountains* (New York: G. P. Putnam's Sons, 1881), Victorian Women Writers Project, Indiana University, accessed 30 July 2018, http://webapp1.dlib.indiana.edu/vwwp/welcome.do.

56. Taylor, *In Search of the Racial Frontier*; Campbell Gibson and Kay Jung, "Historical Census Statistics on Population Totals by Race, 1790 to 1990," Population Division Working Paper No. 56 (Washington, DC: US Census Bureau, 2002), Table 20.

57. *The Rocky Mountain Directory and Colorado Gazetteer, for 1871*, 12. On African Americans in the nineteenth-century West; see, for example, Taylor, *In Search of the Racial Frontier*; Savage, *Blacks in the West*; Billington and Hardway, eds., *African Americans on the Western Frontier*. For studies of the Black town movement, see also George O. Carney, "Oklahoma's All-Black Towns," in *African Americans on the Western Frontier*, 147–160; Melissa Stuckey, "All Men Up: Race, Rights, and Power in the All-Black Town of Boley, Oklahoma, 1903–1939" (PhD diss., Yale University, 2009).

58. Peter Decker, *The Utes Must Go!: American Expansion and the Removal of a People* (Golden, CO: Fulcrum Publishing, 2004), 8; West, *The Contested Plains*, 252, 286.

59. "An Extract," *Colorado Miner* (Georgetown, CO), 24 January 1880, p. 2, Colorado Historic Newspapers Collection, Colorado State Library.

60. "Indian Troubles in Colorado," *Rocky Mountain News* (Denver, CO), 11 March 1865, p. 2, Colorado Historic Newspapers Collection, Colorado State Library.

61. James B. Belford on 18 December 1879, as quoted in *Congressional Record: Containing the Proceedings and Debates of the Forty-Sixth Congress, Second Session, Volume X* (Washington, DC: Government Printing Office, 1880), 179.

62. Elliott West's concept of "Greater Reconstruction" in the nineteenth-century United States provides a valuable framework for interpreting Indian policy in the American West after the Civil War. See West, "Reconstructing Race."

63. See in particular Hyde, *Empires, Nations, and Families*.

64. For a discussion of the role of African Americans in settler colonial processes in the American West, see Tiya Miles, "Beyond a Boundary: Black Lives and the Settler-Native Divide," *William and Mary Quarterly* 76, no. 3 (July 2019): 417–426. On American settler colonialism more broadly, see, for example, Hyde, *Empires, Nations, and Families*; West, *The Contested Plains*; Margaret Jacobs, *White Mother to a Dark Race: Settler Colonialism, Maternalism, and the Removal of Indigenous Children in the American West and Australia, 1880–1940* (Lincoln: University of Nebraska Press, 2009).

65. W. Sherman Savage, *Blacks in the West* (Westport, CT: Greenwood Press, 1976), 85.

66. Liston E. Leyendecker, Christine A. Bradley, and Duane A. Smith, *The Rise of the Silver Queen: Georgetown, Colorado, 1859–1896* (Boulder: University Press of Colorado, 2005), 70; Cynthia Neverdon-Morton, *Finding History's Forgotten People: The Presence of African Americans in Colorado, c. 1534 to 1954* (Denver, CO: US Department of the Interior, Bureau of Land Management, 2008).

67. Clara Brown appears in virtually every Clear Creek County history and state history of Colorado from the late nineteenth century onward, including Frank Hall's *History of the State of Colorado* (1889) and Francis Crissey Young's memoir of Central City, *Echoes from Arcadia* (1903). Francis Crissey Young, *Echoes from Arcadia: The Story of Cental City, as told by one of 'The Clan,'* (Denver: Lanning Bros., 1903). For modern examples, see William Loren Katz, *The Black West: A Documentary and Pictorial History of the African American Role in the Westward Expansion of the United States* (New York: Touchstone, 1996); Leyendecker et al., *The Rise of the Silver Queen*; Neverdon-Morton, *Finding History's Forgotten People*; Glenda Riley, "American Daughters: Black Women in the West" in *African Americans on the Western Frontier;* Savage, *Blacks in the West.*

68. Eugene H. Berwanger, "Reconstruction on the Frontier: The Equal Rights Struggle in Colorado," in *African Americans on the Western Frontier,* 39.

69. "That Protest," *Rocky Mountain News* (Denver, CO), 15 January 1866, p. 1, Colorado Historic Newspapers Collection, Colorado State Library.

70. William Austin Townsend, 1870 United States Federal Census, accessed 24 August 2018, www.ancestry.com.

71. Henry Townsend, 1870 United States Federal Census, accessed 24 August 2018, www.ancestry.com.

72. William Austin Townsend, 1870 United States Federal Census, accessed 24 August 2018, www.ancestry.com.

73. Taylor, *In Search of the Racial Frontier,* 203.

74. Stephen J. Leonard and Thomas J. Noel, *Denver: Mining Camp to Metropolis* (Niwot: University Press of Colorado, 1990); "1870 Census: Volume 1. The Statistics of the Population of the United States," United States Census Bureau, accessed 24 August 2018, https://www.census.gov/library/publications/1872/dec/1870a.html.

75. Osborne Townsend to S. D. Cabaniss, letter dated 26 September 1867, Septimus D. Cabaniss Papers.

76. Osborne Townsend to S. D. Cabaniss, letter dated 27 March 1866, Septimus D. Cabaniss Papers.

77. Osborne Townsend to S. D. Cabaniss, letter dated 26 September 1867, Septimus D. Cabaniss Papers.

78. "Regards It as Settled," *Rocky Mountain News* (Denver, CO), 16 November 1868, p. 1, Colorado Historic Newspapers Collection, Colorado State Library.

79. *The Rocky Mountain Directory and Colorado Gazetteer for 1871,* 112; *The Bessel Directory Co.'s Clear Creek and Gilpin County Directory for the Years 1892–3*

(Trinidad, CO: Bessel Directory Company, 1893); *Ballenger & Richards Denver City Directory, 1894* (Denver, CO: Ballenger & Richards, 1894); *Ballenger & Richards Denver City Directory, 1895* (Denver, CO: Ballenger & Richards, 1895); *Clear Creek County, Colorado, Mining and Business Directory* (Denver, CO: Redman & Hart, 1898); *Ballenger & Richards Denver City Directory, 1901* (Denver, CO: Ballenger & Richards, 1901).

80. Henry Townsend, 1870 United States Federal Census; Henry and Nancy Townsend, Colorado, Divorce Index, 1851–1985, accessed 24 August 2018, www.ancestry.com.

81. Leyendecker et al., *The Rise of the Silver Queen,* 21.

82. Frank Hall, *History of the State of Colorado,* vol. 1 (Chicago: Blakely Printing Company, 1889), 279.

83. Frank Fossett, *Colorado, Its Gold and Silver Mines: Farms and Stock Ranges, and Health and Pleasure Resorts: Tourist's Guide to the Rocky Mountains* (New York: C. G. Crawford, 1880), 315.

84. Fossett, *Colorado, Its Gold and Silver Mines,* 318.

85. John Codman, *The Round Trip by way of Panama through California, Oregon, Nevada, Utah, Idaho, and Colorado; with Notes on Railroads, Commerce, Agriculture, Mining, Scenery, and People (New York: G. P. Putnam's Sons, 1879),* 310.

86. "Georgetown Local," *Daily Register Call* (Central City, CO), 23 June 1869, p. 4, Colorado Historic Newspapers Collection, Colorado State Library; Fossett, *Colorado, Its Gold and Silver Mines,* 314.

87. *The Rocky Mountain Directory and Colorado Gazetteer, for 1871,* 375; Leyendecker et al., *The Rise of the Silver Queen,* 69.

88. *The Rise of the Silver Queen,* 69; *The Rocky Mountain Directory and Colorado Gazetteer, for 1871,* 375.

89. Bird, *A Lady's Life in the Rocky Mountains.*

90. Codman, *The Round Trip,* 288, 315–318.

91. Bird, *A Lady's Life in the Rocky Mountains.*

92. See Thomas G. Andrews, *Killing for Coal: America's Deadliest Labor War* (Cambridge, MA: Harvard University Press, 2008); Leyendecker et al., *The Rise of the Silver Queen,* 31, 62; Savage, *Blacks in the West,* 83.

93. Leyendecker et al., *The Rise of the Silver Queen,* 65, 32.

94. Leyendecker et al., *The Rise of the Silver Queen,* 88.

95. Photograph of five Chinese men taken in Georgetown, Randall Collection, X-21660, Western History Collection, Denver Public Library; Leyendecker et al., *The Rise of the Silver Queen* 209, 70.

96. Georgetown, Clear Creek County, Colorado, 1870 United States Federal Census, accessed 24 August 2018, www.ancestry.com.

97. Georgetown, Clear Creek County, Colorado, 1870 United States Federal Census, accessed 24 August 2018, www.ancestry.com.

98. 25 July 1874 *Colorado Miner* article as quoted in Leyendecker et al., *The Rise of the Silver Queen*, 106.

99. Leyendecker et al., *The Rise of the Silver Queen*, 90.

100. "The Council," *Colorado Miner* (Georgetown, CO), 5 April 1879, p. 3, Colorado Historic Newspapers Collection, Colorado State Library.

101. Neverdon-Morton, *Finding History's Forgotten People*.

102. Georgetown Grantee Index volumes 4 to 13 (1868–1899) and Grantor Index volumes 5 to 14 (1870–1902), Clear Creek County Department of Archives and Records (hereafter CCCDAR).

103. Willis, Osborne's full brother, referred to Osborne as "Charley" in letters to S. D. Cabaniss. Other half-brothers, Thomas, for example, used "Osborne" in letters to Cabaniss, though whether they called him Charles among themselves is uncertain. Willis Townsend to S. D. Cabaniss, letter dated 8 February 1860, Septimus D. Cabaniss Papers.

104. S. D. Cabaniss to R. S. Rust, letter dated 12 July 1860, Septimus D. Cabaniss Papers. In Wilberforce's 1860–61 printed catalogue, Osborne appears as "Charles Townsend."

105. "Married," *Daily Colorado Miner* (Georgetown, CO), 28 February 1873, p. 4, Colorado Historic Newspapers Collection, Colorado State Library.

106. "Georgetown Local," *Daily Register Call* (Central City, CO), 23 June 1869, p. 4, Colorado Historic Newspapers Collection, Colorado State Library.

107. *Daily Register Call* (Central City, CO), 29 September 1871, p. 4, Colorado Historic Newspapers Collection, Colorado State Library.

108. *Georgetown Courier* (Georgetown, CO), 3 January 1878, p. 2; *Colorado* Miner (Georgetown, CO), 1 September 1877, p. 3; *Daily Register Call* (Central City, CO), 29 September 1871, p. 4, Colorado Historic Newspapers Collection, Colorado State Library.

109. *Daily Register Call* (Central City, CO), 29 September 1871, p. 4, Colorado Historic Newspapers Collection, Colorado State Library.

110. John McMurdy, 1870 United States Federal Census, accessed 27 August 2018, www.ancestry.com.

111. *Colorado Miner* (Georgetown, CO), 19 January 1878, p. 2, Colorado Historic Newspapers Collection, Colorado State Library.

112. "Trial of Kerwin," *Colorado Miner* (Georgetown, CO), 25 August 1877, p. 3, Colorado Historic Newspapers Collection, Colorado State Library.

113. Georgetown Grantee Index vol. 4 (July 1868–April 1872), book 11, p. 88, CCCDAR.

114. William C. Randolph, 1880 United States Federal Census, accessed 27 August 2018, www.ancestry.com.

115. Georgetown Grantee Index vol. 6 (April 1, 1876–January 1, 1880), book 59, p. 12, CCCDAR.

116. "Married," *Daily Colorado Miner* (Georgetown, CO), 28 February 1873, p. 4, Colorado Historic Newspapers Collection, Colorado State Library; Georgetown Grantee Index, vol. 5 (April 1, 1872–April 1, 1876), book 29, p. 366, CCCDAR; Georgetown Grantor Index, vol. 7 (April 1876–January 1880), book 39, p. 542, CCCDAR.

117. "Married," *Daily Colorado Miner* (Georgetown, CO), 28 February 1873, p. 4, Colorado Historic Newspapers Collection, Colorado State Library.

118. For George O'Connor, see "Tragedy in Leadville," *Colorado Miner,* 4 May 1878, p. 3, Colorado Historic Newspapers Collection, Colorado State Library; "Marshal George O'Connor," *Officer Down Memorial Page,* accessed 27 August 2018, http://www.odmp.org/officer/10094-marshal-george-oconnor. For Charles Yates, see the 1870 United States Federal Census, accessed 27 August 2018, www.ancestry.com.

119. C. O. Townsend to Thomas Townsend and Wesley Townsend, letter dated 19 January 1876, Septimus D. Cabaniss Papers. Osborne writes that John Armstrong arrived "some three months" earlier, putting his arrival in October 1875.

120. John A. Townsend, 1880 United States Federal Census, accessed 27 August 2018, www.ancestry.com; "County Commissioners," *Georgetown Courier* (Georgetown, CO), 20 January 1881, p. 3; *Georgetown Courier* (Georgetown, CO), 14 March 1878, p. 3, Colorado Historic Newspapers Collection, Colorado State Library.

121. "Matrimonial," *Colorado Miner* (Georgetown, CO), 16 March 1878, Colorado Historic Newspapers Collection, Colorado State Library.

122. Amos Townsend to S. D. Cabaniss, letter dated 19 June 1877, Septimus D. Cabaniss Papers; Amos Townsend, 1880 Federal Census, accessed 27 August 2018, www.ancestry.com. On the oil discovery in Cañon City, see Francis M. Van Tuyl and Arthur E. Brainerd, "Historical Summary" in *Mineral Resources of Colorado, First Sequel* (Denver, CO: Colorado Mineral Resources Board, 1960), 491–492.

123. Amos Townsend, 1870, 1880, and 1910 United States Federal Censuses, accessed 27 August 2018, www.ancestry.com.

124. "Nabbed," *Colorado Miner* (Georgetown, CO), 6 April 1878, p. 3, Colorado Historic Newspapers Collection, Colorado State Library.

125. Leyendecker et al., *Rise of the Silver Queen,* 90.

126. "Martha Townsend's Will," *Leavenworth Standards,* 19 February 1898; "Mrs. Townsend Dead," *Leavenworth Times* (Leavenworth, KS), 9 February 1898. Special thanks to Mary Ann Brown at the Leavenworth County Historical Societyfor sharing these newspaper articles.

127. Georgetown Grantor Index vol. 6 (January 1, 1873–April 1876), book 27, p. 6, CCCDAR.

128. Georgetown Grantee Index volumes 4 to 13 (1868–1899) and Grantor Index volumes 5 to 14 (1870–1902), CCCDAR.

129. C. O. Townsend to Thomas and Wesley Townsend, letter dated 3 December 1872, Septimus D. Cabaniss Papers.

130. C. O. Townsend to Thomas Townsend, letter dated 12 December 1882, Septimus D. Cabaniss Papers.

131. C. O. Townsend to Thomas Townsend, letter dated 5 March 1883, Septimus D. Cabaniss Papers.

132. C. O. Townsend to Thomas Townsend, letter dated 12 December 1882, Septimus D. Cabaniss Papers.

133. Georgetown Grantor Index, vol. 5 (April 1870–January 1873), book 10, p. 392, CCCDAR.

134. Georgetown Grantee Index volumes 4 to 13 (1868–1899) and Grantor Index volumes 5 to 14 (1870–1902), CCCDAR.

135. Georgetown Grantor Index, vol. 9 (May 1882–1884), book 74, p. 104, CCCDAR.

136. C. O. Townsend to Thomas Townsend, letter dated 5 March 1883, Septimus D. Cabaniss Papers.

137. C. O. Townsend to Thomas Townsend, letter dated 12 December 1882, Septimus D. Cabaniss Papers.

138. See Georgetown Grantor Index, vols. 9, 10, 11 (1882–1892), CCCDAR.

139. C. O. Townsend to Thomas Townsend, letter dated 12 December 1882, Septimus D. Cabaniss Papers.

140. C. O. Townsend to Thomas Townsend as quoted in Roberts, "An Experiment in Emancipation of Slaves by an Alabama Planter," 96.

141. C. O. Townsend to Thomas Townsend, letter dated 5 March 1883, Septimus D. Cabaniss Papers.

142. C. O. Townsend to Thomas and Wesley Townsend, letter dated 3 December 1872, Septimus D. Cabaniss Papers.

143. "Married," *Daily Colorado Miner* (Georgetown, CO), 28 February 1873, p. 4, Colorado Historic Newspapers Collection, Colorado State Library.

144. C. O. Townsend to Thomas and Wesley Townsend, letter dated 19 January 1876, Septimus D. Cabaniss Papers.

145. "Margarit Hall," Colorado, County Marriage Records and State Index, 1862–2006; "Maggie Townsend," 1880 United States Federal Census, accessed 4 September 2018, www.ancestry.com. From census records and Osborne's letters, Maggie and Osborne appear to have had at least five children: Charles Osborne, Willis A., Thomas Clarence, Lony, and Roy. Josephine and Osborne's child likely died sometime before the 1880 Federal Census, the first in which any of Osborne's children appear, which lists Maggie as their eldest child's mother.

146. *Colorado Miner* (Georgetown, CO), 1 September 1877, p. 3, Colorado Historic Newspapers Collection, Colorado State Library.

147. C. O. Townsend to Thomas Townsend, letter dated 16 November 1883, Septimus D. Cabaniss Papers.

148. C. O. Townsend to Thomas Townsend, letter dated 18 May 1883, Septimus D. Cabaniss Papers. Osborne mentioned Thomas's "neglectful" habit in a number of letters. In addition, he asked Thomas to send photographs of himself and his

wife and wrote in 1888 that he would like to "fix some date in the near future to see each other." By then, Osborne likely hadn't seen Thomas in person since 1871 and would not before 1896 (if at all) when their extant letters stop. See C. O. Townsend to Thomas Townsend, letters dated 18 May 1883 and 16 November 1883, Septimus D. Cabaniss Papers.

149. *Huntsville Gazette* (Huntsville, AL), 11 February 1888, America's Historical Newspapers.
150. C. O. Townsend to Thomas Townsend, letter dated 14 February 1888, Septimus D. Cabaniss Papers.
151. C. O. Townsend to Thomas Townsend, letter dated 18 May 1883, Septimus D. Cabaniss Papers.
152. C. O. Townsend to Thomas Townsend, letter dated 27 July 1889, Septimus D. Cabaniss Papers.
153. For the erasure of Black veterans in the narrative of the Civil War, see Blight, *Race and Reunion: The Civil War in American Memory*; W. Fitzhugh Brundage, "White Women and the Politics of Historical Memory in the New South, 1880–1920," in *Jumpin' Jim Crow: Southern Politics from Civil War to Civil Rights*, ed. Jane Dailey, Glenda Elizabeth Gilmore, and Bryant Simon (Princeton, NJ: Princeton University Press, 2000).
154. C. O. Townsend to Thomas Townsend, undated continuation of letter (likely 1896), Septimus D. Cabaniss Papers.
155. *Colorado Miner* as quoted in Leyendecker et al., *The Rise of the Silver Queen*, 88–89.
156. C. O. Townsend to Thomas Townsend, letter dated 14 February 1888, Septimus D. Cabaniss Papers.
157. *Colorado Miner* as quoted in Leyendecker et al., *The Rise of the Silver Queen*, 88–89.
158. For case studies of Chinese migrants and miners from the 1850s through early 1900s, see Randall E. Rohe, "After the Gold Rush: Chinese Mining in the Far West, 1850–1890," *Montana: The Magazine of Western History* 32, no. 4 (Autumn 1982): 2–19; Liping Zhu, *A Chinaman's Chance: The Chinese on the Rocky Mountain Mining Frontier* (Niwot: University Press of Colorado, 1997). On anti-Chinese prejudice and its legislative consequences, see Sucheng Chan, ed., *Entry Denied: Exclusion and the Chinese Community in America, 1882–1943* (Philadelphia: Temple University Press, 1991); Erika Lee, "The Chinese Exclusion Example: Race, Immigration, and American Gatekeeping, 1882–1924," *Journal of American Ethnic History* 21, no. 3 (Spring 2002): 36–62; Mae Ngai, *Impossible Subjects: Illegal Aliens and the Making of Modern America* (Princeton, NJ: Princeton University Press, 2004).
159. Rohe, "After the Gold Rush," 4; Roy T. Wortman, "Denver's Anti-Chinese Riot, 1880," *Colorado Magazine* 42, no. 4 (Fall 1965), 275.
160. Gibson and Jung, "Historical Census Statistics on Population Totals by Race, 1790 to 1990."
161. Wortman, "Denver's Anti-Chinese Riot, 1880," 276–277.

162. Chan, ed., *Entry Denied*; Lee, "The Chinese Exclusion Example"; Ngai, *Impossible Subjects.*

163. Mark Twain, "Disgraceful Persecution of a Boy," *Galaxy Magazine* (May 1870), accessed 1 February 2019, http://twain.lib.virginia.edu/onstage/playscripts/galax yo1.html.

164. "Police Court," *Daily Colorado Miner* (Georgetown, CO), 10 October 1872, p. 4, Colorado Historic Newspapers Collection, Colorado State Library.

165. 18 December 1880 *Colorado Miner* article as quoted in Leyendecker et al., *The Rise of the Silver Queen*, 189–90.

166. "Miners' Meeting in Decatur," *Colorado Miner* (Georgetown, CO), 12 June 1880, p. 3, Colorado Historic Newspapers Collection, Colorado State Library.

167. "A Frozen Celestial," *The Silver Standard* (Silver Plume, CO), 15 January 1887, Colorado Historic Newspapers Collection, Colorado State Library.

168. *The Silver Standard* (Silver Plume, CO), 26 May 1894, p. 3, Colorado Historic Newspapers Collection, Colorado State Library.

169. Charles Gow, 1920 United States Federal Census, accessed 30 August 2018, www. ancestry.com; photograph of Charles Gow and nine men taken in Georgetown, Randall Collection X-6569, Western History Collection, Denver Public Library.

170. The ways in which African Americans were complicit in establishing racial hier-archies in the West ("othering" ethnic groups such as the Chinese, or Native Americans) are particularly visible in studies of the "Buffalo Soldiers" who fought in the Indian Wars from the 1860s and '70s forward—earning the respect that military service traditionally brought African American men while at the same time enforcing a regime of white supremacy through Indian removal. See Taylor, *In Search of the Racial Frontier.*

171. On the Sand Creek massacre as well as the conflicting ways in which it has been remembered by historians and Native American tribes, see Kelman, *A Misplaced Massacre.*

172. *Report of the Joint Committee on the Conduct of the War at the Second Session Thirty-Eighth Congress* (Washington, DC: Government Printing Office, 1865), accessed 4 September 2018, Making of America Digital Library, http://name. umdl.umich.edu/ABY3709.0003.001.

173. *Colorado Miner* (Georgetown, CO), 14 April 1870, as quoted in Leyendecker et al., *Rise of the Silver Queen*, 188–189.

174. "Indian Troubles in Colorado, *Rocky Mountain News* (Denver, CO), 11 March 1865, p. 2, Colorado Historic Newspapers Collection, Colorado State Library.

175. Leyendecker et al., *Rise of the Silver Queen*, 189. Sarah Rowe Corbett was likely born in 1875 or 1876. See Sarah J. Rowe, 1880 United States Federal Census; Sarah J. Corbett, 1910 United States Federal Census, accessed 3 June 2021, www. ancestry.com.

176. "Indian Troubles in Colorado, *Rocky Mountain News* (Denver, CO), 11 March 1865, p. 2, Colorado Historic Newspapers Collection, Colorado State Library.

177. "Middle Park. Mines, Utes and a Bear Story," *Colorado Miner* (Georgetown, CO), 15 November 1879, p. 1, Colorado Historic Newspapers Collection, Colorado State Library.

178. "An Extract," *Colorado Miner* (Georgetown, CO), 24 January 1880, p. 1, Colorado Historic Newspapers Collection, Colorado State Library.

179. See Decker, *The Utes Must Go!*; Virginia McConnell Simmons, *The Ute Indians of Utah, Colorado, and New Mexico* (Boulder: University Press of Colorado, 2000).

180. "The Utes," *Colorado Miner* (Georgetown, CO), 20 September 1879, p. 2, Colorado Historic Newspapers Collection, Colorado State Library.

181. "Middle Park. Mines, Utes and a Bear Story," *Colorado Miner* (Georgetown, CO), 15 November 1879, p. 1, Colorado Historic Newspapers Collection, Colorado State Library.

182. C. O. Townsend to Thomas Townsend, letter dated 12 December 1882, Septimus D. Cabaniss Papers.

183. C. O. Townsend to Thomas Townsend, letter dated 21 March 1884, Septimus D. Cabaniss Papers.

184. C. O. Townsend to Thomas Townsend, letter dated 30 June 1893, Septimus D. Cabaniss Papers.

185. C. O. Townsend to Thomas Townsend, continuation of undated letter (likely 1896), Septimus D. Cabaniss Papers. In light of the unity of Black and white Coloradans on economic issues such as Greenbackism and "Free Silver," it's interesting to consider Elizabeth Sanders's argument that agrarianism has served as "a basis for social democracy" in American history more generally. Sanders argues that agrarian populism mobilized farmers and laborers (or, in the case of Colorado, miners) to oppose industrial and financial capitalism, leading people on the "periphery" of the American economy in the late nineteenth and early twentieth centuries to exert influence in national politics. Elizabeth Sanders, *Roots of Reform: Farmers, Workers, and the American State, 1877–1917* (Chicago: University of Chicago Press, 1999).

186. For specific details on legislation and the voting patterns of Republicans and Democrats, see Sanders, *Roots of Reform*.

187. "The Silver Question," *Colorado Miner*, 12 January 1878, p. 2, Colorado Historic Newspapers Collection, Colorado State Library.

188. Sanders, *Roots of Reform,* 109.

189. Richardson, *West from Appomattox*. On the growth of Greenbackism, Populism, and other independent political movements throughout the late nineteenth and early twentieth centuries—particularly their origins in the South—see Edward L. Ayers, *The Promise of the New South: Life After Reconstruction* (New York: Oxford University Press, 1992); Lawrence Goodwyn, *Democratic Promise: The Populist Movement in America* (New York: Oxford University Press, 1976); Robert C. McMath Jr., *American Populism: A Social History* (New York: Hill and Wang, 1993); Sanders, *Roots of Reform*; Nell Irvin Painter, *Standing at Armageddon: The*

United States, 1877-1919 (New York: Norton, 1987); C. Van Woodward, *Origins of the New South, 1877–1913* (Baton Rouge: Louisiana State University Press, 1971).

190. C. O. Townsend to Thomas and Wesley Townsend, letter dated 19 January 1876, Septimus D. Cabaniss Papers.

191. C. O. Townsend to Thomas Townsend, letter dated 12 December 1882, Septimus D. Cabaniss Papers.

192. C. O. Townsend to Thomas Townsend, letter dated 18 May 1883, Septimus D. Cabaniss Papers.

193. C. O. Townsend to Thomas Townsend, letter dated 21 March 1884, Septimus D. Cabaniss Papers.

194. C. O. Townsend to Willis Townsend, letter dated 8 July 1889; C. O. Townsend to Thomas Townsend, letter dated 27 July 1889, Septimus D. Cabaniss Papers. Willis A. Townsend, Osborne's second-eldest son, disappears from the historical record after appearing in the 1880 Federal Census.

195. C. O. Townsend to Thomas Townsend, letter dated 5 August 1890, Septimus D. Cabaniss Papers.

196. C. O. Townsend to Thomas Townsend, letter dated 30 June 1893, Septimus D. Cabaniss Papers.

197. C.O. Townsend to Thomas Townsend, continuation of undated letter (likely 1896), Septimus D. Cabaniss Papers.

198. C. O. Townsend to Thomas Townsend, letter dated 5 March 1883, Septimus D. Cabaniss Papers.

199. Item 30, payments to legatees of the first class as of 1 April 1879, Cabaniss vs. Townsend Reports (2), 1872–1883, Septimus D. Cabaniss Papers.

200. C. O. Townsend to Thomas Townsend, letter dated 16 November 1883, Septimus D. Cabaniss Papers.

201. C. O. Townsend to Thomas Townsend, letter dated 12 December 1882; C. O. Townsend to Willis Townsend, letter dated 8 July 1889, Septimus D. Cabaniss Papers.

202. "National Greenback County Convention," *Georgetown Courier* (Georgetown, CO), 4 July 1878, p. 1; "GREENBACKERS. They Meet in County Convention," *Colorado Miner* (Georgetown, CO), 6 July 1878, p. 3, Colorado Historic Newspapers Collection, Colorado State Library.

203. C. O. Townsend to Thomas Townsend, letter dated 30 June 1893, Septimus D. Cabaniss Papers.

204. "National Greenback County Convention," *Georgetown Courier* (Georgetown, CO), 4 July 1878, p. 1; "GREENBACKERS. They Meet in County Convention," *Colorado Miner* (Georgetown, CO), 6 July 1878, p. 3, Colorado Historic Newspapers Collection, Colorado State Library.

205. C. O. Townsend to Thomas Townsend, letter dated 30 June 1893, Septimus D. Cabaniss Papers.

206. C. O. Townsend to Thomas Townsend, continuation of undated letter (likely 1896), Septimus D. Cabaniss Papers.

207. William Jennings Bryan's 1896 "Cross of Gold" speech as quoted in Sanders, *Roots of Reform*, 143. For Bryan and populism in the American West, with particular attention to the Rocky Mountain region, see Nathan Jessen, *Populism and Imperialism: Politics, Culture, and Foreign Policy in the American West, 1890–1900* (Lawrence: University Press of Kansas, 2017); David R. Berman, *Radicalism in the Mountain West, 1890–1920: Socialists, Populists, Miners, and Wobblies* (Boulder: University Press of Colorado, 2007).

208. C. O. Townsend to Thomas Townsend, letter dated 30 June 1893, Septimus D. Cabaniss Papers.

209. C. O. Townsend to Thomas Townsend, letter dated 14 February 1888, Septimus D. Cabaniss Papers.

210. Georgetown Grantee Index, vol. 13 (May 1895–May1899), book 128, p. 381, CCCDAR.

211. Charles O. Townsend, 1910 United States Federal Census, accessed 4 September 2018, www.ancestry.com; Clarence T. Townsend (also "Clarence Thomas" and "Thomas Clarence" Townsend), 1910 and 1920 United States Federal Censuses, accessed 4 September 2018, www.ancestry.com.

212. Boosterism continued in Colorado during the early twentieth century, though it was now led by African American residents, with local chapters of organizations such as the National Negro Business League promoting Black migration westward. They were likely influenced by the hardening racial lines and decreasing opportunities elsewhere in the country, including Kansas, the destination for mass migration in the late 1870s and '80s. See "Colorado Springs Chapter of the National Negro Business League, 1905," Booker T. Washington Papers, Library of Congress Manuscript Collection, Box 847, as reproduced in Katz, *The Black West*, 188.

CHAPTER 6

1. Item 2, Pardon, dated 27 October 1865, Septimus D. Cabaniss Papers.

2. Item 1, Pardon, undated, Septimus D. Cabaniss Papers.

3. According to US census records, Alabama had a population of 964,201 in 1860: 437,770 African Americans lived in the state, 435,000 of whom were slaves. Enslaved people, therefore, comprised 45 percent of the total state population at that time. In Madison County, the proportion was even higher, with enslaved people comprising 55 percent of the total population in 1860. Rogers et al., *Alabama: The History of a Deep South State*, 227–228; Margaret M. Storey, *Loyalty and Loss: Alabama's Unionists in the Civil War and Reconstruction* (Baton Rouge: Louisiana State University Press, 2004), 254; "Classified Population of the States and Territories, By Counties, on the First Day of June 1860, State of Alabama," United States Census Bureau, accessed 17 December 2018, https://www2.census.gov/library/publications/decennial/1860/population/1860a-04.pdf.

4. Quantitative studies of the economics of slavery have calculated that enslaved people comprised 44 percent of capital investment in Alabama, Georgia, Mississippi, and South Carolina in 1859, as compared to land (25 percent) and manufacturing (1 percent). Roger Ransom and Richard Sutch calculate the total value of enslaved people in 1860 as more than $3 billion across the South. See Stanley L. Engerman, Richard Sutch, and Gavin Wright, "Slavery," *Historical Statistics of the United States: Millennial Edition Online,* accessed 1 February 2019, https://hsus.cambri dge.org; Roger Ransom and Richard Sutch, "Capitalists without Capital: The Burden of Slavery and the Impact of Emancipation," *Agricultural History* 62, no. 3 (Summer 1998): 133–160; Roger L. Ransom and Richard Sutch, *One Kind of Freedom: The Economic Consequences of Emancipation* (Cambridge: Cambridge University Press, 2001).

5. S. D. Cabaniss to Elizabeth Yerger, letter dated 31 January 1866, Septimus D. Cabaniss Papers.

6. S. D. Cabaniss, outgoing letter dated 12 February 1866, Septimus D. Cabaniss Papers.

7. Item 3, "Bill of Revision" filed 12 March 1866, Cabaniss v. Townsend; S. D. Cabaniss to Elizabeth Yerger, letter dated 31 January 1866, Septimus D. Cabaniss Papers.

8. S. D. Cabaniss, outgoing letter dated 10 December 1867 to 14 January 1868, Septimus D. Cabaniss Papers.

9. S. D. Cabaniss to A. F. Callahan, letter dated 13 March 1866, Septimus D. Cabaniss Papers.

10. S. D. Cabaniss to Wesley Townsend, letter dated 28 March 1861, Septimus D. Cabaniss Papers.

11. S. D. Cabaniss to Elizabeth Yerger, letter dated 31 January 1866, Septimus D. Cabaniss Papers.

12. Andrew Kull's article in the *Chicago-Kent Law Review* provides a detailed account of the debate over the enforceability of debts for slaves in the Reconstruction era South—addressing arguments in favor of and against this and other debt relief measures, as well as paying special attention to the unusual convergence in opinion of freedpeople and former slave-owners. Kull cites political scientist Otto Kirchheimer's concept of "political justice" to describe the underlying motives of supporters of slave debt nullification: they used legal procedure " 'to bolster or create new power positions,' most notably in the trial and condemnation of a vanquished regime by its victorious successor." For Republicans, treating contracts for slave purchases as different from other contracts effectively made emancipation "retro-active," altering the nature of property relations and effectively stating that slavery had always been illegal. At the same time, it represented a particularly narrow form of political justice as compared to land redistribution or mass treason trials, neither of which occurred after the Civil War. Andrew Kull, "The Enforceability after Emancipation of Debts Contracted for the Purchase of Slaves—Freedom: Personal Liberty and Private Law," *Chicago-Kent Law Review* 70, no. 2 (December 1994), 493–538.

13. Item 6, Cabaniss v. Townsend, Reports to Court (1), 1866–71, item dated 8 December 1866, Septimus D. Cabaniss Papers.

14. S. D. Cabaniss to John Pope, letter dated 10 December 1867, Septimus D. Cabaniss Papers.

15. Alabama's constitutional convention passed a "stay law" in 1868, halting the collection of all debts until January 1869. Michael W. Fitzgerald, *Reconstruction in Alabama: From Civil War to Redemption in the Cotton South* (Baton Rouge: Louisiana State University Press, 2017), 161; Kull, "The Enforceability after Emancipation of Debts Contracted for the Purchase of Slaves," 498.

16. S. D. Cabaniss to Elizabeth Yerger, letter dated 31 January 1866; Item 3, "Bill of Revision" filed 12 March 1866, Cabaniss v. Townsend; S. D. Cabaniss, outgoing letter dated 11 December 1866, Septimus D. Cabaniss Papers.

17. Elvira Townsend to S. D. Cabaniss, letter dated 10 September 1865, Septimus D. Cabaniss Papers.

18. D. L. Lakin to S. D. Cabaniss, letter dated 19 March 1861, Septimus D. Cabaniss Papers.

19. Elvira Townsend to S. D. Cabaniss, letter dated 10 September 1865, Septimus D. Cabaniss Papers.

20. Willis Townsend to S. D. Cabaniss, letter dated 2 September 1866, Septimus D. Cabaniss Papers.

21. Willis Townsend to S. D. Cabaniss, letter dated 1 October 1867, Septimus D. Cabaniss Papers.

22. Willis Townsend to S. D. Cabaniss, letter dated 2 September 1866, Septimus D. Cabaniss Papers.

23. Item dated 4 June 1870, Cabaniss v. Townsend, Orders/decrees/judgments, 1866–1883, Septimus D. Cabaniss Papers.

24. Roberts, "An Experiment in Emancipation of Slaves by an Alabama Planter," 69–72.

25. Wesley Townsend to S. D. Cabaniss, letter dated 28 October 1866, Septimus D. Cabaniss Papers.

26. S. D. Cabaniss to Osborne Townsend, letter dated 23 December 1866, Septimus D. Cabaniss Papers.

27. Willis Townsend to S. D. Cabaniss, letter dated 1 October 1867, Septimus D. Cabaniss Papers.

28. S. D. Cabaniss to Milcha Caldwell, letter dated 25 April 1866, Septimus D. Cabaniss Papers.

29. S. D. Cabaniss to Willis Townsend, letter dated 14 February 1860, Septimus D. Cabaniss Papers.

30. Cabaniss v. Townsend, Reports to court (1), 1866–1871; Cabaniss v. Townsend, Reports to Court (2), 1872–1883; Cabaniss v. Townsend, Orders/decrees/judgments, 1866–1883, Septimus D. Cabaniss Papers. See also Roberts, "An Experiment in Emancipation of Slaves by an Alabama Planter," 69–72.

31. S. D. Cabaniss to Thomas Townsend, letter dated 11 December 1866, Septimus D. Cabaniss Papers.

32. S. D. Cabaniss to Elvira (Townsend) Clay, letter dated 28 March 1867, Septimus D. Cabaniss Papers.

33. S. D. Cabaniss to Leroy Pope Walker, letter dated October 1861, Septimus D. Cabaniss Papers.

34. Thomas Townsend to S. D. Cabaniss, letter dated 20 March 1866, S. D. Cabaniss.

35. S. D. Cabaniss to Thomas Townsend, letter dated 11 December 1866, Septimus D. Cabaniss Papers.

36. In 1865, roughly one sixth of the state's Black population (and accordingly, a considerably larger proportion of Black men) had served or were serving in the Union Army. Cunningham, "Douglas's Battery at Forth Leavenworth," 207; Taylor, *In Search of the Racial Frontier: African Americans in the American West, 1528–1990*, 99; Sheridan, "From Slavery in Missouri to Freedom in Kansas: The Influx of Black Fugitives and Contrabands into Kansas," 46.

37. Cunningham, "Douglas's Battery at Fort Leavenworth," 205.

38. "NO COMPROMISE WITH TRAITORS," *Leavenworth Daily Conservative* (Leavenworth, KS), 18 February 1864, KHS.

39. General Townsend, U.S. Colored Troops Military Service Records, 1863–1865; General Townsend, General Index to Pension Files, 1861–1934, accessed 2 June 2015, www.ancestry.com; Item 1, dated 10 February 1896, General Townsend, Department of the Interior, Bureau of Pensions, Septimus D. Cabaniss Papers.

40. *Catalogue of the Wilberforce University, 1859–60. Xenia, Ohio* (Cincinnati, OH: Methodist Book Concern, 1860), 12. In one letter to Cabaniss, Thomas signed off with the phrase "View this not with a critic's eye but pass my imperfections by," a line from a poem first published in Caleb Bingham's essay and poetry collection *The Columbian Orator*—giving insight into the books the Townsend children read at Wilberforce. Frederick Douglass described encountering this book while still enslaved, writing, "the more I read, the more I was led to abhor and detest my enslavers." See Thomas Townsend to S. D. Cabaniss, letter dated 20 January 1866, Septimus D. Cabaniss Papers; Caleb Bingham, *The Columbian Orator: Containing a Variety of Original and Selected Pieces Together with Rules Calculated to Improve Youth and Others in the Ornamental and Useful Art of Eloquence* (Boston: Caleb Bingham and Co., 1817); Frederick Douglass, *Narrative of the Life of Frederick Douglass, An American Slave, Written By Himself*, 39–40, accessed at docsouth.unc.edu.

41. Thomas Townsend to S. D. Cabaniss, letters dated 20 January 1866, 20 March 1866, 9 March 1868, Septimus D. Cabaniss Papers.

42. Thomas Townsend to S. D. Cabaniss, unsigned letter dated 20 March 1866, Septimus D. Cabaniss Papers.

43. Thomas Townsend to S. D. Cabaniss, letter dated 20 April 1866, Septimus D. Cabaniss Papers.

44. Thomas Townsend to S. D. Cabaniss, letter dated 9 March 1868, Septimus D. Cabaniss Papers.

45. D. L. Lakin to S. D. Cabaniss, letter dated 22 August 1860, Septimus D. Cabaniss Papers. Wesley came to regret his actions in Ohio and took steps to ensure that Jane, Rainey, and Martha were repaid from his portion of the Townsend estate—a change of heart that pleased Cabaniss, who praised Wesley's "manly acknowledgement of your past errors." S. D. Cabaniss to Wesley Townsend, letter dated 20 January 1866, Septimus D. Cabaniss Papers; Roberts, "An Experiment in Emancipation of Slaves by an Alabama Planter," 94.

46. S. D. Cabaniss to the Jail of Leavenworth Co., letter dated 16 May 1866; S. D. Cabaniss to Woodson Townsend, letter dated 16 May 1866, Septimus D. Cabaniss Papers.

47. Thomas Townsend to S. D. Cabaniss, letter dated 20 April 1866, Septimus D. Cabaniss Papers.

48. Thomas Townsend to S. D. Cabaniss, letter dated 21 September 1867, Septimus D. Cabaniss Papers.

49. Susanna Townsend to S. D. Cabaniss, letter dated 4 June 1868, Septimus D. Cabaniss Papers.

50. Milcha Townsend to S. D. Cabaniss, letter dated 3 December 1865, Septimus D. Cabaniss Papers.

51. Martha Townsend to S. D. Cabaniss, letter dated 12 December 1881, Septimus D. Cabaniss Papers. Emphasis in original.

52. Thomas Townsend to S. D. Cabaniss, unsigned letter dated 20 March 1866, Septimus D. Cabaniss Papers.

53. Thomas Townsend to S. D. Cabaniss, letter dated 21 September 1867, Septimus D. Cabaniss Papers.

54. See, in particular, Thomas Townsend to S. D. Cabaniss, unsigned letter dated 20 March 1866, Septimus D. Cabaniss Papers.

55. Thomas Townsend to S. D. Cabaniss, letter dated 9 March 1868, Septimus D. Cabaniss Papers.

56. S. D. Cabaniss to Thomas Townsend, letter dated 31 January 1866, Septimus D. Cabaniss Papers.

57. S. D. Cabaniss to Thomas Townsend, letter dated 11 December 1866, Septimus D. Cabaniss Papers.

58. S. D. Cabaniss, outgoing letter dated 8 February 1866, Septimus D. Cabaniss Papers.

59. S. D. Cabaniss to Thomas Townsend, letter dated 20 March 1868, Septimus D. Cabaniss Papers. Emphasis in original.

60. Item 4, "Bill of Revision supplement" dated 17 June 1868, Cabaniss v. Townsend, Septimus D. Cabaniss Papers.

61. Thomas Townsend to S. D. Cabaniss, letter dated 21 February 1866; item dated 31 May 1871, Cabaniss v. Townsend, Reports to court (1), 1866–1871, Septimus D. Cabaniss Papers.

62. Thomas Townsend to S. D. Cabaniss, letter dated 21 September 1867, Septimus D. Cabaniss Papers.

63. S. D. Cabaniss to Woodson Townsend, letter dated 16 May 1866, Septimus D. Cabaniss Papers.

64. S. D. Cabaniss to Thomas Townsend, letter dated 30 April 1866, Septimus D. Cabaniss Papers.

65. S. D. Cabaniss to Osborne Townsend, letter dated 30 March 1866, Septimus D. Cabaniss Papers. For his part, Willis denied that he was the father, claiming that he "didn't know her till six month before" and that "there was a man after her at the same time." Willis Townsend to S. D. Cabaniss, letter dated 2 September 1866, Septimus D. Cabaniss Papers.

66. S. D. Cabaniss to Thomas Townsend, letters dated 31 January 1866 and 12 March 1862 [1866], Septimus D. Cabaniss Papers. Martha was reunited with her daughter in either 1866 or 1867, with Emeline relocating to Leavenworth, Kansas. At some point, Emeline became a devout Catholic, as did her mother. Emeline died in November 1867. Martha Townsend to S. D. Cabaniss, letter dated 25 November 1867, Septimus D. Cabaniss Papers.

67. As with many aspects of Lizzy Perryman's story, details of her life in Tennessee and reunion with her daughters remain a mystery. According to Cabaniss, Lizzie and Jennie Townsend had planned to move to west Tennessee permanently to live with their mother, but for unknown reasons "staid only a few days." S. D. Cabaniss to Thomas Townsend, letter dated 6 July 1868, Septimus D. Cabaniss Papers.

68. S. D. Cabaniss to Osborne Townsend, letter dated 23 December 1866, Septimus D. Cabaniss Papers.

69. Thomas Townsend to S. D. Cabaniss, letter dated 21 February 1866, Septimus D. Cabaniss Papers.

70. Milcha Townsend to S. D. Cabaniss, letter dated 3 December 1865, Septimus D. Cabaniss Papers.

71. Thomas Townsend to S. D. Cabaniss, letter dated 21 February 1866, Septimus D. Cabaniss Papers.

72. Wesley Townsend to S. D. Cabaniss, letter dated 13 October 1865; Thomas Townsend to S. D. Cabaniss, letter dated 20 January 1866, Septimus D. Cabaniss Papers.

73. Thomas Townsend to S. D. Cabaniss, letter dated 20 January 1866, Septimus D. Cabaniss Papers.

74. Wesley Townsend to S. D. Cabaniss, letter dated 8 February 1860; D. L. Lakin to S. D. Cabaniss, letters dated 19 March 1861 and 19 March 1860, Septimus D. Cabaniss Papers.

75. S. D. Cabaniss to William Clay, letter dated 28 February 1867; S. D. Cabaniss to Elvira Clay, letter dated 28 March 1867; Item 3, Residences and Marriages, Biographical Information of Legatees, Miscellaneous, dated between February 1868 and 1869, Septimus D. Cabaniss Papers.

76. Thomas Townsend to S. D. Cabaniss, letter dated 9 March 1868, Septimus D. Cabaniss Papers.

77. Thomas Townsend to S. D. Cabaniss, letter dated 20 January 1866, Septimus D. Cabaniss Papers.

78. Thomas Townsend to S. D. Cabaniss, letter dated 20 January 1866, Septimus D. Cabaniss Papers.

79. Thomas made oblique references to complications with Elvira's 1866 pregnancy in his letters to Cabaniss. In March he wrote that she'd been suffering from "neuralgia" (intense nerve pain that, at the time, may have referred to migraines) for weeks. By April she was "in convalescence," recovering perhaps from a miscarriage. Thomas Townsend to S. D. Cabaniss, letter dated 20 March 1866; Thomas Townsend to S. D. Cabaniss, letter dated 20 April 1866, Septimus D. Cabaniss Papers.

80. Elvira's third child with Woodson, a daughter named Julia, was recorded in an 1865 census but disappeared from the historical record thereafter. By the time of Elvira's death, she had only two living children: Elizabeth and Sarah Townsend. Julia Townsend, 1865 Kansas State Census, accessed 28 September 2020, www.ancestry.com.

81. Thomas Townsend to S. D. Cabaniss, letter dated 9 March 1868, Septimus D. Cabaniss Papers.

82. S. D. Cabaniss to Thomas Townsend, letter dated 11 December 1866, Septimus D. Cabaniss Papers.

83. Descriptions of events in Madison County derive from *Testimony Taken by the Joint Select Committee to Inquire Into the Condition of Affairs in the Late Insurrectionary States. Report No. 41, pt. 8. Alabama*, vol. 1–3 (Washington, DC: Government Printing Office, 1872), accessed 1 December 2018, ProQuest Congressional. In fall 1871, a congressional committee held public hearings on Ku Klux Klan activity in the South, taking testimony from both white and Black witnesses. The published reports provide valuable first-person accounts of Klan violence, with details on the methods and members of local Klan groups; they also illustrate the ways in which the "first Klan," active in the immediate postwar period, was less a centralized organization than a collection of independent vigilante gangs building off antebellum slave patrols and local militias and motivated by a white supremacist ideology. Northern Alabama witnessed Klan activity as early as 1867, nearly a year before it became common elsewhere in the South—perhaps because of its close proximity to Pulaski, Tennessee, where the KKK originated. Huntsville is fewer than fifty miles from Pulaski. See also Rogers, *Alabama: History of a Deep South State*; Fitzgerald, *Reconstruction in Alabama*; Hahn, *A Nation Under Our Feet*. For Alabama's Klan trials in particular, see Christopher Lyle McIlwain Sr., "United States District Judge Richard Busteed and the Alabama Klan Trials of 1872," *Alabama Review* 65, no. 4 (October 2012): 263–289.

84. Testimony of Joseph Gill in *Testimony Taken by the Joint Select Committee to Inquire into the Condition of Affairs in the Late Insurrectionary States*, 813–814.

85. Testimony of Job Kelley in *Testimony Taken by the Joint Select Committee to Inquire Into the Condition of Affairs in the Late Insurrectionary States*, 917.

86. Testimony of James M. Moss in *Testimony Taken by the Joint Select Committee to Inquire into the Condition of Affairs in the Late Insurrectionary States*, 922.

87. Testimony of Joseph Gill in *Testimony Taken by the Joint Select Committee to Inquire into the Condition of Affairs in the Late Insurrectionary States*, 812–813.

88. The man named Parks Townsend who was a member of the Ku Klux Klan in the late 1860s was the son of Samuel C. Townsend and grandson of the first Parks Townsend (Edmund and Samuel's brother); he was also the nephew of a third Parks Townsend, Samuel C.'s brother. His father Samuel C. was named co-executor of Samuel Townsend's estate with S. D. Cabaniss in 1856 and inherited a large portion of Samuel's estate as an incentive to uphold the controversial will. When Samuel C. died in 1861, the property passed to his widow Virginia H. Townsend, who served as executor of her husband's will and successfully managed the property herself. Despite the financial losses caused by emancipation, Virginia appeared to fare better than most Madison County planters after the Civil War: census records listed the postwar cash value of her farm as $15,000. In Alabama Klan hearing records, locals referred to Virginia and Samuel C.'s son as "Young Park" to differentiate him from his uncle Parks S. Townsend. As one white Republican in Madison County remarked in 1871, in contrast to Young Parks, "the older one I guess is a pretty nice man." For landholdings and property values, see Virginia H. Townsend, Parks Townsend, and Parks S. Townsend, Township 1, Madison, Alabama: U.S., Selected Federal Census Non-Population Schedules, 1850–1880, accessed 4 January 2019, www.ancestry.com.

89. Testimony of Joseph Gill in *Testimony Taken by the Joint Select Committee to Inquire into the Condition of Affairs in the Late Insurrectionary States,* 814.

90. Fitzgerald, *Reconstruction in Alabama,* 176, 180, 187–189, 197.

91. Testimony of Peyton Lipscomb in *Testimony Taken by the Joint Select Committee to Inquire into the Condition of Affairs in the Late Insurrectionary States*, 951–952.

92. Testimony of James M. Moss in *Testimony Taken by the Joint Select Committee to Inquire into the Condition of Affairs in the Late Insurrectionary States*, 919, 917.

93. Testimony of Joseph Gill in *Testimony Taken by the Joint Select Committee to Inquire into the Condition of Affairs in the Late Insurrectionary States*, 813.

94. Testimony of James M. Moss in *Testimony Taken by the Joint Select Committee to Inquire into the Condition of Affairs in the Late Insurrectionary States*, 922.

95. S. D. Cabaniss to Thomas Townsend, letter dated 17 December 1868, Septimus D. Cabaniss Papers.

96. Virginia H. Townsend, Township 1, Madison, Alabama: U.S., Selected Federal Census Non-Population Schedules, 1850–1880, accessed 4 January 2019, www.ancestry.com.

97. Parks S. Townsend, Township 1, Madison, Alabama: U.S., Selected Federal Census Non-Population Schedules, 1850–1880, accessed 4 January 2019, www.ancestry.com.

98. Testimony of James M. Moss in *Testimony Taken by the Joint Select Committee to Inquire into the Condition of Affairs in the Late Insurrectionary States,* 923.

99. Thomas Townsend, Alabama, Agriculture, 1870, Limestone, Subdivision 13, U.S. Federal Census Non-population Schedules 1850–1880, accessed 7 January 2018, www.ancestry.com.

100. Fitzgerald, *Reconstruction in Alabama*, 130, 132, 235.

101. Sharecropping initially seemed like a step toward independence, with tenant farmers hoping to eventually purchase land outright with their profits. When property prices rebounded from their postwar low, however, independent land ownership moved out of freedpeople's reach. See Fitzgerald, *Reconstruction in Alabama*, 130; Rogers et al., *Alabama: History of a Deep South State*, 237.

102. Rogers et al., *Alabama: History of a Deep South State*, 237, 271; Fitzgerald, *Reconstruction in Alabama*, 132.

103. Thomas Townsend, Alabama, Agriculture, 1870, Limestone, Subdivision 13, U.S. Federal Census Non-population Schedules 1850–1880, accessed 7 January 2018, www.ancestry.com.

104. Item 30, Cabaniss v. Townsend, Reports to court (1), 1866–1871; Item 3, "Inventory and Appraisement" dated February–March 1858, Inventories, Septimus D. Cabaniss Papers.

105. "Hazel Green Dots," *Huntsville Gazette* (Huntsville, AL), 5 December 1891, p. 3, America's Historical Newspapers.

106. Fitzgerald, *Reconstruction in Alabama*, 109–110

107. "Thos W. Townsend," Teacher's Monthly School Report, April, May, and June 1869, United States, Freedmen's Bureau, Records of the Superintendent of Education and the Division of Education, 1868–1872, accessed 7 January 2018, www.familysearch.org.

108. T. W. Townsend, "Genl Townsend," Spencer Townsend, Osborne Townsend, Wesley Townsend, "Shedrick Townsend," Freedman's Bank Records, 1865–1874, accessed 7 June 2016, www.familysearch.org. On the Freedman's Bank and African American community finances, see Richard Bailey, *Neither Carpetbaggers Nor Scalawags: Black Officeholders during the Reconstruction of Alabama, 1867–1878* (Montgomery, AL: NewSouth Books, 2010); L. Olmstead, *Freedmen Philanthropy, and Fraud: A History of the Freedman's Savings Bank* (Urbana: University of Illinois Press, 1976); Barbara P. Josiah, "Providing for the Future: The World of the African American Depositors of Washington, DC's Freedmen's Savings Bank, 1865–1874," *Journal of African American History* 89, no. 1 (Winter 2004): 1–16.

109. "A Duty of Congress," *Huntsville Gazette* (Huntsville, AL), 17 December 1881, p. 2; "Freedman's Bank," *Huntsville Gazette* (Huntsville, AL), 20 May 1882, p. 2, America's Historical Newspapers.

110. Virginia H. Townsend to Thomas W. Townsend, Deed, 1878, Surname T-Z Reverse Index to Real Property, MCRC.

111. Ivey Beard to Thomas W. Townsend, Mortgage, 1887, Surname T-Z Reverse Index to Real Property, MCRC.

112. Alfred Clay to "Thos Townsend," Mortgage, 1872; Ivey Beard to Thomas W. Townsend, Mortgage, 1887, Surname T-Z Reverse Index to Real Property, MCRC. Historian Michele Mitchell coined the term "aspiring class" as an alternative to the "black middle-class." According to Mitchell, the Black aspiring class included "workers able to save a little money as well as those who worked multiple jobs to attain class mobility." While they had a starkly different lifestyle from Black elites, they adopted similar ideologies of racial uplift and respectability. Heather Cox Richardson similarly discusses a pattern of freedpeople and other marginal groups seeking social and economic mobility by adopting the nation's "mainstream vision" of self-help and self-reliance. Mitchell, *Righteous Propagation*; Richardson, *West from Appomattox*.

113. "House and Lot for Sale," *Huntsville Gazette* (Huntsville, AL), 7 July 1881, p. 2; "Administrator's Sale," *Huntsville Gazette* (Huntsville, AL), 28 September 1889, p. 2, America's Historical Newspapers; Roberts, "An Experiment in Emancipation of Slaves by an Alabama Planter," 100; Wm. Fletcher & Co. to Thomas Townsend, letter dated 29 August 1906, Septimus D. Cabaniss Papers; Thomas W. Townsend, U.S. City Directories, 1822–1995, Huntsville, Alabama, City Directory, 1908, accessed 29 September 2020, www.ancestry.com.

114. "The People's Paper," *Huntsville Gazette* (Huntsville, AL), 25 March 1882, p. 3, America's Historical Newspapers.

115. *Huntsville Gazette* (Huntsville, AL), 18 June 1881, p. 3; "The People's Paper," *Huntsville Gazette* (Huntsville, AL), 25 March 1882, p. 3, America's Historical Newspapers.

116. Thomas Townsend, 1880 United States Federal Census, accessed 1 October 2018, www.ancestry.com; "Officers of the Gazette Company," *Huntsville Gazette* (Huntsville, AL), 4 February 1882, p. 3; "The People's Paper," *Huntsville Gazette* (Huntsville, AL), 25 March 1882, p. 3, America's Historical Newspapers.

117. "The People's Paper," *Huntsville Gazette* (Huntsville, AL), 25 March 1882, p. 3, America's Historical Newspapers.

118. "News and Sentiment. (From Colored Exchanges)," *Huntsville Gazette* (Huntsville, AL), 29 July 1882, p. 2, America's Historical Newspapers.

119. Bailey, *Neither Carpetbaggers Nor Scalawags*, 287, 152, 268; Allen J. Going, "The South and the Blair Education Bill," *Mississippi Valley Historical Review* 44, no. 2 (September 1957), 268.

120. Fitzgerald, *Reconstruction in Alabama*, 232.

121. Rogers et al., *Alabama: History of a Deep South State*, 269.

122. *Huntsville Gazette* (Huntsville, AL), 22 July 1882, p. 2, America's Historical Newspapers.

123. Going, "The South and the Blair Education Bill," 267–290.

124. "Notice," *Huntsville Gazette* (Huntsville, AL), 11 November 1882, p. 3, America's Historical Newspapers. Huntsville schools at this time included the Huntsville Normal School (later called the State Normal and Industrial School) and the

Rust Normal Institute, established in 1867 by the Freedmen's Aid Society of the Methodist Episcopal Church. The Rust Institute, where Wesley Townsend and Thomas's first wife Mary Mastin worked as teachers for a time, was named for former Wilberforce University president Richard S. Rust, who served as the Freedmen's Aid Society secretary. See G. Ward Hubbs, *Searching for Freedom after the Civil War: Klansman, Carpetbagger, Scalawag, and Freedman* (Tuscaloosa: University of Alabama Press, 2015), 77–78, 191 fn 39.

125. *Report of the Commissioner of Education for the Year 1884–'85* (Washington, DC: Government Printing Office, 1886), 5.

126. "Wisdom of an Industrial School," *Huntsville* Gazette (Huntsville, AL), 7 May 1884, p. 2, America's Historical Newspapers.

127. William H. Gaston, "What We Might, and Should Do for Ourselves," *Huntsville Gazette* (Huntsville, AL), 28 October 1882, p. 3, America's Historical Newspapers. For an account of Gaston's life and career as a Black community leader in Huntsville, see Stephen R. Robinson, "Rethinking Black Urban Politics in the 1880s: The Case of William Gaston in Post-Reconstruction Alabama," *Alabama Review* 66, no. 1 (January 2013); Joshua Guthman, *Strangers Below: Primitive Baptists and American Culture* (Chapel Hill: University of North Carolina Press, 2015).

128. Gaston, "What We Might, and Should Do for Ourselves," p. 3.

129. "News and Sentiment. (From Colored Exchanges.)," *Huntsville Gazette* (Huntsville, AL), 29 July 1882, p. 2, America's Historical Newspapers.

130. Gaston, "What We Might, and Should Do for Ourselves," p. 3.

131. "Colored Stockholders," *Huntsville Gazette* (Huntsville, AL), 5 July 1884, p. 3, America's Historical Newspapers.

132. *Huntsville Gazette* (Huntsville, AL), 7 May 1884, p. 2, America's Historical Newspapers.

133. For Nelson Hendley, see 1880 United States Federal Census, accessed 8 January 2019, www.ancestry.com.

134. 1874 was a pivotal election year for the nation at large, not only Alabama. Democrats seized a majority in the House of Representatives for the first time since before the Civil War and won nineteen of twenty-five governor's races (including Massachusetts). The "redemption" of the South—as well as the nation's wider acceptance of white supremacist politics—had been in progress for years before the conventional end of Reconstruction. Blight, *Race and Reunion*, 130.

135. Rogers et al., *Alabama: History of a Deep South State*, 251–252; McIlwain, "United States District Judge Richard Busteed and the Alabama Klan Trials of 1872," 263.

136. Fitzgerald, *Reconstruction in Alabama*, 285–286, 315.

137. Rogers et al., *Alabama: History of a Deep South State*, 226, 261–263.

138. "News and Sentiment. (From Colored Exchanges.)," *Huntsville Gazette* (Huntsville, AL), 29 July 1882, p. 2, America's Historical Newspapers.

139. Allen Johnston Going, *Bourbon Democracy in Alabama, 1874–1890* (Tuscaloosa: University of Alabama Press, 1952, 1992), 37.

140. "Duty of Colored Voters," *Huntsville Gazette* (Huntsville, AL), 29 July 1882, p. 2, America's Historical Newspapers.

141. Going, *Bourbon Democracy in Alabama,* 35.

142. Bailey, *Neither Carpetbaggers Nor Scalawags,* 71.

143. Guthman, *Strangers Below,* 104.

144. Throughout the 1880s, independent movements polled 40 percent or more of the vote in seven southern states, undercutting the idea of a "solid Democratic South." Biracial political alliances were particularly fragile, however, as they required Black politicians to maintain the trust of white community leaders as well as their constituents. The "Readjuster" or "Liberal" party, which governed Virginia from 1879 to 1883, was arguably one of the most successful Black-white coalitions of the period. Readjusters pushed for Black suffrage, jury service, and Black elected officials while also accepting a "separate spheres doctrine" which permitted segregation and discrimination in the private sphere. See Richardson, *West from Appomattox,* 200–201; Robinson, "Rethinking Black Urban Politics in the 1880s"; Hahn, *A Nation Under Our Feet*; Jane Dailey, "The Limits of Liberalism in the New South: The Politics of Race, Sex, and Patronage in Virginia, 1879–1883 in *Jumpin' Jim Crow.*

145. Fitzgerald, *Reconstruction in Alabama,* 169.

146. Rogers et al., *Alabama: History of a Deep South State,* 291–292, 283–284.

147. David D. Shelby was the second son of Dr. David Shelby, a wealthy physician who owned two slaves in 1850 and lived adjacent to Samuel C. Townsend. The younger Shelby, seventeen or eighteen years old when the Civil War ended, built a law practice and participated in the Greenbacker movement during the 1880s. Shelby, who ran on the same ticket as African American candidates, was disparaged by some Madison County whites as a "Greenblacker." In 1870, all of Samuel and Edmund Townsend's living children (except for Parthenia and Caroline) and Elvira's daughters Elizabeth and Sarah hired Shelby to represent them in a lawsuit against S. D. Cabaniss. See David Shelby, 1850 and 1860 United States Federal Censuses, accessed 1 January 2019, www.ancestry.com; Frances Cabaniss Roberts, "William Manning Lowe and the Greenback Party in Alabama" in *From Civil War to Civil Rights, Alabama 1860-1960: An Anthology from the Alabama Review,* ed. Sarah Woolfolk Wiggins (Tuscaloosa: University of Alabama Press, 1987); Item 39, Cabaniss v. Townsend, Reports to Court (1), 1866–1871, Septimus D. Cabaniss Papers; Roberts, "An Experiment in Emancipation of Slaves by an Alabama Planter," 91.

148. David D. Shelby "To the Voters of Madison County," *Huntsville Gazette* (Huntsville, AL), 22 July 1882, p. 2, America's Historical Newspapers.

149. "VICTORY. North Ala. Spanks the Bourbons," *Huntsville Gazette* (Huntsville, AL), 12 August 1882, p. 2, America's Historical Newspapers.

150. "The People's Paper," *Huntsville Gazette* (Huntsville, AL), 25 March 1882, p. 3, America's Historical Newspapers.

151. "News and Sentiment," *Huntsville Gazette* (Huntsville, AL), 15 December 1888, p. 2, America's Historical Newspapers.

152. "Coquetry in Politics," *Huntsville Gazette* (Huntsville, AL), 9 August 1884, p. 2, America's Historical Newspapers.

153. Glenda Gilmore writes that the term "best man" likely developed from the term "better classes," which was used in the press as an alternative to "middle class." The "best man" as a model for Black leaders can be seen as an outgrowth of reformers' and racial uplift advocates' promotion of respectability as a means of obtaining white society's acceptance and respect. See Glenda Elizabeth Gilmore, *Gender & Jim Crow: Women and the Politics of White Supremacy in North Carolina, 1896–1920* (Chapel Hill, NC: The University of North Carolina Press, 1996); Kevin K. Gaines, *Uplifting the Race: Black Leadership, Politics, and Culture in the Twentieth Century* (Chapel Hill, NC: University of North Carolina Press, 1996). For a case study of the "better classes" in a southern city, see also Janette Thomas Greenwood, *Bittersweet Legacy: The Black and White 'Better Classes' in Charlotte, 1850–1910* (Chapel Hill: University of North Carolina Press, 1994).

154. Gilmore, *Gender & Jim Crow*, 62–63; Richardson, *West from Appomattox*, 7, 165; Robinson, "Rethinking Black Urban Politics," 7–8.

155. "In Limestone and Jackson," *Huntsville Gazette* (Huntsville, AL), 11 August 1883, p. 2, America's Historical Newspapers.

156. Roberts, "An Experiment in Emancipation of Slaves by an Alabama Planter," 101.

157. "Opening Skirmish. Somewhat of a Bull Run," *Huntsville Gazette* (Huntsville, AL), 18 March 1882, p. 3. America's Historical Newspapers.

158. Nelson Hendley, 1880 United States Federal Census, accessed 8 January 2019, www.ancestry.com; "A Fourth Warder Speaks," *Huntsville Gazette* (Huntsville, AL), 4 April 1891, p. 3. America's Historical Newspapers.

159. "Opening Skirmish. Somewhat of a Bull Run," *Huntsville Gazette* (Huntsville, AL), 18 March 1882, p. 3; "The People's Ticket," *Huntsville Gazette* (Huntsville, AL), 18 March 1882, p. 3; "Announcement," *Huntsville Gazette* (Huntsville, AL), 25 March 1882, p. 3, America's Historical Newspapers.

160. "The City Election," *Huntsville Gazette* Huntsville, AL), 8 April 1882, p. 3, America's Historical Newspapers.

161. "Well Done," *Huntsville Gazette* (Huntsville, AL), 8 April 1882, p. 2, America's Historical Newspapers.

162. "Notes by Jack Daw," *Huntsville Gazette* (Huntsville, AL), 3 June 1882, p. 3, America's Historical Newspapers.

163. Roberts, "An Experiment in Emancipation of Slaves by an Alabama Planter," 101.

164. "A 'Fourth Warder' Speaks," *Huntsville Gazette* (Huntsville, AL), 4 April 1891, p. 3, America's Historical Newspapers.

165. "To Vote by Wards," *Huntsville Gazette* (Huntsville, AL), 17 February 1883, p. 2, America's Historical Newspapers.

166. "A 'Fourth Warder' Speaks," *Huntsville Gazette* (Huntsville, AL), 4 April 1891, p. 3, America's Historical Newspapers.
167. At the time, Thomas Townsend was living with his late wife Mary Mastin's parents on Adams Avenue, which was located in the Third Ward. See Thomas Townsend, 1880 Federal Census, www.ancestry.com. For delineations of the new wards, see "Grin and Endure It. The Ward Bill," *Huntsville Gazette* (Huntsville, AL), 3 March 1883, p. 3, America's Historical Newspapers.
168. "A 'Fourth Warder' Speaks," *Huntsville Gazette* (Huntsville, AL), 4 April 1891, p. 3, America's Historical Newspapers. For Mastin's reputation among Huntsville's African American residents, see Robinson, "Rethinking Black Urban Politics in the 1880s," 12.
169. "Captain Algernon Sidney Fletcher (1833)," Huntsville History Collection, accessed 10 January 2019, www.huntsvillehistorycollection.org; Patrick McCauley, "The Origins of Huntsville's Waterworks Utility Board," *Huntsville Historical Review* 25, no. 1 (Winter–Spring 1998), 2; Ranee' G. Pruitt, ed., *Eden of the South: A Chronology of Huntsville, Alabama, 1805–2005* (Huntsville, AL: Huntsville-Madison County Public Library, 2005), 83.
170. "Grin and Endure It. The Ward Bill," *Huntsville Gazette* (Huntsville, AL), 3 March 1883, p. 3, America's Historical Newspapers.
171. "Republicans and Independents in Conference," *Huntsville Gazette* (Huntsville, AL), 7 May 1884, p. 3; *Huntsville Gazette* (Huntsville, AL), 7 May 1884, p. 2, America's Historical Newspapers.
172. *Huntsville Gazette* (Huntsville, AL), 7 May 1884, p. 2, America's Historical Newspapers.
173. "Neighborhood News and Gossip," *Huntsville Gazette* (Huntsville, AL), 2 August 1884, p. 3.; *Huntsville Gazette* (Huntsville, AL), 2 August 1884, p. 3, America's Historical Newspapers.
174. "Republicans and Independents in Conference," *Huntsville Gazette* (Huntsville, AL), 7 May 1884, p. 3, America's Historical Newspapers.
175. *The Advocate* (Leavenworth, KS), 22 June 1889, KHS. On white Republicans' "retreat" from civil rights activism, see Blight, *Race and Reunion;* Richardson, *West from Appomattox.*
176. "Huntsville Demands a New Charter," *Huntsville Gazette* (Huntsville, AL), 8 December 1888, p. 3; "The Heading of It," *Huntsville Gazette* (Huntsville, AL), 8 December 1888, p. 3, America's Historical Newspapers.
177. "Huntsville Demands a New Charter," *Huntsville Gazette* (Huntsville, AL), 8 December 1888, p. 3, America's Historical Newspapers.
178. See, for example, Rayford Logan, *The Negro in American Life and Thought: The Nadir, 1877-1901* (New York: Dial Press, 1954); W. Fitzhugh Brundage, *Lynching in the New South, 1880-1930* (Urbana, IL: University of Illinois Press, 1993); Paula J. Giddings, *Ida, A Sword Among Lions: Ida B. Wells and the Campaign Against Lynching* (New York: Harper Collins, 2008); Jacquelyn Dowd Hall, *Revolt*

Against Chivalry: Jessie Daniel Ames and the Women's Campaign Against Lynching (New York: Columbia University Press, 1993). For a survey of Jim Crow laws across the country, see Michael J. Klarman, *From Jim Crow to Civil Rights: The Supreme Court and the Struggle for Racial Equality* (New York: Oxford University Press, 2004).

179. Thomas Townsend and "Mary Martin" [Mastin], Alabama County Marriages, 1809–1950, accessed 6 August 2020, FamilySearch.org; "Memoirs," *Huntsville Gazette* (Huntsville, AL), 8 December 1894, p. 2, America's Historical Newspapers.

180. Thomas Townsend and Mary A. Scruggs, Alabama County Marriages, 1809–1950, accessed 6 August 2020, FamilySearch.org.

181. "Distinguished Nuptials," *Huntsville Gazette* (Huntsville, AL), 11 February 1888, p. 3, America's Historical Newspapers.

182. C. O. Townsend to Thomas Townsend, letter dated 14 February 1888, Septimus D. Cabaniss Papers; *Huntsville Gazette* (Huntsville, AL), 18 February 1888, p. 2, America's Historical Newspapers.

183. Roberts, "An Experiment in Emancipation of Slaves by an Alabama Planter," 102; Item 28, Notes on interview with Thomas Townsend Jr., Biographical information of Legatees/ Miscellaneous information, Septimus D. Cabaniss Papers.

184. See, in particular, John Armstrong Townsend to S. D. Cabaniss, letter dated 16 September 1874; Charles Osborne Townsend to Thomas and Wesley Townsend, letter dated 19 January 1876; Charles Osborne Townsend to Thomas Townsend, letters dated 18 May 1883 and 21 March 1884; Wesley Townsend to [Thomas Townsend], letter dated 5 July 1888; Willis Townsend to Thomas Townsend, letter dated 7 September [no year]; Willis Townsend to Thomas Townsend, letter dated 27 July 1889; Willis Townsend to Thomas Townsend, letter dated 5 August 1890; Adelaide Townsend to Thomas Townsend, letter dated 16 November 1900, Septimus D. Cabaniss Papers.

185. Carrie Leontee Townsend to Thomas Townsend, letter dated 19 August 1890, Septimus D. Cabaniss Papers.

186. Roberts, "An Experiment in Emancipation of Slaves by an Alabama Planter," 100–101.

187. Typewritten transcript of "Wealthy Negro Dies," *Huntsville-Mercury Banner* (Huntsville, AL), 31 August 1916, Septimus D. Cabaniss Papers.

188. "War Legislator Dies," *Chicago Defender* (Chicago, IL), 9 September 1916, p. 4; "Former Legislator Dies," *Philadelphia Tribune* (Philadelphia, PA), 16 September 1916, p. 1, America's Historical Newspapers.

189. "Wealthy Negro Dies," *Huntsville-Mercury Banner* (Huntsville, AL), 31 August 1916, Septimus D. Cabaniss Papers; "War Legislator Dies," *Chicago Defender* (Chicago, IL), 9 September 1916, p. 4, America's Historical Newspapers.

190. "War Legislator Dies," *Chicago Defender* (Chicago, IL), 9 September 1916, p. 4, America's Historical Newspapers.

EPILOGUE

1. "The Condition of the Colored People of the South from a Laboring Standpoint," *The Advocate* (Leavenworth, KS), 20 July 1889, KHS.

2. William Bolden is called "Bolling" in Samuel Townsend's 1856 will and in S. D. Cabaniss's inventories of the Townsend estate. He signed some early letters to Cabaniss "Bolden," but began to use the name "William Bolden" or initials "W. B." more regularly in the early-to-mid 1870s. William Bolden calculated his age based on his mother Peggy's estimations. In one letter he wrote Cabaniss that "all that I know is that Mother said I was 6 years old when I reached Kansas." [William] Bolden Townsend to S. D. Cabaniss, letter dated 17 January 1873, Septimus D. Cabaniss Papers.

3. Peggy, her mother Rachel, and Peggy's sisters Jane, Mary, and Lucy were all born in Virginia. They may have been purchased as a family by Samuel Townsend or one of his relatives sometime after the birth of Peggy, the youngest daughter, around 1837; alternatively, they may have already belonged to members of the Townsend family and were sent west to Alabama during this period. "Reggy Armistead" and Rachel Townsend, 1870 United States Federal Census; Mary Eddings, 1880 United States Federal Census, accessed 1 February 2019, www.ancestry.com; Lucy Townsend, Kansas Death Certificates, LHCS.

4. S. D. Cabaniss to Osborne Townsend, letter dated 23 December 1866, Septimus D. Cabaniss Papers.

5. Wesley Townsend and his family moved from Ohio to Huntsville, Alabama, in 1870, and then to Brookhaven, Mississippi, around 1879, where Wesley managed a restaurant and Adelaide worked as a schoolteacher. Census records from 1880 indicate that they had seven living children: Hattie, Ida, Ella, Osborne, Farma, Carrie, and Page. See Wesley Townsend to S. D. Cabaniss, letters dated 16 March 1870 and 24 March 1879, Septimus D. Cabaniss Papers; "Westley Townsend" and Ada Townsend, 1880 United States Federal Census, accessed 1 February 2019, www.ancestry.com.

6. W. D. Chadick to S. D. Cabaniss, letter titled "Mission to Ohio," Septimus D. Cabaniss Papers.

7. The Condition of the Colored People of the South from a Laboring Standpoint," *The Advocate* (Leavenworth, KS), 20 July 1889, KHS.

8. *The Advocate* (Leavenworth, KS), 27 July 1889, KHS.

9. *The Advocate* (Leavenworth, KS), 20 July 1889, KHS.

10. The Condition of the Colored People of the South from a Laboring Standpoint," *The Advocate* (Leavenworth, KS), 20 July 1889, KHS.

11. See Brent M. S. Campney, *This Is Not Dixie: Racist Violence in Kansas, 1861–1927.*

12. See Painter, *Exodusters*; Campney, *This Is Not Dixie*; James N. Leiker, "Race Relations in the Sunflower State: A Review Essay," *Kansas History: A Journal of the Central Plains* 25 (Autumn 2002); Randall Woods, "Integration, Exclusion, or

Segregation?: The 'Color Line' in Kansas, 1878–1900," *Western Historical Quarterly* 14, no. 2 (April 1983).

13. Wesley Townsend to S. D. Cabaniss, letter dated 4 March 1860, Septimus D. Cabaniss Papers.

14. Campney, *This Is Not Dixie,* 74; Woods, "Integration, Exclusion, or Segregation?," 187–188; Leiker, "Race Relations in the Sunflower State," 225.

15. *The Advocate* (Leavenworth, KS), 29 June 1889, as quoted in Woods, "Integration, Exclusion, or Segregation?," 187.

16. Woods, "Integration, Exclusion, or Segregation?," 188.

17. Woods, "Integration, Exclusion, or Segregation?," 192, 195.

18. See, in particular, Gail Bederman, *Manliness & Civilization: A Cultural History of Gender and Race in the United States, 1880–1917* (Chicago: University of Chicago Press, 1995).

19. Campney, *This Is Not Dixie,* 2–6. See also Kidada E. Williams, "Resolving the Paradox of Our Lynching Fixation: Reconsidering Racialized Violence in the South After Slavery," *American Nineteenth Century History* 6 (September 2005): 323–350.

20. "Negro Dies at the Stake," *New York Times,* 16 January 1901, p. 2, America's Historical Newspapers.

21. "Some Kansas History," *Topeka Plaindealer* (Topeka, KS), 4 September 1903, p. 1, America's Historical Newspapers.

22. *The Advocate* (Leavenworth, KS), 10 August 1889, KHS.

23. Richardson, *West from Appomattox,* 204.

24. W. B. Townsend to Harrison Kelley, letter dated 25 May 1889, KHS.

25. Woods, "Integration, Exclusion, or Segregation?," 181.

26. *Leavenworth Daily Conservative,* 20 January 1864, KHS.

27. As William Bolden wrote Cabaniss in 1874: "I have written several times and have never been able to receive an answer. Why? is this." W. B. Townsend to S. D. Cabaniss, letter dated 27 November 1874.

28. [William] Bolden Townsend to S. D. Cabaniss, letters dated 4 February 1870, 29 February 1872, 17 January 1873, 31 January 1873, 15 June 1873, 3 September 1873, 31 May 1874, 15 August 1874, 27 November 1874, 23 February 1875, and telegram dated 26 April 1877, Septimus D. Cabaniss Papers.

29. "Belden Townsend," 1870 United States Federal Census, accessed 1 February 2019, www.ancestry.com; *Ballenger & Howe Fourth Annual City Directory for 1875,* LHCS.

30. William Bolden Townsend to S. D. Cabaniss, letter dated 3 September 1873, Septimus D. Cabaniss Papers.

31. George Armistead, 1870 United States Federal Census, accessed 1 February 2019, www.ancestry.com.

32. [William] Bolden Townsend to S. D. Cabaniss, letter dated 15 August 1874, Septimus D. Cabaniss Papers.

33. W. B. Townsend to S. D. Cabaniss, letter dated 27 November 1874; [William] Bolden Townsend to S. D. Cabaniss, letter dated 15 August 1874, Septimus D. Cabaniss Papers.

34. *Ballenger & Hoye's Fifth Annual City Directory for 1876,* LHCS.

35. Special thanks to Mary Ann Brown for providing information about Margaret "Peggy" Townsend's grave in Greenwood Cemetery, Leavenworth, Kansas.

36. Brent Campney's article "W. B. Townsend and the Struggle Against Racist Violence in Leavenworth" provides an excellent timeline and examination of William Bolden's journalistic and legal career in Kansas. Campney provides intriguing examples of William Bolden's militancy, emphasis on intra-racial solidarity, and identification of white Americans (rather than working-class African Americans) as the chief cause of racial prejudice. Brent M. S. Campney, "W. B. Townsend and the Struggle Against Racist Violence in Leavenworth." *Kansas History: A Journal of the Central Plains* 31 (Winter 2008–2009): 260–273.

37. *Edwin Green's City Directory* (1882, 1884–1889), LHCS; *Historic Preservation in Kansas, Black Historic Sites: A Beginning Point,* 24–25, KHS; *Wichita Reflector* (Wichita, KS), 9 October 1897 in Kansas Scrap-Book Biography, Theis-Tyler, Clippings, T, Volume 2, KHS.

38. "W. B. Townsend Is Prosperous," *Topeka Plaindealer* (Topeka, KS), 14 March 1902, p. 1, America's Historical Newspapers; *Wichita Reflector* (Wichita, KS), 9 October 1897 in Kansas Scrap-Book Biography, Theis-Tyler, Clippings, T, Volume 2, KHS.

39. "ABLE AND WISE," *Topeka Capital* (Topeka, KS), 25 January 1901 in Kansas Scrap-Book Biography, Theis-Tyler, Clippings, T, Volume 2, KHS.

40. "Kansas Club Women," *Topeka Plaindealer* (Topeka, KS), 14 June 1901, p. 1, America's Historical Newspapers; "Local," *The Advocate* (Leavenworth, KS), 8 March 1890, p. 3, KHS. Historian Glenda Gilmore argues that as African American men were increasingly pushed out of electoral and party politics in the late nineteenth century, Black women took on the role of "the black community's diplomats to the white community"—participating in interracial reform clubs and organizations in a "nonpolitical guise." William Bolden's wife Martha Townsend, who served as a leader of multiple philanthropic organizations in Kansas, exemplified this model of political activism. Gilmore, *Gender & Jim Crow,* 119, 147–151. For the activities and ideologies of Black "club women," see also Wander A. Hendericks, *Gender, Race, and Politics in the Midwest: Black Club Women in Illinois* (Bloomington: Indiana University Press, 1998).

41. *Wichita Reflector* (Wichita, KS), 9 October 1897 in Kansas Scrap-Book Biography, Theis-Tyler, Clippings, T, Volume 2, KHS.

42. "Hon. W. B. Townsend"; "ABLE AND WISE," *Topeka Capital* (Topeka, KS), 25 January 1901 in Kansas Scrap-Book Biography, Theis-Tyler, Clippings, T, Volume 2, KHS.

43. "Kansas Club Women," *Topeka Plaindealer* (Topeka, KS), 14 June 1901, p. 1, America's Historical Newspapers.

44. On nineteenth- and early twentieth-century African American newspapers in Kansas, see Gayle K. Berardi and Thomas W. Segady, "The Development of African American Newspapers in the American West, 1880-1914," in *African Americans on the Western Frontier.*

45. *Wichita Reflector* (Wichita, KS), 9 October 1897, in Kansas Scrap-Book Biography, Theis-Tyler, Clippings, T, Volume 2, KHS.

46. "The District Convention," *Topeka Plaindealer* (Topeka, KS), 23 March 1900, p. 2, America's Historical Newspapers.

47. *The Advocate* (Leavenworth, KS), 25 August 1888, KHS.

48. *The Advocate* (Leavenworth, KS), 8 September 1888, KHS.

49. "Tillman Should Help the Negroes," *Topeka Plaindealer* (Topeka, KS), 28 August 1903, p. 1, America's Historical Newspapers; "The Solid South," *The Advocate* (Leavenworth, KS), 4 May 1889, KHS.

50. "The Solid South," *The Advocate* (Leavenworth, KS), 4 May 1889, KHS.

51. *The Advocate* (Leavenworth, KS), 15 September 1888, KHS.

52. *The Advocate* (Leavenworth, KS), 17 August 1889, KHS.

53. Frank Lincoln Mather, ed., *Who's Who of the Colored Race: A General Biographical Dictionary of Men and Women of African Descent*, vol. I (Chicago: 1915), 266. On African American lawyers in the nineteenth and early twentieth centuries, see J. Clay Smith, *Emancipation: The Making of the Black Lawyer, 1844–1944* (Philadelphia: University of Pennsylvania Press, 1993).

54. Campney, *This Is Not Dixie,* 121.

55. "W. B. Townsend Is Prosperous," *Topeka Plaindealer* (Topeka, KS), 14 March 1902, p. 1; "Kansas Mourns for Townsend!," *Topeka Plaindealer* (Topeka, KS), 20 July 1917, p. 1, America's Historical Newspapers.

56. "From Leavenworth," *Topeka Plaindealer* (Topeka, KS), 14 June 1901, p. 4, America's Historical Newspapers.

57. Campney, "W. B. Townsend and the Struggle Against Racist Violence in Leavenworth," 269–271.

58. "ABLE AND WISE," *Topeka Capital* (Topeka, KS), 25 January 1901, in Kansas Scrap-Book Biography, Theis-Tyler, Clippings, T, Volume 2, KHS.

59. William Bolden continued his career as a lawyer and activist in Kansas, rising to the role of clerk of the Judiciary Committee of the House of Representatives within a matter of years—a higher position than he'd achieved after decades in Kansas. His career in Colorado points to the relatively liberal racial climate that had attracted Charles Osborne and other members of the Townsend family earlier in the century. Campney, "W. B. Townsend and the Struggle Against Racist Violence in Leavenworth," 272.

60. "From Leavenworth," *Topeka Plaindealer* (Topeka, KS), 14 June 1901, p. 4, America's Historical Newspapers.

61. "Some Kansas History," *Topeka Plaindealer* (Topeka, KS), 4 September 1903, p. 4, America's Historical Newspapers.

62. "Whites Don't Know the Negro!," *Topeka Plaindealer* (Topeka, KS), 7 April 1905, p 1, America's Historical Newspapers.

63. "From Leavenworth," *Topeka Plaindealer* (Topeka, KS), 14 June 1901, p. 4, America's Historical Newspapers.

64. "Whites Don't Know the Negro!," *Topeka Plaindealer* (Topeka, KS), 7 April 1905, p 1, America's Historical Newspapers.

65. See Jacquelyn Dowd Hall, "The Long Civil Rights Movement and the Political Uses of the Past," *Journal of American History* 91, no. 4 (March 2005): 1233–1263.

66. S. D. Cabaniss to R. S. Rust, letter dated 5 March 1861, Septimus D. Cabaniss Papers.

67. Item 30, payments to legatees of the first class as of 1 April 1879, Cabaniss vs. Townsend Reports (2), 1872–1883, Septimus D. Cabaniss Papers.

68. "Westley Townsend," 1880 United States Federal Census, accessed 25 September 2020, www.ancestry.com.

69. Ada Townsend and Ida Townsend, 1880 United States Federal Census, accessed 25 September 2020, www.ancestry.com; Adelaide Townsend to Thomas Townsend, letter dated 16 November 1900, Septimus D. Cabaniss Papers.

70. Carrie Leontee Townsend to Thomas Townsend, letter dated 19 August 1890, Septimus D. Cabaniss Papers.

71. Stewart E. Tolnay and E. M. Beck, *A Festival of Violence: An Analysis of Southern Lynchings, 1882–1930* (Urbana: University of Illinois Press, 1995), 24.

72. Item 30, payments to legatees of the first class as of 1 April 1879, Cabaniss vs. Townsend Reports (2), 1872–1883, Septimus D. Cabaniss Papers.

73. Thomas C. Townsend, 1910 United States Federal Census, accessed 10 August 2020, www.ancestry.com.

74. "Clarence T. Townsend," 1920 United States Federal Census; Charles O. Townsend, 1920 United States Federal Census; Thomas C. Townsend, 1930 United States Federal Census; Thomas C. Townsend, 1940 United States Federal Census, accessed 25 September 2020, www.ancestry.com.

75. Thomas C. Townsend, 1930 United States Federal Census, accessed 25 September 2020, www.ancestry.com.

76. Thomas Clarence Townsend, U.S., World War II Draft Registration Cards, 1942, accessed 10 August 2020, www.ancestry.com.

77. "Inez Townsen," 1920 United States Federal Census; Inez Townsend, Alabama, County Marriage Records, 1805–1967; Inez P. Smith and Clifton M. D. Smith, 1940 United States Federal Census; Thomas W. Townsend, U.S., World War I Draft Registration Cards, 1917–1918; Thomas W. Townsend, 1930 United States Federal Census, accessed 11 August 2020, www.ancestry.com; Item 28, Notes on Thomas Townsend's children, Miscellaneous file notes, S. D. Cabaniss Papers.

78. Thomas W. Townsend, Alabama, Deaths and Burials Index, 1881–1974, accessed 25 September 2020, www.ancestry.com.

79. Item 30, payments to legatees of the first class as of 1 April 1879, Cabaniss vs. Townsend Reports (2), 1872–1883, Septimus D. Cabaniss Papers.
80. "Mrs. Townsend Dead," *The Leavenworth Times* (Leavenworth, KS), 9 February 1898; "Martha Townsend's Will," *The Leavenworth Standard* (Leavenworth, KS), 19 February 1898. Special thanks to Mary Ann Brown for sharing these articles.
81. "New Orator Comes," *Topeka Plaindealer* (Topeka, KS), 8 November 1901, p. 1, America's Historical Newspapers.
82. "New Orator Comes," *Topeka Plaindealer* (Topeka, KS), 8 November 1901, p. 1, America's Historical Newspapers.

NOTE ON METHODOLOGY

1. See Collection Overview, Septimus D. Cabaniss Papers, The University of Alabama Libraries Special Collections, www.archives.lib.ua.edu.
2. The expansion of the US Postal Service from the 1860s to the early 1900s created a continent-wide network that made frequent correspondence by mail a possibility for more Americans than ever before. Cameron Blevins, *Paper Trails: The US Post and the Making of the American West* (New York: Oxford University Press, 2021). See also Martha Hodes on letter-writing in Hodes, *The Sea Captain's Wife*, 18-19.
3. Trouillot, *Silencing the Past*, 29.
4. Item 44, Jacob Hatton to S. D. Cabaniss, Estate of Samuel Townsend, Envelopes, Septimus D. Cabaniss Papers.
5. See, for example, Item 28, Notes on Thomas Townsend's children, Miscellaneous file notes, Septimus D. Cabaniss Papers.
6. C. O. Townsend to Thomas Townsend, letter dated 12 December 1882, Septimus D. Cabaniss Papers.
7. C. O. Townsend to Thomas Townsend, letter dated 14 February 1888, Septimus D. Cabaniss Papers.
8. David L. Lakin to S. D. Cabaniss, letter dated 29 February 1860, Septimus D. Cabaniss Papers.
9. Caroline Stone, 1870 United States Federal Census; "Mrs. Stone," 1865 Kansas State Census, accessed 19 August 2021, www.ancestry.com.
10. Warren, "'The Cause of Her Grief': The Rape of a Slave in Early New England," 1033.
11. Item 3, "Inventory and Appraisement" dated February–March 1858, Inventories, Septimus D. Cabaniss Papers.
12. Item 10, notes of Samuel Townsend's wills, Legal notes/ strategy/ depositions, Septimus D. Cabaniss Papers; Stevenson, "What's Love Got to Do with It?," 107.
13. See Item 1, will of Samuel Townsend dated 10 September 1853; Item 2, will of Samuel Townsend dated November 1854; Items 4 and 5, wills of Samuel Townsend dated 6 September and 15 October 1856.
14. Item 1, deposition of S. D. Cabaniss, Depositions, 1859 and undated, Septimus D. Cabaniss Papers.

15. L. P. Hartley, *The Go-Between*, ed. David Brooks-Davies (London: Penguin Books, 1997 [1953]), 5.

16. Raymond D. Fogelson, "The Ethnohistory of Events and Nonevents," *Ethnohistory* 36, no. 2 (Spring 1989), 141.

17. Warren, "'The Cause of Her Grief': The Rape of a Slave in Early New England," 1031. Emphasis in original.

18. Natalie Zemon Davis, *Women on the Margins: Three Seventeenth-Century Lives* (Cambridge, MA: Harvard University Press, 1995), 2.

19. Miles, *Ties That Bind*, 2; Fogelson, "The Ethnohistory of Events and Nonevents," 143.

20. Miles, *Ties That Bind,* 3. Miles also draws from Patricia Hill Collins's article "It's All in the Family" for her analysis.

Bibliography

ARCHIVES AND HISTORICAL SOCIETIES

Alabama

Septimus D. Cabaniss Papers, University Library Division of Special Collections, University of Alabama, Tuscaloosa, AL

Frances Cabaniss Roberts Collection, Department of Archives/Special Collections, M. Louis Salmon Library, University of Alabama in Huntsville, Huntsville, AL

[MCRC] Madison County Records Center, Huntsville, AL

Alabama Department of Archives and History, Montgomery, AL

Colorado

[CCCDAR] Clear Creek County Department of Archives and Records, Georgetown, CO

Hart Research Library, History Colorado Center, Denver, CO

Western History Collection, Denver Public Library, Denver, CO

Kansas

[LCHS] Leavenworth County Historical Society at the Carroll Mansion Museum, Leavenworth, KS

DePaul Library, University of St. Mary, Leavenworth, KS

[KHS] State Archives, Kansas Historical Society, Topeka, KS

Richard Allen Cultural Center, Leavenworth, KS

Kentucky

Parker Family Papers, Northern Kentucky University, Highland Heights, KY

Ohio

Historic New Richmond, New Richmond, OH
State Archives, Ohio History Connection, Columbus, OH

ONLINE DATABASES

America's Historical Newspapers, Readex,
    www.readex.com/content/americas-historical-newspapers.
Amon Carter Museum of American Art, Fort Worth, Texas, www.cartermuseum.org.
Ancestry Library Edition, ProQuest, www.ancestry.com.
Colorado Historic Newspapers Collection, Colorado State Library,
    www.coloradohistoricnewspapers.org.
Documenting the American South, University Library of the University of North
    Carolina at Chapel Hill, docsouth.unc.edu.
Family Search, The Church of Jesus Christ of Latter-day Saints, www.familysearch.org.
Fold 3 by Ancestry, ProQuest, www.fold3.com.
Founders Online, National Archives, founders.archives.gov.
Google Books, Google, books.google.com.
HathiTrust Digital Library, HathiTrust, www.hathitrust.org.
Historical Statistics of the United States: Millennial Edition Online, Cambridge
    University Press, hsus.cambridge.org.
Huntsville History Collection, Huntsville-Madison County Public Library,
    huntsvillehistorycollection.org.
Internet Archive, Andrew W. Mellon Foundation, et al., www.archive.org.
Newspapers.com by Ancestry World Collection, ProQuest, newscomwc.newspapers.
    com.
Project Gutenberg, www.gutenberg.org.
ProQuest Congressional, ProQuest, congressional.proquest.com.
Territorial Kansas Online, Kansas State Historical Society, University of Kansas and
    Institute of Museum and Library Services, territorialkansasonline.ku.edu.
Victorian Women Writers Project, Indiana University, http://webapp1.dlib.indiana.
    edu/vwwp/welcome.do.
Virginia Memory, Library of Virginia, http://www.virginiamemory.com/.

PUBLISHED PRIMARY SOURCES

Abbott, Nathan. *A Selection of Authorities on Descent, Wills, and Administration.* St.
    Paul, MN: West Publishing Co., 1894.
Akin, John G. *A Digest of the Laws of the State of Alabama.* Philadelphia: Alexander
    Towar, 1833.

Arnett, B. W. and S. T. Mitchell, eds. *The Wilberforce Annual: A Comprehensive Review of the Origin, Development and Present Status of Wilberforce University*. Xenia, OH, 1885.

Ballenger & Richards Denver City Directory, 1894. Denver, CO: Ballenger & Richards, 1894.

Ballenger & Richards Denver City Directory, 1895. Denver, CO: Ballenger & Richards, 1895.

Ballenger & Richards Denver City Directory, 1901. Denver, CO: Ballenger & Richards, 1901.

The Bessel Directory Co.'s Clear Creek and Gilpin County Directory for the Years 1892–3. Trinidad, CO: Bessel Directory Company, 1893.

Bibb, Henry. *Narrative of the Life and Adventures of Henry Bibb, an American Slave*. New York: 1849.

Bingham, Caleb. *The Columbian Orator: Containing a Variety of Original and Selected Pieces Together with Rules Calculated to Improve Youth and Others in the Ornamental and Useful Art of Eloquence*. Boston: Caleb Bingham and Co., 1817.

Bird, Isabella L. *A Lady's Life in the Rocky Mountains*. New York: G. P. Putnam's Sons, 1881.

Blackmar, Francis W., ed. *Kansas: A Cyclopedia of State History*. Chicago, IL: 1912.

Brown, Hallie Q. *Pen Pictures of Pioneers of Wilberforce*. Xenia, OH: Aldine Publishing Company, 1937.

Bruce, H. C. *The New Man. Twenty-Nine Years A Slave. Twenty-Nine Years a Free Man*. New York: Negro Universities Press, [1895] 1969.

Burke, William S. and J. L. Rock. *The History of Leavenworth, the Metropolis of Kansas, and the Chief Commercial Center West of the Missouri River*. Leavenworth, KS: Leavenworth Times Book and Job Printing Establishment, 1880.

Catalogue of the Wilberforce University. 1859–60. Xenia, Ohio. Cincinnati, OH: Methodist Book Concern, 1860.

Clear Creek County, Colorado, Mining and Business Directory. Denver, CO: Redman & Hart, 1898.

Codman, John. *The Round Trip by Way of Panama through California, Oregon, Nevada, Utah, Idaho, and Colorado; with Notes on Railroads, Commerce, Agriculture, Mining, Scenery, and People*. New York: G. P. Putnam's Sons, 1879.

Congressional Record: Containing the Proceedings and Debates of the Forty-Sixth Congress, Second Session, Volume X. Washington, DC: Government Printing Office, 1880.

Cutler, William G. *History of the State of Kansas*. Chicago: A.T. Andreas, 1883.

Douglass, Frederick. *Narrative of the Life of Frederick Douglass, an American Slave, Written by Himself*. Boston: 1845.

Dyer, Frederick H. *A Compendium of the War of the Rebellion*, vol. 1. Des Moines, IA: Dyer Publishing Company, 1908.

Fossett, Frank. *Colorado, Its Gold and Silver Mines: Farms and Stock Ranges, and Health and Pleasure Resorts: Tourist's Guide to the Rocky Mountains.* New York: C. G. Crawford, 1880.

Hall, Frank. *History of the State of Colorado*, vol. I. Chicago: Blakely Printing Company, 1889.

Hall, Jesse A. and LeRoy T. Hand. *History of Leavenworth County, Kansas.* Topeka, KS: Historical Publishing Company, 1921.

Historical Sketches of the Higher Educational Institutions and also of Benevolent and Reformatory Institutions of the State of Ohio. Philadelphia: 1876.

Jacobs, Harriet. *Incidents in the Life of a Slave Girl: Written by Herself,* ed. L. Maria Child. Boston: 1861.

Jefferson, Thomas. *Notes on the State of Virginia.* Philadelphia: Prichard and Hall, 1788.

Jefferson, Thomas. *The Works of Thomas Jefferson,* vol. 5. Paul Leicester Ford, ed. New York: G. P. Putnam's Sons, 1905.

Locke, John. *Two Treatises on Government, Book II.* London: 1688.

Mather, Frank Lincoln, ed. *Who's Who of the Colored Race: A General Biographical Dictionary of Men and Women of African Descent,* vol. 1. Chicago: 1915.

Moore, H. Miles. *Early History of Leavenworth City and County.* Leavenworth, KS: Sam'l Dodsworth Book Co., 1906.

Olmstead, D. "Observations of the Meteors of November 13, 1833." *American Journal of Science* 25 and 26 (1834).

Pike, Zebulon Montgomery. *The Expeditions of Zebulon Montgomery Pike,* edited by Elliott Coues. New York: Francis P. Harper, 1895.

Report of the Commissioner of Education for the Year 1884–'85. Washington, DC: Government Printing Office, 1886.

The Rocky Mountain Directory and Colorado Gazetteer, for 1871. Denver, CO: S. S. Wallihan and Company, 1871.

Ryan, Daniel J. *A History of Ohio: The Rise and Progress of an American State,* vol. 4. New York: Century History Company, 1912.

Sequestration Act, Passed by The Congress of the Confederate States. Richmond, VA: Tyler, Wise and Allegre, 1861.

Simmons, William J. *Men of Mark: Eminent, Progressive and Rising.* Cleveland, OH: Geo. M. Rewell & Co., 1887.

Sloan, Walter B. *History and Map of Kansas & Nebraska: Describing Soil, Climate, Rivers, Prairies, Mounds, Forests, Minerals.* Chicago: R. Fergus, 1855.

Sumner, Charles. *The Crime Against Kansas. The Apologies for the Crime. The True Remedy. Speech of Hon. Charles Sumner, in the Senate of the United States, 19th and 20th May, 1856.* Boston: John P. Jewett & Company, 1856.

Tanner, Henry. *Directory & Shippers' Guide of Kansas & Nebraska.* Leavenworth City, KS: T. A. Holland & Co., 1866.

Testimony Taken by the Joint Select Committee to Inquire into the Condition of Affairs in the Late Insurrectionary States. Washington, DC: Government Printing Office, 1872.

de Tocqueville, Alexis. *Democracy in America*, vols. 1 and 2, translated by Henry Reeve. New York: Adlard and Saunders, 1838.

Tomlinson, William P. *Kansas in Eighteen Fifty-Eight, Being Chiefly a History of the Recent Troubles in the Territory*. New York: H. Dayton, 1859.

Tower, Reverend Philo. *Slavery Unmasked: Being a Truthful Account*. Rochester, NY: E. Darrot & Brother, 1856.

Turner, Frederick Jackson. "The Significance of the Frontier in American History." *Annual Report of the American Historical Association*. Washington, DC: Government Printing Office, 1894.

Young, Francis Crissey. *Echoes from Arcadia: The Story of Cental City, as told by one of "The Clan."* Denver, CO: Lanning Bros., 1903.

SECONDARY SOURCES

Adams, David Wallace. *Education for Extinction: American Indians and the Boarding School Experience, 1875–1928*. Lawrence: University Press of Kansas, 1995.

Allen, Austin. *Origins of the Dred Scott Case: Jacksonian Jurisprudence and the Supreme Court, 1837–1857*. Athens: University of Georgia Press, 2006.

Andrews, Thomas G. *Killing for Coal: America's Deadliest Labor War*. Cambridge, MA: Harvard University Press, 2008.

Ayers, Edward L. *The Promise of the New South: Life after Reconstruction*. New York: Oxford University Press, 1992.

Bailey, Richard. *Neither Carpetbaggers nor Scalawags: Black Officeholders During the Reconstruction of Alabama, 1867–1878*. Montgomery, AL: NewSouth Books, 2010.

Baptist, Edward E. and Stephanie M. H. Camp, eds. *New Studies in the History of American Slavery*. Athens: University of Georgia Press, 2006.

Baumgartner, Kabria. "Building the Future: White Women, Black Education, and Civic Inclusion in Antebellum Ohio." *Journal of the Early Republic* 37, no. 1 (Spring 2017): 117–145.

Beckert, Sven. *Empire of Cotton: A New History of Global Capitalism*. New York: Alfred A. Knopf, 2014.

Beckles, Hilary McD. "An Economic Life of Their Own." In *Caribbean Slavery in the Atlantic World: A Student Reader*, edited by Verne Shepherd and Hilary McD. Beckles. Kingston, Jamaica: Ian Randle, 2000.

Bederman, Gail. *Manliness & Civilization: A Cultural History of Gender and Race in the United States, 1880–1917*. Chicago: University of Chicago Press, 1995.

Berardi, Gayle K. and Thomas W. Segady. "The Development of African American Newspapers in the American West, 1880-1914." In *African Americans on the Western Frontier*, edited by Monroe Lee Billington and Roger D. Hardaway. Boulder: University Press of Colorado, 1998.

Berlin, Ira. *Generations of Captivity: A History of African-American Slaves*. Cambridge, MA: Harvard University Press, 2003.

Berlin, Ira. *Many Thousands Gone: The First Two Centuries of Slavery in North America*. Cambridge, MA: Belknap Press of Harvard University Press, 1998.

Berlin, Ira. *Slaves Without Masters: The Free Negro in the Antebellum South*. New York: Pantheon Books, 1974.

Berman, David R. *Radicalism in the Mountain West, 1890–1920: Socialists, Populists, Miners, and Wobblies*. Boulder: University Press of Colorado, 2007.

Billington, Monroe Lee and Roger D. Hardaway, eds. *African Americans on the Western Frontier*. Boulder: University Press of Colorado, 1998.

Black, Henry Campbell. *A Dictionary of Law*. St. Paul, MN: West Publishing Company, 1891.

Blackett, R. J. M. *Making Freedom: The Underground Railroad and the Politics of Slavery*. Chapel Hill: University of North Carolina Press, 2013.

Blackhawk, Ned. *Violence over the Land: Indians and Empires in the Early American West*. Cambridge, MA: Harvard University Press, 2008.

Blassingame, John W., ed. *Slave Testimony: Two Centuries of Letters, Speeches, Interviews, and Autobiographies*. Baton Rouge: Louisiana State University Press, 1977.

Blassingame, John W. "Using the Testimony of Ex-Slaves: Approaches and Problems." *Journal of Southern History* 41 (November 1975): 473–92.

Blevins, Cameron. *Paper Trails: The US Post and the Making of the American West*. New York: Oxford University Press, 2021.

Blight, David W. *Race and Reunion: The Civil War in American Memory*. Cambridge, MA: Harvard University Press, 2001.

Bodenhorn, Howard. *The Color Factor: The Economics of African-American Well-Being in the Nineteenth Century South*. New York: Oxford University Press, 2015.

Bradley, Josephine Boyd and Kent Anderson Leslie. "White Pain Pollen: An Elite Biracial Daughter's Quandary." In *Sex, Love, Race: Crossing Boundaries in North American History*, edited by Martha Hodes. New York: New York University Press, 1999.

Brandt, Nat. *The Town that Started the Civil War*. Syracuse, NY: Syracuse University Press, 1990.

Brown, Kathleen M. *Good Wives, Nasty Wenches, and Anxious Patriarchs: Gender, Race and Power in Colonial Virginia*. Chapel Hill: University of North Carolina Press, 1996.

Brown, P. "The Leonid Meteor Shower: Historical Visual Observations." *Icarus* 138, no. 2 (1 April 1999): 287–308.

Brown, Vincent. "Social Death and Political Life in the Study of Slavery. *American Historical Review* 114, no. 5 (December 2009): 1231–1249.

Brundage, W. Fitzhugh. *Lynching in the New South, 1880–1930*. Urbana: University of Illinois Press, 1993.

Brundage, W. Fitzhugh. "White Women and the Politics of Historical Memory in the New South, 1880–1920." In *Jumpin' Jim Crow: Southern Politics from Civil War to Civil Rights*, edited by Jane Dailey, Glenda Elizabeth Gilmore, and Bryant Simon. Princeton, NJ: Princeton University Press, 2000.

Burke, Diane Mutti. "Scattered People: The Long History of Forced Evictions in the Kansas-Missouri Borderlands." In *Civil War Wests: Testing the Limits of the United States*, edited by Adam Arenson and Andrew R. Graybill. Berkeley: University of California Press, 2015.

Camp, Stephanie M. H. *Closer to Freedom: Enslaved Women and Everyday Resistance in the Plantation South*. Chapel Hill: University of North Carolina Press, 2004.

Campitt, Bradley R. *Occupied Vicksburg*. Baton Rouge: Louisiana State University Press, 2016.

Campney, Brent M. S. "'Light Is Bursting Upon the World!': White Supremacy and Racist Violence Against Blacks in Reconstruction Kansas." In *Lynching Beyond Dixie: American Mob Violence Outside the South*, edited by Michael J. Pfeifer. Urbana: University of Illinois Press, 2013.

Campney, Brent M. S. *This Is Not Dixie: Racist Violence in Kansas, 1861–1927*. Urbana: University of Illinois Press, 2015.

Campney, Brent M. S. "W. B. Townsend and the Struggle Against Racist Violence in Leavenworth." *Kansas History: A Journal of the Central Plains* 31 (Winter 2008–2009): 260–273.

Carter, Nancy Carol. "U.S. Federal Indian Policy: An Essay and Annotated Bibliography," *Legal Reference Services Quarterly* 30, no. 3 (2011): 210–230.

Chan, Sucheng, ed. *Entry Denied: Exclusion and the Chinese Community in America, 1882–1943*. Philadelphia: Temple University Press, 1991.

Chaplin, Joyce E. "Creating a Cotton South in Georgia and South Carolina." *Journal of Southern History* 57, no. 2 (May 1991): 171–200.

Chesnut, Mary Boykin and C. Vann Woodward, eds. *Mary Chesnut's Civil War*. New Haven, CT: Yale University Press, 1981.

Clymer, Jeffory A. *Family Money: Property, Race, and Literature in the Nineteenth Century*. New York: Oxford University Press, 2013.

Crifasi, Robert R. *A Land Made from Water: Appropriation and the Evolution of Colorado's Landscape, Ditches, and Water Institutions*. Boulder: University Press of Colorado, 2015.

Cunningham, Roger D. "Douglas's Battery at Fort Leavenworth." *Kansas History* 23, no. 4 (Winter 2000–2001): 201–217.

Dailey, Jane. "The Limits of Liberalism in the New South: The Politics of Race, Sex, and Patronage in Virginia, 1879–1883." In *Jumpin' Jim Crow: Southern Politics from Civil War to Civil Rights*, edited by Jane Dailey, Glenda Elizabeth Gilmore, and Bryant Simon. Princeton, NJ: Princeton University Press, 2000.

Davis, Adrienne D. "The Private Law of Race and Sex: An Antebellum Perspective." *Stanford Law Review* 51, no. 2 (January 1999): 221–288.

Davis, Karl. "'Remember Fort Mims': Reinterpreting the Origins of the Creek War." *Journal of the Early Republic* 22, no. 4 (Winter 2002): 611–636.

Davis, Natalie Zemon. *Women on the Margins: Three Seventeenth-Century Lives*. Cambridge, MA: Harvard University Press, 1995.

Decker, Peter. *The Utes Must Go!: American Expansion and the Removal of a People.* Golden, CO: Fulcrum, 2004.

Deyle, Steven. *Carry Me Back: The Domestic Slave Trade in American Life.* New York: Oxford University Press, 2005.

Diemer, Andrew K. *The Politics of Black Citizenship: Free African Americans in the Mid-Atlantic Borderland, 1817–1863.* Athens: University of Georgia Press, 2016.

Diller, Christopher G. "Introduction." In Harriett Beecher Stowe, *Uncle Tom's Cabin; or, Life Among the Lowly* (1852), edited by Christopher G. Diller. Buffalo, NY: Broadview Press, 2009.

Dorman, John Frederick. *Adventures of Purse and Person, Virginia, 1608–1624/5: Families G-P.* Baltimore, MD: Genealogical Publishing, 2004.

Du Bois, W. E. B. *Black Reconstruction: An Essay Toward a History of the Part Which Black Folk Played in the Attempt to Reconstruct Democracy in America, 1860–1880.* New York: Harcourt, Brace, 1935.

Dupre, Daniel S. *Transforming the Cotton Frontier: Madison County, Alabama, 180–1840.* Baton Rouge: Louisiana State University Press, 1997.

Egerton, Douglas R. "'Its Origin Is Not a Little Curious': A New Look at the American Colonization Society." *Journal of the Early Republic* 5, no. 4 (Winter 1985): 463–480.

Eslinger, Ellen. "The Evolution of Racial Politics in Early Ohio." In *The Center of a Great Empire: The Ohio Country in the Early American Republic,* edited by Andrew R. L. Cayton and Stuart D. Hobbs. Athens: Ohio University Press, 2005.

Etcheson, Nicole. *Bleeding Kansas: Contested Liberty in the Civil War Era.* Lawrence: University Press of Kansas, 2004.

Eubanks, W. Ralph. *The House at the End of the Road: The Story of Three Generations of an Interracial Family in the American South.* New York: Harper Collins, 2009.

Farber, Daniel A. "A Fatal Loss of Balance: *Dred Scott* Revisited." *Pepperdine Law Review* 39, no. 1 (2011): 13–48.

Fields, Barbara J. "Ideology and Race in American History." In *Region, Race, and Reconstruction: Essays in Honor of C. Van Woodward,* edited by J. Morgan Kousser and James McPherson. New York: Oxford University Press, 1982.

Finkelman, Paul. "The Strange Career of Race Discrimination in Antebellum Ohio," *Case Western Reserve Law Review* 55, no. 1 (Fall 2004): 373–408.

Finley, Alexandra. "'Cash to Corinna': Domestic Labor and Sexual Economy in the 'Fancy Trade.'" *Journal of American History* 104, no. 2 (September 2017): 410–430.

Finley, Alexandra. *An Intimate Economy: Enslaved Women, Work, and America's Domestic Slave Trade.* Chapel Hill: University of North Carolina Press, 2020.

Fitzgerald, Michael W. *Reconstruction in Alabama: From Civil War to Redemption in the Cotton South.* Baton Rouge: Louisiana State University Press, 2017.

Fogel, Robert W., Stanley L. Engerman, and James Trussel. "Exploring the Uses of Data on Height: The Analysis of Long-Term Trends in Nutrition, Labor Welfare, and Labor Productivity." *Social Science History* 6, no. 4 (Autumn 1982): 401–421.

Fogelson, Raymond D. "The Ethnohistory of Events and Nonevents," *Ethnohistory* 36, no. 2 (Spring 1989): 133–147.

Folk, Richard Albert. "Black Man's Burden in Ohio, 1849–1863." PhD diss., University of Ohio, 1972.

Foner, Eric. *Forever Free: The Story of Emancipation & Reconstruction*. New York: Vintage Books, 2006.

Foner, Eric. *Gateway to Freedom: The Hidden History of the Underground Railroad*. New York: W. W. Norton, 2015.

Foner, Eric. *A Short History of Reconstruction, 1863–1877*. New York: Harper & Row, 1990.

Foner, Philip S. and Robert James Branham, eds. *Lift Every Voice: African American Oratory, 1787–1900*. Tuscaloosa: University of Alabama Press, 1998.

Forret, Jeff and Christine E. Sears, eds. *New Directions in Slavery Studies: Commodification, Community, and Comparison*. Baton Rouge: Louisiana State Press, 2015.

Fuentes, Marisa J. *Dispossessed Lives: Enslaved Women, Violence, and the Archive*. Philadelphia: University of Pennsylvania Press, 2016.

Fuentes, Marisa J. "Power and Historical Figuring: Rachael Pringle Polgreen's Troubled Archive." *Gender & History* 22, no. 3 (November 2010): 564–584.

Gaines, Kevin K. *Uplifting the Race: Black Leadership, Politics, and Culture in the Twentieth Century*. Chapel Hill: University of North Carolina Press, 1996.

Gerber, David A. *Black Ohio and the Color Line, 1860–1915*. Urbana: University of Illinois Press, 1976.

Gibson, Campbell and Kay Jung. "Historical Census Statistics on Population Totals by Race, 1790 to 1990." Population Division Working Paper No. 56. Washington, DC: US Census Bureau, 2002.

Giddings, Paula J. *Ida, A Sword Among Lions: Ida B. Wells and the Campaign Against Lynching*. New York: Harper Collins, 2008.

Gilmore, Glenda Elizabeth. *Gender & Jim Crow: Women and the Politics of White Supremacy in North Carolina, 1896-1920*. Chapel Hill, NC: University of North Carolina Press, 1996.

Glymph, Thavolia. *Out of the House of Bondage: The Transformation of the Plantation Household*. Cambridge: Cambridge University Press, 2008.

Going, Allen Johnston. *Bourbon Democracy in Alabama, 1874–1890*. Tuscaloosa: University of Alabama Press, 1952, 1992.

Going, Allen Johnston. "The South and the Blair Education Bill." *Mississippi Valley Historical Review* 44, no. 2 (September 1957): 267–290.

Goodman, James. *Stories of Scottsboro*. New York: Vintage Books, 1995.

Goodwyn, Lawrence. *Democratic Promise: The Populist Movement in America*. New York: Oxford University Press, 1976.

Gordon-Reed, Annette. *The Hemingses of Monticello: An American Family*. New York: W. W. Norton, 2008.

Green, Sharony. *Remember Me to Miss Louisa: Hidden Black-White Intimacies in Antebellum America*. Dekalb: Northern Illinois University Press, 2015.

Greene, Lorenzo Johnson. *The Negro in Colonial New England, 1620–1776*. New York: Columbia University Press, 1962.

Greenwood, Janette Thomas. *Bittersweet Legacy: The Black and White 'Better Classes' in Charlotte, 1850–1910*. Chapel Hill: University of North Carolina Press, 1994.

Gross, Ariela J. *Double Character: Slavery and Mastery in the Antebellum Southern Courtroom*. Athens: University of Georgia Press, 2006.

Gross, Ariela J. "Litigating Whiteness: Trials of Racial Determination in the Nineteenth-Century South." *Yale Law Journal* 108 (October 1998): 109–188.

Guardino, Peter. *The Dead March: A History of the Mexican-American War*. Cambridge, MA: Harvard University Press, 2017.

Guyatt, Nicholas. "The Outskirts of Our Happiness": Race and the Lure of Colonization in the Early Republic." *Journal of American History* 95, 4 (March 2009): 986–1011.

Guthman, Joshua. *Strangers Below: Primitive Baptists and American Culture*. (Chapel Hill: University of North Carolina Press, 2015.

Hahn, Steven. *A Nation Under Our Feet: Black Political Struggles in the Rural South from Slavery to the Great Migration*. Cambridge, MA: Belknap Press of Harvard University Press, 2003.

Hall, Jacquelyn Dowd. "The Long Civil Rights Movement and the Political Uses of the Past." *Journal of American History* 91, no. 4 (March 2005): 1233–1263.

Hall, Jacquelyn Dowd. *Revolt Against Chivalry: Jessie Daniel Ames and the Women's Campaign Against Lynching*. New York: Columbia University Press, 1993.

Hamalainen, Pekka. *The Comanche Empire*. New Haven, CT: Yale University Press, 2008.

Hammond, John Craig. *Slavery, Freedom, and Expansion in the Early American West*. Charlottesville: University of Virginia Press, 2007.

Handler, Jerome S. *The Unappropriated People: Freedmen in the Slave Society of Barbados*. Baltimore, MD: Johns Hopkins University Press, 1974.

Hanger, Kimberly S. *Bounded Lives, Bounded Places: Free Black Society in Colonial New Orleans, 1769–1803*. Durham: Duke University Press, 1997.

Harris, Leslie M. *In the Shadow of Slavery: African Americans in New York City, 1626–1863*. Chicago: University of Chicago Press, 2003.

Hartley, L. P. *The Go-Between*, edited by David Brooks-Davies. London: Penguin Books, 1997 [1953].

Hartman, Saidiya. *Scenes of Subjection: Terror, Slavery, and Self-Making in Nineteenth-Century America*. New York: Oxford University Press, 1997.

Hartman, Saidiya. "Venus in Two Acts." *Small Axe* 26, no. 2 (June 2008): 1–14.

Hartog, Hendrik. *The Trouble with Minna: A Case of Slavery and Emancipation in the Antebellum North*. Chapel Hill: University of North Carolina Press, 2018.

Hendericks, Wander A. *Gender, Race, and Politics in the Midwest: Black Club Women in Illinois*. Bloomington: Indiana University Press, 1998.

Heuman, Gad J. *Between Black and White: Race, Politics, and the Free Coloreds in Jamaica, 1792–1865.* Westport, CT: Greenwood, 1981.

Heuman, Gad J. "White Over Brown Over Black: The Free Coloureds in Jamaican Society During Slavery and After Emancipation." *Journal of Caribbean History* (May 1, 1981): 46–69.

Hickman, Russell K. "Lincoln College, Forerunner of Washburn University: Part Two: Later History and Change of Name—Concluded." *Kansas Historical Quarterly* 18, no. 2 (May 1950): 164–204.

Hill, Lynda M. "Ex-Slave Narratives: The WPA Federal Writers' Project Reappraised." *Oral History* 26, no. 1 (Spring 1998): 64–72.

Hobbs, Allyson. *A Chosen Exile: A History of Racial Passing in American Life.* Cambridge, MA: Harvard University Press, 2014.

Hodes, Martha. "Fractions and Fictions in the United States Census of 1890." In *Haunted by Empire: Geographies of Intimacy in North American History*, edited by Ann Laura Stoler. Durham, NC: Duke University Press, 2006.

Hodes, Martha. "The Mercurial Nature and Abiding Power of Race: A Transnational Family Story." *American Historical Review* 108, no. 1 (1 February 2003): 84–118.

Hodes, Martha. *The Sea Captain's Wife: A True Story of Love, Race, and War in the Nineteenth Century.* New York: W.W. Norton, 2006.

Hodes, Martha. *White Women, Black Men: Illicit Sex in the Nineteenth-Century South.* New Haven, CT: Yale University Press, 1999.

Holt, Thomas C. "Marking: Race, Race-making, and the Writing of History." *American Historical Review 100*, No. 1 (February 1995): 1–20.

Horton, James Oliver and Stacy Flaherty. "Black Leadership in Antebellum Cincinnati." In *Race and the City: Work, Community, and Protest in Cincinnati, 1820–1970*, edited by Henry Louis Taylor Jr. Urbana: University of Illinois Press, 1993.

Horton, James Oliver and Lois E. Horton. "A Federal Assault: African Americans and the Impact of the Fugitive Slave Law of 1850." *Chicago-Kent Law Review* 68, no. 3 (1993): 1179–1198.

Horton, James Oliver and Lois E. Horton. *Slavery and the Making of America.* New York: Oxford University Press, 2006.

Howe, Daniel Walker. *What Hath God Wrought: The Transformation of America, 1815–1848.* New York: Oxford University Press, 2007.

Hubbs, G. Ward. *Searching for Freedom after the Civil War: Klansman, Carpetbagger, Scalawag, and Freedman.* Tuscaloosa: University of Alabama Press, 2015.

Hunter, Tera W. *Bound in Wedlock: Slave and Free Black Marriage in the Nineteenth Century.* Cambridge, MA: Harvard University Press, 2017.

Hunter, Tera W. *To 'Joy My Freedom: Southern Black Women's Lives and Labors after the Civil War.* Cambridge, MA: Harvard University Press, 1997.

Hyde, Anne F. *Empires, Nations, and Families: A New History of the North American West, 1800–1860.* New York: Harper Collins, 2011.

Jacobs, Margaret. *White Mother to a Dark Race: Settler Colonialism, Maternalism, and the Removal of Indigenous Children in the American West and Australia, 1880–1940.* Lincoln: University of Nebraska Press, 2009.

Jacoby, Karl. *Shadows at Dawn: An Apache Massacre and the Violence of History.* New York: Penguin Press, 2008.

Jacoby, Karl. *The Strange Career of William Ellis: The Texas Slave Who Became a Mexican Millionaire.* New York: W.W. Norton, 2016.

Jessen, Nathan. *Populism and Imperialism: Politics, Culture, and Foreign Policy in the American West, 1890–1900.* Lawrence: University Press of Kansas, 2017.

Jewett, Clayton E. and John O. Allen, *Slavery in the South: A State-by-State History.* Westport, CT: Greenwood Press, 2004.

Johnson, J. H. III. *Early Leavenworth and Fort Leavenworth: A Photographic History.* Leavenworth, KS: J. H. Johnson III, 1977.

Johnson, Susan. *Roaring Camp: The Social World of the California Gold Rush.* New York: W. W. Norton, 2000.

Johnson, Walter. *River of Dark Dreams: Slavery and Empire in the Cotton Kingdom.* Cambridge, MA: Belknap Press of Harvard University Press, 2013.

Johnson, Walter. *Soul by Soul: Life Inside the Antebellum Slave Market.* Cambridge, MA: Harvard University Press, 1999.

Jones, Bernie D. *Fathers of Conscience: Mixed-Race Inheritance in the Antebellum South.* Athens: University of Georgia Press, 2009.

Jones, Martha S. "Julian Bond's Great-Grandmother a 'Slave Mistress?' How the New York Times Got It Wrong." History News Network. Historynewsnetwork.org.

Jordon, Winthrop D. *White over Black: American Attitudes Toward the Negro, 1550–1812.* Chapel Hill: University of North Carolina Press, 1968.

Josiah, Barbara P. "Providing for the Future: The World of the African American Depositors of Washington, DC's Freedmen's Savings Bank, 1865–1874." *Journal of African American History* 89, no. 1 (Winter 2004): 1–16.

Kansas State Historical Society Historic Sites Survey. *Black Historic Sites: A Beginning Point.* Topeka: Kansas State Historical Society, 1977.

Katz, William Loren. *The Black West: A Documentary and Pictorial History of the African American Role in the Westward Expansion of the United States.* New York: Touchstone, 1996.

Kelman, Ari. *A Misplaced Massacre: Struggling over the Memory of Sand Creek.* Cambridge, MA: Harvard University Press, 2013.

Kesterman, Richard. "The Burnet House: A Grand Cincinnati Hotel." *Ohio Valley History* 12, no. 4 (Winter 2012): 61–63.

King, Thomas. "Black Settlement in Xenia, Ohio, 1850–1880: An Historical Geography." MA thesis, University of Colorado, 1983.

Klarman, Michael J. *From Jim Crow to Civil Rights: The Supreme Court and the Struggle for Racial Equality.* New York: Oxford University Press, 2004.

Kulikoff, Allan. *Tobacco and Slaves: The Development of Southern Cultures in the Chesapeake, 1680–1800.* Chapel Hill: University of North Carolina Press, 1986.

Kull, Andrew. "The Enforceability after Emancipation of Debts Contracted for the Purchase of Slaves—Freedom: Personal Liberty and Private Law." *Chicago-Kent Law Review* 70, no. 2 (December 1994).

Lakwete, Angela. *Inventing the Cotton Gin: Machine and Myth in Antebellum America.* Baltimore, MD: Johns Hopkins University Press, 2003.

LaRoche, Cheryl Janifer. *Free Black Communities and the Underground Railroad: The Geography of Resistance.* Urbana: University of Illinois Press, 2014.

Lawson, Ellen NicKenzie and Marlene D. Merrill. *The Three Sarahs: Documents of Antebellum Black College Women.* New York: Edwin Mellen Press, 1984.

Lee, Erika. "The Chinese Exclusion Example: Race, Immigration, and American Gatekeeping, 1882–1924." *Journal of American Ethnic History* 21, no. 3 (Spring 2002): 36–62.

Leiker, James N. "Race Relations in the Sunflower State: A Review Essay." *Kansas History: A Journal of the Central Plains* 25 (Autumn 2002): 214–236.

Leonard, Stephen J. and Thomas J. Noel, *Denver: Mining Camp to Metropolis.* Niwot: University Press of Colorado, 1990.

Leyendecker, Liston E., Christine A. Bradley, and Duane A. Smith. *The Rise of the Silver Queen: Georgetown, Colorado, 1859–1896.* Boulder: University Press of Colorado, 2005.

Limerick, Patricia Nelson. *The Legacy of Conquest: The Unbroken Past of the American West.* New York: W. W. Norton, 1988.

Litwack, Leon. *North of Slavery: The Negro in the Free States, 1790–1860.* Chicago: University of Chicago Press, 1961.

Logan, Rayford. *The Negro in American Life and Thought: The Nadir, 1877–1901.* New York: Dial Press, 1954.

McCauley, Patrick. "The Origins of Huntsville's Waterworks Utility Board." *Huntsville Historical Review* 25, no. 1 (Winter–Spring 1998).

McGinnis, Frederick Alphonso. *The Education of Negroes in Ohio.* Wilberforce, OH: Frederick A. McGinnis, 1962.

McGinnis, Frederick Alphonso. *A History and An Interpretation of Wilberforce University.* Blanchester, OH: Brown Publishing, 1941.

McIlwain, Christopher Lyle Sr. "United States District Judge Richard Busteed and the Alabama Klan Trials of 1872." *Alabama Review* 65, no. 4 (October 2012): 263–289.

McMath, Robert E. Jr. *American Populism: A Social History.* New York: Hill and Wang, 1993.

Melish, Joanne Pope. *Disowning Slavery: Gradual Emancipation and "Race" in New England, 1780–1860.* Ithaca, NY: Cornell University Press, 1998.

Middleton, Stephen. *The Black Laws: Race and the Legal Process in Early Ohio.* Athens: Ohio University Press, 2005.

Miller, Albert G. *Elevating the Race: Theophilus G. Steward, Black Theology, and the Making of an African American Civil Society, 1865–1924.* Knoxville: University of Tennessee Press, 2003.

Miller, Steven F. "Plantation Labor Organization and Slave Life on the Cotton Frontier: The Alabama-Mississippi Black Belt, 1815–1840." In *Cultivation and Culture: Labor and the Shaping of Slave Life in the Americas*, edited by Ira Berlin and Philip D. Morgan. Charlottesville: University of Virginia Press, 1993.

Mitchell, Michele. *Righteous Propagation: African Americans and the Politics of Racial Destiny after Reconstruction.* Chapel Hill: University of North Carolina Press, 2004.

Miles, Tiya. "Beyond a Boundary: Black Lives and the Settler-Native Divide." *William and Mary Quarterly* 76, no. 3 (July 2019): 417–426.

Miles, Tiya. *Ties That Bind: The Story of an Afro-Cherokee Family in Slavery and Freedom.* Berkeley: University of California Press, 2005.

Morgan, Edmund S. *American Slavery, American Freedom.* New York: W.W. Norton, 1975.

Morgan, Jennifer. *Laboring Women: Reproduction and Gender in New World Slavery.* Philadelphia: University of Pennsylvania Press, 2004.

Morgan, Philip D. *Slave Counterpoint: Black Culture in the Eighteenth-Century Chesapeake and Lowcountry.* Chapel Hill: University of North Carolina Press, 1998.

Morris, Brent. *Oberlin, Hotbed of Abolitionism: College, Community, and the Fight for Freedom and Equality in Antebellum America.* Chapel Hill: University of North Carolina Press, 2014.

Morris, Thomas D. *Free Men All: The Personal Liberty Laws of the North, 1780–1861.* Union, NJ: Lawbook Exchange, 2001.

Nash, Gary B. *Forging Freedom: The Formation of Philadelphia's Black Community, 1720–1840.* Cambridge, MA: Harvard University Press, 1988.

Neverdon-Morton, Cynthia. *Finding History's Forgotten People: The Presence of African Americans in Colorado, c. 1534 to 1954.* Denver, CO: US Department of the Interior, Bureau of Land Management, 2008.

Ngai, Mae. *Impossible Subjects: Illegal Aliens and the Making of Modern America.* Princeton, NJ: Princeton University Press, 2004.

Novkov, Julie. *Racial Union: Law, Intimacy, and the White State in Alabama, 1865–1954.* Ann Arbor: University of Michigan Press, 2008.

O'Hara, Matthew D. and Andrew B. Fisher, eds. *Imperial Subjects: Race and Identity in Colonial Latin America.* Durham, NC: Duke University Press, 2009.

Olmstead, Alan L. *Freedmen Philanthropy, and Fraud: A History of the Freedman's Savings Bank.* Urbana: University of Illinois Press, 1976.

Olson, Donald W. and Laurie E. Jasinski. "Abe Lincoln and the Leonids." *Sky & Telescope* (November 1999): 34–35.

Owens, Emily. "On the Use of 'Slave Mistress.'" *Black Perspectives* (21 August 2015). African American Intellectual History Society.

Painter, Nell Irvin. *Exodusters: Black Migration to Kansas after Reconstruction.* New York: W.W. Norton, 1976.

Painter, Nell Irvin. *Standing at Armageddon: The United States, 1877–1919.* New York: W. W. Norton, 1987.

Pascoe, Peggy. *What Comes Naturally: Miscegenation Law and the Making of Race in America.* New York: Oxford University Press, 2009.

Pashman, Howard. "The People's Property Law: A Step Toward Building a New Legal Order in Revolutionary New York." *Law and History Review* 31, no. 3 (August 2013): 587–626.

Patterson, Orlando. *Slavery and Social Death: A Comparative Study.* Cambridge, MA: Harvard University Press, 1982.

Ponce, Pearl T. *To Govern the Devil in Hell: The Political Crisis in Territorial Kansas.* DeKalb: Northern Illinois University Press, 2014.

Pruitt, Ranee' G., ed. *Eden of the South: A Chronology of Huntsville, Alabama, 1805–2005.* Huntsville, AL: Huntsville-Madison County Public Library, 2005.

Ransom, Roger and Richard Sutch. "Capitalists Without Capital: The Burden of Slavery and the Impact of Emancipation." *Agricultural History* 62, no. 3 (Summer 1998): 133–160.

Ransom, Roger and Richard Sutch. *One Kind of Freedom: The Economic Consequences of Emancipation.* Cambridge: Cambridge University Press, 2001.

Record, James. *A Dream Come True: The Story of Madison County and Incidentally of Alabama and the United States.* Huntsville, AL: John Hicklin, 1970.

Richardson, Heather Cox. *West from Appomattox: The Reconstruction of America after the Civil War.* New Haven, CT: Yale University Press, 2007.

Roberts, Frances Cabaniss. "An Experiment in Emancipation of Slaves by an Alabama Planter." MA thesis, University of Alabama, 1940.

Roberts, Frances Cabaniss. "William Manning Lowe and the Greenback Party in Alabama." In *From Civil War to Civil Rights, Alabama 1860–1960: An Anthology from the Alabama Review,* edited by Sarah Woolfolk Wiggins. Tuscaloosa: University of Alabama Press, 1987.

Robinson, Stephen R. "Rethinking Black Urban Politics in the 1880s: The Case of William Gaston in Post-Reconstruction Alabama." *Alabama Review* 66, no. 1 (January 2013): 3–29.

Robinson, Wilhelmena. "The Negro in the Village of Yellow Springs, Ohio." *Negro History Bulletin* 29, no. 5 (1 February 1966): 103–112.

Rogers, William Warren, et al. *Alabama: The History of a Deep South State.* Tuscaloosa: University of Alabama Press, 2010.

Rohe, Randall E. "After the Gold Rush: Chinese Mining in the Far West, 1850–1890." *Montana: The Magazine of Western History* 32, no. 4 (Autumn 1982): 2–19.

Rohr, Nancy. "Free People of Color in Madison County, Alabama." Huntsville History Collection. Huntsvillehistorycollection.org.

Root, Maria P., ed. *The Multiracial Experience: Racial Borders as the New Frontier*. Thousand Oaks, CA: Sage, 1996.

Rosen, Deborah A. *American Indians and State Law: Sovereignty, Race, and Citizenship, 1790–1880*. Lincoln: Nebraska University Press, 2007.

Rothman, Adam. *Slave Country: American Expansion and the Origins of the Deep South*. Cambridge, MA: Harvard University Press, 2005.

Rothman, Joshua. *Notorious in the Neighborhood: Sex and Families Across the Color Line in Virginia, 1787–1861*. Chapel Hill: University of North Carolina Press, 2003.

Sanders, Elizabeth. *Roots of Reform: Farmers, Workers, and the American State, 1877–1917*. Chicago: University of Chicago Press, 1999.

Sandweiss, Martha A. *Passing Strange: A Gilded Age Tale of Love and Deception Across the Color Line*. New York: Penguin Press, 2009.

Sandweiss, Martha A. *Print the Legend: Photography and the American West*. New Haven, CT: Yale University Press, 2002.

Saunt, Claudio. *Black, White, and Indian: Race and the Unmaking of an American Family*. New York: Oxford University Press, 2005.

Savage, W. Sherman. *Blacks in the West*. Westport, CT: Greenwood Press, 1976.

Saville, Julie. *The Work of Reconstruction: From Slave to Wage Labor in South Carolina, 1860–1870*. New York: Cambridge University Press, 1996.

Scalise Jr., Ronald J. "Undue Influence and the Law of Wills: A Comparative Analysis." *Duke Journal of Comparative & International Law* 19, no. 1 (Fall 2008): 41–106.

Schmidt, Fredrika Teute and Barbara Ripel Wilhelm. "Early Proslavery Petitions in Virginia," *William and Mary Quarterly* 30, no. 1, Chesapeake Society (January 1973): 133–146.

Seeley, Samantha. "Beyond the American Colonization Society." *History Compass* 14, no. 3 (March 2016): 93–104.

Sellers, James Benson. *Slavery in Alabama*. Tuscaloosa: University of Alabama Press, 1950.

Sharfstein, Daniel J. *The Invisible Line: Three American Families and the Secret Journey from Black to White*. New York: Penguin Press, 2011.

Sheehan, Bernard W. *Seeds of Extinction: Jeffersonian Philanthropy and the American Indian*. Chapel Hill: University of North Carolina Press, 1973.

Shepherd, Verne and Hilarly McD. Beckles, eds. *Caribbean Slavery in the Atlantic World: A Student Reader*. Kingston, Jamaica: Ian Randle, 2000.

Sheridan, Richard B. "From Slavery in Missouri to Freedom in Kansas: The Influx of Black Fugitives and Contrabands into Kansas." *Kansas History* 12, no. 1 (Spring 1989): 28–47.

Simmons, Virginia McConnell. *The Ute Indians of Utah, Colorado, and New Mexico*. Boulder: University Press of Colorado, 2000.

Sio, Arnold A. "Marginality and Free Coloured Identity in Caribbean Slave Society." *Slavery & Abolition* 8, no. 2 (1987): 166–182.

Smith, Henry Nash. *Virgin Land: The American West as Symbol and Myth*. Cambridge, MA: Harvard University Press, 1950, 1978.

Smith, J. Clay. *Emancipation: The Making of the Black Lawyer, 1844–1944*. Philadelphia: University of Pennsylvania Press, 1993.

Snell, Joseph W. and Don W. Wilson. "The Birth of the Atchison, Topeka and Santa Fe." *Kansas History* 34, no. 2 (Summer 1968).

Stanley, Amy Dru. *From Bondage to Contract: Wage Labor, Marriage, and the Market in the Age of Slave Emancipation*. Chicago: University of Chicago Press, 1998.

Stevenson, Brenda E. "What's Love Got to Do with It? Concubinage and Enslaved Women and Girls in the Antebellum South." *Journal of African American History* 98, no. 1, Special Issue: "Women, Slavery, and the Atlantic World" (Winter 2013): 99–125.

Storey, Margaret M. *Loyalty and Loss: Alabama's Unionists in the Civil War and Reconstruction*. Baton Rouge: Louisiana State University Press, 2004.

Stuckey, Melissa. "All Men Up: Race, Rights, and Power in the All-Black Town of Boley, Oklahoma, 1903–1939." PhD diss., Yale University, 2009.

Taylor, Henry Louis Jr., ed. *Race and the City: Work, Community, and Protest in Cincinnati, 1820–1970*. Urbana: University of Illinois Press, 1993.

Taylor, Nikki. *Frontiers of Freedom: Cincinnati's Black Community, 1802–1868*. Athens: Ohio University Press, 2005.

Taylor, Judge Thomas Jones. *A History of Madison County and Incidentally of North Alabama, 1732–1840,* edited by W. Stanley Hoole and Addie S. Hoole. Tuscaloosa, AL: Confederate Publishing, 1976.

Taylor, Quintard. *In Search of the Racial Frontier: African Americans in the American West, 1528–1990*. New York: W.W. Norton, 1998.

Tolnay, Stewart E. and E. M. Beck. *A Festival of Violence: An Analysis of Southern Lynchings, 1882–1930*. Urbana: University of Illinois Press, 1995.

Tribe, Ivan M. *Albany, Ohio: The First Fifty Years of a Rural Midwestern Community*. Athens, OH: Athens County Historical Society and Museum, 1985.

Trouillot, Michel-Rolph. *Silencing the Past: Power and the Production of History*. Boston: Beacon Press, 1995.

Trudeau, Noah Andre. *Like Men of War: Black Troops in the Civil War, 1862–1865*. New York: Little, Brown, 1998.

VanderVede, Lea. "The *Dred Scott* Case in Context." *Journal of Supreme Court History* 40, no. 3 (November 2015): 263–281.

Van Tuyl, Francis M. and Arthur E. Brainerd. "Historical Summary." In *Mineral Resources of Colorado, First Sequel*. Denver, CO: Colorado Mineral Resources Board, 1960.

Van Woodward, C. *Origins of the New South, 1877–1913*. Baton Rouge: Louisiana State University Press, 1971.

Wade, Peter. *Race and Ethnicity in Latin America*, 2nd ed. New York: Pluto Press, 2010.

Wallace, Anthony F. C. *The Long, Bitter Trail: Andrew Jackson and the Indians.* New York: Hill and Wang, 1993.

Warren, Wendy. "'The Cause of Her Grief': The Rape of a Slave in Early New England." *Journal of American History* 93, no. 4 (March 2007): 1031–1049.

Waselkov, Gregory A. *A Conquering Spirit: Fort Mims and the Redstick War of 1813–14.* Tuscaloosa: University of Alabama Press, 2006.

West, Elliot. *The Contested Plains: Indians, Goldseekers, and the Rush to Colorado.* Lawrence: University Press of Kansas, 1998.

West, Elliot. "Reconstructing Race." *Western Historical Quarterly* 34, no. 1 (Spring 2003): 6–26.

White, Deborah Gray. *Ar'n't I a Woman? Female Slaves in the Plantation South.* New York: W.W. Norton, 1999.

White, Richard. *Railroaded: The Transcontinentals and the Making of Modern America.* New York: W. W. Norton, 2011.

Wilentz, Sean. *The Rise of American Democracy: Jefferson to Lincoln.* New York: W.W. Norton, 2005.

Williams, Heather Andrea. *Self-taught: African American Education in Slavery and Freedom.* Chapel Hill: University of North Carolina Press, 2005.

Williams, Kidada E. "Resolving the Paradox of Our Lynching Fixation: Reconsidering Racialized Violence in the South After Slavery," *American Nineteenth Century History* 6 (September 2005): 323–350.

Williamson, Joel. *The Crucible of Race: Black/White Relations in the American South Since Emancipation.* New York: Oxford University Press, 1984.

Williamson, Joel. *A Rage for Order: Black/White Relations in the American South Since Emancipation.* New York: Oxford University Press, 1986.

Winch, Julie. *Between Slavery and Freedom: Free People of Color in America from Settlement to the Civil War.* Lanham, MD: Rowman & Littlefield, 2014.

Woods, Randall. "Integration, Exclusion, or Segregation?: The 'Color Line' in Kansas, 1878–1900." *Western Historical Quarterly* 14, no. 2 (April 1983): 181–198.

Wortman, Roy T. "Denver's Anti-Chinese Riot, 1880." *Colorado Magazine* 42, no. 4 (Fall 1965): 275–343.

Writers Program of the Works Project Administration in the State of Ohio. *Cincinnati: A Guide to the Queen City and its Neighbors.* Cincinnati, OH: Wiesen-Hart Press, 1943.

Wrobel, David M. and Michael S. Steiner. *Many Wests: Place, Culture, and Regional Identity.* Lawrence: University Press of Kansas, 1997.

Zhu, Liping. *A Chinaman's Chance: The Chinese on the Rocky Mountain Mining Frontier.* Niwot: University Press of Colorado, 1997.

Index

For the benefit of digital users, indexed terms that span two pages (e.g., 52–53) may, on occasion, appear on only one of those pages.

Note: Page numbers followed by *f* indicate a figure on the corresponding page.